# 2,000 YEARS OF CALLIGRAPHY

A THREE-PART EXHIBITION
ORGANIZED BY

THE Baltimore Museum of Art
Peabody Institute Library
Walters Art Gallery

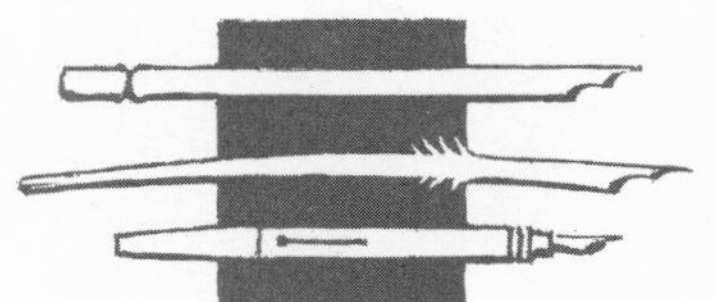

A Comprehensive Catalog

A Pentalic Book TAPLINGER PUBLISHING COMPANY – NEW YORK

Compiled by
Dorothy E. Miner, The Walters Art Gallery, Baltimore
Victor I. Carlson, The Baltimore Museum of Art
P. W. Filby, The Peabody Institute Library, Baltimore

Second printing
First paperback edition published in 1980
by Taplinger Publishing Co. Inc.

ISBN 0-8008-7919-8


LIBRARY OF CONGRESS CARD NUMBER: 65-22689


PRINTED IN THE UNITED STATES OF AMERICA

# Table of Contents

As heads of the three institutions engaged cooperatively in the exhibition, "2000 Years of Calligraphy," and in this present catalogue, we wish to record our gratitude to P. W. Filby, Dorothy Miner and Victor Carlson, whose understanding and labor are manifest. Commencing with Mr. Filby's conception of such a grand cooperative exhibition, each of these scholars has developed a special section for simultaneous presentation in our respective institutions. It is comforting to know that we are buttressed by such competent colleagues whose work, epitomized in the following pages, we regard with admiration and gratification.

FRANK N. JONES, Director
The Peabody Institute Library

EDWARD S. KING, Director
The Walters Art Gallery

CHARLES PARKHURST, Director
The Baltimore Museum of Art

# Foreword

THIS exhibition is an attempt to cover the calligraphy produced during a period of almost exactly 2000 years in the regions using the Latin alphabet. The earliest exhibits are incised monumental inscriptions of the Flavian period in Rome; the latest is an example in italic script written in May, 1965. Considerations of space as well as of unity caused the decision to eliminate the calligraphy of Greece and Islam, and the ancient alphabets of the Middle East and the Far East.

Baltimore has experienced two earlier exhibitions of calligraphy, both held at the Peabody Institute Library: one in 1959, and the other, restricted to American calligraphy and handwriting, in 1961–1962. The former was accompanied only by a mimeographed hand-list, but the interest aroused by the latter display resulted in the publication of a commemorative catalogue, *Calligraphy and Handwriting in America, 1710–1962,* compiled by P. W. Filby, Italimuse, Caledonia, N. Y., 1963. In a sense these two previous exhibitions were rehearsals and experiments for this present ambitious undertaking.

Since World War II, the three institutions, The Walters Art Gallery, The Baltimore Museum of Art and The Peabody Institute Library, have combined together in other ventures so successfully that such a cooperation seemed a natural one for this 1965 exhibition of calligraphy.

Inasmuch as no one institution could mount the entire display effectively, it was decided to present it as a simultaneous three-part showing—Part I: The first century A.D. to the fifteenth century, at The Walters Art Gallery; Part II: The sixteenth to the eighteenth century, at The Baltimore Museum of Art; Part III: The nineteenth century to 1965, at The Peabody Institute Library.

Each part has been organized and prepared entirely by the institution concerned. This catalogue is in effect a combination of three different books, because each section had its own distinct emphasis, requiring appropriate treatment.

Part I is in essence the story of the formal hands required for the worthy production of books, until the printing press gradually assumed that task during the last half of the fifteenth century.

Part II emphasizes the era of the development of fine and elegant scripts suitable for the official purposes of the chanceries and other government offices, as well as for the handwriting of the cultivated gentleman, the intellectual and eventually for the merchant. It was the period of the great writing-masters, whose influence was spread far and wide by the treatises and copy-books which they published.

Part III concentrates on the calligraphy that has been revived and is practiced today as an art in itself. The exhibits are devoted almost entirely to the twentieth century. Since most of the artists comprising this section are still living, few of the pieces have changed hands or had any history, such as characterizes the material in the two earlier sections of the exhibition. Indeed, almost half of the examples are being exhibited for the first time, and of these one quarter were commissioned by collectors expressly for the Baltimore exhibition. More attention is given to the biography and background of the contemporary scribes than is usual in books on calligraphy.

The exhibition was first suggested over a year ago, and for twelve months the organizers have had enthusiastic cooperation from lenders and scribes. It was the intention of the collaborating institutions to have a printed catalogue available at the opening of the exhibition, and in order to make this possible lenders have generously allowed their precious pieces to be away for over six months. Without this cooperation, a catalogue could not have been produced in 1965.

The list of lenders merely indicates those who have allowed their treasures to be shown. It is but scanty recognition of the special efforts put forward by many of them—the work undertaken in the preparation or selection of the loans. The great libraries cooperated in every possible way. As usual, the Pierpont Morgan Library, with generous advice and assistance from the Director, Frederick B. Adams, Jr., and from the respective curators, Dr. John Plummer and Dr. Herbert Cahoon, not only collaborated with precious loans, but made it possible to reach some private owners in the New York area. All of the institutions listed, both in this country and abroad, were gracious and helpful, and our gratitude to their several curators and officers is very deep. However, we cannot pass without special mention the exceptional part played by James M. Wells, Associate Director of the Newberry Library in Chicago. Not only his famous institution, which is a leading one among collections of calligraphy, but he himself actually became a part of the show. In addition to making available the riches of the Newberry collection, with the generous cooperation of Lawrence W. Towner, the Director, and giving all of us the benefit of his extensive knowledge, Mr. Wells helped in the overall selection of most objects in Part II and some in Part I. Furthermore, he graciously read over the entries to the second section of the catalogue.

Harvard, as always, was a generous collaborator and lender, thanks to the Director of the Houghton Library, Dr. William H. Bond, but again we must reserve a special word of heartfelt appreciation for Philip Hofer, who has so often been a partner in these Baltimore exhibitions, and who once more has given us complete choice of his superb collection. Both Mr. Hofer and his assistant, Miss Eleanor Garvey, have added the extensive chores of so generous a loan to a full and exacting schedule.

It is a most distinguished honor to be able to include in our list of lenders Her Majesty Queen Elizabeth II, who has graciously consented to lend the two historic pieces described under nos. 167 and 209.

Among the other private collectors, all of whom were most generous, we must express particular obligation to Stuart B. Schimmel, a recent collector of calligraphy, mainly of British examples, Richard Harrison, who actually commissioned several works especially for this exhibition, Lessing J. Rosenwald, John M. Crawford, Jr. and Harry A. Walton, Jr.

Gabriel Austin, Librarian of the Grolier Club, is accorded special thanks for making available the extensive collection of photographs taken at the time of the Grolier Club calligraphy exhibition a few years ago. Many selections were made with the help of these.

The British scribes who contributed to Part III were put to considerable expense and trouble, and it is only through the magnificent cooperation of the Society of Scribes and Illuminators that the modern calligraphy section is so complete.

The photographs are the work of the photographers of the respective institutions, but many, particularly those illustrating Part III, were made by the printers. The printing of the catalogue and its plates are due to the care and devotion of E. Harold Hugo and Jack Leether of the Meriden Gravure Company, Meriden, Connecticut, while the book design is the work of Roderick D. Stinehour of the Stinehour Press, Lunenburg, Vermont. The proof for all of the catalogue was read by Vera R. Filby.

The cover was designed and written by Byron J. Macdonald; the title-page and the headings were lettered by Raymond F. DaBoll. Their distinguished contributions to the beauty of the catalogue are herewith most gratefully acknowledged by the organizing institutions.

# Preface to Reprint Edition

ON the occasion of the exhibition "2,000 Years of Calligraphy," the third exhibition on calligraphy to be held in Baltimore within the space of six years, Mr. John Carter, bibliophile and arbiter of taste in the arts, referred to Baltimore as "the center of calligraphy in America." Alas, at the end of the 1965 exhibition, Mr. P. W. Filby, who had been responsible for the first two and was the organizer of the third, left the Peabody Institute and went two blocks away to become Librarian and Assistant Director of the Maryland Historical Society. Through him the Peabody had made its mark in the field of calligraphy and had drawn many people to the library. Though the historical society has almost two million manuscripts, few would rank as calligraphy, and since there is no one with the facilities to mount another exhibition, the brief period of fame seems to be at end.

The catalogue for the exhibition became available on the day the show opened. With one thousand copies in soft cover and another thousand hardbound, the edition was quickly exhausted, and there have been many requests for it in the intervening years. It is with much pleasure that the compilers welcome a reprint and congratulate the Walters Art Gallery and Rowman & Littlefield for their parts in the issue, the latter for its realization of the need and the former for allowing it to be reprinted with a minimum of discussion.

The compilers now have the unique opportunity of commenting on the exhibition and the reviews it engendered. There is no doubt that the exhibition was a tremendous success; record crowds visited the three institutions, and overseas visitors were numerous. Reviews were plentiful and mostly glowing with enthusiasm. Some reviewers felt that six weeks was a ridiculously short display period for a gathering of such proportions, and so it was, but the Walters Art Gallery and the Baltimore Museum of Art had prior commitments and these had to be fulfilled. Each of the three institutions took down its section with considerable sadness, and there were many disappointed visitors who had not realized the shortness of the showing.

In general, reviewers reported that the catalogue was one of the best reference tools ever to be produced on calligraphy. Few criticisms were made of Parts I and II; the comments on Part III are dealt with later in this introduction.

Of great satisfaction to the compilers is the fact that not a single typographical error has been pointed out to them, and that no serious factual error occurred.

Reviews were published in about one hundred publications, including such august ones as *The New York Times*, *Times Literary Supplement* (which gave a whole page to it), *The Book Collector*, *Antiquarian Bookman*, *Papers of the Bibliographical Society of America*, *American Artist* (seven pages), *Apollo*, the *Connoisseur* and the *Publishers' Weekly*. The exhibition was also featured for thirty minutes on television.

## PART I: The First to the Fifteenth Century

THE section of the exhibition mounted at the Walters Art Gallery had for the viewer the inherent advantage of the beauty of glowing gold and colors which embellished the majority of the specimens. It did, however, have to labor under the *disadvantage* of attempting to present the development of calligraphy for fifteen hundred years, while the two other sections had to divide less than five hundred years between them. The surprisingly few criticisms offered by thoughtful visitors or reviewers concerned only three matters: (1) Why should an exhibition of calligraphy be initiated by carved Roman inscriptions? (2) Why were Roman cursive examples omitted? (3) Why were no actual examples of third-, fourth-, fifth-century scripts included?

The Roman stone inscriptions are carved calligraphy, since they were written out first with brush and color. More important, they were studied and admired all through the Middle Ages and the Renaissance, and had direct influence on the majuscules and display scripts of the scribes throughout that time. Finally, the tradition has come full circle with the splendid carvings in stone or wood by stars of the twentieth century shown in Part III: David Kindersley, Father Catich, Will Carter, and the Bensons, father and son.

Roman cursive, interesting as it is, cannot rank as calligraphy—"beautiful writing." It did unquestionably have important influence upon certain medieval hands, especially upon some of the provincial pre-Carolingian scripts, as is mentioned in the discussions of such examples in the exhibition.

The truly valid observation as to the gap between Roman and Merovingian inscriptions reproduced in the catalogue can be countered only by reminding the reader that this is the record of an exhibition of actual specimens, selected for their beauty, gathered together, and presented as effectively as possible to the viewer. An exhibition, by its very nature, is limited by what can be shown well, and—even more—by what is available!

These very questions were foreseen and the answers are to be found either in the original foreword to Part I, or in the individual catalogue entries.

DOROTHY E. MINER
Librarian and Keeper of Manuscripts
Walters Art Gallery

## PART II: *The Sixteenth to the Eighteenth Century*

It came as a surprise to find that nearly all the printed desiderata, and many essential manuscripts, could be found in American collections. This circumstance is due to the farsightedness of some private collectors, who for years have sought out calligraphic works, and is a tribute to the scholarship of the directors of the public institutions which had so generously lent to the exhibition. As was noted in the reviews of the exhibition and catalogue, the only point at which the resources of the lenders proved unequal to our needs was the impossibility of locating a work by the Tudor scribe Roger Ascham. Here the practical difficulties of working within the format of an exhibition could not be overcome. His omission is felt all the more since it was possible to locate a letter by Ascham's illustrious pupil Queen Elizabeth I (cat. no. 103).

VICTOR I. CARLSON
Curator of Prints and Drawings
Baltimore Museum of Art

## PART III: *The Nineteenth and Twentieth Centuries*

A few reviewers and visitors expressed some disappointment that Part III passed over nineteenth-century examples of calligraphy, and jumped direct from 1800 to 1900. Alan Fern in *The American Connoisseur* remarked, "Exuberant excesses of the era of Spencerian script and medieval 'illumination' are absent." But it was said by the compiler, "If we accept the definition of calligraphy as 'beautiful handwriting' or as 'handwriting as an art' we must exclude most of the writing of the nineteenth century." Lloyd Reynolds stated that "Compared with Arrighi, the Spencerian systems seem coldly mechanical in nature, quite illegible and thoroughly lacking in character. . . ." The compiler has seen or read nothing in the intervening years which has changed his mind in any way. Another criticism was that a few very fine calligraphers in America and several in Europe were omitted, causing some imbalance. This is true and the fault rests with the compiler's lack of knowledge and on the calligraphers who refused to be included or did not answer his requests. But in the main, it is now seen that there were few serious omissions. It is also realized that the late Mr. Paul Bennett's comments in *Publishers' Weekly* challenging the relative merits of American and English calligraphers and the compiler's conclusions were in part valid. Perhaps it was (and is) the compiler's enthusiasm for the traditional British calligraphic forms rather than for the fresh and dramatic and inventive American layouts which caused him to choose more British than American hands. Another exhibition would probably remedy some shortcomings; the compiler has learned much since then.

The decision to write biographies rather than to attempt to describe the work met with general approval, and Mr. Fern commented, "Mr. Filby has assembled a mass of biographical data on 20th century scribes that is unequalled anywhere."

One remarkable fact is that hardly any new American calligraphers have emerged since 1965. Warren Ferris and Oscar Ogg have departed, but those remaining seem to go from strength to strength. Some, though retired, still continue to teach, to review and to write books. A number of new faces have appeared in Britain, even though the Society of Scribes and Illuminators, after some soul-searching, decided to maintain its very stiff entrance rules. The society continues to hold excellent exhibitions and runs concentrated courses in calligraphy and illumination. It also participated in the Victoria and Albert Museum's great exhibition "The Decorated Page," where two of the compilers were among the eight lecturers. Of the British calligraphers in the catalogue, Ernest Duncombe, T. W. Swindlehurst and Madelyn Walker are no longer with us.

P. W. FILBY
Director
Maryland Historical Society

# List of Lenders

Dorothy Abbe
Hingham, Mass.
Frederick B. Adams, Jr.
New York City
Arthur Baker
Piedmont, Cal.
Stuart Barrie
Edinburgh, Scotland
Esther Fisher Benson
Newport, R. I.
H. J. Blackman
Richmond, England
Boston Public Library
Boston, Mass.
Chris Brand
Breda, Netherlands
William T. Brantman
Tiburon, Cal.
Ann Camp
London, England
Will Carter
Cambridge, England
La Casa del Libro
San Juan, Puerto Rico
Heather Child
London, England
The Chiswick Book Shop
New York City
The Marquess & Marchioness of Cholmondeley
London, England
Lady Churchill, g.b.e.
London, England
Columbia University Libraries
New York City
John M. Crawford, Jr.
New York City
Raymond F. DaBoll
Newark, Ark.
Her Majesty Queen Elizabeth II
London, England
Robert Elwell
New York City
The Essex Institute
Salem, Mass.
Herbert Farrier
Auburndale, Mass.
P. W. Filby
Baltimore, Md.
Catharine Fournier
Brooklyn, N. Y.
Henri Friedlaender
Jerusalem, Israel
William M. Gardner
Wittersham, England
Robert H. I. Goddard, Jr.
Providence, R. I.
Lilian Greif
Baltimore, Md.
Richard Harrison
San Francisco, Cal.
Harvard College Library, Department of Printing and Graphic Arts
Cambridge, Mass.
James F. Hayes
Evanston, Ill.
Mr. and Mrs. Philip Hofer
Cambridge, Mass.
E. Harold Hugo
Meriden, Conn.
Donald Jackson
London, England
Margaret James
Sheffield, England
Fridolf Johnson
New York City
Edward Karr
Boston, Mass.
Charles C. Kerwin
Chicago, Ill.
David Kindersley
Linton, England
The Klingspor Museum
Offenbach, Germany
Mark Lansburgh
Santa Barbara, Cal.
Vera Law
Folkestone, England

Wilmarth S. Lewis
Farmington, Conn.
The Library of Congress,
Lessing J. Rosenwald Collection
J. and E. R. Pennell Collection
Washington, D. C.
The Lilly Library, Indiana University
Bloomington, Ind.
Byron J. Macdonald
San Francisco, Cal.
Egdon H. Margo
Sherman Oaks, Cal.
Charles de Coti Marsh
London, England
The Metropolitan Museum of Art
New York City
Maury Nemoy
Los Angeles, Cal.
The Newberry Library
Chicago, Ill.
Oscar Ogg
New York City
Wendy Parnell
Bristol, England
Enid Eder Perkins
New York City
The Free Library of Philadelphia
Phliadelphia, Pa.
The Pierpont Morgan Library
New York City
Crimilda Pontes
Washington, D. C.
The Princeton University Library
Princeton, N. J.
Mildred M. Ratcliffe
Maidstone, England
Lloyd J. Reynolds
Portland, Ore.
Pat Russell
Abingdon, England
Stuart B. Schimmel
Rye, N. Y.
The School of Medical Science,
University of South Dakota
Vermillion, S. D.
Paul Standard
New York City
Steuben Glass
New York City
Reynolds Stone
Litton Cheney, England
Frank Taylor
Leeds, England
The Right Honourable The Lord Tennyson
Paris, France
The Honorable Vincent Thomas
San Pedro, Cal.
Lewis Trethewey
London, England
Marjorie Tuson
Bristol, England
The Victoria and Albert Museum
London, England
The Walters Art Gallery
Baltimore, Md.
Mr. and Mrs. Harry A. Walton, Jr.
Covington, Va.
Sheila Waters
Froxfield, England
James M. Wells
Chicago, Ill.
Mary White
Llantwit Major, Wales
The Whitworth Art Gallery,
University of Manchester
England
Martin Wilke
West Berlin, Germany
Jeanyee Wong
New York City
Pamela Wrightson
Enfield, England

# *Abbreviations frequently used*

Bonacini: Claudio Bonacini, *Bibliografia delle Arti Scrittorie e della Calligrafia*. Florence, 1953.

Bond and Faye, *Supplement: Supplement to the Census of Medieval and Renaissance Manuscripts in the United States and Canada*, Originated by C. U. Faye, continued and edited by W. H. Bond. New York, The Bibliographical Society of America, 1962.

Cotarelo y Mori: Don Emilio Cotarelo y Mori, *Diccionario Biográfico y Bibliográfico de Calígrafos Españoles*. Madrid, 1913–1916.

De Ricci: Seymour de Ricci and W. J. Wilson, *Census of Medieval and Renaissance Manuscripts in the United States and Canada*, 2 vols. and Index. New York, 1935–1940.

Harvard *Cat.*, 1955: Harvard College Library, *Illuminated and Calligraphic Manuscripts—an Exhibition held at the Fogg Art Museum & Houghton Library*. Cambridge, Massachusetts, 1955.

Heal: Sir Ambrose Heal, *The English Writing-Masters and their Copy-books, 1570–1800*. Cambridge University Press, 1931.

L. C. C.: London County Council.

E. A. Lowe, *C. L. A.*: E. A. Lowe, *Codices Latini Antiquiores*. Oxford, The Clarendon Press. Vols. I–, 1934– (in progress).

*Nomenclature*: Centre National de la Recherche Scientifique, *Nomenclature des écritures livresques du IXe au XVIe siècle: premier colloque international de paléographie latine Paris 28–30 avril 1953*. Paris, 1954.

Portland *Cat.*, 1958: Portland Art Association, *Calligraphy—The Golden Age and its Modern Revival—an Exhibition held at the Portland Art Museum*. Portland, Oregon, 1958.

R. C. A.: Royal College of Art. London.

S. S. I.: The Society of Scribes and Illuminators. London.

B. L. Ullman, *Humanistic Script*: B. L. Ullman, *The Origin and Development of Humanistic Script*. Rome, 1960.

Walters *Cat.*, 1949: Walters Art Gallery, *Illuminated Books of the Middle Ages and Renaissance—an Exhibition held at the Baltimore Museum of Art*. Baltimore, 1949.

Wing: Donald G. Wing, *Short-title Catalogue of Books Printed in England, Scotland, Ireland, Wales and British America, and of English Books Printed in Other Countries, 1641–1700*. New York, 1945–1951.

# PART I: *The First to the Fifteenth Century*

THIS first part of our exhibition seeks to present in survey the general development of the writing of western Europe from the early decades of the Roman Empire up until the time when all classical forms of expression again became the acknowledged ideal. The major proportion of the entries will be found to represent the interim between these two extreme points. Allusion is made by a few exhibits to the local scripts of continental and Insular centers, but the concentration is upon the splendid development and long supremacy of Carolingian minuscule, and then the gradual evolution toward the other great innovation of the medieval scribes, gothic black-letter. The fifteenth-century humanistic return to Carolingian models (nos. 40–55) was both a reaction and in some ways a survival. One thing perhaps will become clear to the attentive observer: during all the fifteen hundred years of this evolution and of the search for a book hand combining practicality with dignity, Roman epigraphy and calligraphy in various forms were seldom remote from the vision of the calligrapher (except in the north during the fourteenth and fifteenth centuries). Sometimes the relationship was clear-cut and strong, at other times it was distant and half-remembered. The pendulum swung back and forth.

There are aspects of the long development which are not represented by the pieces exhibited. Such are the very informal cursives for personal notations and letter-writing, the interesting notary and charter hands, as well as the very cursive text hands used from the thirteenth to the fifteenth century for certain purposes. All of these played an important part and in their turn made contributions to the main stream, an influence touched upon in the catalogue discussions. What we are concentrating upon in all parts of the exhibition is fine and beautiful writing—as the word 'calligraphy' literally signifies. And what sets the calligraphy of the first fifteen centuries of our era apart from the developments presented in Parts II and III of the exhibition is that calligraphy was stimulated, shaped and cultivated because it was required in the production of books. The products of the skilful scribe had been a necessity before this, of course, in order to publish the works of Cicero, Seneca, Plautus and Terence; and before that in the Greek world, most especially where great library projects were under way, as at Athens and Alexandria and Pergamum. But during our period there were a number of driving forces, working either in succession or simultaneously. First and foremost was the need to multiply copies of the Scriptures and the service books required for Christian religious observance—a need which continued up to the day of the first printing with moveable type. It is no accident that the first true book to come from the printing press was a Bible. Hardly less urgent during the earlier Middle Ages was the multiplication of the works of the Church Fathers who expounded and interpreted the Scriptures. These were a necessity to the missionaries who began to fan out over Europe and set up hardy Christian communities on heathen soil. Each such community required a library of sorts, and as time went on a good many of these grew into centers not only of scholarship, but essentially of book production. The writing and compiling of new works and the copying out of older ones became an ever more important activity, and by the time we reach the ninth and tenth centuries, it had reached prodigious proportions. This activity embraced the reproduction not only of Christian literature but of pagan, transferring classical texts upon crumbling papyrus to the more durable surface of vellum.

So the story goes without break into the time when the guilds of the later Middle Ages took up the task of multiplying the books needed. And the humanists, as the renaissance impetus to individual scholarship got under way, were the ones who created a new book hand based upon the fine old ones in which their beloved classics had been copied down upon vellum five centuries earlier.

The concern with the fine writing of our fifteen hundred years is thus explained. However, in an exhibition of this sort, such an aim by its very nature must fall far short of complete accomplishment. Not all that one would wish for can be transferred from its permanent home to a temporary display. One will note the lack of any early manuscript written entirely in one of the most monumental scripts of all—the square capitals. But after all, this was a script of very brief duration—only four manuscripts—always a Vergil, and all fragments—exist in this fourth-century writing. No manuscript written entirely in Rustic capitals is to be seen. In the case of this letter as well as of square capitals, its long survival as a display script is, however, abundantly illustrated. Half-uncial also is represented only by its ninth-century revival. Uncial itself, that script of special dignity and authority, is to be studied here in a historical example of the seventh century (no. 3) and an imperial revival of the tenth (no. 11), even though we are unable to present a specimen from its greatest era, the fifth century. Irish majuscules are to be seen only in reflection (no. 6), not in full majesty.

However, all of these gaps can be filled through the study of one of the great compilations of calligraphical specimens, such as those of Traube, Chroust, The Palaeographical Society, and of Professor Lowe. Such works may select what they wish of the greatest monuments, and no exhibition can rival them in this respect. The point of an exhibition is not completeness—but the physical presence of objects which are living witnesses of history and of human endeavor. Each one of these parchment volumes or fragments—be it a royal gift or the provincial production of some monk in a remote mission—represents all that went before and all that was to emerge in the effort to preserve the loftiest thoughts and aspirations of humanity in clear and worthy form. That this effort succeeded is clear. The spark which it kept alive during the dark ages was to be fanned into flames. The need for the written word so early felt grew ever greater. In the fifteenth century, the unquenchable thirst for books could not be satisfied even by the ceaseless efforts of the scribes. Man was forced to invent a way to multiply texts 'without the exertion of any pen whatosever'—and so came the printing press.

Since this exhibition concerns the forms of writing, I have tried to assign a name to the script of each volume described in Part I. This causes little difficulty in the earlier scripts, so thoroughly explored by Professor E. A. Lowe, nor in fact in most of those up to the twelfth century or so. I have used the term 'Carolingian minuscule' for the examples that descend from that hand named in honor of its inception in Charlemagne's time, but whose development and survival was, like many cultural matters, far more immortal than historical or political things. This is a usage accepted by everyone. When it comes to designating the transitional scripts that led toward gothic writing, or indeed the different kinds of gothic script itself, there is no such unanimity. The greatest experts disagree in naming them. In fact a symposium on the *Nomenclature des Écritures Livresques*, called in Paris in 1953 to settle these very points, only proved again how diverse are the opinions of the specialists. Although the symposium settled nothing, I have found its published papers enlightening for the expert analysis of significant features of the various scripts. Grateful allusion to these discussions will be found cited in various entries, as well as reflected in at least some of the nomenclature I have adopted. Especially helpful has been Stanley Morison's essay on '*Black Letter*' *Text*, which survived the wartime bombing of London as a fragment of a partially completed work on calligraphy whose destruction can only be lamented. Only one hundred copies of this invaluable work were printed.

Any effort such as this is by its nature a compilation and absorption of the more specialized labors of others. My debts to many will become clear in the bibliographical references. The prefaces provided by Professor E. A. Lowe for the volumes of his monumental work on the earliest Latin manuscripts, *Codices Latini Antiquiores*, have been an invaluable fountainhead of information and wisdom. The volume concerning early manuscripts in American collections is even now in preparation. Had I the advantage of using it, my remarks concerning nos. 3–6 would have benefited greatly.

If this exhibition should stimulate some to seek a fuller introduction to the mysteries and beauties of the subject, I can suggest that they begin with two very readable and informative surveys by the foremost authorities: the chapter by Professor Lowe on 'Handwriting' in *The Legacy of the Middle Ages*, edited by C. G. Crump and C. F. Jacob, Oxford, 1951; and Professor B. L. Ullman, *Ancient Writing and its Influence*, New York, 1932. And of course, the classic handbook in the field, E. M. Thompson, *Introduction to Greek and Latin Paleography*, Oxford, 1912, is indispensable and has lately been reprinted.

It only remains for me to thank those who have labored especially over this initial section of the catalogue, making its production possible under the pressures always attendant upon such an undertaking: my assistants, Mrs. Thomas Butterbaugh and Mrs. Martin Vogelhut, as well as Mrs. Edward McCracken, all of the Walters Art Gallery. Their loyalty and alertness has saved me many an error. For the abundant ones that may still remain, I refer the reader to the scribal colophon reproduced in no. 42.

DOROTHY MINER, Keeper of Manuscripts
The Walters Art Gallery

## *Incised Square Capitals*

1 FUNERAL ALTAR

Rome (?), 1st century A.D.

No. 23.16. In Latin. Carved in marble, H. 25¾; W. 22¼; D. 18 inches.

Provenance: Don Marcello Massarenti Collection, Rome. Acquired by Henry Walters in 1902.

*The Walters Art Gallery*

The carved monumental inscriptions of the Romans had a long development, but reached a pinnacle of artistry in the late first and early second centuries A.D. In the estimation of later ages, the apogee of perfection was the inscription carved in A.D. 114 or slightly earlier, for the base of the Column of Trajan in the Forum of that emperor. The structure, proportions and spacing of its letters were the subject of study from the early Renaissance to modern times (cf. nos. 54, 55). The incised capitals had a continuous influence on the majuscules and especially the display script in books produced throughout the Middle Ages.

The present example is several generations earlier than the Trajanic inscription. It is an altar dedicated by a Marcus Ogulnius to his young son of the same name, a monument which he intended also to serve as his own memorial. The inscription reads: D. M. | M. OGVLNIO | IVSTO FILIO | PIENTISSIMO | VIX ANN. XV MENSII D. XXII | M. OGVLNIVS | IVSTVS PATER | ET SIBI FECIT | .

An inscription of this kind was first written out with brush and color on the marble. Some of the qualities developed by carved inscriptions reflect this calligraphic origin, such as the shading of the strokes of the letters in thick and thin parts. Other characteristics are due to the use of the chisel—such as the small serifs to be seen at the tops and bases of F, M and N, T, etc. The swelling parts of round letters like G, O and S are incised more deeply than their light lines. The squarish bottom of the G occurs in other first-century inscriptions, but was rounded more gracefully by the early second century. The gently splayed lines of the M, which blended well with adjacent rounded letters, were an especially subtle Roman device, not always repeated.

Bibliography: *Corpus Inscriptionum Latinarum*, VI, no. 23414; *Catalogue du Musée de peinture, sculpture et archéologie au Palais Accoramboni*, II, Rome, 1897, p. 151, no. 61.

## *Incised Square Capitals*

### 2 DEDICATORY ALTAR

Rome (?), 2nd half of 1st century A.D.

No. 23.184. In Latin. Marble. H. 32⅛; W. 18¼; D. 15¾ inches.

Provenance: Don Marcello Massarenti Collection, Rome. Acquired by Henry Walters in 1902.

*The Walters Art Gallery*

This altar betrays the calligraphic design which guided the stonecutter much more clearly than does no. 1. The most obvious features are the adjustments in size and spacing which allow the last four letters of the top line to be accommodated. The slightly larger T has an upward-curving top which shelters the end of the C, a dwarfed I and part of the S. Likewise, toward the end of the fourth line, the outermost horizontals of F and L flare gracefully above or under the adjacent letter. However, a close inspection will reveal that some of the lines of other letters, such as A and V, are subtly curved, and the D shows an undulation not to be found in that letter on no. 1. The possibility of adapting letters in an ornamental way to the space available was attentively studied by medieval letterers. In the monogram-pages of Carolingian Gospel books, and even more noticeably in the 'display script' of romanesque volumes, the opportunities are exploited to a wonderful degree (cf. no. 19).

This altar was dedicated by a lady to the goddess Mother Earth. The inscription reads: DEAE SANCTIS | SIMAE TER | RAE MATRI | AVRELIA FLA | VIA IVLIANA | C E VOTVM | SOLVIT |

Bibliography: *Catalogue du Musée de peinture, sculpture et archéologie au Palais Accoramboni*, II, Rome, 1897, p. 150, no. 53 (?).

## *'Natural' Uncials*

### 3 SAINT AUGUSTINE, HOMILAE DECEM IN EPISTOLAM SANCTI JOANNIS

Benedictine Abbey of St. Peter, Luxeuil, France, A.D. 669.

Ms. M. 334. In Latin. 133 vellum leaves, 10×6⅞ inches. Written in uncial script in long lines, with some use of square capitals for captions. Brown ink with occasional rubrication in minium (now oxidized). One large initial decorated with typical Merovingian fish-and-bird-motives; pen-work ornamentation around quire letters. Binding: 20th-century tan crushed levant by Duprez Lahey.

Provenance: Abbey of Luxeuil; Cathedral of St. Peter, Beauvais, from the 11th century until the French Revolution (15th cent. cat., MS. 79); then Louis de Caron, Château de Troussures; J. Pierpont Morgan, 1907.

*Lent by the Pierpont Morgan Library*

The uncial script as developed in Italy was one of the most majestic bookhands ever devised. Formal, balanced, clear, sumptuous in its rounded and stable proportions, it originated in the fourth or perhaps even the third century A.D. It gained authority in subsequent centuries not only for its beauty, but because it was the writing in which were handed down the oldest and finest copies of the Scriptures—the revision of the Bible by St. Jerome in the fourth century, the works of the great Early Church Fathers, such as Augustine. The fullest flowering of its development occurred in the fifth century—and many manuscripts in this writing were carried from Italy to Gaul and England. These became the foundation of local emulation—sometimes, as in England, so skilful as to puzzle the connoisseur. In Gaul the script was adopted and 'naturalized,' remaining for several centuries in use as the letter for major books—a script of dignity and authority and honor. This concept of the rank of uncial was not forgotten even as new cursive and minuscule forms were developed in the scriptoria (cf. nos. 4–8).

The present venerable volume is written in what has been termed the 'natural' uncials of Gaul. The lettering, executed by two scribes, is not as elegant and uniform as that of the great scriptoria of fifth-century Italy. But it has dignity and character. The book is the earliest surviving copy of this text of St. Augustine. It was executed in the Benedictine Abbey of St. Pierre de Luxeuil in Burgundy, which Professor E. A. Lowe has termed "the first great writing center of Merovingian Gaul." Of the production of its scriptorium, this is the earliest manuscript to have survived, being dated 669. It is a key to the recognition of other manuscripts of Luxeuil. Evidence for the exact date and place of origin is furnished by the colophon, which may be translated: "The work was finished, by the grace of God, in the monastery of Luxeuil, the twelfth year of Clothaire, thirteenth indiction, the fortieth year of our father." The two persons referred to are Clothaire III, King of Burgundy (ruled 656–670) and Waldebert, third abbot of Luxeuil. Luxeuil had been founded by the Irish missionary, St. Columban, in A.D. 590, but he and his immediate followers soon moved on to other enterprises, and no Irish influence survives in the Luxeuil manuscripts which have come down to us.

An indication of the development of uncials along natural lines may be seen here in the tendency to ascenders and descenders as tall again as the main body of each letter. In earlier uncial, the length of such ascending and descending

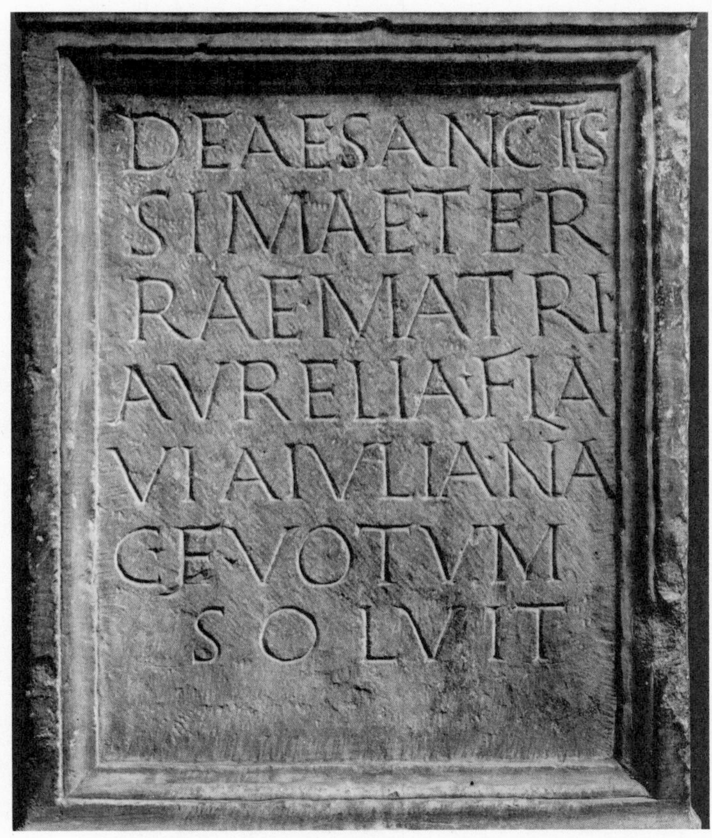


2. Dedicatory Altar. Rome (?), 1st century A.D.

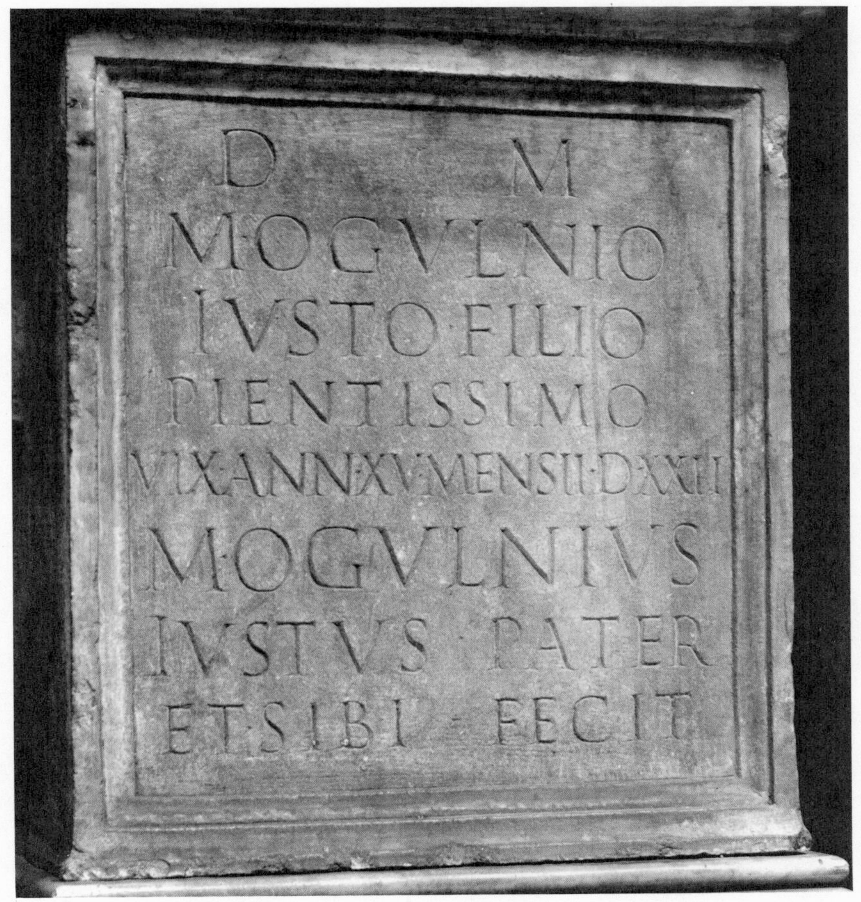


1. Funerary Altar. Rome (?), 1st century A.D.

3. St. Augustine: *Homilae Decem*. Luxeuil, A.D. 669

4. Haggai (fragment). Luxeuil, beginning of 8th century

elements was restricted, and in the 'artificial' uncials revived in the ninth and tenth centuries, this early requirement of an even body was emphasized still further (cf. nos. 7, 8, 11).

Bibliography: Of the extensive literature on this important manuscript, one may cite: J. Mabillon, *De re diplomatica*, Paris, 1681, Lib. v, p. 359, facs.; Migne, *Patrologia Latina*, vol. 35, 1845, col. 1979; J. Havet, "La date d'un manuscrit de Luxeuil . . . ," *Bibliothèque de l'École des Chartes*, XLVI, 1855, p. 429; L. Delisle, "Notice sur un manuscrit de l'abbaye de Luxeuil," *Notices et extraits des manuscrits*, 31, pt. 2, 1886, p. 149, pls. I–III; F. Traube, *Vorlesungen und Abhandlungen*, I, Munich, 1909, p. 242; E. M. Thompson, *Introduction to Greek and Latin Palaeography*, Oxford, 1912, p. 289, facs. 92; H. Omont, "Recherches sur la bibliothèque de . . . Beauvais," *Mémoires de l'Institut national de France, Académie des Inscriptions et Belles-Lettres*, XL, 1916, pp. 2, 14, 27, 83, 85; E. H. Zimmermann, *Vorkarolingischen Miniaturen*, Berlin, 1916, p. 47; E. A. Lowe, "A List of the Oldest Extant Mss. of St. Augustine," *Miscellanea Agostiniana*, II, 1931, p. 235; B. L. Ullman, *Ancient Writing and its Influence*, New York, 1932, pp. 69–71, pl. VIIb; De Ricci, II, p. 1428, with further references; E. A. Lowe, *Revue Bénédictine*, nos. 1–2, 1953; *idem*, *C.L.A.*, VI, 1953, pp. xv–xvii.

## *Merovingian Minuscules*

### 4 THE PROPHETS: HAGGAI

Abbey of St. Peter, Luxeuil, or an affiliated house, France (Burgundy), beginning of the 8th century.

Ms. in Latin. Upper half (14 lines) of 1 vellum leaf. Written in advanced Luxeuil minuscule in 2 columns, without horizontal ruling. Running title in uncial on the verso. Brown ink. Merovingian fish-form and other decorative initials in red, green and yellow. Unbound.

Provenance: Luxeuil (?); Benedictine abbey of Admont, Austria.

*Lent by the Newberry Library*

This example of Merovingian minuscules may serve to represent the many different kinds of script which developed locally during the confused period after the breakup of the Roman Empire, due to the barbarian migrations. The formal book hands, such as uncial (cf. no. 3) and half-uncial, had been developed out of long-established literary usage. As events disrupted the even course of such traditions, other forms became current, especially writing based upon the script of the notaries. These scripts were of some antiquity, going back at least to the fourth century. They differed from the more stately book hands in that they were cursive, being written more rapidly; they tended to be more compressed and thus saved space, and to the same end they could develop systems of ligatures and abbreviations. Although originally not as formal in intention as the more ancient book hands, in the scriptoria of the monasteries the cursive achieved many local qualities of regularity and beauty. The difficulty eventually lay in the peculiarities of the scripts, which made them of doubtful legibility in other centers—a factor of crucial importance when each new book had to be copied from an earlier exemplar.

The first calligraphic minuscule of France was developed at Luxeuil, and was a script of great character, although short-lived. The Luxeuil minuscule reached its apogee toward the last decades of the seventh century. The best examples had a more regular *ductus* than the present fragment, greater angularity, and a more pronounced tendency to lateral compression.

Minuscule may be defined as the equivalent of our 'lowercase' letter, being combined with capital initial letters. Its ultimate nature in contrast to majuscule writing will become clear in the discussion and illustrations of nos. 7 and 8.

This fragment is one of eleven surviving folios of a manuscript of the Books of the Prophets which are to be found in Admont (MS. 261 and Frag. 12), Munich (Clm. 29158a), Yale University (Branford College), Pierpont Morgan Library (M. 798 and M. 825) and Princeton University Library (Garrett Collection). All of these fragments had been used during the later Middle Ages as fly-leaves or pastedowns in the bindings of books. The Newberry fragment is the upper half of one of the leaves preserved in Admont Frag. 12, and it contains the text of Haggai I: 7–9, 11–14; II: 2–5, 7–10. The first three lines at the top of the left column in the illustration read: "Hec dicit dn̄s exercituum ponite corda vestra super bias (i.e. vias) vestras."

Bibliography: E. A. Lowe, *C.L.A.*, VI, 1953, p. xvi; IX, 1959, p. 29, no. 1337; X, p. 2, no. **1337.

## *Anglo-Saxon Minuscules*

### 5 ST. ISIDORE OF SEVILLE, SYNONYMA

Probably region of Würzburg, Franconia, end of 8th century.

Plimpton MS. 129. In Latin. 1 vellum leaf, written in 21 long lines. Unbound.

Provenance: From an Anglo-Saxon center in Germany. Said to have been in a fire at the Hotel de Cluny, Paris; J. Martini; acquired from him by George A. Plimpton, New York City. Presented by the latter to Columbia University in 1936.

*Lent by Columbia University Libraries*

Insular manuscripts and Insular scribes accompanied the Anglo-Saxon missionaries who pushed into the German regions in the eighth century, founding new monasteries or taking over ones established earlier by the Irish. The habits of Insular scribes were carried on in these centers for several generations. Such a fragment as this demonstrates well the main characteristics of this script.

It was the Irish who are thought to have been the first to develop minuscule writing. The English scribes were in close touch with them at an early date, both in Ireland and in Northumbria. They adopted the angular and vertical *ductus* of the Irish, the closely packed letter sequence, the abundant ligatures and abbreviations. Many of the peculiarities of Irish script continued in Anglo-Saxon establishments, although modified in the direction of somewhat less crowding and fewer bizarre forms. The present example shows the kind of script written in Anglo-Saxon foundations such as Fulda and Würzburg.

This leaf, which contains the *Synonyma*, I, cap. 65–68, was originally conjugate with another leaf from the same codex which is now in the Pierpont Morgan Library, MS. M. 599.

Bibliography: E. A. Lowe in *Revue Bénédictine*, XXXIX, 1927, pp. 193–194; De Ricci, II, p. 1775, no. 129.

## *Irish Majuscules*

6 ST. ISIDORE OF SEVILLE, ETYMOLOGIAE

Irish-founded continental center, late 8th or early 9th century.

Plimpton MS. 127. In Latin. 4 cut-down vellum leaves, 8¼×5½ inches. Written in Irish majuscule in long lines, originally 25 to the page; simple capital letters, the fields picked out with red or yellow. Black ink.

Provenance: Monastery of St. Emmeram, Regensburg (reused in bindings); Ernst Fischer; G. Martini; George A. Plimpton, New York City; presented by him in 1936.

*Lent by Columbia University Libraries*

The date and nature of the origin of Insular calligraphy is a matter of conjecture. The Irish, in contrast to their Insular contemporaries, the English, never wrote in uncial (cf. no. 3). But perhaps the ancient script known as half-uncial was the root of the peculiarly individual script that developed in Ireland after the foundation of its Christian monastic activity in the fifth century and up to the time when we begin to have a few definitely dateable Irish paleographical documents, at the very end of the seventh and beginning of the eighth century. Ireland never knew the occupation of the Romans, as England and Gaul did. So she was not influenced by the magnificent Italian uncial, by the fluent Rustic capital script or by the monumental square capitals, and other venerable and well-established Italian scripts which had made their way at an early date to Gaul and to England, and which played a significant part in the development of their book hands.

Despite the lack of relatively early dateable examples, there still seems a basis for the belief that the Irish monastic scriptoria had a significant influence upon foundations in England and upon the continent, by reason of the exchange of scholars and by missionary effort. What came to be known as the 'Insular hand' of England and English foundations is thought by many scholars to have developed its special qualities thanks to Irish instruction. Especially noteworthy is the fact that as early as the seventh century the Irish had developed a true minuscule script, which may have contributed not a little to the ultimate triumph of minuscule (see nos. 7, 8).

The most outstanding example of the Irish formal script, or majuscule, is that in the renowned Book of Kells of about A.D. 800. That book in every way is an exceptional and extraordinary achievement. More characteristic of the Irish majuscule book hand, especially as it reached the continent and was perpetuated in the many missionary foundations of the Irish, is the present example, although by a somewhat inexpert scribe.

Eighteen leaves from this Isidore manuscript survive, some in Munich, and others formerly in the Sir Thomas Phillipps Collection—their existence due to the fact that they were reused as paste-downs or fly-leaves in various books bound in the fifteenth century at the library of the monastery of St. Emmeram at Regensburg. The Columbia leaves are from Book I of the *Etymologiae*.

Bibliography: De Ricci, II, p. 1775, no. 127; E. A. Lowe, *C.L.A.*, II, 1935, p. 8, no. 144; IX, 1959, p. 28, no. **144.

## *Carolingian Minuscules*

7 LEAF OF A BIBLE

Abbey of St. Martin, Tours, about A.D. 850.

Ms. 30. In Latin. 1 vellum leaf, cut down, 15½×10⅝ inches. Written in Carolingian minuscule in 2 columns, with ornamental initial in red, grey, violet and yellow; title in square capitals in alternating lines of minium and brown; introductory lines in uncials; text in half-uncial and minuscule; *explicits* and running heading in Rustic capitals. Brown ink. Unbound.

Provenance: St. Martin's, Tours; Abbey of St. Maximin, Trier; acquired in Kiel ca. 1930 by Professor Rörig of Berlin University; acquired from his widow in 1953 by H. P. Kraus, New York, from whom purchased by

5. St. Isidore: *Synonyma*. Würzburg (?), end of 8th century

6. St. Isidore: *Etymologiae*. Irish Center on Continent, ca. A.D. 800

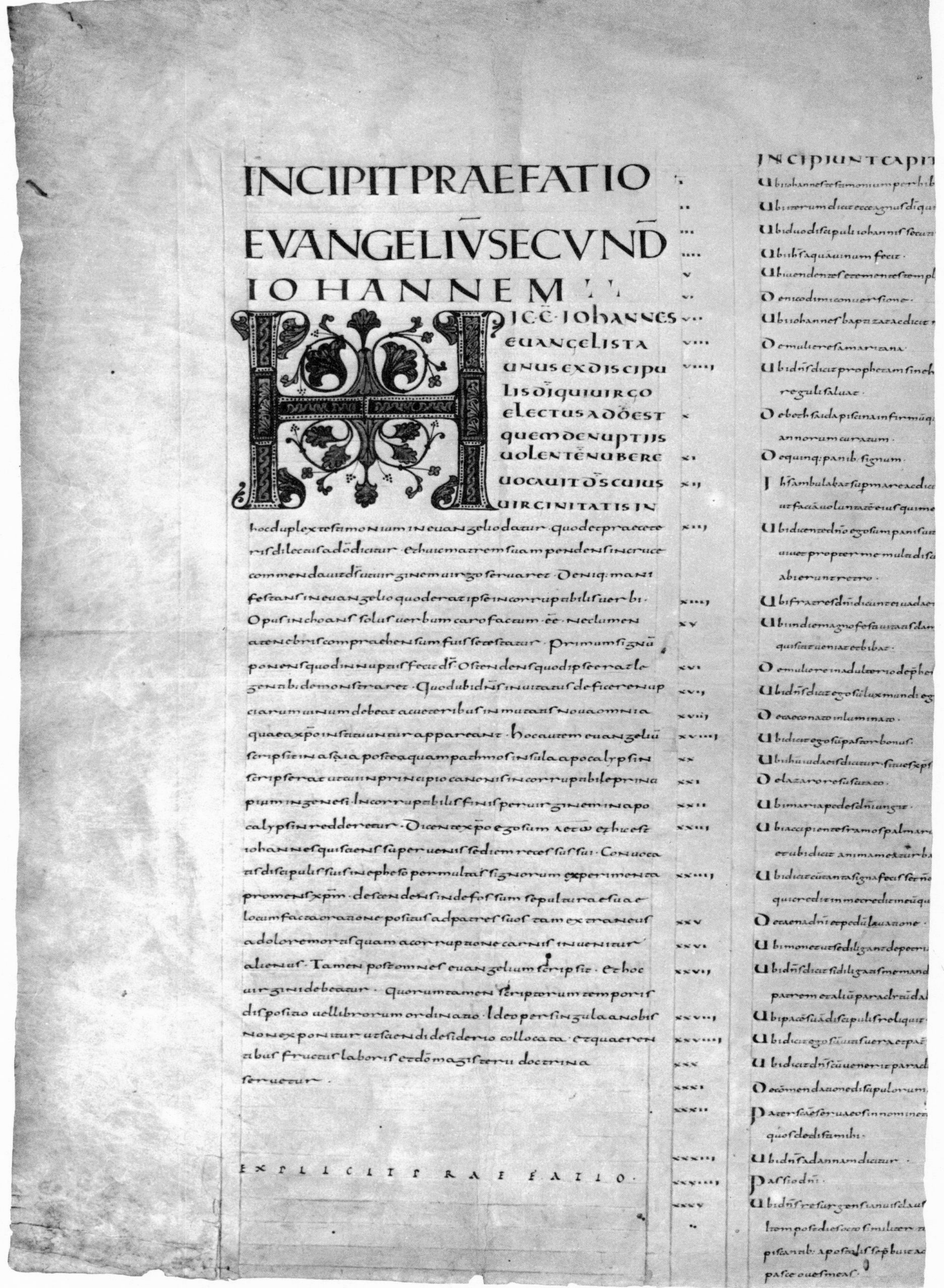


7. Bible (fragment). Tours, ca. A.D. 850

George A. Poole, Jr. in 1954. Acquired by Indiana University with his collection, 1958.

*Lent by the Lilly Library, Indiana University*

During the eighth century experiments were made in various French writing centers to develop a minuscule script which would be clearer and somewhat more formal than the pointed Insular minuscules (no. 5) or the complicated cursive minuscule of Luxeuil (no. 4). The move was in the direction of greater roundness of form, fewer ligatures and abbreviations and the elimination of cursive features. The scribes of Charlemagne's Court School and the scriptorium of Corbie (near Amiens), a daughter-house of Luxeuil, both achieved an essentially 'Carolingian' minuscule by around A.D. 780. The tremendous activity in the production of fine books, which began in the last two decades of the eighth century and proceeded throughout the ninth, is generally attributed to the active interest and patronage of Charlemagne, which concerned itself with all phases of literary and artistic development, both secular and religious. In 782 he invited the renowned British scholar, Alcuin of York (ca. 732–804), to take charge of the Court School and his educational program. One facet of this program was the critical revision of the current Vulgate text of the Bible and also of the Mass-book for the services of the church. In 796 Alcuin became abbot of St. Martin's at Tours, which was destined to become the foremost center of the new style of minuscule writing and to bring it during the course of the ninth century to its highest state of perfection.

The present example, although but a fragment, illustrates perfectly the characteristics of the Carolingian script developed at Tours. This part of a leaf gives some idea of the majestic dimensions of the great folio Bibles that were prepared at Tours during the first half of the ninth century to circulate the text as revised by Alcuin. The leaf was reused in later times as a fly-leaf—evidently in a binding in the library of St. Maximin's at Trier—but, despite the cutting away of half the width of the inner column of writing and at least three or four inches of the lower text and margin, the surface of script and ornament have not been impaired. The text originally ran to about 52 lines per page, as in the other great Tours Bibles. This leaf contains, on the recto, Luke XXIII: 41–XXIV: 20, 23–53; and on the verso (illustrated) the preface and capitula to St. John's Gospel. Another fragmentary leaf from the same Bible, also in the collection of Indiana University, containing part of the text of John, had been reused as a paste-down and retains a fourteenth- or fifteenth-century ex-libris: *Codex monasterii sancti maximini archiepiscopi Treverim.*

The fragment demonstrates well the distinction between different styles of writing for different purposes: the major titles in square capitals, the opening lines and rubricated captions in uncials, the prefaces in the characteristic half-uncial of Tours, *explicits* and running headings in Rustic capitals, the capitula and text in Touronian minuscule. The use of these various scripts implies a consciousness of rank among them—what has been termed 'the hierarchy of scripts.' To a degree, this indicates a recognition of the antiquity as well as the relative formality of the lettering styles. The square capitals hark back to monumental Roman letters (cf. no. 1), and had been used as a script for entire books only in the fourth century and dedicated specifically to Vergil (so far as we can tell from the four fragmentary examples which survive). The Rustic capital was a classical book hand of second rank, being slightly less formal, more compact and more rapidly written, but still the hand in which the earliest manuscripts of many classical authors descended to the Middle Ages. The uncial, as the formal book hand of major manuscripts in Italy, Gaul and Britain up to the beginning of the eighth century, is discussed elsewhere (no. 3). It should be noted that the ninth-century version of uncial reverts to the more even-bodied proportions of the fifth century, with the ascenders and descenders of only a very few of the letters breaking the line of writing (cf. nos. 3, 8, 11). The half-uncial as used here is an especially characteristic Tours form. It derives from one of the more formal hands of earlier centuries that was a rival of uncial, but which originally offered certain cursive elements. It resembles its offspring, minuscule, in the length of its ascenders and descenders, in the forms of e, r, s, d, and b, for instance. The Insular flat-topped g is peculiar and the round a; the N preserves the capital form. The minuscule (seen at the right of the illustration) retains many of these characters, including the clubbed ascenders and tapering descenders—perhaps a souvenir of Insular practices. But forms of e, n, g, b, d, r and s are full-fledged minuscule.

The great importance of this Carolingian minuscule lay in its influence upon the book hand of western Europe and England, an influence which was to extend for seven centuries and to affect even the forms of typography in the Renaissance.

Bibliography: Bond and Faye, *Supplement*, p. 180, no. 30.

## *Carolingian Minuscules*

### 8 THE FOUR GOSPELS

Abbey of St. Martin, Tours, ca. A.D. 857–860.

Ms. M. 860. In Latin. 205 vellum leaves, 11⅝×8½ inches.

Written in Carolingian minuscule in 2 columns, with use of burnished gold square capitals on purple at head of each Gospel, uncial and half-uncial for the prefaces, run-

ning headings and *explicits* in Rustic capitals, the text in Touronian minuscule. Ink brown to black. Richly illuminated in gold, silver and colors with 6 ornamented Canon Tables, 5 framed decorative title pages, 4 elaborate *incipit* pages with large initials, 7 smaller ornamental initials. Binding: modern red velvet with silver clasps. Provenance: St. Martin's, Tours; Lucienne Delamarre; Henry Yates Thompson, London; A. Chester Beatty, London. Acquired from Mrs. Chester Beatty in 1952.
*Lent by the Pierpont Morgan Library*

This volume is an excellent example of the nobility of the fully developed calligraphic style of Tours. It is a luxurious book with richly illuminated Canon Tables of architectural aspect, and with the first letters or words of each Gospel presented in the form of a monumental monogram of gold and silver enlivened with green, red, blue and purple. These sumptuous 'parade pages' are not exhibited nor are they illustrated herewith, since the emphasis of this exhibition is upon the book hand, rather than upon the book ornamentation. The volume has been opened to reveal the ordered and disciplined calligraphy that evolved during the ninth century at Tours. The 'hierarchy of scripts' described under no. 7 is magnificently in evidence here: square capitals, Rustic capitals, uncials, half-uncials and minuscule. Like the previous entry, the text is written upon the thin, polished vellum characteristic of fine Tours volumes. Here is achieved the calligraphic quality that caused the works of this scriptorium to have such an immediate and lasting impact upon the ateliers of western Europe: the spaciousness of format in terms of margins (at least one-third of the width of the page), of interlinear allowance, of amplitude and roundness of letter-forms. Deliberate, unhurried, the script virtually eliminates ligatures, is sparing of abbreviations. Lightly shaded, the clubbed ascenders and tapering descenders project a distance just equal to the height of the main round body of the script. The requirements of square capitals and uncials had meant that they were always written with a broad pen held straight, with the flat edge of the nib kept in all its movements parallel to the top of the page. Despite the deliberate avoidance of haste, the scribes of Tours adopted one practice of cursive workmanship. For the half-uncials and also for the minuscules of the main text they held the pen somewhat on a slant—effecting greater ease, even if haste was outlawed. For this the nib would have been cut on a slant also, so that the edge could continue to remain parallel to the top of the page. The slight tendency to a slope in the ascenders, and an occasional light joining of one letter to the next, betray this more comfortable method—which could in careless hands lead to quite another effect.

This Gospel book, in the opinion of the late Wilhelm Köhler, belongs to the production of the monastery just after A.D. 853, when the community returned from a period of exile due to the depredations of the Norman invaders. It still retains, both in script and illumination, close relationship to the achievement of the period just before the exile, when, under Abbot Vivian (ruled 845–851), the most distinguished books of Tours were executed.

Bibliography: H. Y. Thompson, *A Descriptive Catalogue of Fourteen Illuminated Manuscripts . . .*, Cambridge, 1912, p. 53, MS. C; *idem, Illustrations from One Hundred Manuscripts in the Library of Henry Yates Thompson*, London, 1912, p. 1, pls. I–VIII; E. K. Rand, *A Survey of the Manuscripts of Tours*, Cambridge, 1921, vol. I, p. 154, no. 115, vol. II, pls. CXXVIII, CXXIX; Eric G. Millar, *The Library of A. Chester Beatty . . .*, Oxford, 1927, pp. 42–43, no. 8, pls. XVI–XIX; W. Köhler, *Die Schule von Tours*, Berlin, 1930, I, pt. 1, p. 429, I, pt. 2, pp. 296–298, 409, pls. 115 a–e; E. K. Rand, in *Theological Review*, XXIV, no. 4, 1931, p. 332, no. 47; F. B. Adams, Jr., *Third Annual Report to the Fellows of the Pierpont Morgan Library*, New York, 1952, pp. 11–13, illus.; Bond and Faye, *Supplement*, p. 365, no. 860.

## *Carolingian Minuscules*

9 THE FOUR GOSPELS

Diocese of Freising, Bavaria, ca. A.D. 875.
Ms. W. 4. In Latin. 215 vellum leaves, 7×4¾ inches. Written in Carolingian minuscule in long lines; titles of Matthew in square capitals in minium and brown; other titles, running headings, captions, first lines and *explicits* in Rustic capitals. Uncials occur only in captions of Canon Tables. Brown ink. 18 ornamented Canon Tables. 4 full-page miniatures of the Evangelists. Binding: 16th-century velvet over boards, with vestiges of old manuscript paste-downs (12th and 14th century).
Provenance: Diocese of Freising; subsequently in a 19th-century German collection, when page numbers were inserted. Acquired in Paris by Henry Walters, probably around 1917.
*The Walters Art Gallery*

The success of the Carolingian minuscule as developed at Tours and certain other French centers was immediate. It became the favored writing in scriptoria in Germany, Italy and—in the tenth century—England. Of course, local variations developed, which often presented scripts quite distinct in effect. The most frequent variation was, not unnaturally, a tendency to abandon some of the spaciousness and unhurried quality which characterized the Tours script in its own home. The pen held at a slant produced letters not

8. Gospels. Tours, ca. A.D. 857–860

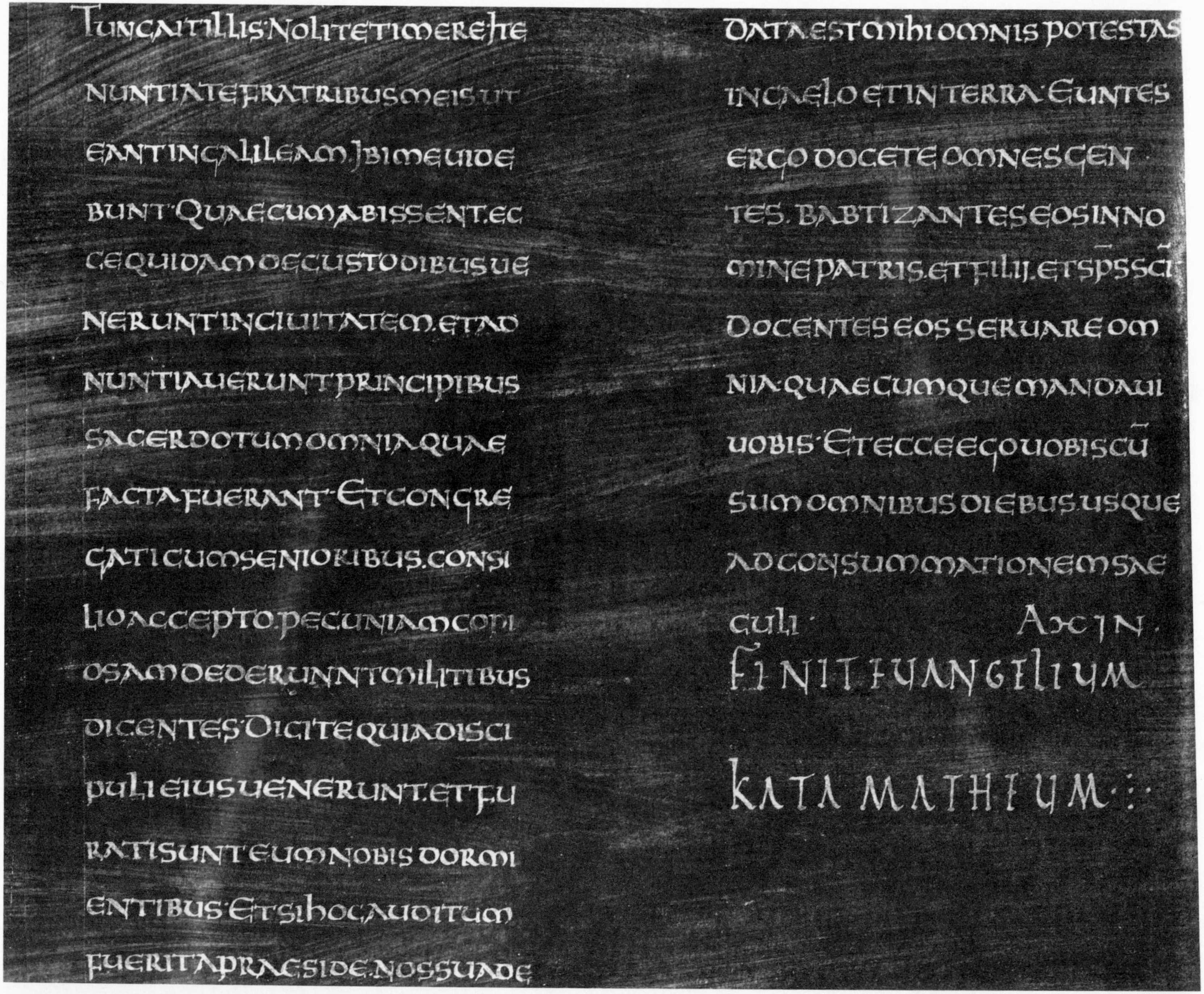

TUNCAITILLIS·NOLITETIMEREITE
NUNTIATEFRATRIBUSMEISUT
EANTINGALILEAM.IBIMEUIDE
BUNT·QUAECUMABISSENT.EC
CEQUIDAMDECUSTODIBUSUE
NERUNTINCIUITATEM.ETAD
NUNTIAUERUNTPRINCIPIBUS
SACERDOTUMOMNIAQUAE
FACTAFUERANT·ETCONGRE
GATICUMSENIORIBUS.CONSI
LIOACCEPTO.PECUNIAMCOPI
OSAMDEDERUNTMILITIBUS
DICENTES·DICITEQUIADISCI
PULIEIUSUENERUNT.ETFU
RATISUNTEUMNOBISDORMI
ENTIBUS·ETSIHOCAUDITUM
FUERITAPRAESIDE.NOSSUADE

DATAESTMIHIOMNISPOTESTAS
INCAELOETINTERRA·EUNTES
ERGODOCETEOMNESGEN
TES.BABTIZANTESEOSINNO
MINEPATRIS.ETFILII.ETSPSSCI
DOCENTESEOSSERUAREOM
NIAQUAECUMQUEMANDAUI
UOBIS·ETECCEEGOUOBISCU
SUMOMNIBUSDIEBUS.USQUE
ADCONSUMMATIONEMSAE
CULI· AXCIN·

FINIT EUANGELIUM

KATA MATHEUM·:·

11. Gospels in Gold Uncials on Purple. Trier, last quarter of 10th century

only with a somewhat sloping *ductus*, but which tended to become more compressed laterally.

The present example illustrates these points well. It is a splendid specimen of what Stanley Morison happily christened 'rustic' Carolingian minuscules. As the name suggests, the script partakes of certain of the qualities of the venerable Rustic capitals—condensed laterally, more rapidly penned than fully round forms, less shading, a tendency to slope—although carefully controlled. The scribe is conscious enough of his more 'rustic' tendencies and has fitly used Rustic capitals for his majuscules, except for the beginning of each verse, where a square capital is employed: in minium, dark red, violet or blue.

This little Gospels, unusually small for an altar-book, was executed in the diocese of Freising in Bavaria, perhaps at the time of Bishop Anno (ruled 854–875), according to an unpublished opinion of Dr. Bernhard Bischoff of Munich. In script and in textual peculiarities it is linked to a Gospel-book written at the order of Bishop Anno, now in Munich (MS. Clm. 6215), as well as to another closely related Freising book also in Munich (Clm. 17011). The style of its miniatures, as in these other examples, shows a derivation from the rapid, expressive painting-style which had been developed at Reims in northern France earlier in the century.

Bibliography: W. H. Frere, *Studies in Early Roman Liturgy*, II, *The Roman Gospel-Lectionary*, London, 1934, p. 147; De Ricci, I, p. 767, no. 62; Walters *Cat.*, 1949, no. 6, pl. II; Bond and Faye, *Supplement*, p. 195, no. 62, with other references. For an analysis of 'rustic' Carolingian minuscules, see Stanley Morison, *'Black-Letter' Text*, Cambridge, 1942, pp. 9–11; for the Freising scriptorium in the ninth century, see B. Bischoff, *Die südostdeutschen Schreibschulen und Bibliotheken in der Karolingerzeit*, Teil I, 2nd ed., Wiesbaden 1960, pp. 68–70.

## *Carolingian Minuscules*

### 10 ST. GREGORY THE GREAT, HOMILIES

North Italy, ca. 900.

Ms. in Latin. Part of 1 vellum leaf, 12¼×5¼ inches. Written in Carolingian minuscules in what were originally 2 columns; mixed use of uncials and Rustic capitals for *explicits* and *incipits*. Large ornamental initial with lacertines and interlace in colors introduces the first word of text in fancifully interplaced letters (cf. no. 19). Unbound.

*Lent by Mr. and Mrs. Philip Hofer*

This fragment represents the migration of Tours minuscule beyond the Alps, where, indeed, it lasted far longer than in its native land. The scribe of this specimen has been at pains to emulate something of the expansive, unhurried aspect of Tours script. He betrays his more provincial status in several ways—the lack of a truly disciplined *ductus*, the omission of clubbed ascenders, the preservation of various ligatures belonging to more cursive script: st, et, ct, fe, fi. A later example of Carolingian minuscule in Italy is discussed under no. 15.

Bibliography: Portland *Cat.*, 1958, no. 3, illus.

## *'Artificial' Uncials*

### 11 THE GOLDEN GOSPELS ON PURPLE VELLUM

Trier, Abbey of St. Maximin's, last quarter of the 10th century.

Ms. M. 23. In Latin. 144 vellum leaves, 14¼×10¼ inches. Written in gold uncials in 2 columns upon heavy vellum painted purple, in shades varying from mauve to slate-blue. Occasional use of rustic capitals; one decorative initial. Binding: English 18th-century red morocco. Provenance: St. Maximin's, Trier; Ralph Palmer of Little Chelsea (18th cent.); Alexander, 10th Duke of Hamilton (until 1882); Theodore Irwin, Oswego, New York (1889); J. Pierpont Morgan (1901).

*Lent by the Pierpont Morgan Library*

The opulence of golden letters inscribed upon purple was a practice developed in classical times, which continued during the days of the Church Fathers (who frowned upon such ostentation). The earliest surviving manuscripts on purple are of the fifth and sixth centuries (six in Latin, six in Greek and one in Gothic), but all except one are written in silver letters, which, being subject to oxidization, are far less splendid in appearance than the gold. During the Carolingian era chrysography upon purple was revived for especially sumptuous manuscripts and was continued in the Ottonian period. Through the ninth century the coloring of the vellum was achieved by dyeing the sheets. In Ottonian times, as seen in the present manuscript, the leaves were painted purple. The burnished gold letters are upon a yellow size.

During the eighth century, uncial script gradually gave way to minuscule, except for captions and display purposes (cf. nos. 7, 8, 12). Display uncials of the ninth and tenth centuries tend to be more regular and uniform in height than the 'natural' uncials just preceding them, avoiding long ascenders and descenders, permitting the incorporation of some capital forms, such as Q, and some embellishing with serifs. On these points it is instructive to compare a seventh-century example of 'natural' uncials (no. 3).

In any case, the use of uncials for an entire volume in the tenth century was an artificial one, and underscores the very special nature of this particular Gospels. For a very long time this manuscript, because of its archaic writing, was attributed to dates as early as the seventh century. A decade ago, Professor E. A. Lowe demonstrated by means of peculiarities in the uncial forms that this Gospels belongs to a group of splendid manuscripts produced in the monastic scriptorium at Trier during and just after the rule of Archbishop Egbert (977–993). A sixteenth-century inscription apparently copied from an original dedication gives rise to the possibility that the volume was intended as a gift to the young Emperor Otto III. There is evidence that it was prepared for a special occasion, perhaps in some haste, as sixteen different scribes participated in the work.

Bibliography: De Ricci, II, p. 1369. From the very extensive literature one may cite: W. Wattenbach in *Sitzungsberichte der Akademie der Wissenschaften zu Berlin*, 1889, pp. 151 ff.; Walters *Cat.*, 1949, no. 2, frontispiece in color; E. A. Lowe, "The Morgan Golden Gospels: The Date and Origin of the Manuscript," in *Studies in Art and Literature for Belle da Costa Greene*, Princeton, 1954, pp. 266–279, figs. 191–219; Meta Harrsen, *Central European Manuscripts in the Pierpont Morgan Library*, New York, 1958, no. 7, pls. 4, 18, with complete bibliography.

## *Carolingian Minuscules*

### 12 EPISTOLARY

Atelier of the Master of the *Registrum Gregorii*, Trier, ca. 1000.

Ms. W. 9. In Latin. 361 vellum leaves, 5 7/16×4 1/4 inches. Written by several hands in Carolingian minuscules in long lines, with opening words in uncials, rubricated captions in Rustic capitals, rubricated square capitals as initials for main passages. Ornamental foliate letters illuminated in gold and colors at beginning of the volume and at opening of Easter Epistle and lesson. Dark brown ink. Binding: black morocco, inlaid, by Gruel.

Provenance: Trier. Acquired in Paris by Henry Walters.

*The Walters Art Gallery*

This little service-book was made in the same center as the Golden Gospels described under no. 11. The uncial forms have much in common with those used in that sumptuous manuscript. However, the present book is written in the natural script of the place and period, a delicate and competent minuscule. Dr. Carl Nordenfalk, who first recognized the affiliations of this volume, has attributed it to the atelier presided over by the foremost book-artist of the era—the anonymous master who executed the surviving illuminated pages of a codex of the Epistles of Pope Gregory the Great, now divided between the Trier municipal library and Chantilly. Not only his miniatures, but his ornamental initial pages show a genius for spatial and clearly organized, symmetrical but dynamic composition. The books which he executed or supervised are always of the utmost refinement of execution, of script and of carefully selected vellum.

This little book cannot be supposed to be by the master himself, but the conception, the thin, polished vellum, the beauty of the script and of the few illuminated passages all relate to the standards and the style set by him. Closest, perhaps, is the script of a Sacramentary written in his atelier for a Trier church and now in Paris (Bibliothèque Nationale, MS. lat. 10501).

Our manuscript was written by several scribes, and the script of each of them has close connections with other productions of the atelier. This is an unusual volume in several ways: for one thing, it is surprisingly small and compact for an altar-book—although one must make full allowance for the fact that rebindings during the centuries have clipped away much of the marginal area which originally enhanced its dignity. Its height must originally have been about six and one-half inches, and its width five and three-quarters. The contents are exceptional: they comprise the complete text of the readings throughout the year from the Epistles, Acts, Apocalypse and the Old Testament; Gospel readings are given only in abbreviated capitular form, which means that this was intended to be used in conjunction with a regular book of Gospels.

Bibliography: De Ricci, I, p. 768, no. 69; C. Nordenfalk in *Münchner Jahrbuch der bildenden Kunst*, Folge 3, I, 1950, p. 64, fig. 7; Bond and Faye, *Supplement*, p. 195, no. 69.

## *Carolingian Minuscules*

### 13 THE FOUR GOSPELS

Abbey of St. Peter, Reichenau or an affiliated house, ca. A.D. 1030.

Ms. W. 7. In Latin. 202 vellum leaves, 9 1/16×6 1/2 inches. Written by three hands in Carolingian minuscule in long lines, with burnished gold uncials at first lines of chapters and gold marginal uncial initials to each verse. Illuminated in gold and colors are 16 Canon Tables, 4 *incipit* pages, each with large ornamental branching initial and beginning passage in gold majuscules on purple, 4 smaller illuminated branching initials at the prefaces. 5 full-page miniatures. Ink dark to light brown. Binding: modern white vellum.

Provenance: Reichenau or an affiliated house; a 19th-

10. St. Gregory the Great: *Homilae* (fragment). North Italy, ca. A.D. 900

9. Gospels. Freising, ca. A.D. 875

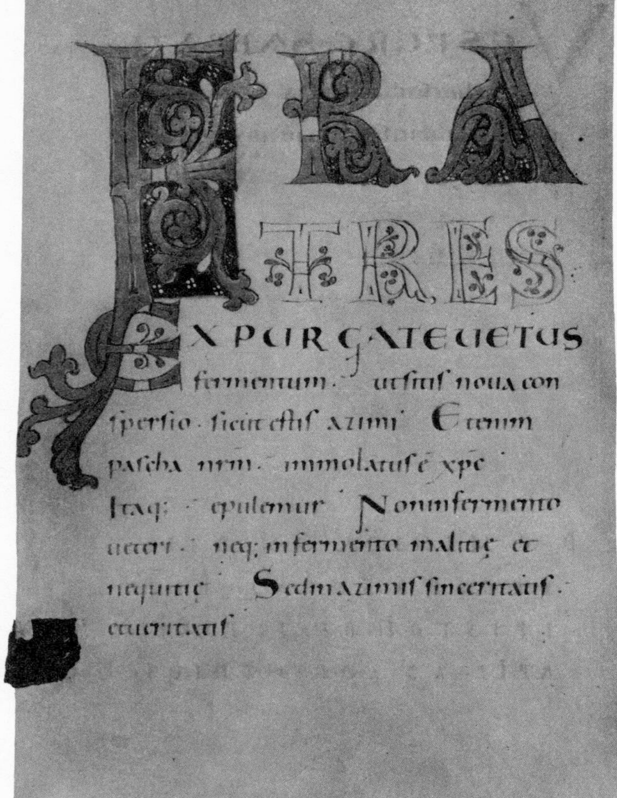

FRA
TRES
EXPURGATEUETUS
fermentum. ut sitis noua con
spersio. sicut estis azimi. Etenim
pascha nrm. immolatus e xpc.
Itaq; epulemur. Non in fermento
ueteri. neq; in fermento malitie et
nequitie. Sed in azimis sinceritatis.
et ueritatis

12. Epistolary. Trier, ca. A.D. 1000

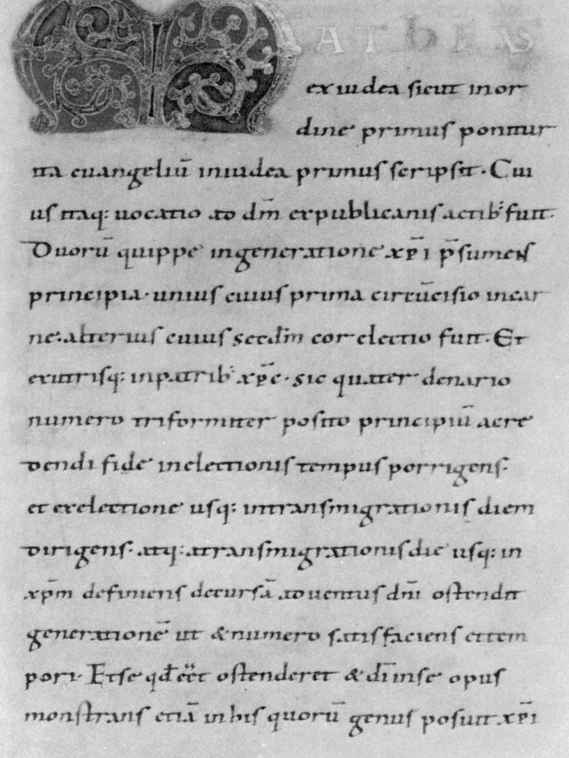

MATHEUS
ex iudea sicut in or
dine primus ponitur
ita euangeliu in iudea primus scripsit. Cui
us itaq; uocatio ad dm ex publicanis actib; fuit.
Duoru quippe in generatione xpi psumens
principia. unius cuius prima circucisio in car
ne. alterius cuius secdm cor electio fuit. Et
ex utrisq; in patrib; xpc. sic quaterdenario
numero triformiter posito principiu a cre
dendi fide in electionis tempus porrigens.
et ex electione usq; in transmigrationis diem
dirigens. atq; a transmigrationis die usq; in
xpm definiens decursa aduentus dni ostendit
generatione ut & numero satisfaciens et tem
pori. Et se qd eet ostenderet & di in se opus
monstrans etia in his quoru genus posuit xpi

13. Gospels. Reichenau, ca. A.D. 1030

century German collection; Sir Thomas Brooke, Huddersfield, Yorkshire, until 1913. Acquired from Leon Gruel, Paris, by Henry Walters.
*The Walters Art Gallery*

The direction in which Carolingian minuscules were to develop in south German and Swiss centers is well illustrated by this manuscript. It is a fine book, the thick suede-surfaced white vellum carefully selected and prepared, the margins and interlinear interval ample, the illumination rich. However, a close inspection of the fine, regular script shows that here we have to do with a 'rustic' variety of minuscule, even though the effect is far more stately than that of no. 9. Although the impression is one of spaciousness, the slightly sloping script tends to stress straight rather than curved forms and there is a more compact grouping of the letters, so that the words are separated more clearly than in previous examples. The shading is of the sort that betrays the slanting pen, being noticeable only in the curved forms. The ascenders are no longer clubbed, but the descender of the q has now acquired a finishing serif. The g is characteristic of this stage of minuscule—for the first time it shows us both the upper and lower bowls fully closed. Despite the luxurious character of this manuscript and its meticulous layout, the carefully ordered 'hierarchy of scripts' promoted at Tours does not here prevail. No Rustic capitals occur for any purpose. The beautiful golden uncials that introduce the sections of the text are actually a mixture of uncials with square capitals, even on the sumptuous purple *incipit* pages of the Gospels.

This book was probably produced in one of the most renowned scriptoria of the Middle Ages. The abbey of Reichenau was founded on an island in the Lake of Constance by monks from St. Gall, around A.D. 700. It was to become famous as a center of literary and musical achievement, and during the late tenth and first half of the eleventh centuries its scribes and painters were the foremost in western Europe. The Ottonian emperors made it an imperial abbey, and under their patronage a series of fabulously rich books was produced, often as gifts to other establishments. Artists and scribes migrated from Reichenau to other centers such as Trier and Echternach. The greatest period of the Reichenau atelier was just before and after the year 1000.

Bibliography: G. I. Ellis, *A Catalogue of the Manuscripts and Printed Books Collected by Thomas Brooke*, London, 1891, vol. I, p. 196, plate; J. Prochno, *Das Schreiber- und Dedikationsbild in der deutschen Buchmalerei*, Leipzig, 1929, I, p. 38, plate; De Ricci, I, p. 767, no. 64, II, p. 2289; D. Miner in *The Art Bulletin*, XVIII, 1936, pp. 168–185, 16 figs., citing other literature; Walters *Cat.*, 1949, no. 12, pl. VII; W. Gernsheim, *Die Buchmalerei der Reichenau* (Diss.), Munich, 1934, p. 105; Peter Bloch in *Kunst in Hessen und am Mittelrhein*, III, 1963, p. 43; Bond and Faye, *Supplement*, p. 195, no. 64; W. Wixom in Cleveland Museum *Bulletin*, LI, 3, 1964, pp. 44 f., illus.

## *Carolingian Minuscules*

### 14 THE FOUR GOSPELS

Switzerland (?), late 10th century.
Ms. W. 3. In Latin. 148 vellum leaves, 12⅛×7 inches. Written in Carolingian minuscules in long lines, with rubricated *incipits* in uncials, *explicits* in Rustic capitals; square capitals introduce the first sentence of each Gospel. 12 ornamented Canon Tables in simple colors, large ornamental initials with interlace, lacertine and foliate designs in minium, blue, yellow and green, sometimes upon violet grounds, at beginning of each Gospel; one drawing. Brown ink. Binding: early 19th-century French morocco, gilt.
Provenance: Acquired by Henry Walters in Paris in 1903.
*The Walters Art Gallery*

This manuscript is characteristic of the many competent but not luxurious books produced in scattered monasteries which were not in themselves great centers. The degree to which these out-of-the-way houses were receptive to current movements is suggested by the present volume. Its charming but provincial ornamentation is quite old-fashioned for its time, but the scribes have naturalized the current Carolingian minuscule with ability. Again we have here a 'rustic' version of this script, as is seen in the lighter weight of the pen strokes, the more compact alignment of the letters, the gently sloping *ductus*. The ascenders are a good deal taller than the round body of the letter, and instead of clubbing, there is sometimes a tendency to spread the tops in a slight wedge.

The location of this manuscript, as often with provincial products whose history is lost, presents a puzzle. It has been attributed to the north of France and also to the south. Recently, however, one of the most experienced French scholars in the field rejected a French origin, casting out a tentative suggestion of Swiss connection. It has not yet been possible to substantiate this. However, one may point out that the rather striking format, long in proportion to width, characterizes a number of manuscripts produced at the monastery of St. Gall.

Bibliography: De Ricci, I, p. 766, no. 60; Walters *Cat.*, 1949, no. 7; Bond and Faye, *Supplement*, p. 195, no. 60, with further references.

## *Carolingian Minuscules*

### 15 MISSAL

Probably Sant'Apollinare in Classis, Ravenna, mid-11th century.

Ms. W. 11. In Latin. 263 vellum leaves (imperfect at end), 11⅛×ca. 6¾ inches. Written by several hands in Carolingian minuscules in long lines; rubricated captions in both square capitals and uncials; subordinate rubrics in Rustic capitals. Uncials and Rustic capitals used for initials. Musical notation. Ink dark to light brown. 2 full-page drawings, 1 tinted with color. Preface to the Canon illuminated in gold, silver and color upon violet ground. Binding: modern red velvet.

Provenance: Sant'Apollinare in Classis (?); Sant'Ambrogio di Ranchio (?). Acquired by Henry Walters in Paris.

*The Walters Art Gallery*

The development of Carolingian minuscule in Italy may be surmised by comparing no. 10 with the present example. The spacious, almost sprawling lettering of the former has given way to a more compact rhythm with some of the letters joined or touching in one way or another. The ascenders are now all finished with an incipient serif. Ligatures and abbreviations are more numerous. Most of the subordinate initials are Rustic capitals. The words to be sung are smaller in size that the rest of the text and are accompanied by musical neumes.

This manuscript, although by no means a sumptuous production, is of exceptional interest liturgically and musically. It was executed in an atelier accustomed to the martyrology of Ravenna and for a monastery dedicated to St. Ambrose. On the basis of liturgical and paleographical evidence, Dom Anselm Strittmatter has proposed that it may have been written in the scriptorium of Sant'Apollinare in Classis, but for the specific use of the monastery of Sant'Ambrogio di Ranchio near Sarsina, a suffragan see of Ravenna.

Bibliography: De Ricci, I, p. 744, no. 111, II, p. 2290; Leo F. Miller in *Traditio*, II, 1944, pp. 123–154; Dom Anselm Strittmatter, *ibid.*, III, 1945, pp. 392–394; *idem*, *ibid.*, VI, 1948, pp. 328–340; *idem* in *Miscellanea Liturgica in Honorem L. Cuniberti Mohlberg*, Rome, 1949, vol. II, pp. 139–146; Bond and Faye, *Supplement*, p. 196, no. 111.

## *Carolingian Minuscules*

### 16 LECTIONARY OF THE GOSPELS

St. Emmeram, Regensburg, Bavaria, mid-11th century.

Ms. W. 8. In Latin. 228 vellum leaves, 11×8½ inches. Written in long lines by at least two scribes in Carolingian minuscules; uncials mixed with square capitals for first lines of lections, Rustic capitals for second lines and rubrics. 1 large and 4 smaller ornamental foliate capitals illuminated in gold and silver (not oxidized). Other initials large red square capitals. Binding: early 12th-century treasure-binding of thick boards, the top covered with silver and ornamented with silver-filigree, nielli, rock-crystal and carved ivories, the bottom set with a gilt-copper plaque engraved with a representation of St. Michael; the spine covered with a 'Regensburg' silk-and-linen damask.

Provenance: Scriptorium of Regensburg. Traditionally said to have been at Mondsee, in the Austrian Tyrol, but in any case from an Austrian or south German monastery perhaps dedicated to St. Michael; in the 19th century in a German archducal collection. Acquired by Henry Walters from Jacques Rosenthal of Munich after 1926, and probably around 1930.

*The Walters Art Gallery*

This sumptuous service-book, containing lessons from the Gospels arranged in the order of their use throughout the year, is written by two or more scribes in a very large minuscule. Large script especially characterizes medieval books intended to be read aloud, as it permitted easy and effective delivery by the officiant (cf. nos. 22, 23, 24, 29, 30).

Despite the amplitude of scale and the spacious margins, the script (especially that of the chief hand) has a noticeable tendency toward lateral compression, permitting increased text per line. This results in a strong vertical rhythm—a harbinger of the developments of the next century (cf. nos. 18, 21, 22, 23, etc.). One may note the bevelled slope at the ends of ascenders and descenders, which now are much shorter in relation to the main body of the letter. The long s and f perform a gentle double-curve; the third stroke of m terminates with a serif which has been taken over from the analogous form of n.

It has been informally suggested by Dr. Bernhard Bischoff that the chief hand in this lectionary may be recognized as that of Othlon of Regensburg, a Benedictine scribe who learned his craft at the Bavarian monastery of Tegernsee and from 1032 to about 1055 was a scholar and eventually dean at St. Emmeram of Regensburg. He wrote a book listing the service-books which he had copied out (including two Gospel-lectionaries).

Bibliography: Jacques Rosenthal, *Catalogue* 83, Munich, 1926, no. 40, pls. I, IX, X; Adolf Goldschmidt, *Die Elfenbeinskulpturen aus der Zeit der karolingischen und sachsischen Kaiser*, Berlin, 1914–26, IV, p. 58, no. 30, pl. LXXV, fig. 40; De Ric-

15. Missal. Ravenna, mid-11th century

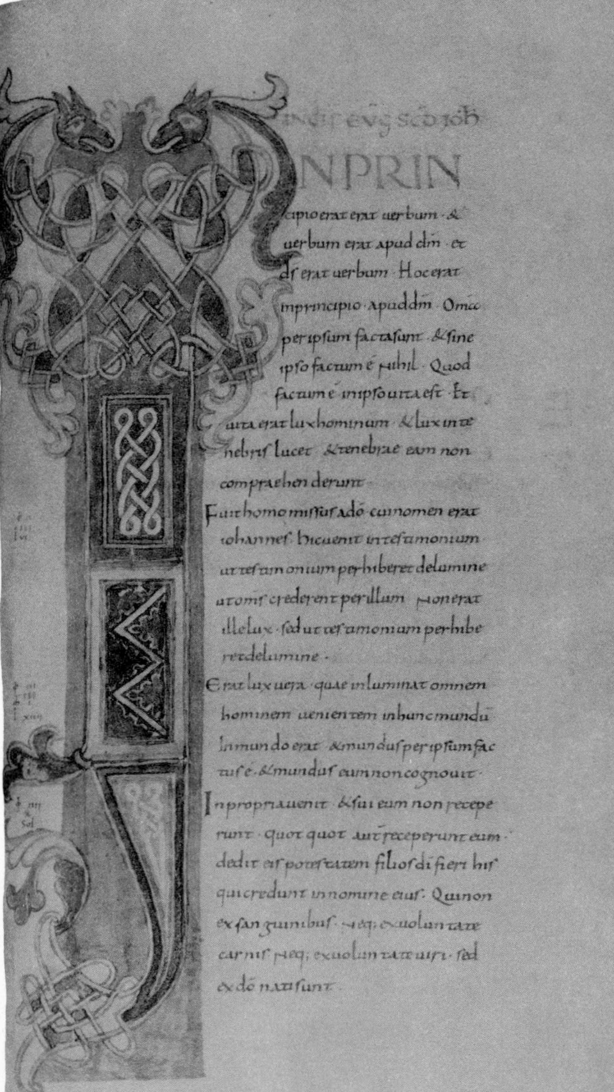

14. Gospels. Switzerland (?), late 10th century

17. Missal. South Italy, mid-11th century

ci, I, p. 768, no. 71, II, p. 2290; David Rosen in *The Journal of the Walters Art Gallery*, XV–XVI, 1952–53, pp. 87 f., figs. 5–12; Walters Art Gallery, *The History of Bookbinding 525–1950 A.D.*, Baltimore, 1957, pp. 8–9, no. 10, pl. VII.

## *Beneventan Minuscules*

17 MISSAL

South Italy, perhaps Canosa or Sant'Angelo on Monte Gargano, mid-11th century.

Ms. W. 6. In Latin. 232 vellum leaves, 7½×4¾ inches. Written by several hands in Beneventan minuscule in long lines; rubrics all in Beneventan minuscule. Major initials drawn in fanciful shapes and colored yellow, blue and green, the larger ones ornamented with interlace and animal and bird designs. Large and elaborate ornamented and historiated initials at opening of Preface and Canon of the Mass. Musical notation. Black ink. Binding: modern green velvet.

Provenance: Acquired in Paris by Henry Walters before 1917.

*The Walters Art Gallery*

Some of the more isolated areas of western Europe remained untouched by the triumph of Carolingian minuscule, and their own local writing systems, developed out of cursive scripts, were pursued undisturbed—as in Spain, for instance, and southern Italy. Until well into the thirteenth century, the monastic scribes of southern Italy wrote an extremely individual and highly developed hand which is termed Beneventan, after the duchy of Benevento, which was its locale. The chief center was the famous Benedictine monastery of Monte Cassino, but it was practiced in other places and even in Dalmatia.

Although a formal hand possessing great style, it is difficult for us to read without study, since it has so many peculiar forms. The pen, held on a slant, shaded the letters heavily and moved in a systematically jerky fashion. Although an erect hand, the forms of many of the letters are 'broken,' as the c, e, i, etc. The cursive ancestry of the script betrays itself not only in numerous ligatures and abbreviations, but in a tendency toward what is termed 'union,' that is the contact of the round strokes with adjacent round letters—a practice more fully exploited in gothic writing. The most characteristic letters are the a which resembles two c's, a t which looks very much like the a, a long-shafted r which often flows into a smooth ligature with i.

In the illustration, the first three lines introduced by the ornamental initial may be transcribed:

"In illo t(empore). Dicebat ih̄s (Jesus) ad eos qui in se confidebant tam quam iusti et aspernabantur . . ." (Luke XVIII:9).

The musical parts of the service are accompanied by the Beneventan neumes which also have a very individual character.

The place in which this book was executed has not yet been determined exactly. It has been suggested by the Benedictine scholars of Solesmes that it was written for the church of Canosa near Mount Gargano in the southernmost part of Italy near the east coast, or perhaps for the sanctuary of Sant'Angelo on the mountain.

Bibliography: De Ricci, I, p. 775, no. 112; Walters *Cat.*, 1949, no. 13, pl. XII; Benedictines of Solesmes, *Paléographie Musicale*, XV, p. 76 and p. 176, *corrigenda*; Bond and Faye, *Supplement*, p. 196, no. 112, with further references.

## *Advanced Carolingian Minuscules*

18 HONORIUS AUGUSTODUNENSIS, EXPOSITIO IN CANTICA CANTICORUM; SIGILLUM SANCTAE MARIAE; NEOCOSMUS.

Western Austria (Salzburg school), ca. 1170.

Ms. W. 29. In Latin. 150 vellum leaves, 10⅜×7⅛ inches. Written in advanced Carolingian minuscules, with first two lines of each Book in an adaptation of Rustic capitals. Black ink; rubricated titles. 3 miniatures, 3 historiated initials and 5 ornamental branching initials, all executed in colored inks and flat colors. Binding: original blind-stamped deerskin over boards.

Provenance: Benedictine monastery at Lambach (MS. 94) since an early date and until around 1926. Acquired by Henry Walters from Jacques Rosenthal, Munich, around 1928.

*The Walters Art Gallery*

The clear, harmonious forms of Carolingian minuscule continued strongly in Germany and Austria up to the beginning of the thirteenth century. As in this handsomely written volume, the trend continues toward a narrower letter, yet written with a broad pen, so that the block of script appears darker in general color. The ascenders of b, d and l spread into a wedge at the top, but these and the descenders of p and q are shorter than in the earlier Carolingian script. This again enhances the effect of compactness. One notes an angular tendency in the strokes which form what used to be the rounded parts of c, e, f, r and s.

The script is eminently legible and presents an effect of great dignity, which is not disturbed even by flaws in the heavy, suede-like vellum, such as the enlarged follicle hole visible in the illustration. The words simply skip across such interferences with no loss of assurance. Faulty or damaged sheets of vellum, which would have been avoided so far as possible for a *de luxe* liturgical volume, were not discarded in preparing a scholastic text, such as this, during the first half of the Middle Ages, when each writing center had to prepare its own materials from whatever was at hand. The simple colors of the allegorical illustrations and of the ornamental initials—red, blue, green and violet, as well as the rubricated captions and subordinate initials, provide a lively foil to the black script.

Bibliography: J. A. Endres, *Das St. Jacobsportal im Regensburg*, Kempton, 1903, pp. 32–33; Georg Swarzenski, *Die Salzburger Malerei*, Leipzig, 1913, pp. 94–95, note 1; Jacques Rosenthal, *Bibliotheca Medii Aevi Manuscripta* (Cat. 90), Munich, 1928, pp. 48–51, no. 144, pl. VIII; G. Hobson in *The Library*, the Bibliographical Society, London, XV, 1934, p. 202, no. LXXIV; De Ricci, I, p. 821, no. 387, II, p. 2292, no. 387; Walters *Cat.*, 1949, pp. 12–13, no. 27, pl. XVIII; Walters Art Gallery, *The History of Bookbinding 525–1950 A.D.*, Baltimore, 1957, p. 47, pl. XXV (erroneously attributed to Seittenstetten); Bond and Faye, *Supplement*, p. 196, no. 387, with further literature.

## *Romanesque Display Capitals*

### 19 THE FOUR GOSPELS

Northern Spain, ca. 1100.

Ms. W. 17. In Latin. 161 vellum leaves, 10¾×8¾ inches. Written in 'early gothic' minuscules in 2 columns. Brown ink. Square capitals mixed with some uncial forms used as a display script in alternating lines or letters of red and blue on the first page of each Gospel, at the beginning of each preface, and for most *explicits*. The rubricated square capitals introducing each verse are also usually touched with strokes or dots of blue. Rustic capitals are used for only one *explicit* and for running headings. 1 full-page miniature; 1 historiated initial; 3 large ornamental initials. Binding: modern red velvet.

Provenance: Acquired in Paris by Henry Walters.

*The Walters Art Gallery*

The pages of large capitals which introduce each Gospel present a monumental effect which is enlivened in three ways: (1) The first one or two letters, which, as in Carolingian times, are enlarged ornamentally, are composed of interlaced vine-like strands that bud into leaves and involve fantastic or playful animal or human forms. (2) Red and blue are used alternately for the lines of letters. (3) The lettering accommodates characters of smaller size which are enclosed or sheltered within the larger forms, as well as monogram-like combinations of letters or abbreviations. Some of the pages carry this latter tendency further than that shown in the illustration. This intricate interrelation of letter forms had the virtue of decorative variety, and also it permitted the use of a larger scale than would have been possible if the entire text had to be accommodated in a single size. The practice, which occurs notably in south French manuscripts also, was used with great effect in carved stone inscriptions of the romanesque period, and was in fact a descendant of certain Roman epigraphical methods (no. 2). It must be remembered that Roman inscriptions in stone existed throughout Gaul and Spain, as well as Britain, and provided an ever-ready model for letterers of subsequent times.

The contrasting use of red and blue in the inscription combines to fine effect with the strongly stylized picture of the Evangelist Matthew on the facing page.

The script used for the body of the text, which does not appear in the illustration, is at first glance a variety of late Carolingian minuscule, with perhaps a touch of Visigothic influence in the height of the ascenders. However, the tendency of all verticals in m, n and long r to have a rightward turn or serif at the base, of both strokes of u to bend leftward at the top, and the shafts of d, h and b to be spread at the top into the suggestion of a serif—these all hint at the coming of gothic forms, according to distinctions set forth by Dr. Bernhard Bischoff and explained more fully in connection with no. 22.

Bibliography: De Ricci, I, p. 767, no. 65; Walters *Cat.*, 1949, p. 10, no. 21, pl. XIII, with other references; Council of Europe, *El Arte Románico*, Barcelona & Santiago de Compostela, 1961; Bond and Faye, *Supplement*, p. 195, no. 65, with other literature.

## *'Early Gothic' Text Script*

### 20 JUVENAL, SATYRAE

Northern France, 12th century.

Ms. W. 20. In Latin. 55 vellum leaves, 9½×6 inches. Written in 'early gothic' minuscules in single column. One ornamental branching letter on a blue ground, other smaller ornamental red initials at head of each Satire. Light brown ink. Many interlinear and marginal glosses added. Binding: French stiff vellum, ca. 1600.

Provenance: A note of ca. 1300 refers to Amiens; owned ca. 1570 by Antoine Loisel; Pierre Pithou, MS. 65; Duchesse de Berry sale, Paris, 1837, no. 2419; Joseph Barrois coll., no. 192; purchased 1849 by the Earl of Ashburn-

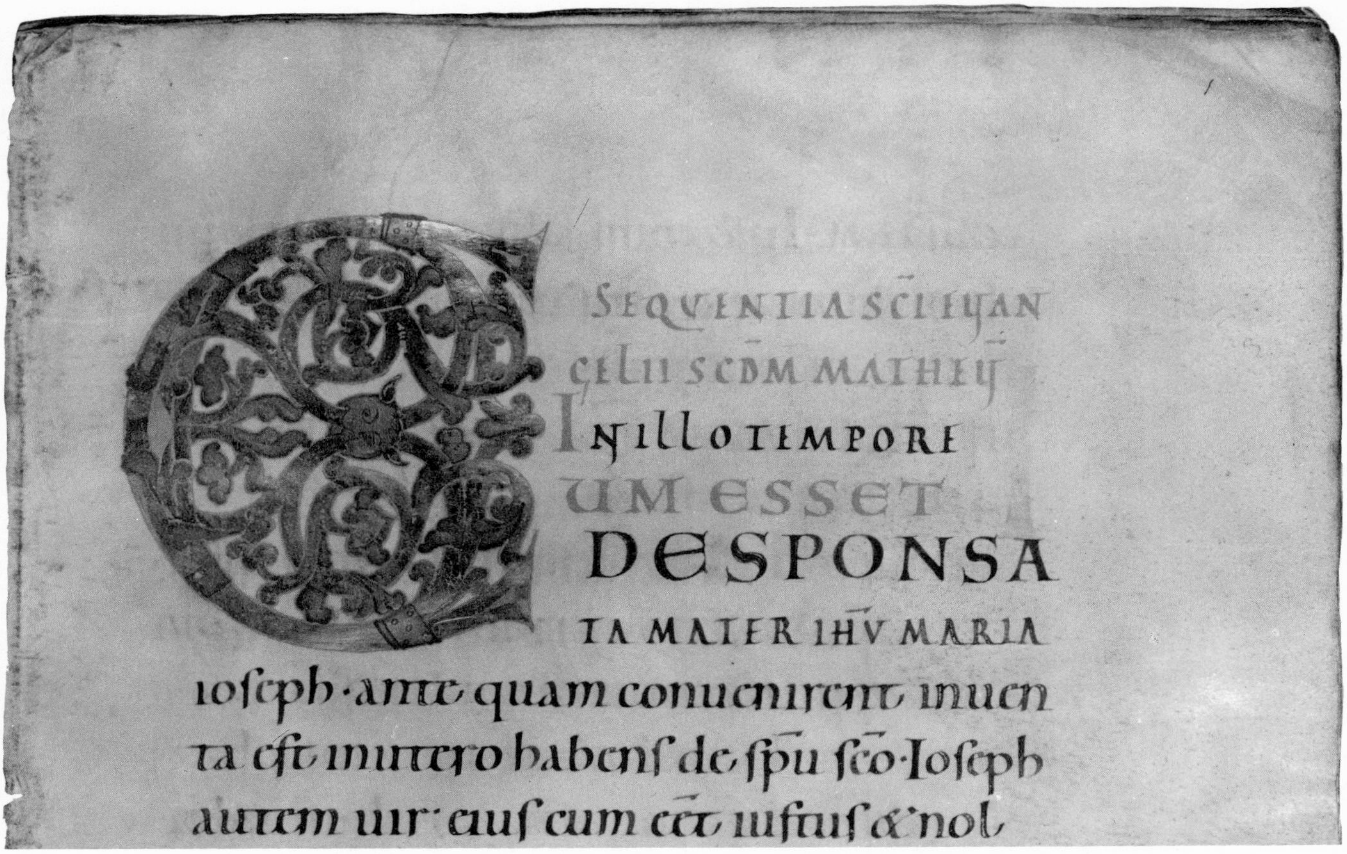

16. Gospel-Lectionary. Regensburg, mid-11th century

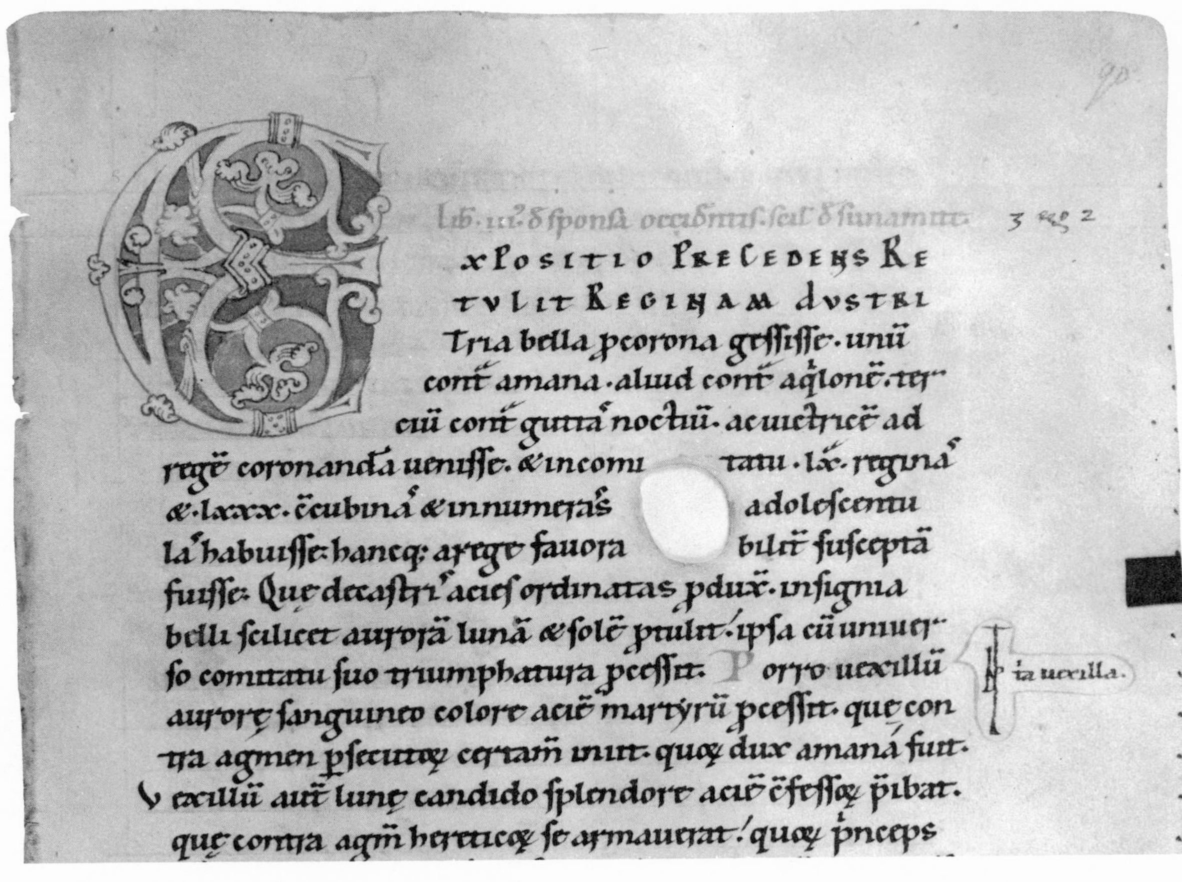

18. Honorius Augustodunensis, *Opera*. Austria, ca. 1170

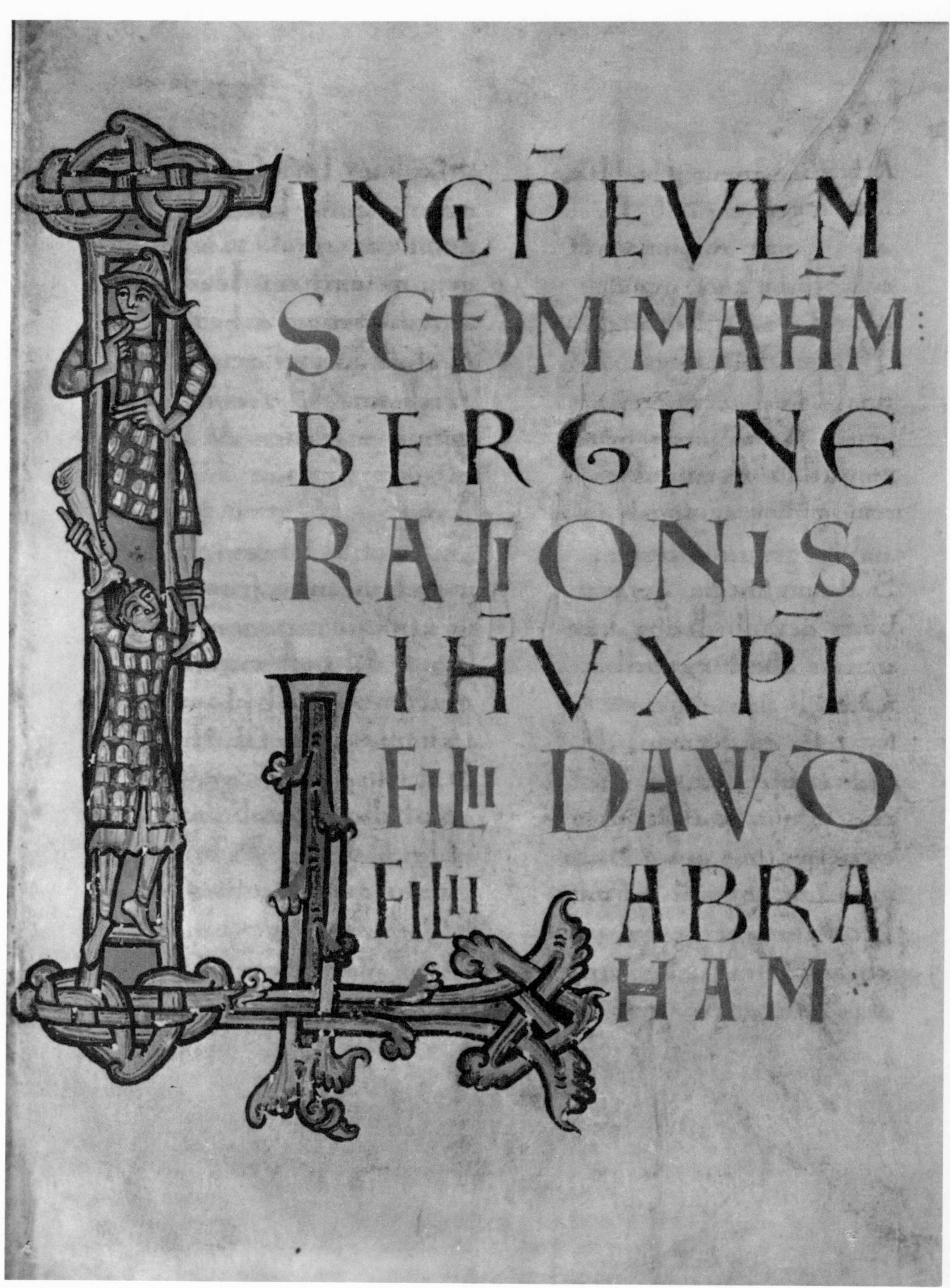


19. Gospels. Northern Spain, ca. 1100

ham (his sale, London, 1901, no. 317). Acquired by Henry Walters early in this century.
*The Walters Art Gallery*

A small, but rather carefully executed script. The initials to each line of verse, set somewhat apart, represent a convention in the writing of classical and other poetry which seems to have started in the eighth century. It was continued by the early printers of the fifteenth and sixteenth centuries.

The wide margins and interlinear spaces are to accommodate glosses, which indeed have been added on many of the pages of the manuscript. The most interesting is a gloss to parts of the first three Satires in a minute gothic *notula*. Professor Raymond Klibansky has identified this gloss as a composition by the twelfth-century scholastic, William of Conches.

The plate shows the first lines of Satire XI, beginning: "Aticus eximie si cenat lautus habetur . . ."

Bibliography: De Ricci, I, p. 833, no. 448; R. Klibansky in *The Warburg Institute: Annual Report*, London, 1946–47, p. 12; *idem* in *Proceedings of the British Academy: Annual Report*, London, 1947–48, p. 7; Bond and Faye, *Supplement*, p. 196, no. 448.

## 'Early Gothic' Minuscules

21 SACRAMENTARY FOR USE OF REIMS CATHEDRAL

Reims, northern France, ca. 1150–75.

Mss. W. 28 and W. 28 Add. In Latin. 73 plus 45 vellum leaves, 9×5⅝ inches. Written in 'early gothic' minuscules in long lines, with rubrics in fanciful narrow capitals and in adaptation of Rustic capitals. Light brown ink. 2 large ornamental initials in gold and colors and many smaller ones, displaying foliate and some animal ornament. Each passage begins with a large capital in red, blue or green. 2 full-page miniatures. Binding: W. 28: modern green velvet; W. 28 Add., green portfolio-case.

Provenance: Reims Cathedral; Chapter Library of Beauvais Cathedral from at least the early 15th century until the French Revolution; Louis de Caron, Château de Troussures, no. 304 (his sale, July 9, 1909, no. 14). W. 28 acquired thereafter by Henry Walters from Leon Gruel, Paris; the 45 leaves comprising W. 28 Add. acquired in two lots in 1950, one by purchase and one by gift of Philip B. Perlman.

*The Walters Art Gallery*

The carefully selected white vellum, regular script and delicately painted miniatures and ornament accord with the execution of a manuscript intended for the exclusive use of the Archbishop of Reims. The erect narrow letters show only certain of the features which were to characterize developed gothic script. Neither 'union' nor fusion occurs.

The manuscript is remarkable liturgically, having very full rubricated directions for such proto-dramatic ceremonies as the washing of the feet of twelve paupers on Maundy Thursday, an Exultet hymn for Pentecost as well as for the Saturday before Easter, etc. In the seventeenth century this book, like many other manuscripts belonging to Beauvais, suffered severely from neglect. When in the Troussures sale in 1909, it was incomplete and mutilated by mould and damp, but it retained 130 leaves. Fifty-seven of the most badly damaged leaves were subsequently removed when the manuscript was rebound for the market. W. 28 Add. consists of forty-five of these discarded leaves which have so far been tracked down and acquired.

Bibliography: H. Omont in *Mémoires de l'Académie des Inscriptions et Belles Lettres*, XL, 1916, p. 80; C. Niver in *Speculum*, X, 1935, pp. 33–37; De Ricci, I, p. 775, no. 113, II, p. 2290, no. 113; P. E. Schramm in *Archiv für Urkundenforschung*, XVI, 1939, p. 283; Walters *Cat.*, 1949, pp. 10 f., no. 22, pl. XIV; D. Miner in *Bulletin of the Walters Art Gallery*, III, Nov. and Dec., 1950, and March, 1951, illus.; Dom Anselm Strittmatter in *Studies in Art and Literature for Belle da Costa Greene*, Princeton, 1954, pp. 384–400, illus.; Bond and Faye, *Supplement*, p. 198, nos. 565–566, with other literature.

## English 'Early Gothic' Minuscules

22 THE NEW TESTAMENT

Cathedral of Rochester, Kent, first half 12th century.

Ms. W. 18. In Latin. 248 vellum leaves, 14½×10⅝ inches. Written in 'early gothic' letters in 2 columns, with *incipits* in square capitals, sometimes mixed with uncial forms, in alternating lines of red, blue, dull rose and green; large capitals in color at beginning of verses and *capitula*; rubrics in minuscule. 26 large ornamental initials with foliate, animal, etc., forms executed in colors, without gold. Black or very dark brown ink. Binding: modern rose silk over old boards.

Provenance: Cathedral Priory of St. Andrew, Rochester (?). Acquired by Henry Walters in Paris.

*The Walters Art Gallery*

Although in decoration and in general appearance this is certainly to be considered a romanesque book, the criteria which Dr. Bernhard Bischoff has laid down for identifying the first intimations of gothic tendencies force us to classify the handsome script of this volume as 'early gothic' minuscule. Chiefly to be noted are the right turns or hairline serifs at the end of all the vertical strokes in d, f, i, m, n, p, q, r, long s, also of the first stroke of h. A slight tendency to a broken arc in the last stroke of m and n can also be detected, as well as a growing taste for hair-lines as a finish. These traits had appeared in some Norman scripts as early as the third quarter of the eleventh century and it perhaps was from such sources that they took root in south-English writing after the Norman conquest. Also warning of gothic development are the occasional instances of 'union,' i.e., touching round letters—as for instance the p and o of *tempore* in the next to last line at the right, of o and g just above it, etc. The vertical rhythm is accompanied here by an increasing angularity of stroke as the sloping pen emphasizes height and lateral contraction in the proportions of the letters. Despite the former concern, the ascenders and descenders continue to be reduced in relative projection (cf. nos. 16, 18); it is the body of the letter which gains in vertical proportion.

A general impression of triangularity is due not only to the shapes of such letters as c, e, o, but also to the regularity of alignment of the script at the top, the emphasis on the horizontal of t and the expanded ends of the ascenders. All this may well be considered the heritage of the indigenous Insular minuscules of four or five centuries earlier (cf. no. 5).

As in the case of other books of large script and format (nos. 16, 23) the presentation of this manuscript indicates that it was designed for reading aloud, either in the services or the refectory. It is an imposing volume, even though no gold is used. The decoration consists of robust initials composed of foliate scrolls, sometimes inhabited by animals or occasional human figures. The colors, blue, red, green and yellow, are picked up in the lines of capitals giving the first passage of the texts, as well as in the initials of the *capitula*.

The manuscript used to be attributed to the scriptorium of Christ Church priory, Canterbury; but Dr. C. R. Dodwell, who has made the most intensive study of twelfth-century Canterbury manuscripts, considers that although, the script is that of Christ Church, the decoration indicates that this book was actually executed in Rochester, where a cell was established from Canterbury. It is clear that some Canterbury monks moved to Rochester, and therefore the identity of script is explicable.

Bibliography: De Ricci, I, p. 766, no. 57; N. R. Ker, *Medieval Libraries of Great Britain*, London, 1941, p. 18; Walters *Cat.*, 1949, pp. 9–10, no. 20; T. S. R. Boase, *English Art 1100–1226*, The Oxford History of English Art, Oxford, 1953, pp. 63–65, fig. 19b; C. R. Dodwell, *The Canterbury School of Illumination, 1066–1200*, Cambridge, 1954, pp. 65, 74, 119, pl. 37g; Bond and Faye, *Supplement*, pp. 194 f., no. 57, with other references. For analysis of the symptoms of 'early gothic' script, see Bernhard Bischoff in *Nomenclature*, pp. 11 f.

## *'Early Gothic' Minuscules*

### 23 S. PETRUS CHRYSOLOGUS, SERMONES CLXXV.

Monastery of Ste. Marie de Citeaux, Burgundy, 12th century.

Ms. W. 19. In Latin. 170 vellum leaves, 14½×10⅛ inches. Written in 'early gothic' minuscules in 2 columns, title in fanciful capitals in lines alternating red and green, some of rubrics in same fanciful capitals, the rest in 'early gothic' minuscules. *Capitula* initials alternately blue, red and green. Large ornamental initials in green, blue, red, salmon, olive, tan or lavender introduce each sermon. Binding: 18th-century French green morocco, gilt.

Provenance: Ste. Marie de Citeaux; evidently passed during the mid-18th century into a private library in Dijon; seized by the revolutionary authorities *le 20 Prairial l'an 3* (June 8, 1793); said to have belonged to Count Mac-Carthy Reagh; sold ca. 1830 by De Bure to Sir Thomas Phillipps (no. 4360) (his sale, London, 1908, no. 606). Acquired by Henry Walters, probably shortly thereafter.

*The Walters Art Gallery*

A handsome book whose large format and script proclaim it to be intended for reading aloud in services or in the refectory. The general aspect—robust script and well-selected suede-surfaced vellum, simple but effective ornamental initials—is characteristic of Cistercian volumes. Its origin in Citeaux is indicated by an ex-libris at the end in the same hand as the rest of the rubrication, and by a fourteenth-century ex-libris on folio 1.

The script is compact laterally, but there is little indication of the 'union' or fusion of adjacent rounded forms which characterizes fully developed gothic writing; an exception is the fusion of the two p's in the abbreviated word for *populis* nine lines from the bottom. Four lines above this appears a double tick over the two i's in *abiit*, so as to distinguish them from u or y. Single i's are not yet ticked. Note the tendency to fork the top of the ascenders, as well as to treat the lower ends of all vertical strokes harmoniously. The notes of the scribe for the rubricator and illuminator are still visible on a number of pages. These were inserted at the very edges of the margins in the expectation that they

20. Juvenal, *Satyrae*. Northern France, 12th century

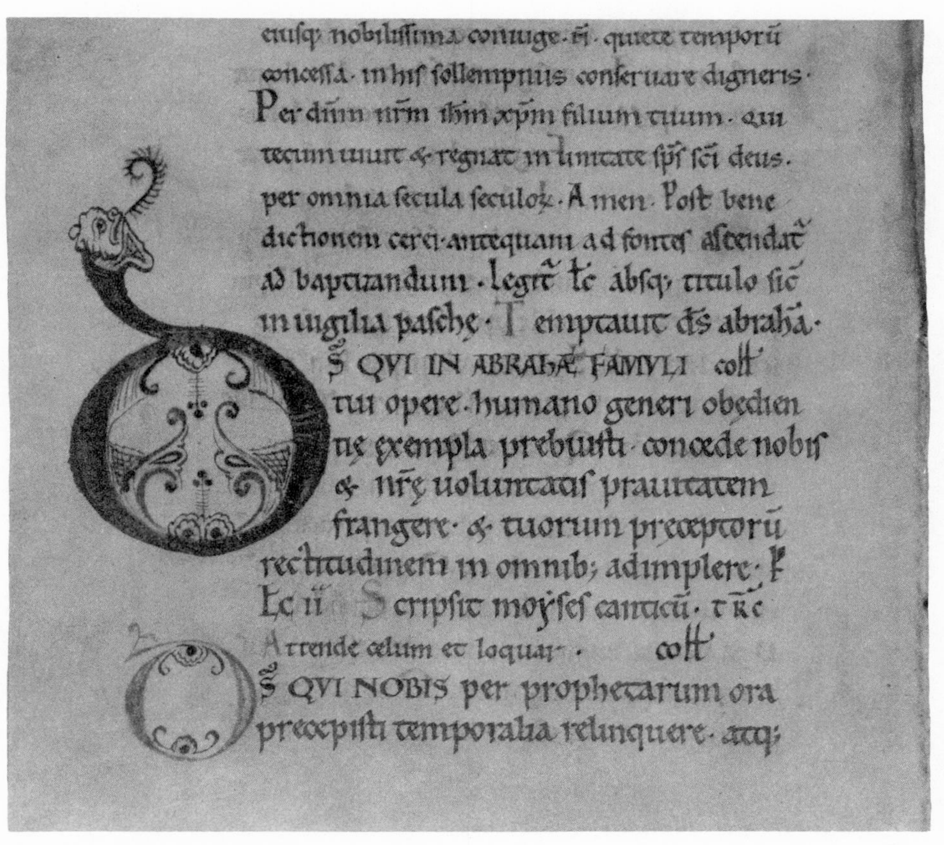
eiusq; nobilissima coniuge . & . quiete temporū
concessa . in his sollempniis conseruare digneris .
Per dnm nrm ihm xpm filium tuum . qui
tecum uiuit & regnat in unitate sps sci deus .
per omnia secula seculoꝝ . Amen . Post bene
dictionem cerei . antequam ad fontes ascendat
ad baptizandum . legit te absq; titulo sic
in uigilia pasche . Temptauit ds abrahā .
DS QVI IN ABRAHÆ FAMVLI coll
tui opere . humano generi obedien
tie exempla prebuisti . concede nobis
& nre uoluntatis prauitatem
frangere . & tuorum preceptorū
rectitudinem in omnib; adimplere . P
Lc ii Scripsit moyses canticū . t R̄c
Attende celum et loquar . coll
DS QVI NOBIS per prophetarum ora
precepisti temporalia relinquere . atq;

21. Sacramentary. Reims, ca. 1150–75

22. New Testament. Rochester, first half of 12th century

23. S. Petrus Chrysologus, *Sermones*. Citeaux, 12th century

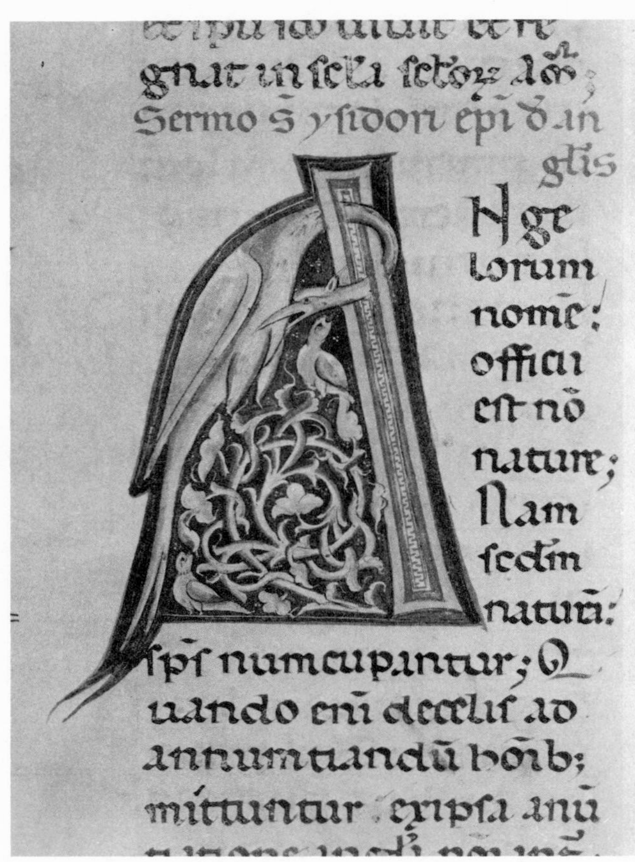

24. *Sermones et Vitae*. Northern Italy, early 13th century

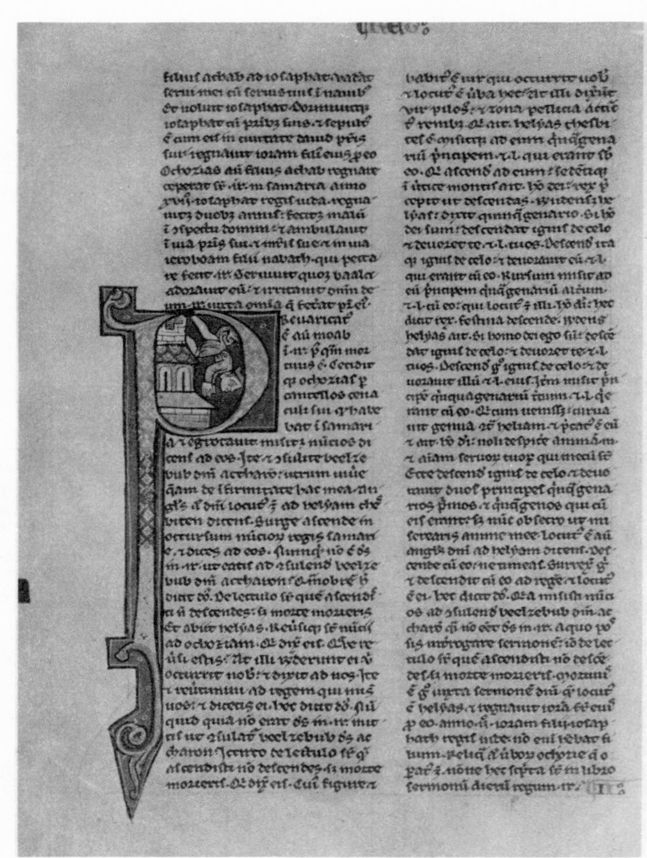

25. Small Bible. England (?), late 13th century

would eventually be cut off when the pages were trimmed by the binder, but some have escaped.

Bibliography: De Ricci, I, p. 823, no. 396; A. J. Dunstan in *Scriptorium*, VII, 1953, pp. 217–218.

## *Gotica Rotunda*

24 SERMONS AND LIVES OF SAINTS

North Italy, early 13th century.

Ms. W. 27. In Latin. 145 vellum leaves, 19¼×11¾ inches. Written in 2 columns in round gothic script. Black ink; rubricated captions. Numerous ornamental initials with foliate and animal designs. Binding: Italian wood boards backed with calf.

Provenance: Acquired in Paris by Henry Walters.

*The Walters Art Gallery*

The compression and angular breaking of strokes which characterized developed gothic script north of the Alps never took hold in Italy. Carolingian minuscule continued for a long period. The gothic writing which finally developed retained a strong memory of the round and spacious forms of Carolingian, but in its heavy shading, slightly angular formation of the bows of some letters, eventual tendency to fusion, it displays its gothic flavor. Elegant hairlines and similar trimmings of fully developed northern gothic were never affected—although elaborately flourished penwork became a special feature of border ornament in the fifteenth century (cf. nos. 38, 39).

Bibliography: De Ricci, I, p. 821, no. 389.

## *Minute Textus Formata*

25 BIBLE

England (?), late 13th century.

Ms. W. 51. In Latin. 525 vellum leaves, 5¾×3¾ inches. Written in a developed formal gothic script in 2 columns. Brown ink. Historiated or illuminated initial introduces each Book. 2 full-page miniatures inserted at beginning. Binding: French 18th-century red morocco, gilt.

Provenance: English 16th-century ownership inscription; modern French bookplate of Baron D. G. Acquired by Henry Walters in Paris.

*The Walters Art Gallery*

This little book contains the entire Bible written in a minute but carefully formed script upon leaves of very thin vellum. The impetus to the production of such handy personal Bibles came during the thirteenth century when the lectures at the universities of Paris and Oxford were concerned with textual criticism.

The gothic practice of the fusion of letters obtains here, but with restraint. It may be noted chiefly in instances of d or h followed by an e or o. The d is in the uncial form. The r is shaped like a 2 when it follows o. The tops of ascenders are wedge-shaped or even forked. Double i is always ticked and sometimes the single i, when it adjoins an n or a u, the component strokes of which are now so similar that ambiguity is possible.

Bibliography: De Ricci, I, p. 765, no. 46; Walters *Cat.*, no. 45.

## *Compressed 'Early Gothic' Minuscules*

26 PSALTER

Southwest Germany, diocese of Constance, first half of 13th century.

Ms. W. 70. In Latin. 68 vellum leaves, 8⅝×6¼ inches. Written in 'early gothic' minuscules in long lines. 89 historiated and illuminated initials. Black ink. Binding: modern red velvet.

Provenance: Acquired in Paris by Henry Walters in 1905.

*The Walters Art Gallery*

The extreme lateral compression and thick strokes of this example result in a page so dark in color that it presents an impression of developed gothic script. A close analysis of the letters, however, shows the forms of the minuscule to be essentially simple and free from mannerism. The bases of the verticals are treated harmoniously but without exaggeration. The double p's near the top of the illustration are fused, but otherwise there is no tendency toward 'union.' An interesting contrast is provided by the marginal note in fourteenth-century *textus quadratus*.

Bibliography: De Ricci, I, p. 769, no. 79.

## *Textus Prescissus*

27 THE ANTIPHONARY OF BEAUPRÉ

Cistercian abbey of Cambron, Flanders, A.D. 1290.

Ms. W. 759–762. In Latin. 4 vols.: vol. I: 223 vellum leaves, 19×13½ inches; vol. II: 258 vellum leaves, 19×12½ inches; vol. III: 270 vellum leaves, 16½×12¼ inches; vol. IV: 62 vellum leaves, 19×13½ inches. Vols. I–III written in long lines in *textus prescissus*, with a few later insertions in *textus quadratus*. Vol. IV composed of a collection of the later (15th–17th cent.) contributions to the antiphonary. 49 large historiated initials, many smaller

illuminated ones and abundant red and blue initials with penwork. Black ink. Bindings: modern half morocco and red velvet.
Provenance: Executed at the order of Lady Marie de Viane apparently at Cambron for its daughter-house, the convent of St. Marie de Beaupré near Grammont in Belgium, where it remained until the French Revolution; John Ruskin, by ca. 1853; Henry Yates Thompson, London (his sale, London, June 22, 1921, III, no. 67, illus.); A. Chester Beatty (his sale, June 7, 1932, I, no. 15, pls. 18–20); William Randolph Hearst. Presented to the Gallery by the Hearst Foundation in 1957.
*The Walters Art Gallery*

The steady trend toward formality and lateral compression reached its apogee in the gothic scripts achieved in the thirteenth to fifteenth centuries. *Textus prescissus*, as the medieval calligraphers called it, was written with a very broad pen held straight. The emphasis was on the regular, strictly parallel reiteration of the verticals. The upright strokes (excluding descenders) of nearly all letters terminate abruptly at the base line (*prescissus* means 'cut off'). Only l, t and u retain a very slight angular turn to the right at the foot of the shaft—a vestige of the curved base of these letters in Carolingian minuscule. In developed gothic script like this, even essentially bowed letters such as b, c, d, e and round s have had their curves fractured into a combination of straight lines.

The plate shows the opening pages of volume I. The script, like the format, is of great size in order to be legible to a group of singers clustered around a lectern in the choir. The left page is lettered in a display script, even more exaggerated in its compressed and vertical mannerisms than is the writing used for the services. This inscription gives details of the ownership of the book ("Liber ecclesie beate marie de bello prato"), the date of the writing, an anathema against theft and a blessing on pious use. The extremely tall and embellished ascenders and the flourished descenders in the last line reflect the style of the formal chancery hands used in contemporary official documents. The lines are written alternately in red and blue.

Bibliography: The antiphonary is fully described in Henry Yates Thompson, *Catalogue of... Manuscripts*, vol. III, Cambridge, 1907, pp. 55–74, no. LXXXIII, and reproduced in his *Illustrations from One Hundred Manuscripts*, London, 1916, VI, pp. 4–8, pls. XII–XXIII; also in Eric Millar, *The Library of A. Chester Beatty: A Descriptive Catalogue of the Western Manuscripts*, Oxford, 1930, II, pp. 88–103, no. 63, pls. CXXXIII–CXXXIX; De Ricci, II, p. 1688, no. 4, giving additional history and bibliography; Bond and Faye, *Supplement*, p. 199, no. 574–577, with more recent references. For a valuable discussion of *textus prescissus*, see Stanley Morison, '*Black Letter*' *Text*, Cambridge, 1942, pp. 19–25.

## *Textus Semiquadratus*

28 PSALTER WITH LITURGICAL ADDITIONS
North France, late 13th century.
Ms. W. 47. In Latin. 203 vellum leaves, 12×9 inches. Written in gothic minuscule in long lines. 2 full-page miniatures, 9 historiated initials and numerous large ornamental illuminated initials. Black ink. Binding: modern red velvet set with *champlevé* enamel plaque.
Provenance: Given in 1589 by Henri Jordain to Frater Johannes Guymier. Acquired in Paris by Henry Walters in 1903.
*The Walters Art Gallery*

The script of this volume does not insist upon the precise parallel regularity of the vertical strokes seen in nos. 27 and 29. The bending of the ends of the strokes at tops and bases, while consistent, is not fractured at a sharp angle. The final stroke of m and n retains a bow shape. The whole effect is softer and less 'mechanical' than in nos. 27, 29 and 30. Note the smaller script used for the passages of the responses.

Bibliography: De Ricci, I, p. 770, no. 85.

## *Textus Quadratus*

29 MISSAL, SUMMER PART
Northeast France, 1300.
Ms. W. 127. In Latin. 211 vellum leaves, 13⅝×9½ inches. Written in formal gothic minuscules in 2 columns. Black ink with rubricated captions, illuminated initials with flourished penwork. 11 historiated initials. Binding: modern red velvet.
Provenance: Acquired in Paris by Henry Walters.
*The Walters Art Gallery*

The kind of script represented by no. 28 soon developed a formality and precision to rival that of the *textus prescissus* (nos. 27, 30). When used for a ceremonial altar-book, such as the present example, the closely-spaced verticals maintain a strictly parallel relationship, the formerly rounded letters, such as b, c, d, e, p, q, o, etc., are reduced to straight elements almost as severely as in *textus prescissus*. Furthermore, the bases of letters which once had ended in a curve to the right or a serif, now are bent sharply at an angle, or terminated by a diamond. This gives a uniformity to the bases

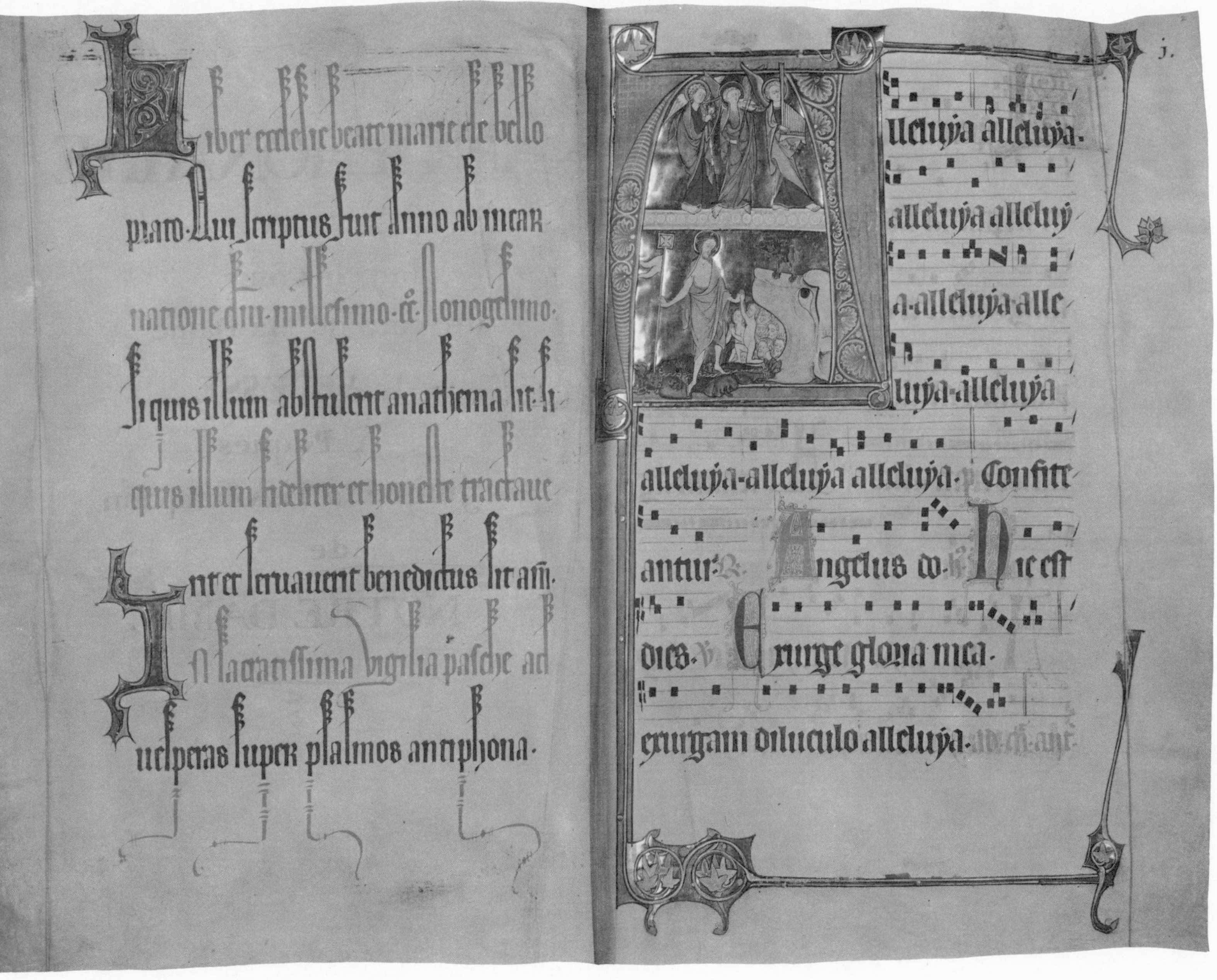

27. Antiphonary for Beaupré. Cambron, A.D. 1290

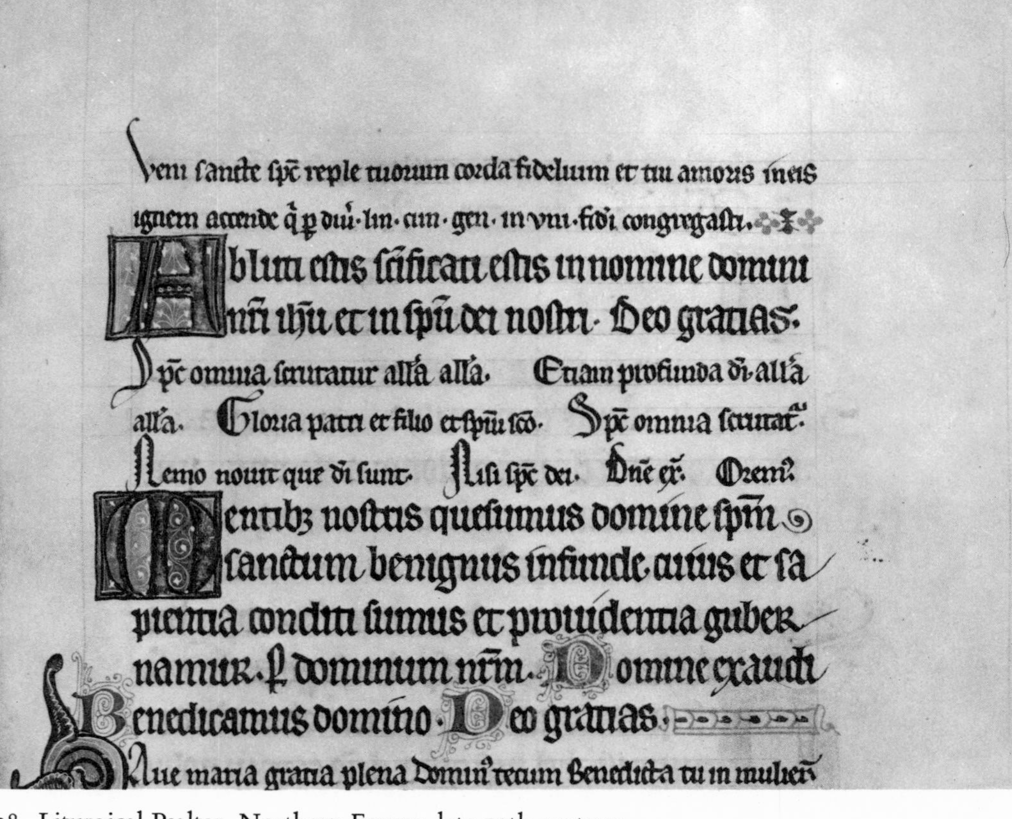

28. Liturgical Psalter. Northern France, late 13th century

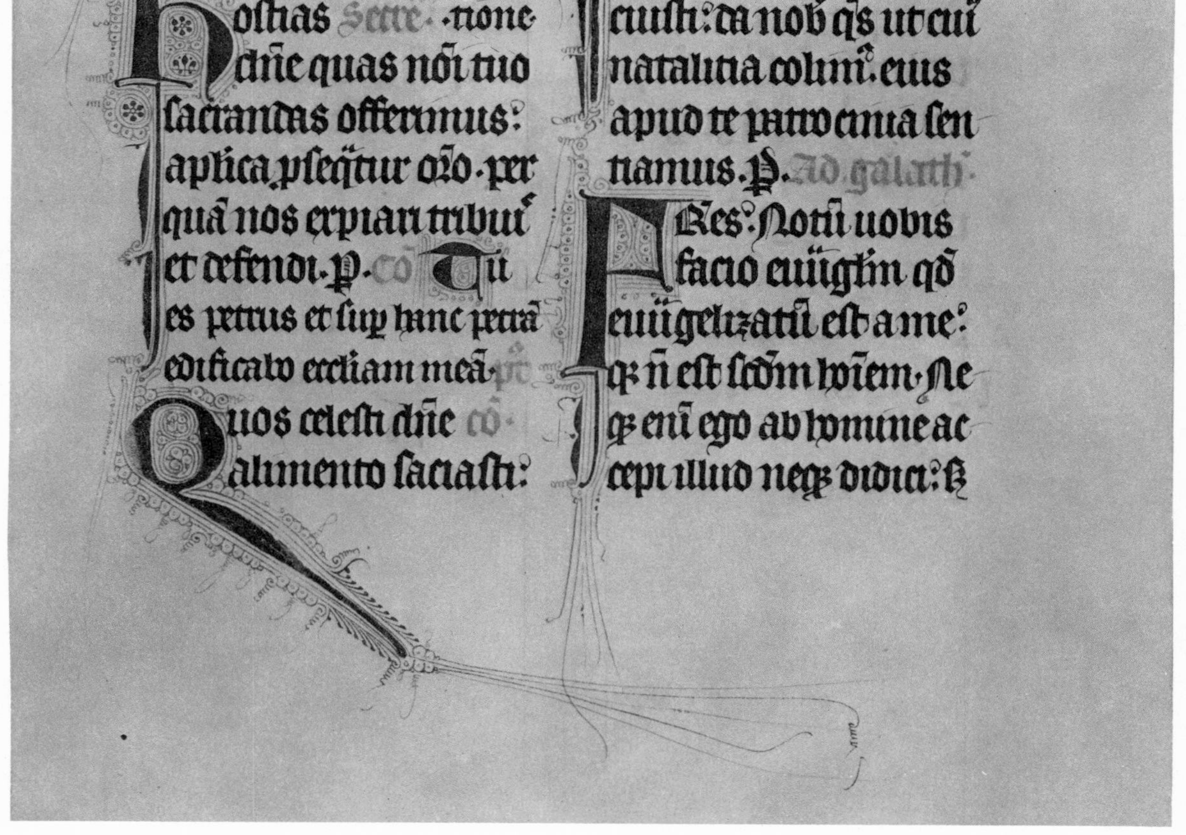

29. Missal. Northeast France, 1300

which contributes greatly to the sharp-cut and angular appearance of the line of script. The reduction of the space between verticals, the fusion of many combinations of letters (as the h and o of *hominem* in the next to last line at the right in the illustration) all enhance the effect of blackness and of trim regularity. Whereas the pen was held straight to write *textus prescissus*, for *quadratus* it was held on a slant.

This kind of script, by its compression and abundant use of abbreviations, could present much text in a short space. This and its architectural rhythm caused it to be adopted for monumental inscriptions in stone and metal during the fourteenth and fifteenth centuries. It was the basis of the 'psalter' types designed by Johann Gutenberg—the earliest of all moveable type.

Bibliography: De Ricci, I, p. 775, no 116. For an enlightening discussion of *textus quadratus* see Stanley Morison, '*Black Letter*' *Text*, Cambridge, 1942, pp. 25–30.

## *Textus Prescissus*

30 PSALTER AND HOURS

England, early 14th century.

Ms. W. 79. In Latin. 193 vellum leaves, 13⅝×9½ inches. Written in formal gothic minuscules, with rubricated captions. Black ink. Large and small initials ornamented with elaborate pen-flourishing in red and blue. Decorative line-fillers. First words at the main divisions inscribed in raised burnished gold. 3 historiated initials (several missing). Marginal drolleries. The last 2 leaves contain prayers written in a fine 15th-century humanist hand. Binding: black English morocco, blind tooled by Rivière.

Provenance: Col. Cotes (sale, London, March 18, 1900, no. 289). Acquired by Henry Walters from Wilfred M. Voynich.

*The Walters Art Gallery*

The extreme, almost mechanical regularity achieved by *textus prescissus* in the fourteenth century is well illustrated by this fine large Psalter. The relentless sharpness of the lettering has been relieved—as is usual in English manuscripts of this kind—not only by the gaiety of color and burnished gold in historiated initials and in line-fillers, but most notably by the fluent and abundant use of marginal pen-embellishments. This kind of ornamentation by its very nature is a calligraphic one, and was developed to a high degree in England.

Bibliography: De Ricci, I, p. 773, no. 103.

## *Gotica Rotunda*

31 OVID, METAMORPHOSES: I–VII

Northern Italy (Padua or Venice), end of 14th century.

Ms. W. 162. In Latin. 72 vellum leaves, 11×8 inches. Written in single column in the round gothic minuscules described by some scholars as *gotico-antiqua*. Black-brown ink, with the lists of contents of each Book in red. 2 historiated initials and 4 large ornamental initials illuminated in gold and colors. Binding: early 19th-century stamped brown calf by Larrivière.

Provenance: Joseph Barrois coll., MS. 80; acquired from him in 1849 by the Earl of Ashburnham (his sale, London, 1901, lot 445). Acquired by Henry Walters from Leo S. Olschki in Florence.

*The Walters Art Gallery*

The Italian variety of gothic script had a particularly significant development in northern Italy, thanks to the scribal activities in connection with the great universities, such as those of Bologna and Padua. This was the book hand known to the earliest humanists of the fourteenth century, Petrarch, Coluccio Salutati and others. The works of classical literature copied out for them by professional scribes looked not unlike the fine Ovid manuscript shown in our illustration, and the book hand used by such early humanist scholars themselves was a less formal version of this script. One notes that it is not only more rounded and less acutely angular than the contemporary gothic hands used north of the Alps, but the words are more widely and clearly spaced. Being a work of literature, it resembles in this last quality, as well as in the smaller scale of the script, the secular literary manuscripts of the north, such as no. 33, a good deal more than the formal liturgical script of France and England represented by nos. 30 and 32. However, the comparison with no. 33 also brings out the essential differences in the *ductus*. Despite the impression of less crowding, the Italian script is still a gothic one because of the contrast between thick and thin lines in the shading, and the fusion of certain combinations of letters.

The convention of separating the first initial of each line of verse, seen in no. 20, still obtains here.

Bibliography: De Ricci, I, p. 832, no. 445.

## *Textus Quadratus*

32 MISSAL FOR PARIS USE

France, Paris, ca. 1380.

Ms. W. 124. In Latin. 295 vellum leaves, 10¼×7 inches. Written by several hands in a regular gothic minuscule in 2 columns. Light brown ink, with rubrication. Nu-

merous initials alternately blue and burnished gold with red or blue penwork. Some scribal initials in the top lines extended vertically and embellished with droll faces, etc. 6 historiated initials and 12 other miniatures. The main pages embellished with bar and ivy borders in gold and colors with drolleries. Binding: white vellum over boards, brass trimmed; edges gilt and painted in mid-15th century style.
Provenance: Arms of an owner connected with the Dorigny family inserted in the 16th century; in the 17th century belonged to the Chartreuse de Beaune. Acquired in Paris by Henry Walters.
*The Walters Art Gallery*

This is a characteristic example of the Paris version of *textus quadratus*—daintier and not as monumental as the kind favored for liturgical books in England in the fourteenth century. Here the close array of the letters and the fusion of such combinations as de, he, pe, oc, etc., is abundantly evident, as well as the greatly increased number of abbreviations. The similarity of the verticals and bases of such letters as i, m, n, and u causes these letters to look so much alike as to be confusing—note, for instance *miniam* in the top line of the right column. The rubricated passages were inserted by another scribe, as is clear even in the black and white illustration (note the *Ad romanos* in the eleventh line of the first column, and the three-and-a-half-line rubric starting in the fourteenth line at the right).

The particular mannerisms of the marginal pen-flourishes are a hall-mark of the Paris scriptoria of the fourteenth century. The abbreviated *expectate* with its fanciful head is a catch-word to connect this gathering of the book with the first line of the next gathering—a device to assist the binder. The fine, even vellum of the book is the kind selected for the best Paris guild productions of the period. By this time it was commercially prepared, in contrast to the practice necessary in the monastic scriptoria of earlier centuries (cf. no. 18).

Bibliography: De Ricci, I, p. 776, no. 119; Walters *Cat.*, 1949, p. 29, no. 72; Walters Art Gallery, *The International Style*, Baltimore, 1962, pp. 42–43, no. 40, pl. LIII.

## *Littera Textualis*

### 33 GUILLAUME DE LORRIS AND JEAN DE MEUNG, ROMAN DE LA ROSE; ANONYMOUS, LA CHÂTELAINE DE VERGI.

Northern France (Artois or Picardy), ca. 1325.
Ms. A–2200. In French. 162 vellum leaves, 11⅝×8⅝ inches. Written in 2 columns in a northern gothic book hand. Brown ink. The larger initials in red or blue with penwork. 1 miniature and 1 historiated initial. Binding: French red morocco, ca. 1700.
Provenance: Sir Henry Spelman (1564–1641); Rev. Cox Macro (1638–1769); John Patterson (his sale, 1820); Hudson Gurney (1775–1864); Maggs Bros., London (Cat. 830, no. 486, pl. XXXI); C. C. Rattey.
*Lent by Mr. and Mrs. Harry A. Walton, Jr.*

The fourteenth century saw a great increase in the production of copies of secular literary texts intended for entertainment and diversion. The ateliers of Artois and Picardy seem to have specialized in such works. As in all books intended to meet a popular demand, the quality varied from quite fine and well-finished productions to hastily written-out examples on rough vellum. The illustrations, also lively and amusing, varied similarly in calibre.

The present example of such a literary volume is not *de luxe*, but it is of exceptional quality: the vellum has been carefully selected and well ruled, the margins are wide and well balanced, the script fairly regular, and the little illustrations dainty and delightful. The first text was one of the most popular of the fourteenth and fifteenth centuries. This is, however, one of only three manuscripts of the *Roman de la Rose* to contain also *La Châtelaine de Vergi.*

Specialists never seem to agree on a satisfactory name for this kind of French gothic script—careful, but far less formal than the liturgical letters, narrow in proportion, although not extremely so as in the formal scripts, of an angular *ductus* but not sharply fractured at the ends of the strokes as in *textus quadratus*. The whole appearance is softer. For the caption of this entry I have adopted the designation suggested by Professor G. I. Lieftinck. Note the separation of the first letter of each verse (cf. nos. 20, 31, 52).

Bibliography: Ernest Langlois (ed.), *Le Roman de la Rose*, Paris, 1914, I, p. 51, note; Frederick Whitehead, *La Chastelaine de Vergi*, Manchester, 1944, p. xlv; C. E. Pickford in *Bulletin of the John Rylands Library*, XXXIV, 1951–52, pp. 344–349; Bond and Faye, *Supplement*, p. 524, no. A–2200. For a discussion of the term *Littera textualis*, see Dr. G. I. Lieftinck in *Nomenclature*, pp. 17 ff.

## *Littera Textualis Formata*

### 34 BOOK OF HOURS FOR USE OF UTRECHT

Holland, diocese of Utrecht, ca. 1450.
Ms. A–1015. In Dutch. 152 vellum leaves, 5½×4 inches. Written in long lines in careful gothic minuscules.

26. Psalter. Southwest Germany, first half of 13th century

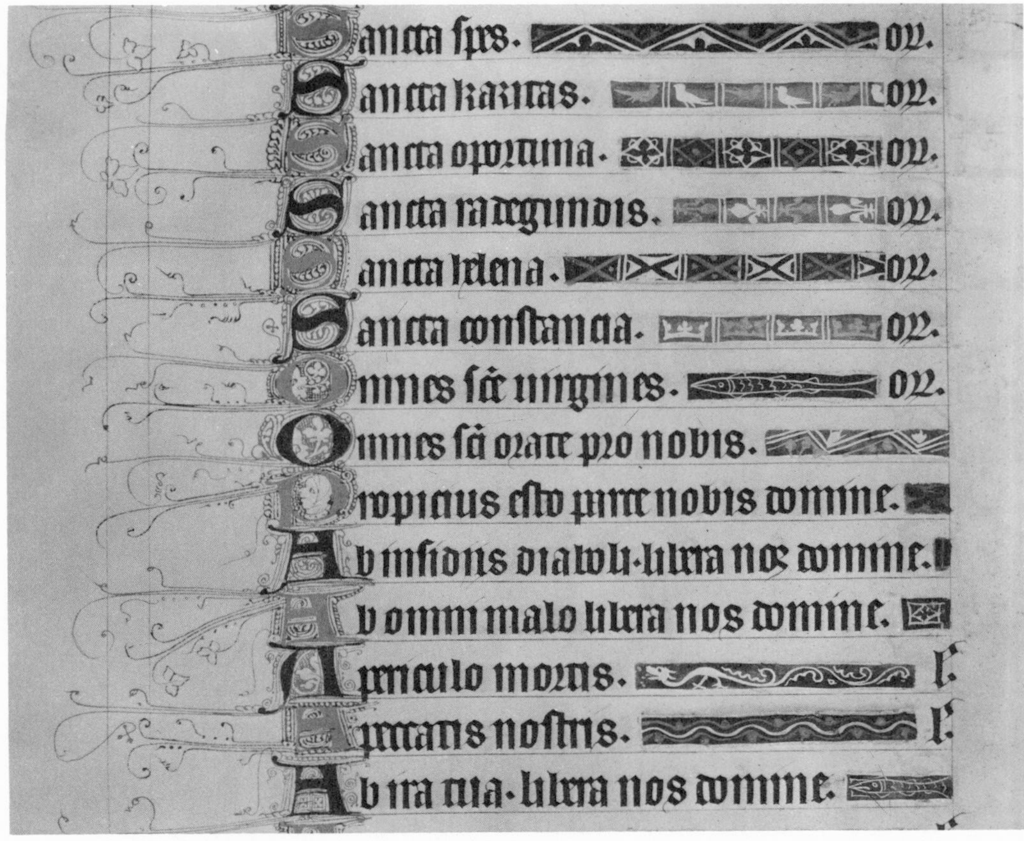
Sancta spes. or.
Sancta karitas. or.
Sancta oportuna. or.
Sancta radegundis. or.
Sancta helena. or.
Sancta constancia. or.
Omnes sce uirgines. or.
Omnes sci orate pro nobis.
Propicius esto parce nobis domine.
Ab insidiis diaboli libera nos domine.
Ab omni malo libera nos domine.
A periculo mortis. l.
A peccatis nostris. l.
Ab ira tua libera nos domine.

30. Psalter and Hours. England, early 14th century

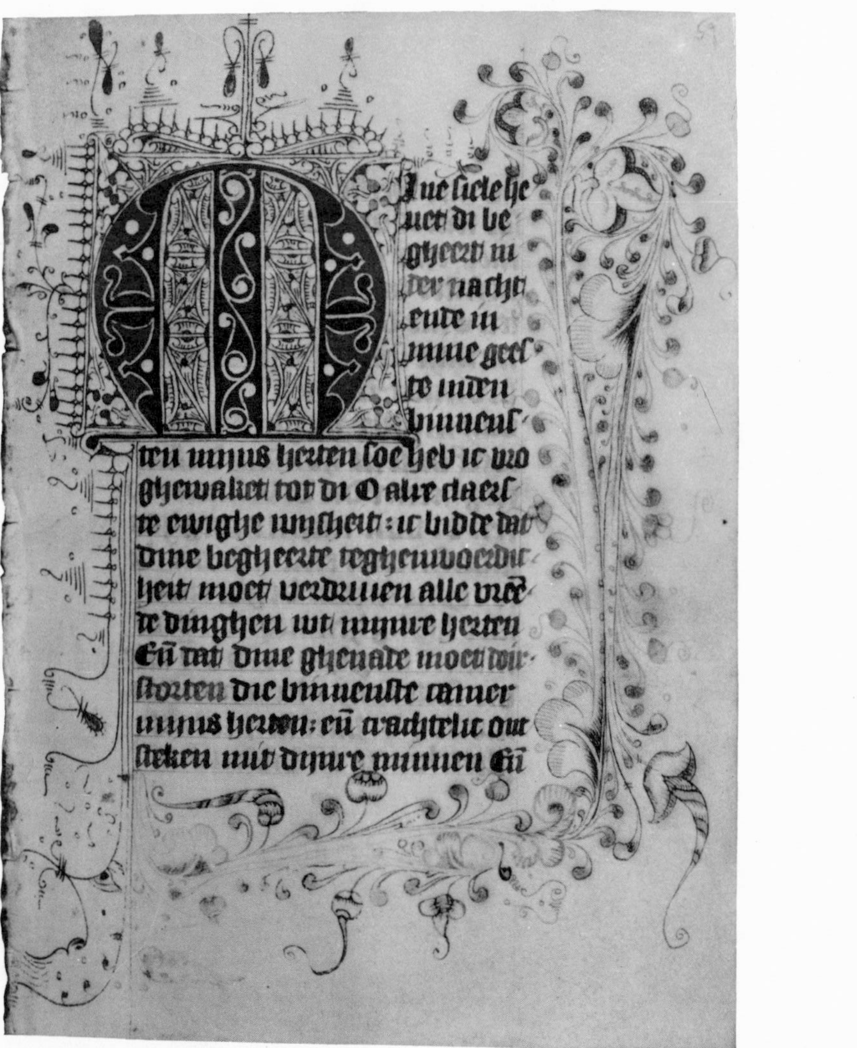

34. Book of Hours. Utrecht diocese, ca. 1450

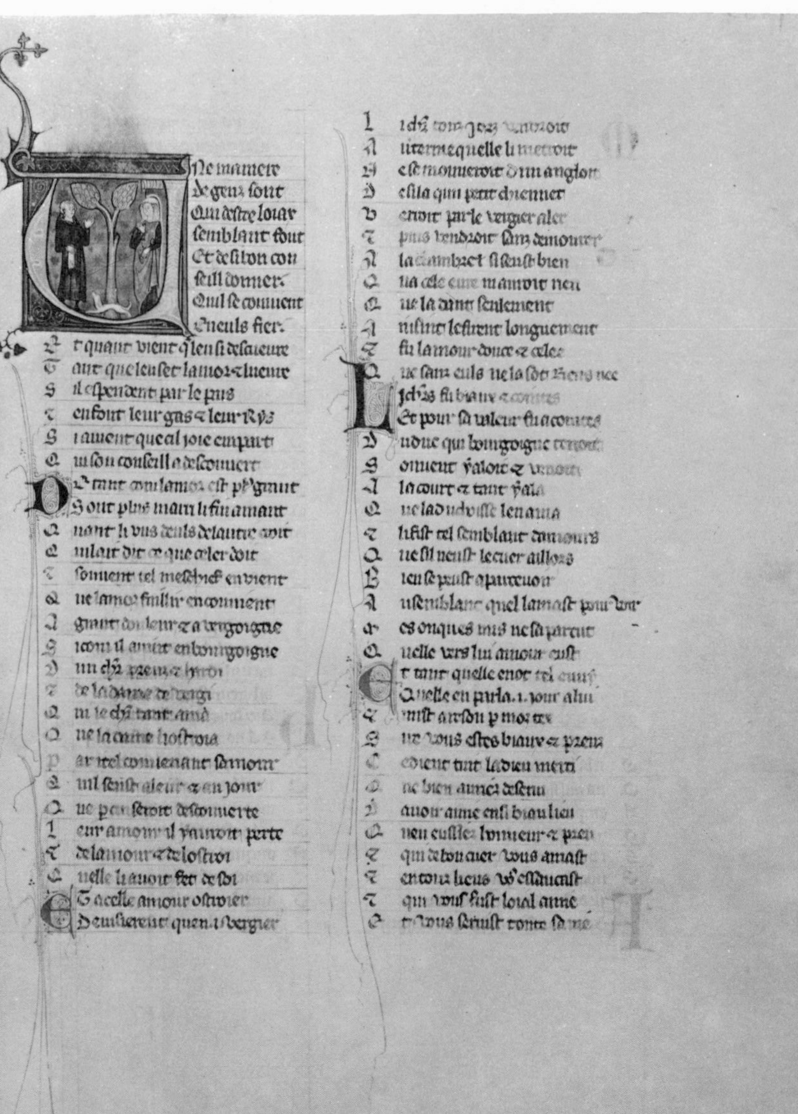

33. *La Châtelaine de Vergi*. Northern France, ca. 1325

Brown ink. Rubrics and red and blue text initials, and some with penwork. 4 large initials ornamented with colors and elaborate penwork in colored inks forming full or partial frames, the first one enhanced with gold. Binding: early 19th-century brown straight-grain morocco, stamped.
Provenance: Two ownership inscriptions on fly-leaves, one in Dutch dated 1561 and one in Latin dated 1570.
*Lent by Mr. and Mrs. Harry A. Walton, Jr.*

This competent, carefully inscribed book hand is characteristic of the kind produced for middle-class lay use in the Netherlands. Uncomplicated by insistent fracture and by finishing hair-lines, it simply does not have the sharp, angular quality of *textus quadratus* (the latter script was, of course, produced in the Netherlands at this time, but was reserved for Missals and other formal altar-books and for *de luxe* productions). The *ductus* gives a square and slanting impression. The term I have adopted for the caption of this entry again follows the proposals of Dr. Lieftinck (cf. no. 33).

Bibliography: Bond and Faye, *Supplement*, p. 521, no. A–1015.

## *Littera Bastarda by David Aubert*

35 GUY DE THURNO, LA VISON DE L'ÂME
Flanders (Ghent), 1474.
Ms. Typ. 235 H. In French. 34 vellum leaves, 14⅜×10½ inches. Written in large *lettres bâtardes* in 2 columns. Illuminated initials. 1 miniature with full illuminated border. Binding: modern brown morocco, by Trautz-Bauzonnet.
Provenance: Executed for Margaret of York, wife of Charles the Bold, Duke of Burgundy; Marquis de Ganay (his sale, Paris, 1881, lots 38–39); Comte de Lignerolles (his sale, Paris, 1894, lot 17); Baron Vitta. Acquired in 1951 from H. P. Kraus, New York.
*Lent by Mr. and Mrs. Philip Hofer*

Contemporary with the formal gothic book hands such as *textus prescissus*, *textus quadratus* and others that can be grouped as *littera textualis formata*, there were practiced many less formal and more rapidly written hands. These had the qualities of all cursive: sloping, closely joined, the exactions of angular precision giving way to curved strokes, and so on. Again, as so often in the history of calligraphy, the characteristics of informal writing moved into the field of formal script. In France and Flanders, where this style had a special development, the script was called 'bastard.' Variations of it, of course, appeared in England and elsewhere. The distinguishing characteristics are the inclination toward curved and sometimes flourished forms, the preservation of fused letters, the lack of serifs and a preference for tapering terminals to the strokes. It is a heavily shaded writing. Noticeable is the prominent long s.

In Flanders it reached a special status as the hand for large, *de luxe* volumes in French, intended for the new class of aristocratic bibliophiles. These were showy volumes, written upon heavy, white, suede-surfaced vellum in script of large size.

The fifteenth century saw a new development in the production of books for secular needs—the growth of establishments which were really editorial or publishing houses. The head of such an establishment would select the kind of texts most in demand, translate or edit them, assemble scribes, rubricators and illuminators to put them into presentable form. Such offices tended to move to whatever location offered the best business. When an aristocrat was developing his library, the miniaturists and other artists would come from many places of origin, and might move on as other opportunities beckoned, but the general aspect of the works of such a 'publishing house' would tend toward a uniform standard.

One of the most distinguished of all such 'publishers' in the fifteenth century was the scribe David Aubert, native of Hesdin. He established himself at Bruges around 1460 and then at Brussels, drawn by the commissions of Philip the Good, Duke of Burgundy, and of his courtiers. Just before 1475, he moved to Ghent, where he undertook especially the production of some luxurious works for Margaret of York, the wife of Charles the Bold, now Duke of Burgundy. The present example is the earliest dated manuscript surely to be located in Aubert's Ghent studio. It was commissioned by Margaret of York, and its illuminated border bears her motto and the cipher of herself and her husband. It is signed by David Aubert, and dated at Ghent, February 1st, 1474. The miniature is attributed to the great Valenciennes painter, Simon Marmion. A companion volume, dated by Aubert in March of the same year, is also in the collection of the lender. As in the case of all fine books prepared by Aubert for Margaret, these are spiritual treatises.

Bibliography: Harvard *Cat.*, p. 27, no. 89, pl. 53; L. M. J. Delaissé, *La Miniature Flamande*, Brussels, 1959, p. 59, no. 191, pl. 59, and introductions to sections on Bruges, Brussels and Ghent; Bond and Faye, *Supplement*, p. 273, MS. Typ. 235 H.

## *'Notula' or Bastard Minuscules*

36 MODUS SCRIBENDI
Austria (Melk ?), ca. 1440.
Ms. Typ. 111 H. In Latin. 8 paper leaves, 8⅝×5⅝

inches. Written in various styles of gothic 'bastard' minuscule or 'secretary hand' in long lines. Black and brown ink. Binding: modern red crushed morocco by Rivière and Son.
Provenance: Benedictine Abbey of Melk from an early date, and perhaps written there (MS. 4.G.16); procured from Melk by E. P. Goldschmidt; acquired from him in 1937 by Stanley Morison. Acquired from Scribner's, New York, 1947.
*Lent by Mr. and Mrs. Philip Hofer*

This is one of only five or six known fifteenth-century writing manuals, as distinct from calligrapher's specimen sheets. This little treatise was designed not so much to introduce a beginner to the art of calligraphy as to assist the instructor in presenting basic rules. Much of the text is in verse form, and illustrates different kinds of secretary hands current in Germany at the time. All, whether a formal, fractured and flourished hand, as at the left of the illustration, or a more current hand in letters of small size as at the right, are basically a 'bastard' script (cf. no. 35).

Bibliography: Martinus Kropff, *Bibliotheca Mellicensis*, Vienna, 1747, p. 459; Bernhard Bischoff, *Ein neuentdeckten Modus Scribendi des XV. Jahrhunderts aus der Abtei Melk*, Berlin, 1939; Stanley Morison, *A Fifteenth Century Modus Scribendi from the Abbey of Melk*, Cambridge, 1940; S. H. Steinberg in *The Library*, Ser. 4, XXIII, 1943, pp. 191–194; Walters *Cat.*, 1949, p. 84, no. 229; Portland *Cat.*, p. 12, no. 6, pl. 4.

## *Joannis Ranizi*

37 LEGAL DOCUMENT
Milan, 1461.
Ms. Wing f Z W 1. 469. In Latin. 1 paper sheet inscribed in long lines in a careful secretary hand. Brown ink. Unbound.
*Lent by the John M. Wing Foundation of the Newberry Library*

This *supplicatio*, addressed to Duke ('principe') Galeazzo Maria Sforza, is written out in a careful secretary hand of the kind termed *brevitura* in the well-known advertisement compiled for his atelier in 1447 by the writing master Hermann Strepel of Münster (The Hague, Bibl. Roy. MS. 76 D 45: 4 B). Our specimen is in fact also the production of a professional writing master, as it is signed on the address side of the missive: "Johannis de ranitis Magr scola scribendi" and dated in Milan, November 28, 1461.

## *Guinifortus de Vicomerchato*

38 ILLUMINATOR'S SAMPLE BOOK
Northern Italy (Milan), 1450.
Ricketts MS. 240. Latin inscriptions. 19 vellum leaves, 13½×9 inches. A variety of ornamental letters executed in color and penwork. Binding: old stiffened vellum.
Provenance: Sale of Sir Thomas Gage and others (London, 1867, no. 457); W. H. Crawford in 1867 (his sale, London, 1891, no. 3248); Robert Hoe, New York, 1892 (his sale, New York, 1911, I, no. 2182); C. L. Ricketts, Chicago. Acquired from his collection by the Library of Indiana University in 1961.
*Lent by the Lilly Library, Indiana University*

This fascinating book is a compilation of ornamental alphabets of various sizes and degrees of elaboration, which might be suitable for use in various kinds of productions from small Books of Hours to huge antiphonaries. Most of the letters are executed in red or blue upon contrasting blue or red penwork *maiblümen* or other grounds. These are developed with penwork flourishes ranging from simple vertical passages of pen-play in red, blue or lavender, to most elaborate and involved geometrical and floral ornament—all executed with the pen freely or by construction with ruler and compass. In these designs olive, violet, minium and black are introduced, in addition to the red and blue. Also, use is made of imitation or false gold, known as 'mosaic gold' in the medieval Italian recipe-books (*aurum musicum* or *purpurina*). There are two examples of complete page-designs for tiny Books of Hours. Some of the larger initials incorporate microscopic inscriptions in the formal ornament around the letter-fields. In just such a microscopic hand the artist has signed in one of the ornaments: "Guinifortus de vicomerchato mediolanensis fecit hoc opus 1450 die primo aug'i" (see illustration). Another artist has added some less imaginative antiphonary initials in blue and red and 'mosaic gold,' one of which is signed "Basilius de Gallis." Later on, probably after 1500, a third and clumsy hand has inserted some passages of renaissance floral ornament.

Such a volume as this is not a sketch-book, but is rather a compilation of designs intended to show what the artist could do. Thus the samples include ideas for various kinds of work, as well as pure exhibition-pieces to display his virtuosity. Presumably Guinifortus travelled about to towns outside Milan, wherever he thought bibliographical projects might offer a field for his services.

Bibliography: Quaritch, *General Catalogue*, London, 1868, p. 1080; Grolier Club, *Catalogue of an Exhibition of Illuminated and Painted Manuscripts . . .*, New York, 1892, p. 15, no. 34; O. A. Bierstadt, *The Library of Robert Hoe*, New

32. Missal. Paris, ca. 1380

31. Ovid, *Metamorphoses*. Northern Italy, end of 14th century

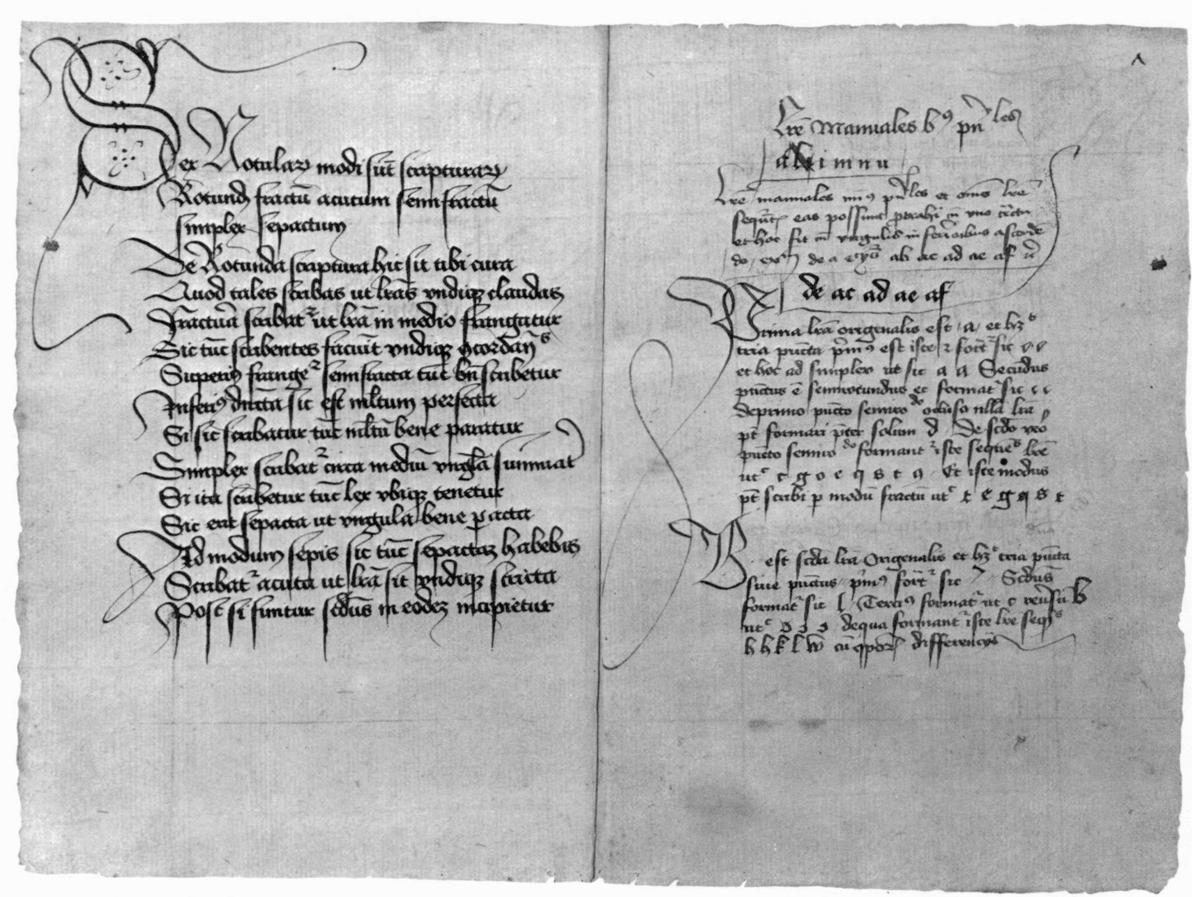

36. *Modus Scribendi*. Austria, ca. 1440

37. Joannis Ranizi, *Supplicatio*. Milan, 1461

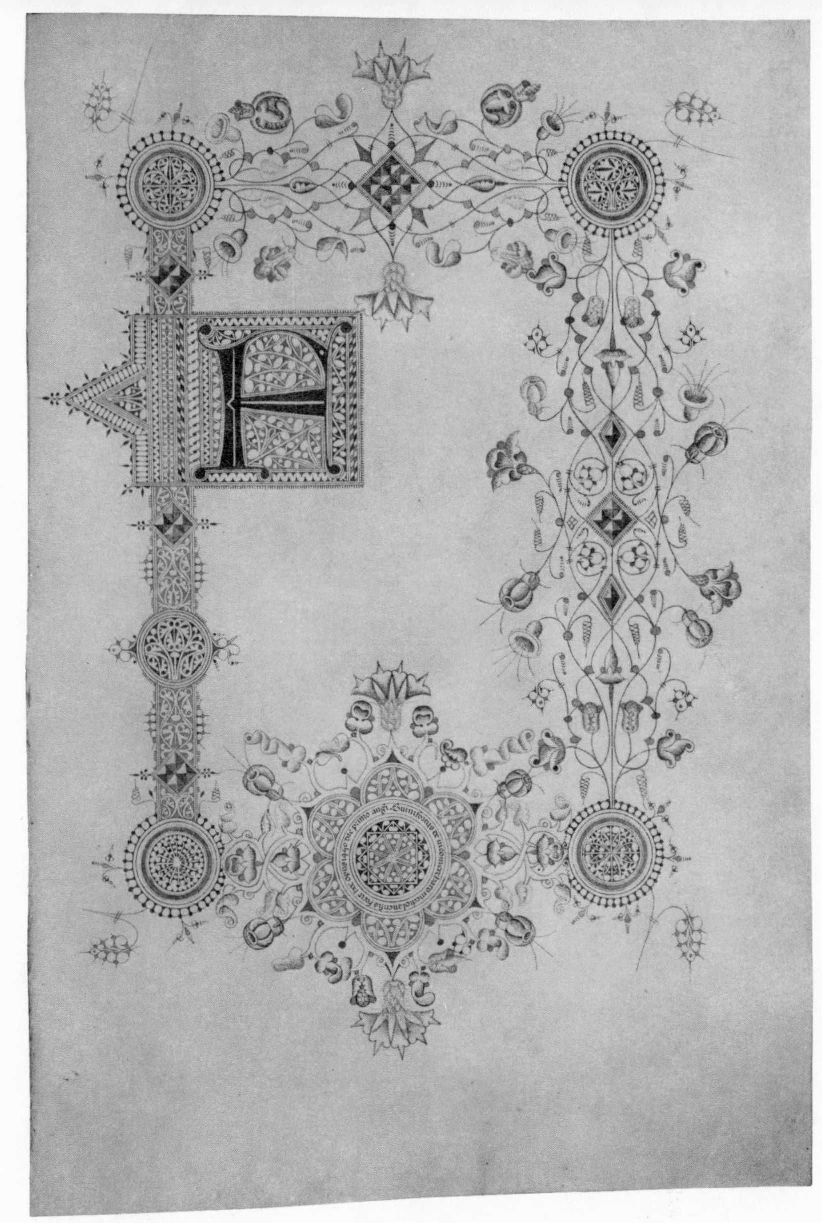

38. Guinifortus de Vicomerchato, Sample Book. Milan, 1450

39. Breviary. Florence, ca. 1480

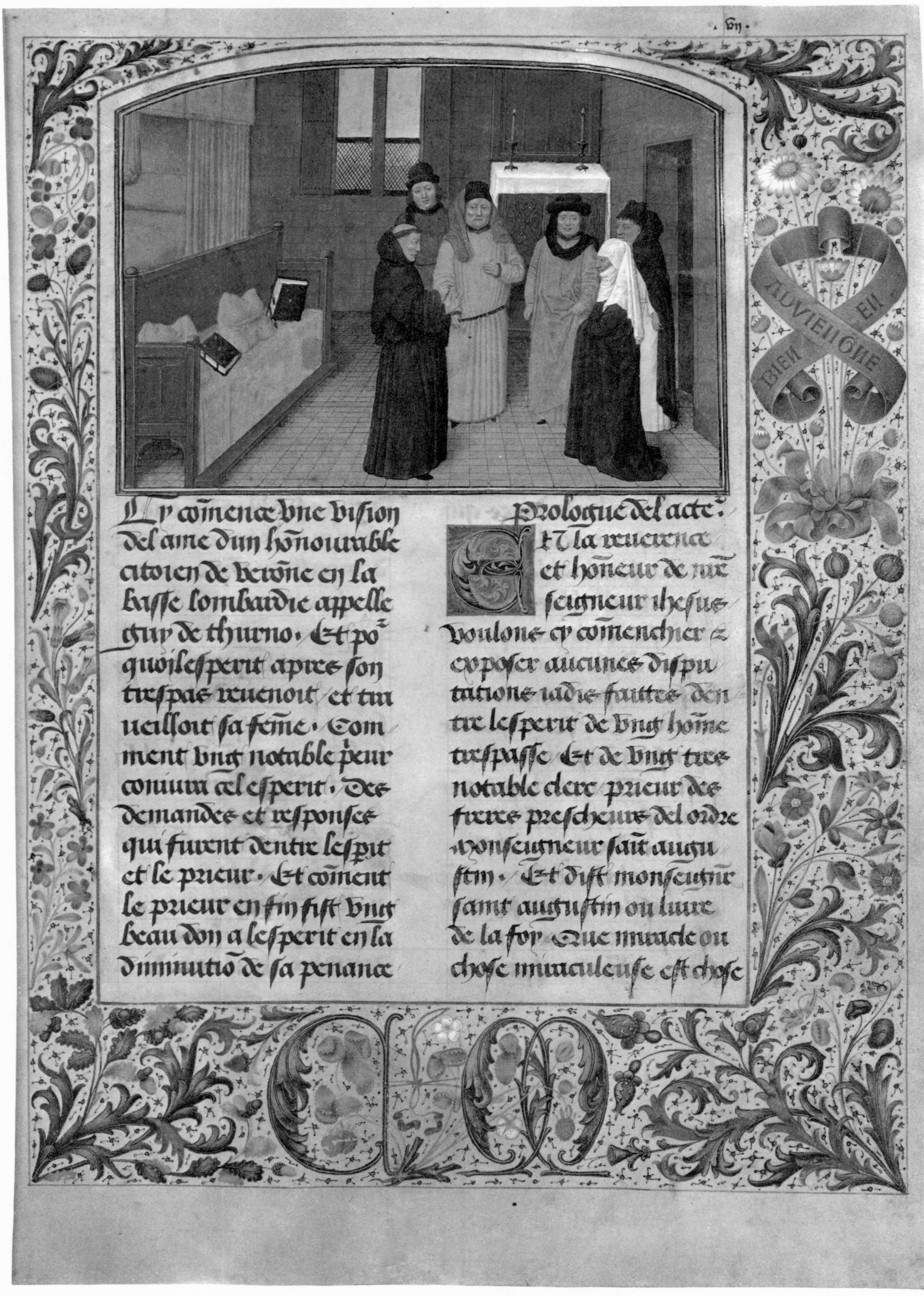

Cy comence une vision  
del ame dun honnourable  
citoien de beronne en la  
basse lombardie appelle  
guy de thurno. Et pour  
quoi lesperit apres son  
trespas revenoit et tra  
veilloit sa feme. Com  
ment ung notable peur  
conivra cel esperit. Des  
demandes et responses  
qui furent dentre lespit  
et le prieur. Et coment  
le prieur en fin fist ung  
beau don a lesperit en la  
diminutio de sa penance

Prologue del acteur.

Et la reverence  
et honeur de nre  
seigneur ihesus  
voulons cy comenchier &  
exposer aucunes dispu  
tations iadis faittes den  
tre lesperit de ung home  
trespasse. Et de ung tres  
notable clerc prieur des  
freres prescheurs del ordre  
monseigneur saint augu  
stin. Et dist monseignr  
saint augustin ou livre  
de la foy Que miracle ou  
chose miraculeuse est chose

35. Guy de Thurno, *La Vision de l'Âme*. By David Aubert. Ghent, 1474

York, 1895, p. 24; De Ricci, I, p. 655, no. 240; Bond and Faye, *Supplement*, p. 539.

## *Gotica Rotunda*

39 BREVIARY FOR USE OF ROME

Italy (Florence), ca. 1480.

Ms. W. 334. In Latin. 501 vellum leaves, 10×6½ inches. Written in 2 columns in round gothic minuscules. Black ink; rubricated captions and liturgical directions. Numerous historiated initials and illuminated borders. The other initials in red and blue with freely-drawn marginal penwork in the contrasting color. The signatures of the gatherings are embellished with illuminated ornament. Binding: modern Italian sprinkled calf with metal bosses.

Provenance: Arms of Cardinal Giovanni Battista Savelli of Rome (cardinal 1480–98). Acquired from Leo S. Olschki, Florence, by Henry Walters after 1912.

*The Walters Art Gallery*

This book is characteristic of Florentine liturgical volumes of the period. The vellum is soft and silky, the penwork is in patterns characteristic of Florentine ateliers, the illumination is dainty. The *gotica rotunda* remained in use for liturgical volumes long after Italian scribes had adopted humanistic letter forms for most other kinds of text.

Bibliography: L. S. Olschki in *La Bibliofilia*, XII, 1910–11, p. 341; De Ricci, I, p. 779, no. 334, with further references.

## *Early Humanistic Minuscules*

40 CICERO, RHETORICA NOVA ET RHETORICA VETUS

Italy (perhaps Padua or Verona), first quarter of 15th century.

Ms. W. 367. In Latin. 133 paper leaves, 10⅜×8 inches. Written in humanistic minuscules in long lines; rubricated initials and captions. Brown ink. Binding: early 19th-century French blue straight-grained morocco, gilt.

Provenance: Abate Mateo Celotti (his sale, London, March 14, 1875, no. 87); Sir Thomas Phillipps, MS. 916 and 2705 (his sale, London, 1898, no. 205). Acquired by Henry Walters probably in London.

*The Walters Art Gallery*

Although the early Italian humanists of the fourteenth century themselves wrote a round gothic hand (cf. no. 31), it is clear that they were the ones who reintroduced an appreciation of Carolingian minuscules and eventually fostered a new script based on the *lettera antica*. By the latter term they meant the fine clear writing which they found in the best copies of the classical authors that their agents were assembling from the oldest libraries. These good, correct copies almost invariably were manuscripts written in Carolingian minuscules, and dating from the ninth, tenth or eleventh centuries.

Professor Ullman has demonstrated that it was the Florentine humanist Coluccio Salutati who first experimented tentatively with a form of a new 'antique' script in his own writing and then sought out professional scribes who could learn to practice a round hand based upon Carolingian exemplars. He evidently found such a man in the young scholar and notary, Poggio Bracciolini, who soon after 1400 was working for Coluccio and gained a reputation for his skill as a copyist in *littera antiqua*, executing several books for him before Coluccio's death in 1406.

The manuscript on display is by no means as early as the pioneer work just referred to, but it belongs to the early phase of humanistic script. It has already shaken off some of the gothic mannerisms that lingered for a while. Fusion has been abandoned, the uncial d with curved top has definitely been replaced by the minuscule d with a tall stem, the s is always the long form. A glance at the illustration of no. 31 will serve to show what a leap has been made. The g, as in many fairly early humanist manuscripts, has an awkward form. The rather tall proportions of the script suggest that the models selected by our scribe were those of the tenth or eleventh century, rather than earlier (cf. nos. 14, 15).

A feature of this manuscript—which caused the late James Wardrop to suggest, informally, that the manuscript originates not in Florence but in the north of Italy—is the nature of the rubricated titles. The rather fanciful handling of these letters is reminiscent of the byzantinizing characteristics which Stanley Morison has discussed in connection with no. 43.

The marginal notations seen in the illustration provide a good example of a neat humanistic cursive.

Bibliography: De Ricci, I, p. 835, no. 457. For the discussion of the contributions of Coluccio and Poggio to the earliest development of humanistic script see B. L. Ullman, *Humanistic Script*, Rome, 1960, pp. 15–57.

## *Antonio di Mario (?), (active 1417–56)*

41 PETRARCH, SONETTI, CANZONI E TRIONFI

Italy (Florence), 1440.

Richardson MS. 43. In Italian. 186 vellum leaves, 9½×

6½ inches. Written in humanistic minuscules in dark brown ink; rubrics in pale red. 3 illuminated initials and others in red and blue. Binding: modern brown calf, stamped and gilt.

Provenance: William King Richardson, who acquired it of E. P. Goldschmidt, London. Bequeathed to Harvard in 1951.

*Lent by Harvard College Library, Dept. of Printing and Graphic Arts*

One of the Florentine sponsors of the new humanistic script was Niccolò Niccoli, a scholar who was also a friend of Poggio Bracciolini and of Coluccio. He seems to have encouraged Florentine scribes to imitate the style of Poggio, who as early as 1403 had left Florence for Rome. One of these scribes was Antonio di Mario, who was active for about forty years. He signed and dated forty-one manuscripts, but it is supposed that unsigned ones also exist. Professor Ernest H. Wilkins has suggested that the script of this Petrarch resembles that of Mario. It seems clear, however, that more than one scribe is involved in this manuscript or else one who was learning as he wrote, for the first fifty leaves or so display many gothic survivals, such as consistent use of uncial d and of some fusion. Thereafter, the scribe seems to be making an effort to adopt the correct humanistic forms, long-stemmed d is introduced, but the uncial one keeps creeping in inadvertently. Eventually in the last part of the manuscript, uncial d is abandoned entirely. The long s throughout is like the bastard form. Professor Ullman, in pointing out variations from signed Mario manuscripts, notes that the latter are all in Latin, while perhaps a variant script was reserved for the vernacular.

Bibliography: Bond and Faye, *Supplement*, p. 248, MS. Richardson 43; B. L. Ullman, "Petrarch Manuscripts in the United States," *Censimento dei Codici Petrarcheschi*, I, Padua, 1964, p. 448, no. 14 and note 1. For an account of Antonio di Mario see, *idem, Humanistic Script*, pp. 98–109.

## *Pietro Cennini (1444–ca. 1481)*

42 PLAUTUS, COMEDIAE VIII

Italy (Florence), ca. 1462–67.

Ms. Lat. 43. In Latin. 130 paper leaves, 8⅝×5¾ inches. Written in humanistic cursive in brown ink. Illuminated initials at beginning of each play; others in color. Rubricated captions. Binding: Italian 18th-century printed paper.

Provenance: Ms. F. VI.32 in an 18th-century Italian Library; acquired in 1829 by Sir Thomas Phillipps, MS. 6332 (his sale, London, 1896, no. 955). Acquired by Harvard from Quaritch in 1897, with the Minot Fund.

*Lent by Harvard College Library, Dept. of Printing and Graphic Arts*

The scribe of this manuscript was one of a number of professionals active in Florence during the last half of the fifteenth century. A number of his manuscripts are signed and dated from 1462 to 1474. His most characteristic script is a cursive one, as in the present case, and he wrote usually on paper.

This manuscript is one of four or five which are signed with verses disclaiming responsibility for errors, which he blames upon a faulty exemplar:

"Hoc opus, o lector, transcripsit Petrus, avorum
Cuius Cennina est nomine dicta domus.
Error si quis inest, exemplar semina sevit.
Si secus esse putas, invidiosus abi."

Bibliography: De Ricci, I, p. 981, MS. Lat. 43; B. L. Ullman, *Humanistic Script*, p. 125, no. 14.

## *Milanus Burrus*

43 AULUS GELLIUS, NOCTES ATTICAE

Italy (probably Milan), 1445.

Ms. 90. In Latin with quotations in Greek. 272 vellum leaves, 10¼×6¾ inches. Written in long lines in humanistic minuscules. Illuminated initials. Rubricated titles. Binding: 18th-century calf.

Provenance: Biblioteca Molza, Modena. Acquired from Ulrico Hoepli, Milan, in 1949.

*Lent by the Newberry Library*

Milanus Burrus (Italian: Borro) was the scribe of several elegant manuscripts, some of which were executed for the Visconti family of Milan. He had the commendable habit of signing and dating his books. Besides the present example, three others have been pointed out: a luxurious copy of Suetonius, *Vitae Duodecim Caesarum*, dated 1433, now at Princeton, another Suetonius in the McClean collection of the Fitzwilliam Museum, Cambridge, dated 1443, and a Leonardo Bruni, *De Primo Bello Punico*, in the Philadelphia Free Library, dated 1444.

As Stanley Morison has written, Burrus is "highly competent and well instructed. He writes, effortlessly, a humanistic minuscule which is regularly well formed, spaced and paragraphed." It is indeed a beautiful script, and its mellowness becomes apparent when compared with no. 40, for instance. Mr. Morison points out that so accomplished a minuscule would, if not dated, be assigned to the latter half of the century. Burrus understands humanistic refinements as

41. Petrarch, *Sonetti*, etc. By Antonio di Mario (?). Florence, 1440

40. Cicero, *Rhetorica*. Northern Italy, first quarter of 15th century

45. Breviary. Florence, ca. 1470

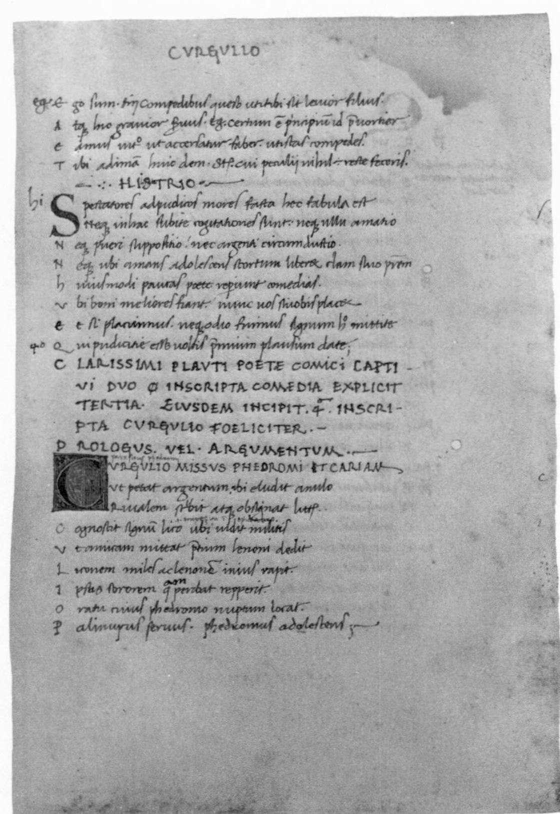

42. Plautus, *Comediae*. By Pietro Cennini. Florence, ca. 1462–67

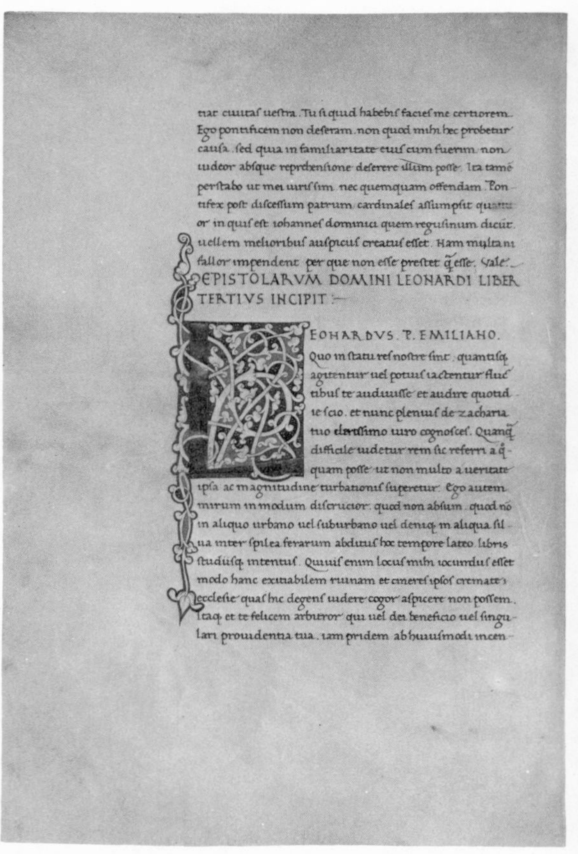

46. Leonardo Bruni Aretino, *Epistolae*. Florence, ca. 147

well as the Florentines. He provides us, however, with a valuable demonstration of the spread of humanistic script to other parts of Italy, not only by the evidence of his connection with the Visconti library, but by another interesting circumstance studied by Mr. Morison. As the illustration shows, the titles used in the manuscript are executed in a fantastic lettering. Included among the forms are several of Byzantine Greek origin, especially an M formed like an H with a median vertical below the cross-bar (the latter form does not appear in the illustration). That such a taste would obtain in the north where contacts with Byzantine scholarship flourished seems natural.

Bibliography: Hans Baron in *Studies in Philology*, XLVIII, 1951, pp. 107–125; *idem, ibid.*, XLIX, 1952, pp. 248–250; Stanley Morison, *Byzantine Elements in Humanistic Script . . . the Aulus Gellius of 1445* . . . , Chicago, 1952. Cf. also Walters *Cat.*, 1949, pp. 62 f., nos. 169, 170, pl. LXVI.

## *Collected Inscriptions*

### 44 GIOVANNI MARCANOVA, ANTIQUITATES

Northern Italy (probably Padua), 1465.

Garrett MS. 158. In Latin. 209 vellum leaves, 14¼×10¼ inches. Written in humanistic minuscule in 2 columns. 15 full-page illustrations and numerous text drawings and copies of inscriptions. Brown ink. Binding: 18th-century Italian vellum.

Provenance: M. Antonius Muretus; bequeathed by his nephew to the Collegio Romano, Rome; there until about 1870; acquired by Robert Garrett of Wilfred Voynich, New York, in 1924. Presented by him to Princeton University in 1942.

*Lent by Princeton University Library*

The monumental Roman inscriptions, dotted about western Europe wherever the Empire had established its hold, exerted a fascination upon later generations. In the ninth century a pilgrim to Rome brought back across the Alps a collection of seventy or so ancient inscriptions, and these were circulated in copies made during the same era. In the Renaissance the humanists turned to the monuments with especial devotion—studying them for their historical evidence, for their Latinity, for the perfection of their letter forms, copying and transcribing them.

The present work is just such a compilation of transcribed inscriptions, of drawings of stele and altars, and sculptured monuments. It also contains a group of wash drawings of more or less capricious assemblages of ancient or pseudo-ancient monuments, a description of Rome, and selections from classical authors. It was produced by the labors and at the expense of a Paduan physician, Giovanni Marcanova, who worked upon it from 1457 to 1465. Marcanova first completed the text and the transcription of the inscriptions in 1460 in a manuscript without drawings which he presented to a monastery in Padua and which is now in Bern. He then revised and enlarged the work, seeing to it that the text drawings and the illustrations were added, completing this 'second edition' in 1465, according to a colophon. The manuscript of it, which was also in his own autograph, is now in the Biblioteca Estense in Modena. Two copies were immediately made: one now in Paris and the present example.

It seems to have been the humanists of northern Italy rather than those of Florence who dedicated themselves to the study of inscriptions. Ciriaco d'Ancona, among other things, made an extensive collection of inscriptions in Verona, and these are quite completely represented in the present compilation. So we have the possibility that Marcanova appropriated collections that had been already assembled by his fellow-archeologists. Our collection also includes the twenty-seven inscriptions copied by an antiquarian of Verona, Felice Feliciano, and his companions on the shores of the Lake of Garda in September, 1464, just a year before the completion of this version of Marcanova's work. A charming letter of Feliciano's, describing the excursion to the lake, was first published by Paul Kristeller in his monograph on Mantegna (1901), and has often been quoted since. His companions on the idyllic outing included the painter Mantegna (who often introduced classical inscriptions into his frescoes) and a certain Giovanni Antenori, who is thought to be identical with Marcanova. Feliciano compiled a collection of inscriptions which he dedicated to Mantegna, but more important was a little treatise which he composed perhaps as early as the 1460's, as a result of his researches into the forms of classical letters (cf. nos. 54, 55).

The present copy of Marcanova's work is one of the greatest elegance. Its vellum is silky and pliant, the script the finest of humanistic minuscule. The inscriptions are, for the most part, transcribed in capitals closely imitating ancient forms, sometimes within areas outlined to suggest the shapes of stelae, etc., other times within renderings of monuments in which mouldings and sculpture are suggested by sepia wash. This manuscript has been known to the scholars concerned with epigraphical studies since the eighteenth century.

Bibliography: Holmes Van Meter Dennis and Elizabeth Lawrence in *Memoirs of the American Academy in Rome*, VI, 1927, pp. 113–131, pls. 23–48, where are cited all the older references of Dorez, Mommsen, Heulsen and others; De

Ricci, I, p. 897, no. 158; Walters *Cat.*, 1949, no. 185, pl. LXXII. For a discussion of Mantegna's concern with ancient carved letters, see M. Meiss, *Andrea Mantegna as Illuminator*, New York, 1957, pp. 55–67.

## *Humanistic Minuscules*

### 45 BREVIARY FOR ROME USE

Italy (Florence), ca. 1470.

Ms. Typ 182 H. In Latin. 450 vellum leaves, 10½×6 inches. Written in minuscules in long lines with plain square capitals in color introducing each verse. 12 small historiated initials. Binding: Italian mottled boards and sprinkled calf.

Provenance: Bookplate of an unidentified cardinal. Acquired from Davis and Orioli in 1949.

*Lent by Mr. and Mrs. Philip Hofer*

The pages of this manuscript seem to have returned to the serene and spacious ideals created by the scribes of Tours in the ninth century, although even after humanistic script was developed in Italy, the *gotica rotunda* was for long retained there as the letter for liturgical manuscripts. In the second half of the fifteenth century, we note a tendency to turn to humanistic letters occasionally for works of this kind. By the sixteenth century the new fashion became fairly general.

Bibliography: Harvard *Cat.*, 1955, no. 83, pl. 39; Bond and Faye, *Supplement*, p. 268, MS. Typ 182 H.

## *Humanistic Minuscules*

### 46 LEONARDO BRUNI ARETINO, EPISTOLARUM LIBRI OCTO

Italy (Florence), ca. 1470.

Ms. Typ 9. In Latin. 100 vellum leaves, 13¼×9¼ inches (about 20 leaves lacking). Written in long lines in humanistic minuscules. Brown ink. Titles of Books in gold capitals. One white-vine border and 8 illuminated initials. Binding: French late 18th-century dull purple morocco, gilt.

Provenance: Sold from the shop of Vespasiano da Bisticci in Florence; Chardin (his sale, Paris, 1825, lot 2128); Sir Thomas Phillipps, MS. 862. Acquired in 1947 from William H. Robinson, London, with the Hofer Fund.

*Lent by Harvard College Library, Dept. of Printing and Graphic Arts*

Written in a regular and authoritative hand which is characterized by the insistence with which serifs and other finishing marks are used, giving a rather 'bumpy' quality to the script. In this respect the hand is quite similar to that of no. 49 and several of the manuscripts prepared for King Matthias Corvinus of Hungary. The type of white-vine ornament in this beautifully produced manuscript is purely Florentine.

On the last vellum leaf, which was originally a pastedown, is inscribed in red humanistic capitals: VESPASIANVS LIBRARIVS FLORENTINVS VENDIDIT. This is the mark of the famous Florentine bookseller and 'stationer,' Vespasiano da Bisticci (1421–98). He himself was not a scribe but essentially a procurer and supplier of books. He sold some medieval manuscripts to various scholars, and, when the great rush of humanist collecting and aristocratic library development got under way, he met the expanded demand by furnishing copies of books made to order. These he commissioned from many different scribes, who probably worked at their own homes or ateliers, and who accepted commissions from other sources as well. Vespasiano played an important role in the promotion of humanistic script. He wrote a biographical work on the famous men of the fifteenth century, which is of great value to our knowledge of the personalities of the period.

Bibliography: Harvard *Cat.*, 1955, p. 26, no. 84; Bond and Faye, *Supplement*, p. 251, MS. Typ 9. For Vespasiano, see B. L. Ullman, *Humanistic Script*, pp. 131–134.

## *Humanistic Minuscules*

### 47 ARISTEAS, EPISTOLA AD PHILOCRATEM

Italy (Urbino ?), ca. 1475.

Ms. W. 356. In Latin. 49 vellum leaves, 8⅞×5⅝ inches. Written in humanistic minuscule in long lines. Dark brown ink; captions in blue and in red. One illuminated white-vine border and large initial; I historiated initial; numerous smaller illuminated initials. Binding: contemporary red-brown morocco, elaborately gilt, executed for the ducal library at Urbino.

Provenance: Federico di Montefeltro, Duke of Urbino (his arms); MS. no. 389 in the *Indice vecchio* of the ducal library, compiled between 1482 and 1487; Count Eugenio Minutoli Tegrimi, Lucca (cat. 1871, p. 27, no. 142); A. Firmin-Didot (his sale, Paris, 1883, no. 23); Eugène Piot (his sale, Paris, 1890); Marshall C. Lefferts, New York until 1901 (check-list, p. 56). Acquired by Henry Walters from George H. Richmond, New York in 1901.

*The Walters Art Gallery*

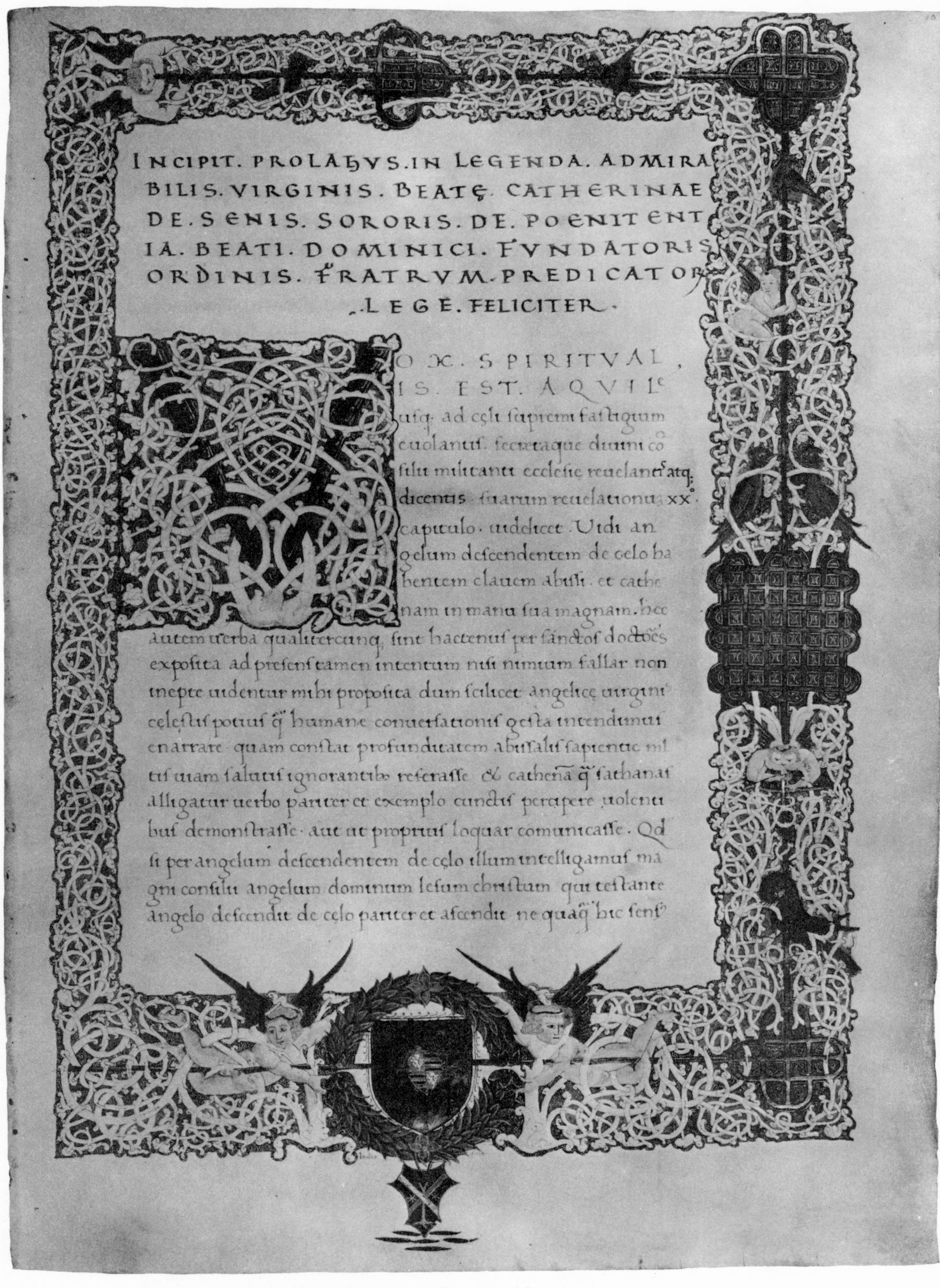


49. *Legenda S. Catharinae.* By Jacobus Macharius. Florence (?), ca. 1470

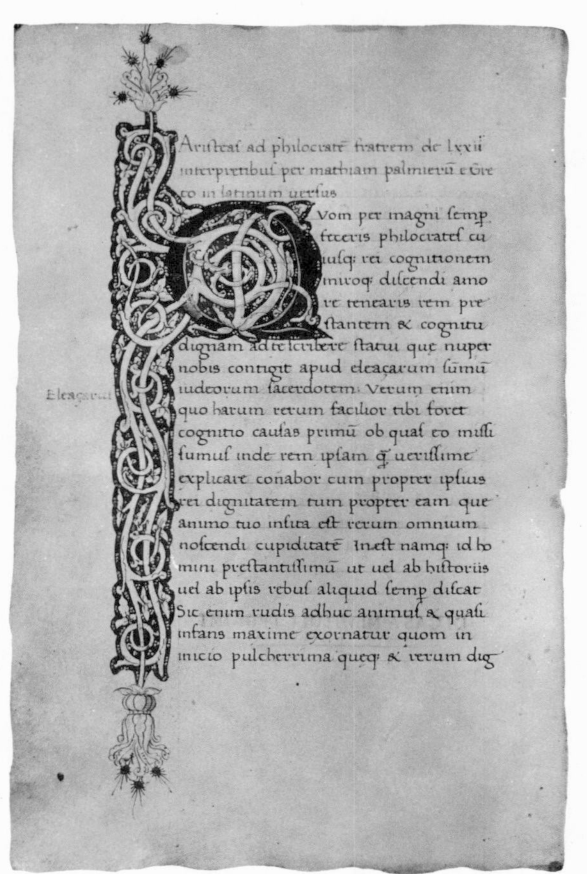

Aristeas ad philocratē fratrem de lxxii interpretibus per mathiam palmierū e Gre co in latinum uersus

Quom per magni semp fecerim philocratē cu iusq; rei cognitionem miroq; discendi amo re tenearis rem pre stantem & cognitu dignam ad te scribere statui que nuper nobis contigit apud eleaçarum summū iudeorum sacerdotem. Verum enim quo harum rerum facilior tibi foret cognitio causas primū ob quas eo missi sumus inde rem ipsam q̄ uerissime explicare conabor cum propter ipsius rei dignitatem tum propter eam que animo tuo insita est rerum omnium noscendi cupiditatē. Inest namq; id ho mini prestantissimū ut uel ab historiis uel ab ipsis rebus aliquid semp discat. Sic enim rudis adhuc animus & quasi infans maxime exornatur quom in initio pulcherrima queq; & rerum dig

Eleaçarus

47. Aristeas, *Epistola ad Philocratem*. Urbino (?), ca. 1475

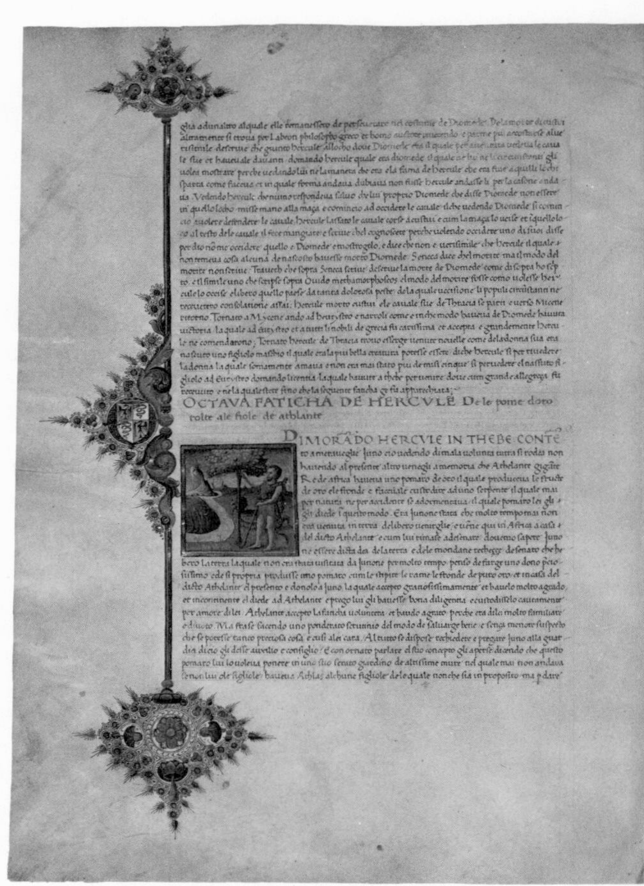

OCTAVA FATICHA DE HERCVLE De le pome doro tolte ale fiole de athlante

DIMORADO HERCVLE IN THEBE CONTE

48. Pietro Andrea di Bassi, *Le Fatiche de Hercule*. Ferrara, ca. 1

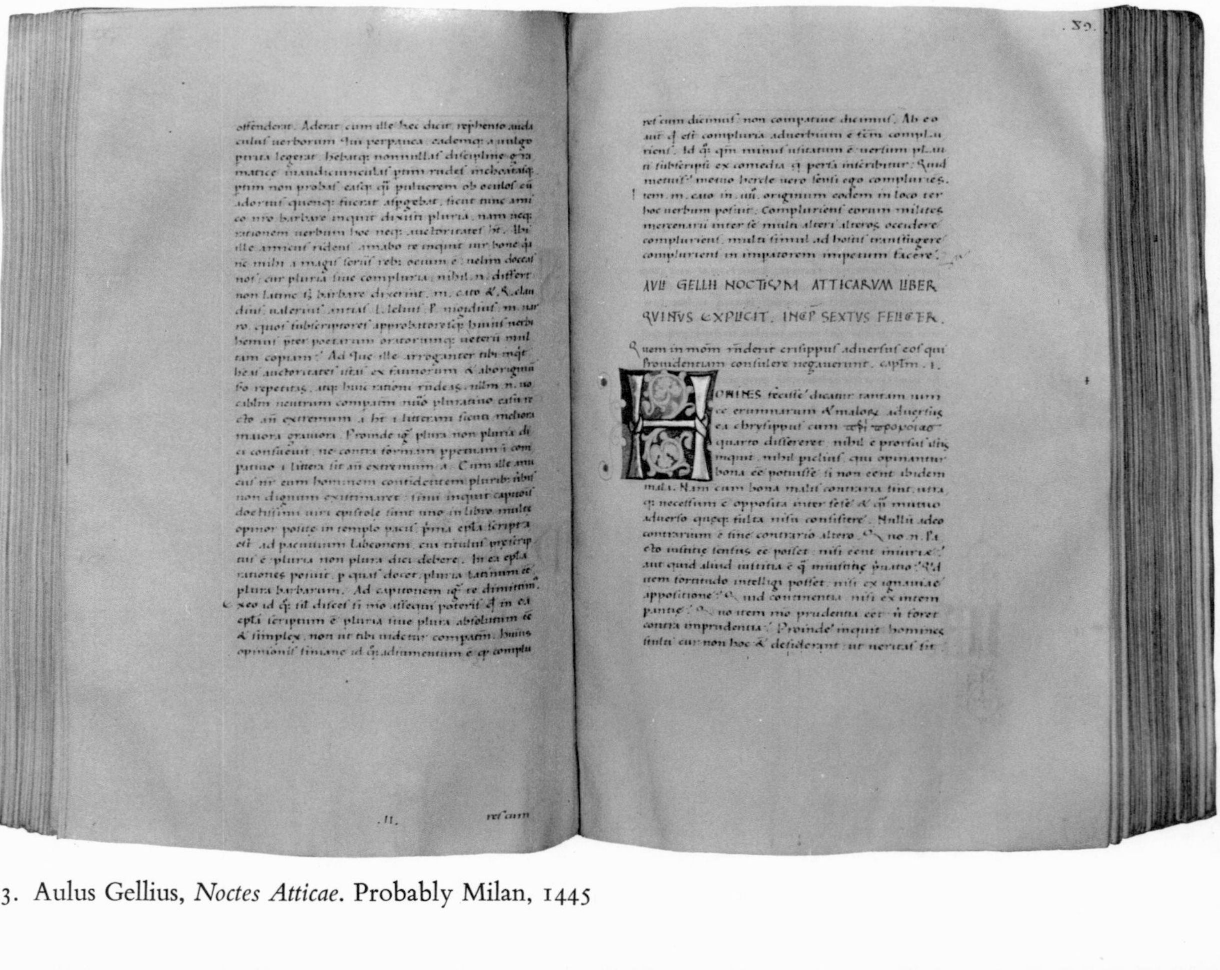

43. Aulus Gellius, *Noctes Atticae*. Probably Milan, 1445

This text is a translation into Latin by Mathias Palmieri of Pisa from the original Greek of Aristeas, which he made between 1464 and 1471 under the patronage of Pope Paul II. The present volume must have been copied out for the library of the Duke of Urbino very soon after the completion of the papal dedication volume. The Duke was eager to emulate the bibliographical activities of the Popes, of the Aragonese Kings of Naples and of the Medici. He began to develop a very rich library, calling upon the services of Vespasiano da Bisticci (cf. no. 46) and others. Signor de Marinis, when writing upon the especially rich and distinctive bindings executed for the library at Urbino, identified this manuscript in the list known as the *Indice vecchio* drawn up after the death of Federico in 1482.

Bibliography: De Ricci, I, p. 817, no. 371; Walters Art Gallery, *The History of Bookbinding 525–1950 A.D.*, 1957, p. 90, no. 201, pl. XL; T. de Marinis, *La legatura artistica in Italia nei secoli XV e XVI*, Florence, 1960, vol. I, pp. 84, 86, no. 951 F., pl. C 5; *idem*, in *Festschrift Ernst Kyriss*, Stuttgart, 1961, p. 319.

## *Humanistic Minuscules*

48 PIETRO ANDREA DI BASSI, LE FATICHE DE HERCULE

Italy (Ferrara), ca. 1471.

Ms. Typ 226 H. In Italian. 38 vellum leaves, 14¼×10½ inches (lacking some at end). Written in a compressed minuscule in long lines. Brown ink. The title of each Book in capitals and minuscules of burnished gold; the first line of each in red capitals. One full white-vine border and 20 half-borders of filigree and foliage in a characteristic Ferrarese style, each with a small miniature. Binding: 18th-century Austrian sprinkled calf, gilt.

Provenance: Galeazzo Maria Sforza (his arms and emblems); Harrach (?) library, Vienna. Acquired from W. H. Schab, New York, in 1954.

*Lent by Mr. and Mrs. Philip Hofer*

This book presents a script rather different in effect from the round humanistic minuscule of other examples described. It is small and relatively compressed laterally, but still with no cursive tendencies. The whole aspect of the book, with its deep but luminous rose-reds and blues and a green highlighted with yellow, is quite different from that of Florentine productions. The splendid little miniatures are related in style to the works of the painter Cosimo Tura.

Bibliography: Harvard *Cat.*, 1955, p. 26, no. 85, pl. 30; Bond and Faye, *Supplement*, p. 272, MS. Typ 226 H.

## *Jacobus Macharius Venetus*

49 LEGENDA S. CATHERINAE SENENSIS

Italy (Florence ?), ca. 1470.

Ms. W. 350. In Latin. 236 vellum leaves, 13¼×9¼ inches. Written in humanistic minuscules in long lines, with titles rubricated; first title in burnished gold capitals; the first words of each chapter in regular ink capitals. One full illuminated white-vine border signed by 'India'; numerous large white-vine initials. Binding: 19th-century Italian brown russia.

Provenance: The Library of the Gonzagas, Dukes of Mantua (arms); Museo Cavaleri, Milan; Charles Butler of Hatfield; William Morris (his sale, London, 1898, no. 345); Laurence W. Hodson (his sale, London, 1906, no. 109). Acquired by Henry Walters in Florence from L. S. Olschki, after 1912.

*The Walters Art Gallery*

This splendid volume is very similar in its script to no. 46, sharing some of the same peculiarities. However, the divergences suffice to prevent us from attributing no. 46 with assurance to Jacobo Machario of Venice, the scribe of our book. His name indicates the cosmopolitan nature of the production in Florence, whither scribes were attracted from everywhere, because of the activity in supplying the new libraries being developed by the aristocrats. The signature on the white-vine border: 'India fecit,' is perhaps unique.

Bibliography: De Ricci, I, p. 822, no. 392, with other references.

## *P. Hippolytus of Luni*

50 ONOSANDER, DE OPTIMO IMPERATORE; FRONTINUS, DE RE MILITARI

Italy (Naples ?), ca. 1470.

Ms. Typ 179 H. In Latin. 174 vellum leaves, 8½×5¾ inches. Written in long lines in rather cursive humanistic minuscules. Brown ink. 2 framed title-pages lettered in alternate lines of blue and gold capitals; 2 full illuminated white-vine borders, with large white-vine initials. Binding: 19th-century blue morocco.

Provenance: Guglielmo Libri (his sale, 1859, lot 740); Sir Thomas Phillipps, MS. 23619. Acquired from William H. Robinson, London in 1947.

*Lent by Mr. and Mrs. Philip Hofer*

The script is sloping and fairly rapid—the kind of controlled humanistic cursive which developed into the prototype of italic type-fonts (cf. no. 52). This book contains two ancient treatises on military matters. The first, on the duties of a general, by Onosander, a Greek philosopher of the first century A.D., was translated into Latin for Pasiello Malipiero, Doge of Venice (1457–62), by his secretary, Nicolo Sagundino. The work was dedicated by the translator to Alphonse of Aragon, King of Naples. The other work, on military strategy, was written by a Roman general who was once governor of Britain.

Bibliography: Walters *Cat.*, 1949, p. 68, no. 187; Harvard *Cat.*, 1955, p. 23, no. 73, pl. 37; T. de Marinis, *La Biblioteca Napoletana dei Re d'Aragona*, Milan, 1952, vol. I, p. 57, no. 17, illus., p. 58; Portland *Cat.*, 1958, p. 13, no. 9, pl. 5; Bond and Faye, *Supplement*, p. 267, MS. Typ 179 H.

## *Humanistic Minuscules*

51 CHRONICA REGNI ARAGONUM

Italy (Naples), ca. 1470.

Ms. Typ 242 H. In Latin. 102 vellum leaves, 13×9 inches. Written in long lines in humanistic minuscule. One full illuminated white-vine border with white-vine initial. Binding: contemporary brown morocco, gilt and blind tooled.

Provenance: Ferrante I, King of Aragon and Naples (his arms); Ramón de Mesonero Romanos; presented by him in 1853 to Joaquín Gómez de la Cortina, Marqués de Morante (his sale, Paris, 1872, lot 1719); Rowland Gibson Hazard, 2nd (d. 1918). Acquired from Walter Schatzki, New York in 1951.

*Lent by Mr. and Mrs. Philip Hofer*

The exceptional intricacy and richness of the white-vine border on the first page of this manuscript bespeaks the care with which it was prepared for the Royal Library of Naples.

Bibliography: Richard C. Christie, *Selected Essays and Papers*, London, 1902, pp. 257–290; Harvard *Cat.*, 1955, p. 26, no. 87, pl. 38; Bond and Faye, *Supplement*, p. 273, MS. Typ 242 H.

## *Humanistic Cursive*

52 VERGIL, OPERA

Italy (Naples), ca. 1470.

Ms. W. 400. In Latin. 220 vellum leaves, 5½×2¾ inches. Written in a small humanistic cursive. Brown ink. Titles in burnished gold capitals on red base. 2 full-page miniatures; 3 historiated borders.

*The Walters Art Gallery*

This little pocket-size Vergil is an example of the elegant books of the classics in handy format produced in the second half of the fifteenth century for aristocratic humanists. The fine, closely written script made it possible to include in this small volume the entire *opus* of Vergil. Such script as this was the model upon which the Venetian printer Aldus Manutius designed his italic type, around 1500, so that printed classics also could appear in compact pocket editions. Such manuscripts as ours appear to have been prepared in sets. The late James Wardrop identified a little Martial manuscript in the collection of Major J. R. Abbey as a companion volume to our Vergil.

Bibliography: De Ricci, I, p. 832, no. 440; Walters *Cat.*, 1949, p. 71, no. 195, pl. LXXIV.

## *Alexander Verazanus*

53 NALDUS NALDII, VITA ZENOBII JULIANI DE GIROLAMIS ANTISTITIS URBIS FLORENTIAE

Italy (Florence), 1499.

Ms. W. 406. In Latin. 84 vellum leaves, 9⅜×6 inches. Written in long lines in humanistic minuscules; one title in gold capitals. Full illuminated and historiated border; 1 historiated initial. Binding: contemporary Florentine red morocco, stamped and gilt.

Provenance: Raphael de Girolami of Florence; Abate Mateo Canonici Collection, MS. 273; sold in 1835 to Rev. Walter Sneyd (his sale, London, 1903, no. 530). Acquired by Henry Walters of L. S. Olschki, Florence.

*The Walters Art Gallery*

Alexander Verazanus was an accomplished Florentine scribe, who also worked at the Aragonese Chancery in Naples. Our manuscript is signed: ALEXANDER VERAZANVS ESCRIPSIT MCCCCLXLVIIII. This particular text was apparently commissioned by Raphael de Girolami as an account of his ancestor, St. Zenobius, Bishop of Florence from around A.D. 418 to 428. Naldus Naldii was a Florentine poet and biographer who died around 1470. Another manuscript signed by Verazanus in 1494 is now in the Princeton University Library, Kane MS. 15.

Bibliography: De Ricci, I, p. 842, no. 486; Walters Art Gallery, *The History of Bookbinding 525–1950 A.D.*, Baltimore, 1957, p. 95, no. 212. For Alexander Verazanus see T. de Marinis, *La Biblioteca Napoletana dei Re d'Aragona*, Milan, 1952, vol. I, pp. 87 ff. and notes, with several illustrations. Neither this manuscript nor the Princeton one is listed.

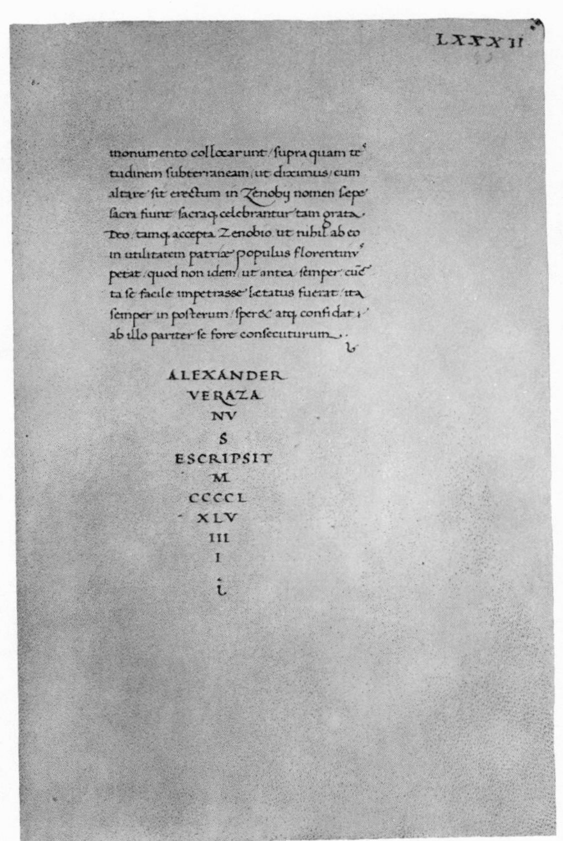

LXXXII

monumento collocarunt / supra quam te-
tudinem subterraneam, ut diximus, cum
altare sit erectum in Zenoby nomen sepe
sacra fiunt sacraq. celebrantur tam grata
Deo tamq. accepta Zenobio ut nihil ab eo
in utilitatem patriae populus florentinus
petat, quod non idem ut antea semper cunc-
ta se facile impetrasse letatus fuerat, ita
semper in posterum speret atq. confidat
ab illo pariter se fore consecuturum.

ALEXANDER
VERAZA
NV
S
ESCRIPSIT
M
CCCCL
XLV
III
I

53. Nałdus Naldii, *Vita Zenobii*. By Alexander Verazanus. Florence, 1499

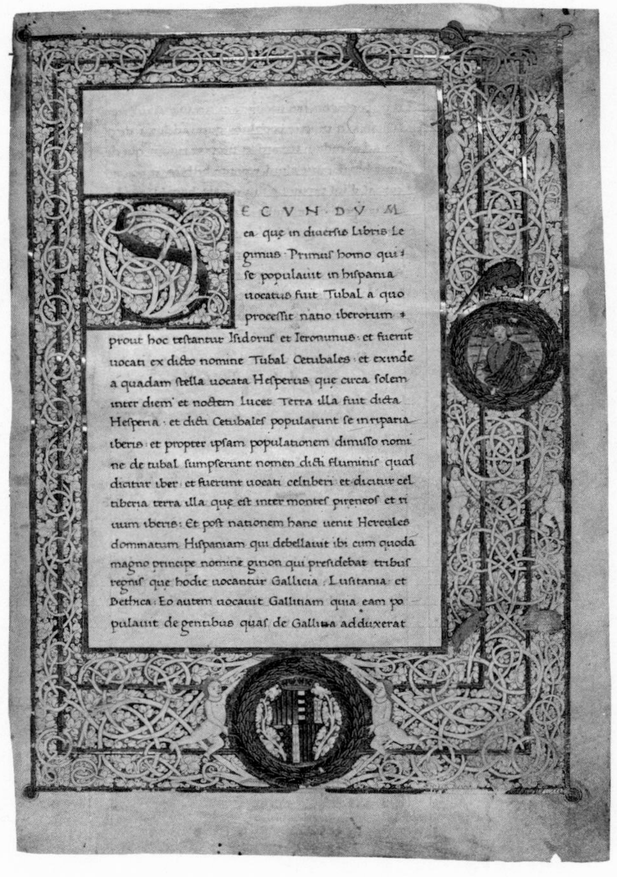

SECVNDVM
ea que in diversis Libris Le
gimus Primus homo qui
se populavit in hispania
vocatus fuit Tubal a quo
processit natio iberorum
prout hoc testantur Isidorus et Ieronimus et fuerit
vocati ex dicto nomine Tubal Cetubales et exinde
a quadam stella vocata Hesperus que circa solem
inter diem et noctem lucet Terra illa fuit dicta
Hesperia et dicti Cetubales popularunt se in riparia
iberis et propter ipsam populationem dimisso nomi
ne de tubal sumpserunt nomen dicti fluminis quod
dicitur iber et fuerunt vocati celtiberi et dicitur cel
tiberia terra illa que est inter montes pireneos et ri
vum iberis: Et post nationem hanc venit Hercules
dominatum Hispaniam qui debellavit ibi cum quoda
magno principe nomine girion qui presidebat tribus
regnis que hodie vocantur Gallicia Lusitania et
Bethica Eo autem vocavit Gallitiam quia eam po
pulavit de gentibus quas de Gallitia adduxerat

51. *Chronica Regni Aragonum*. Naples, ca. 1470

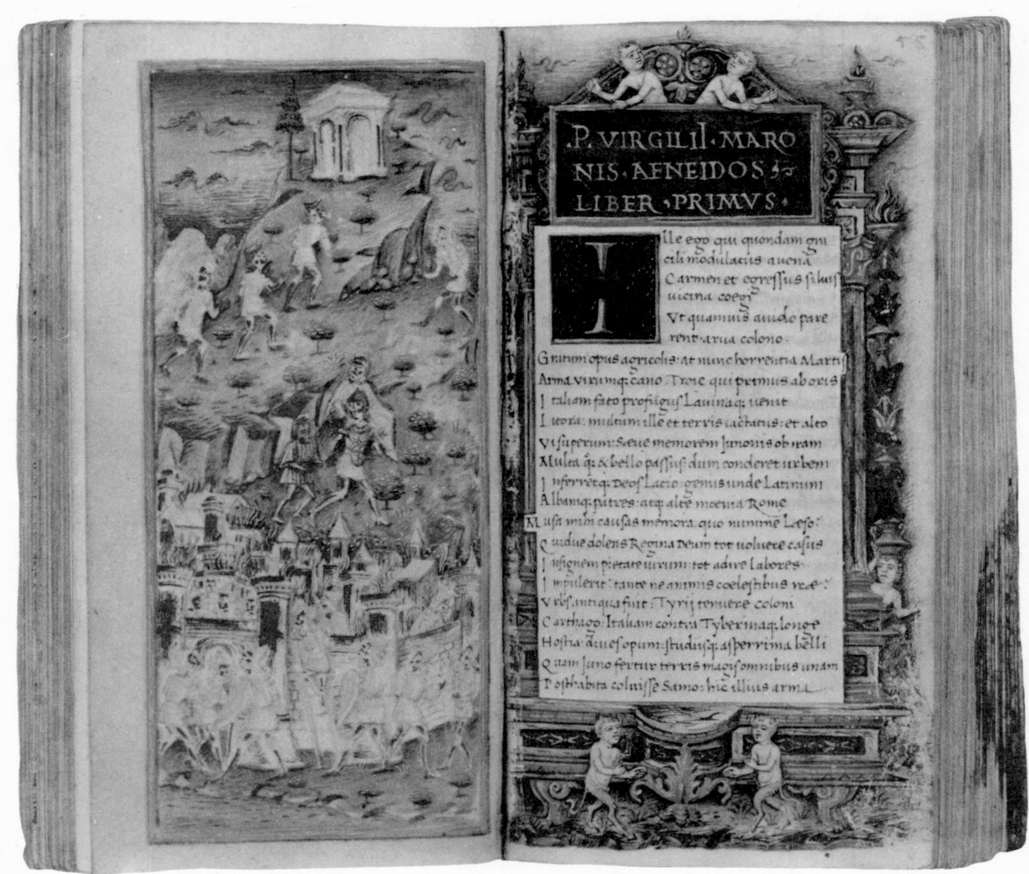


52. Vergil, *Opera*. Naples, ca. 1470

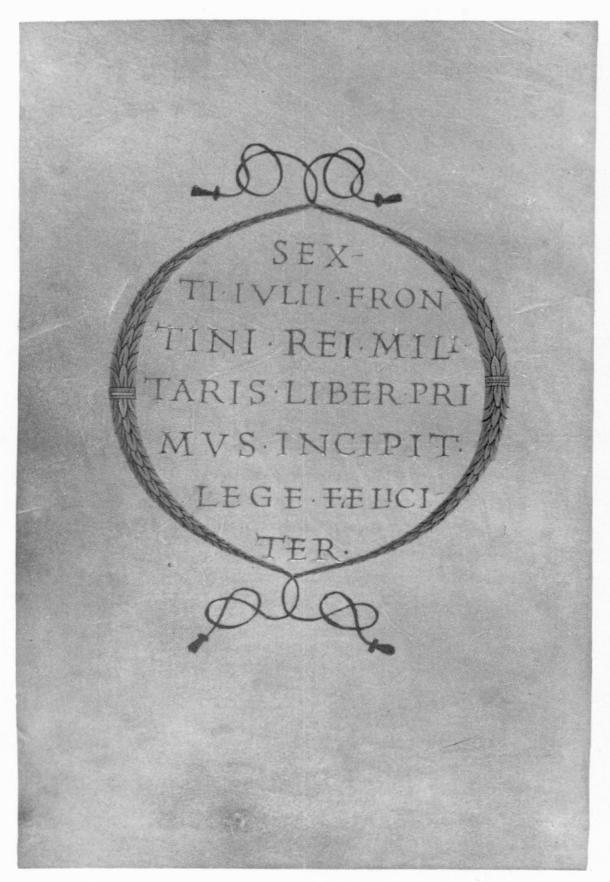


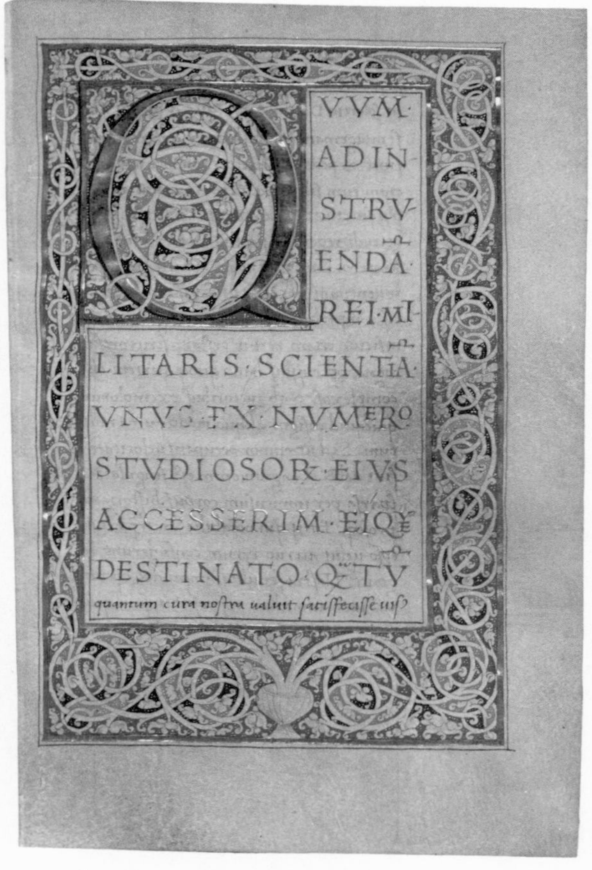


50. Onosander and Frontinus. By P. Hippolytus of Luni. Naples (?), ca. 1470

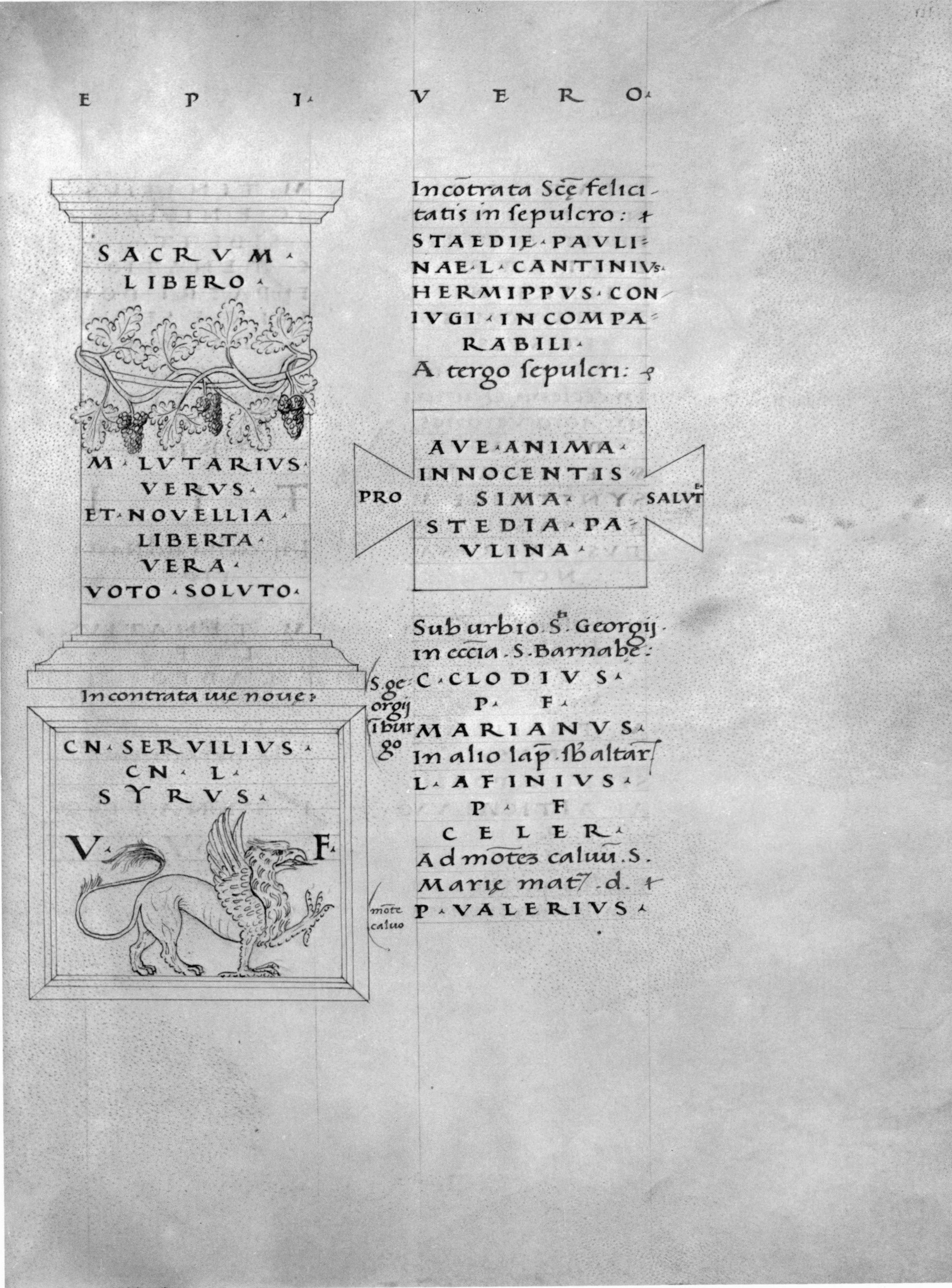


44. Giovanni Marcanova, *Antiquitates*. Northern Italy, 1465

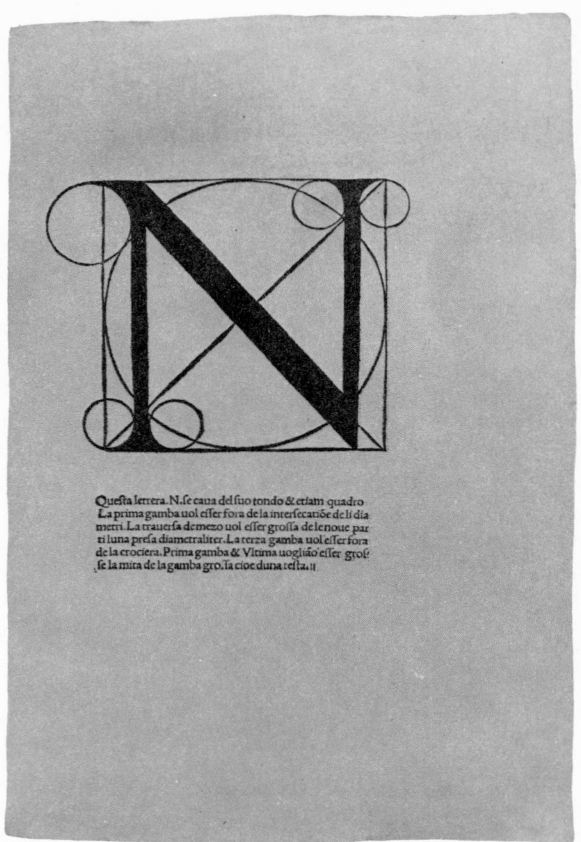

Queſta lettera. N. ſe caua del ſuo tondo & etiam quadro La prima gamba uol eſſer fora de la interſecatiõe de li diametri. La trauerſa de mezo uol eſſer groſſa de le noue parti luna preſa diametraliter. La terza gamba uol eſſer fora de la crociera. Prima gamba & Vltima uoglião eſſer groſſe la mita de la gamba groſſa cioe duna teſta.

55. Pacioli, *De Divina Proportione*. Venice, 1509

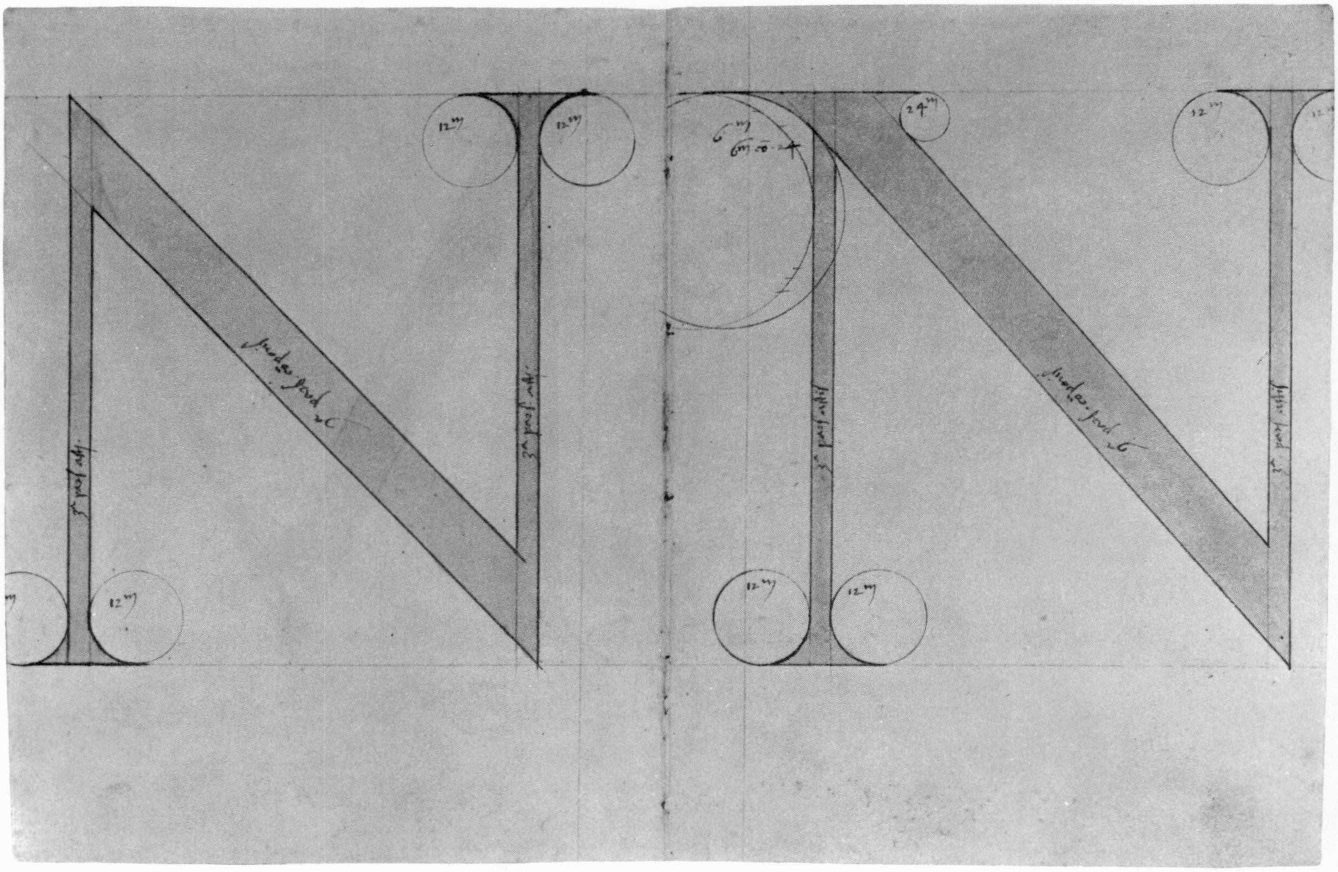

54. Construction of Roman Letters. Northern Italy, ca. 1480

## *Anonymous*

54 CONSTRUCTION OF ROMAN LETTERS

Northern Italy, ca. 1480.

Ms. Z W. 141.481. 23 paper leaves, 6¼×5½ inches. Inscriptions in gothic cursive. Pen and ink with washes in color. Unbound.

Provenance: Andrea Teissier, Venice (his sale, Munich, May 21, 1900, no. 895); acquired 1907 from Jacques Rosenthal by C. L. Ricketts, Chicago. Purchased from his estate in 1941.

*Lent by the John M. Wing Foundation of the Newberry Library*

The studies of extant Roman inscriptions by the fifteenth-century humanists led to speculation concerning canons of proportions and methods of construction. Felice Feliciano (cf. no. 44) believed that he could detect on some of the Roman marbles the marks of ruler and compass by which the letters were constructed. He inferred that they were drawn upon a square field divided horizontally, diagonally and so on. Feliciano wrote the first renaissance treatise on the proportions of classical letters, the manuscript of which survives in the Vatican, Lat. 6852. His discussions of the numerical relations of the proportions merely extend in a way the kind of mystical interpretations of numbers to be found in the treatises of renaissance architects. His manuscript is illustrated with letters modelled in light and shade to indicate that they are carved.

Another of the few extant manuscripts of this genre is the present anonymous alphabet. The letters are represented as flat, but the indications of construction and of the proportions of the members approach the subject in the same way, although the principle differs from that of Feliciano, in the opinion of Mr. Morison. This authority suggests a date as early as the middle of the century.

Bibliography: F. W. Goudy in *Ars Typographica*, II, 1926, pp. 202–205 (erroneously attributed to Leonardo da Vinci); Stanley Morison, *Fra Luca de Pacioli of Borgo S. Sepolcro*, New York, The Grolier Club, 1933, p. 19; De Ricci, I, p. 655, no. 241; Stanley Morison in G. B. Verini, *Luminario*, Cambridge and Chicago, 1947, pp. 1–3; Millard Meiss, *Andrea Mantegna as Illuminator*, New York, 1957, p. 97, note 1, fig. 96; Bond and Faye, *Supplement*, p. 158, no. 37. For the theories of Feliciano and the literature on him, see Meiss, *op. cit.*, esp. pp. 68–76 and notes.

## *Fra Luca da Pacioli (ca. 1440–after 1509)*

55 DE DIVINA PROPORTIONE

Printed by Paganino de Paganini, Venice, June 1, 1509. In Italian. Parts I–IV; 153 paper leaves, folio. Binding: vellum on boards.

Provenance: C. L. Ricketts, Chicago.

*Lent by the John M. Wing Foundation of the Newberry Library*

The Franciscan friar who composed this treatise was a teacher and writer on mathematics. He published three other works, all in the mathematical field, one being a pioneer essay on double-entry book-keeping.

The three manuscript presentation copies of *De Divina Proportione*, which were completed in 1497 and dedicated to Gian Galeazzo di San Severino, to Ludovico Sforza and to Pietro Soderini, respectively, had to do with geometrical solids only. It was when the treatise was being prepared for this printing of 1509 that Pacioli added a supplement concerning the ideal proportions of letters. The woodcut alphabet of twenty-three letters illustrating this addition shows construction-lines based upon squares and circles and is furnished with comments upon the theoretical proportions of Roman capitals.

For a long period students ranked this as the first printed treatise on the subject. In 1927, however, there was discovered a unique example of a treatise on classical letter design printed at Parma by Damianus Moyllus. The date is not given in the colophon, but since Moyllus, who was also an illuminator, printed three other books at dates between 1477 and 1483, it is to be presumed that his printed alphabet must be placed around the same period—and thus precede Pacioli's publication by two or three decades. The Moyllus alphabet is on six sheets, folded in fours and printed on one side of the paper only. Therefore, it appears to have been intended to be used as working or teaching models by a master—which doubtless accounts for the almost total disappearance of the edition.

Pacioli's more substantial publication is rare enough. It was the forerunner of a series of renaissance treatises on the proportions and construction of letters: Fanti in 1514, Vicentino in 1523, Dürer in 1525 and Tory in 1529.

Bibliography: Stanley Morison, *Fra Luca de Pacioli of Borgo S. Sepolcro*, New York, The Grolier Club, 1933. For Moyllus, see *idem*, *A Newly Discovered Treatise on Classic Letter Design . . . by Damianus Moyllus*, Paris, 1927.

# PART II: *The Sixteenth to the Eighteenth Century*

## INTRODUCTION—PART II—

BEGINNING at about 1500, the second part of this exhibition spans a period of slightly more than three centuries. There was good reason to begin an exhibition of mature Renaissance and Baroque calligraphy at this point. The period inaugurates a new era in the history of the book. Scarcely fifty years earlier, the first books using moveable type had been printed. The effect of this innovation on calligraphy is not commonly realized. No longer was it necessary to write a book by hand or to cut on woodblocks the text for an entire page, both laborious and costly processes. As printed works became more accessible, calligraphy lost its preponderant role as a book hand.

During the period under discussion, script served a variety of functions. Foremost, it became the vehicle of personal correspondence to a degree which surpasses the surviving evidence of earlier centuries. It was also customary that official documents, Papal bulls, and manuscripts commemorating important events would be written in a fine, cultivated hand. And manuscripts continued to be produced, often richly illuminated, to delight the fortunate owner and give pleasure to the bibliophile. By the late seventeenth and eighteenth centuries, books were even written to imitate the refined printed works from earlier presses.

Dominating this section of the exhibition is a series of printed calligraphy manuals or copy-books, published to spread a knowledge of scripts among a wide audience. The skill and knowledge won from a study of these pages gave to an unprecedentedly large number of people a means of communication which might have been denied to them before the production of printed books. A variety of manuals appeared in every part of cultivated Europe from the sixteenth century onward, and the number and frequency of some of the editions is sufficient indication that they satisfied a widely felt need.

It would be redundant to trace here the history of the important copy-books. As the catalogue describes most of the important treatises produced during the three centuries covered by this part of the exhibition, the historic development of these books and of the scripts contained within their pages will unfold itself to the reader. However, the catalogue entries cannot emphasize the basic role of printed copy-books in the development of High Renaissance and Baroque scripts. As calligraphers in Europe and America modified existing hands or developed new scripts, their innovations were reproduced on the pages of these printed manuals. Spreading a knowledge of beautiful scripts throughout the civilized world, printed calligraphic manuals became a means of enhancing one of the most personal and basic forms of communication.

It came as a surprise to find that nearly all the printed desiderata, and many essential manuscripts, could be found in American collections. This circumstance is due to the farsightedness of some private collectors, who for years have sought out calligraphic works, and is a tribute to the scholarship of the directors of the public institutions which have so generously lent to the exhibition.

It is a great pleasure to record here my indebtedness to several experts who have been of constant help throughout the preparation of this section of the catalogue. Mr. James M. Wells, Associate Director of The Newberry Library, Chicago, undertook to read all of the catalogue entries. Whatever merit they have is due in large part to his advice and stimulating suggestions. My Baltimore colleagues, Miss Dorothy Miner, Librarian and Keeper of Manuscripts, The Walters Art Gallery, and Mr. P. W. Filby, Assistant Director, The Peabody Institute Library, were selfless in sharing with me their vast knowledge of calligraphy. Without their encouragement, this section of the catalogue could not have achieved its present form. The Baltimore Museum of Art participated in this joint venture at the suggestion of the Director, Mr. Charles Parkhurst, whose support of the project is greatly appreciated.

VICTOR CARLSON, Curator of Prints and Drawings
The Baltimore Museum of Art

Note: Where more than one copy of a book has been borrowed, the copy described is owned by the lender listed first in the credit line.

## *Bartolomeo Sanvito*

ITALY 1435–1518 (?)

56 PETRARCH'S *TRIONFI*

Rome or Florence, ca. 1480–1490.

Ms.W.755. In Italian. Formal "antica" script. 70 vellum leaves, 8½×5⅜ inches. In ink with gold. 6 full page miniatures and 6 borders with historiations.

Provenance: Sir George Holford (sale, London, Sotheby's, July 29, 1929, no. 6, pls. II–III); B. Quaritch, *A Catalogue of Illuminated and Other Mss.*, 1931, pp. 98–99; Harvey Frost, until 1955.

*Lent by The Walters Art Gallery*

Although the scribe is one of the principal calligraphers and illuminators of his age, until recently his identity remained unknown. The rediscovery of this artist is an achievement described at length by James Wardrop; some forty manuscripts in European and American collections are now attributed to Sanvito.

The Walters manuscript is a particularly sumptuous example, written in Sanvito's formal "antica" hand, as Wardrop calls it. Two artists of quite different styles are responsible for the illustrations. The first two Triumphs have frontispieces and borders by a Paduan artist; the rest are by one of the brothers, Gherardo and Monte del Fora of Florence. Although this manuscript has usually been attributed to Rome, because of Bartolomeo's recorded activity there, it is known that he worked for the Medici, the Gonzagas, and other non-Roman clients. So far, there is no sure evidence that the del Fora brothers were active outside of Florence.

Bibliography: Burlington Fine Arts Club, *Exhibition of Illuminated Manuscripts*, London, 1908, no. 194, pl. 128; James Wardrop, *The Script of Humanism, 1460–1560*, Oxford, 1963, pp. 32, 51, pl. 35; Bond and Faye, *Supplement*, p. 199, n. 171; William Wixom in *Bulletin of the Cleveland Museum of Art*, LI, no. 3, 1964, pp. 56–58; B. Ullman, "Petrarch Manuscripts in The United States," *Censimento dei Codici Petrarcheschi*, I, Padua, 1964, p. 446, no. 6.

## *Anonymous*

57 CEREMONIAL OF DOGE LEONARDO LAUREDANO: GESTANDERUM INSIGNIUM TRIUMPHALIUM RITUS

Venice, 1508, with later additions.

Ms.W.486. In Latin. Venetian chancery script. 28 vellum leaves, 9¾×6 inches. Black ink with rubrication; illuminated with the arms of Lauredano. Binding: contemporary Venetian binding in oriental style.

*Lent by The Walters Art Gallery*

The official illuminated account of the ceremonial of the accession of Leonardo Lauredano as Doge of Venice. Written in a fine humanistic cursive hand, the manuscript is a distinguished example from the Chancery of Lauredano. Calligraphy from that Chancery formed a high point in Venetian official writing.

Bibliography: De Ricci, I, p. 853, no. 539; Walters Art Gallery, *The History of Book Binding*, Baltimore, 1957, no. 209, pl. XLVI.

Iui fra glialtri tincto era virginio
Del sangue di sua figlia: onde á que dieci
Tyranni tolto fu lempio dominio.
Elarghi duo di lor sangue: e tre deci
E i duo gran scipion che spagna oppresse:
Et martio che sostenne ambe lor ueci.
Et come á suoi par che ciaschun sappresse
Lasiatico iui era: e quel perfecto
Choptimo solo il buon senato elesse.
Et lelio á suoi cornelii era ristrecto:
Non cosi quel metello, al qual arrise
Tanto fortuna, che felice e decto.
Parean uiuendo lor menti diuise:
Morendo ricongionte: & seco il padre
Era el suo seme che sotterra il mise.
Vespasian poi alle spale quadre
Riconobbi: á guisa dhuom che ponta
Con tito suo da lopre alte e leggiadre.

56 Petrarch: *Trionfi*, by Bartolomeo Sanvito, ca. 1480–1490

THEORICA ET PRATICA PER SPI
CACISSIMI SIGISMVNDI DE
FANTIS FERRARIENSIS IN
ARTEM MATHEMATICE
PROFESSORIS DE MO
DO SCRIBENDI FA,
BRICANDI Q VE
OMNES LIT,
TERARVM
SPECIES.

✠

Cum Gratia & Priuilegio.

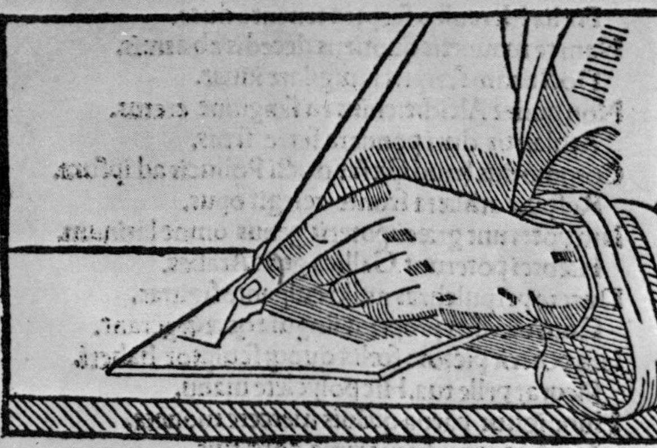

58 Sigismondo Fanti, *Theorica et Pratica*, Venice, 1514

i

GESTANDORVM

INSIGNIVM TRIVMPHALIVM

RITVS QVO SERENISS. PRINC.

D. DVX VENETIARVM INCEDERE
CONSVEVIT.

PRIMVM Praecones anteeunt.

OCTO vexilla Imperialia serica auro distincta cum imagine S. Marci sub Leonis specie: quorum Duo priora candida sunt: Duo succedentia caelestis coloris: Duo tertio loco delata, ametisti et sanguinei coloris, seu subrubri: Vltima duo coloris chermesini, seu rubri: et eorum quodque crucem habet deauratam in superiori parte hastae.

SEX Tubae argenteae longae, quarum cuique pendet signum unum sericeum auro distinctum, cum insigni peculiari et domestico Domini Ducis cum Ducali corona suprapositâ.

DVAE aliae argenteae tubae intortae: quarum utrique pendet signum purpureum cum D. Ducis insigni: et tres Tybiae, seu vulgo dicunt pifari.

FAMILIARES et Scutiferi Domini Ducis.

COMMILITONES eius. SCRIBAE Carcerum.

CAPITANEI eorumdem GASTALDIONES D. Ducis.

NOTARII Curiae Maioris.

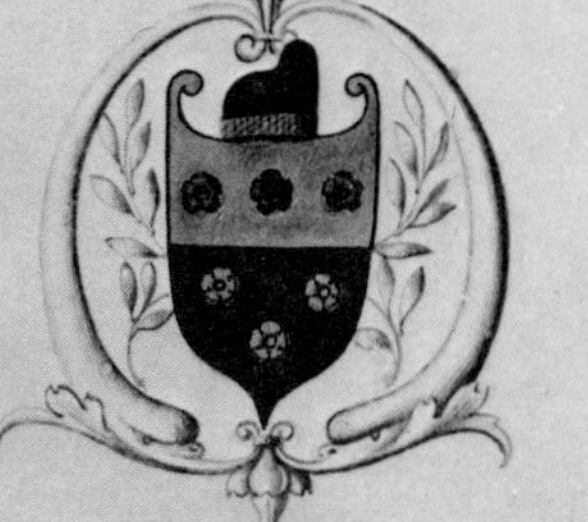

[illegible] (with later additions)

## *Sigismondo Fanti*

ITALY ACTIVE 1514–1535

58 THEORICA ET PRATICA...

Venice, 1514, I. Rubeus.

In Latin. 76 paper leaves, 7⅞×5½ inches. Type and woodcuts. Binding: modern.

*Lent by The John M. Wing Foundation of The Newberry Library*

The earliest printed writing book, Fanti's work illustrates geometrically constructed capitals and gothic lower case letters. In the text are the first printed instructions on how to form the chancery hand. Apparently Fanti could not find a cutter to provide blocks for the chancery examples, as none are illustrated. However, there are blank spaces in the text on the chancery hand. Perhaps calligraphers were supposed to fill the spaces with manuscript examples, but no copy is known where the blanks are completed. Little is known about the author, a nobleman from Ferrara, who also practised architecture and mathematics.

Bibliography: Bonacini, 607.

## *Ludovico degli Arrighi (Vicentino)*

ITALY BEFORE 1510–1527 (?)

59 LA OPERINA

Rome, 1522.

In Italian and Latin. Chancery cursive script. 16 paper leaves, 5¾×8½ inches. Woodcuts. Binding: limp vellum.

Provenance: Carl Ullman.

*Lent by Esther Fisher Benson (1522 and 1533 editions); Mr. and Mrs. Philip Hofer (1522 edition)*

Considered by many to be the finest of all writing books, this treatise is the first illustrated set of instructions on the formation of chancery letters written for a general audience. Fanti's earlier volume (no. 58) gave only written instructions, without illustrations. Chancery cursive script had been developed in the Papal Chancery for writing briefs and other less formal documents where a speedier and readily legible hand was desired. Arrighi was employed as a writer of briefs in the Apostolic Chancery. It is now known that when Arrighi undertook the publication of this copybook he enlisted the help of Ugo da Carpi. The latter was one of the foremost woodblock cutters in Rome and is famous for his early experiments in color woodblock printing.

Although Arrighi was from Vicenza, nothing is known of his life there. The surviving documents list only the scribe's years in Rome, beginning in 1510 until the sack of Rome, in which Arrighi died. Three manuscripts written by Arrighi have survived and a number of works in various collections bear attributions to the calligrapher. He was a bookseller for a while, worked in the Camera Apostolica, but much of his known activity was concerned with the writing and publication of books. An aspect of his interest in publishing is Arrighi's activity as a type designer. His models of italic type are among the finest of their time. The possibility of printing italic script from moveable type also inspired Tagliente to design models.

Bibliography: A. F. Johnson and Stanley Morison, "The Chancery Types of Italy and France," *Fleuron*, no. 3, 1924, pp. 23–51; *The Calligraphic Models of Ludovico degli Arrighi, Surnamed Vicentino*, A Complete Facsimile and Introduction by Stanley Morison, Paris, 1926; James Wardrop, "Arrighi Revived," *Signature*, no. 12, 1939, pp. 26–46; A. F. Johnson, "A Catalogue of Italian Writing-Books of the Sixteenth Century," *Signature*, n.s. 10, 1950, pp. 24–26; John Howard Benson, *The First Writing Book: An English Translation & Facsimile of Arrighi's "Operina,"* New Haven, 1954; Philip Hofer, "Variant Issues of Ludovico Arrighi's *Operina*," *Harvard Library Bulletin*, 14, no. 3, 1960, pp. 334–342.

60 IL MODO DE TEMPERARE LE PENNE...

Venice, 1523.

In Italian and Latin. Various scripts and constructed letters. 16 paper leaves, quarto. Woodcuts and italic type. Bound with a copy of the 1522 edition of *La Operina*.

*Lent by The Library of Congress (Lessing J. Rosenwald Collection)*

The second of Arrighi's writing manuals, first printed in the year following the publication of *La Operina*, differs substantially from the earlier treatise. *Il Modo* contains a greater variety of scripts and several complex alphabet designs. Whereas the 1522 volume was intended to spread a knowledge of italic script among a wide audience, presupposing no professional skill, this work would seem to be of greatest value to the reader with a practised hand.

Some copies of *Il Modo* state on the colophon that the book was printed in Venice, while *La Operina* had been printed in Rome. The woodblock cutter for *Il Modo* was Eustachio Celebrino, who also acted in the same capacity for Tagliente's 1524 manual, thereby providing a link between Arrighi's publication of 1523 and Tagliente's (no. 63) of the following year.

Bibliography: A. F. Johnson, "A Catalogue of Italian

Writing-Books of the Sixteenth Century," *Signature*, n.s. 10, 1950, pp. 24–26; Alfred Fairbank and Berthold Wolpe, *Renaissance Handwriting*, London, 1960, pp. 82–83.

## *Attributed to Arrighi*

61 LETTER FROM CARDINAL PIETRO BEMBO TO OCTAVIO FREGIOSO
Rome, 1516.
In Latin. Chancery script. 1 vellum leaf, 6¼×9¹¹⁄₁₆ inches.
Provenance: Stanley Morison.
*Lent by The John M. Wing Foundation of The Newberry Library*

The letter, dated May 31, 1516, was written in the Papal Chancery during the period when Arrighi was a scribe there, and may be by his hand.

## *John Howard Benson*

UNITED STATES 1901–1956

62 MS TRANSLATION OF ARRIGHI'S *LA OPERINA*
In English. Italic script. 32 paper leaves, 10⅝×8½ inches. Pen and black ink on white laid paper. Unbound.
*Lent by Mr. and Mrs. Philip Hofer*

This is the manuscript from which was reproduced, in 1955, the first English translation of Arrighi's manual. In addition to his command of Arrighi's italic script, Benson imitated with great success the earlier scribe's especially beautiful placement of the letters on the page, a difficult feat when dealing with a translation. The renaissance copy-book's instructions on the formation of italic letters were written with such clarity that they remain one of the best guides to a command of that script.

Bibliography: see no. 59 and Portland *Cat.*, no. 151 and pl. 65.

## *Giovanantonio Tagliente*

ITALY ACTIVE 1491–1524

63 LO PRESENTE LIBRO INSEGNA...
Venice, 1524.
In Italian. Various scripts and alphabets. Woodcuts and type, on paper. Binding: paper on boards.
*Lent by Esther Fisher Benson*

Perhaps encouraged by the great success of Arrighi's two copy-books of 1522 and 1523, in the following year Tagliente published the above volume, one of the most important treatises of its time and place. In addition to various cursive scripts, the work illustrates several alphabets and a set of constructed letters. However much Arrighi's volume impressed Tagliente, the latter's scripts have their sources in Venetian and Paduan models. It is worth noting that eight pages of Tagliente's text are set in a type cut to imitate italic script. Two years before, when Arrighi published *La Operina*, moveable type was not used. Instead, each page was printed from a woodblock, the text for that page being cut on the block.

Little is known of Tagliente's life, which seems to have been spent largely as a writing master. In that capacity he taught calligraphy to the Venetian Chancery. In addition to the present volume, he published works on various subjects, including a book of lace designs. Although Tagliente claimed that he taught throughout Italy, his recorded activity was in Venice. There he trained a generation of scribes, and through them influenced the calligraphy of the Veneto.

Bibliography: James Wardrop, "A Note on Giovanantonio Tagliente," *Signature*, n.s. 8, 1949, pp. 57–61; A. F. Johnson, "A Catalogue of Italian Writing-Books of the Sixteenth Century," *Signature*, n.s. 10, 1950, pp. 26–30; James M. Wells, editor, *Opera di Giovanni Tagliente*, Chicago, 1952.

## *Anonymous*

64 PAPAL BULL. POPE PAUL III
Rome, signed December 19, 1537.
In Latin. Scribal hand. 18 vellum leaves, folio. In ink.
Binding: cloth wrapper.
Provenance: Azzolini Collection.
*Lent by The Pierpont Morgan Library*

An elaborate and formal example of the script used in the Papal Chancery, the bull illustrates the difficulty of reading such documents. For minor documents and briefs the Chancery developed a less formal, more speedily written hand which became known as the chancery cursive. It is this hand which is seen in Arrighi's writing; for a time the author of the first copy-book to illustrate the chancery hand was employed as a scribe in the Chancery.

Bibliography: De Ricci, II, p. 1610; Portland *Cat.*, 1958, no. 12, pl. 8.

## *Giovanni Battista Palatino*

ITALY ACTIVE 1538–1574

65 LIBRO NUOVO D'IMPARARE A SCRIVERE...
Rome, 1540, by Baldassare di Francesco Carolari Perugino for M. Benedetto Gionta (colophon).

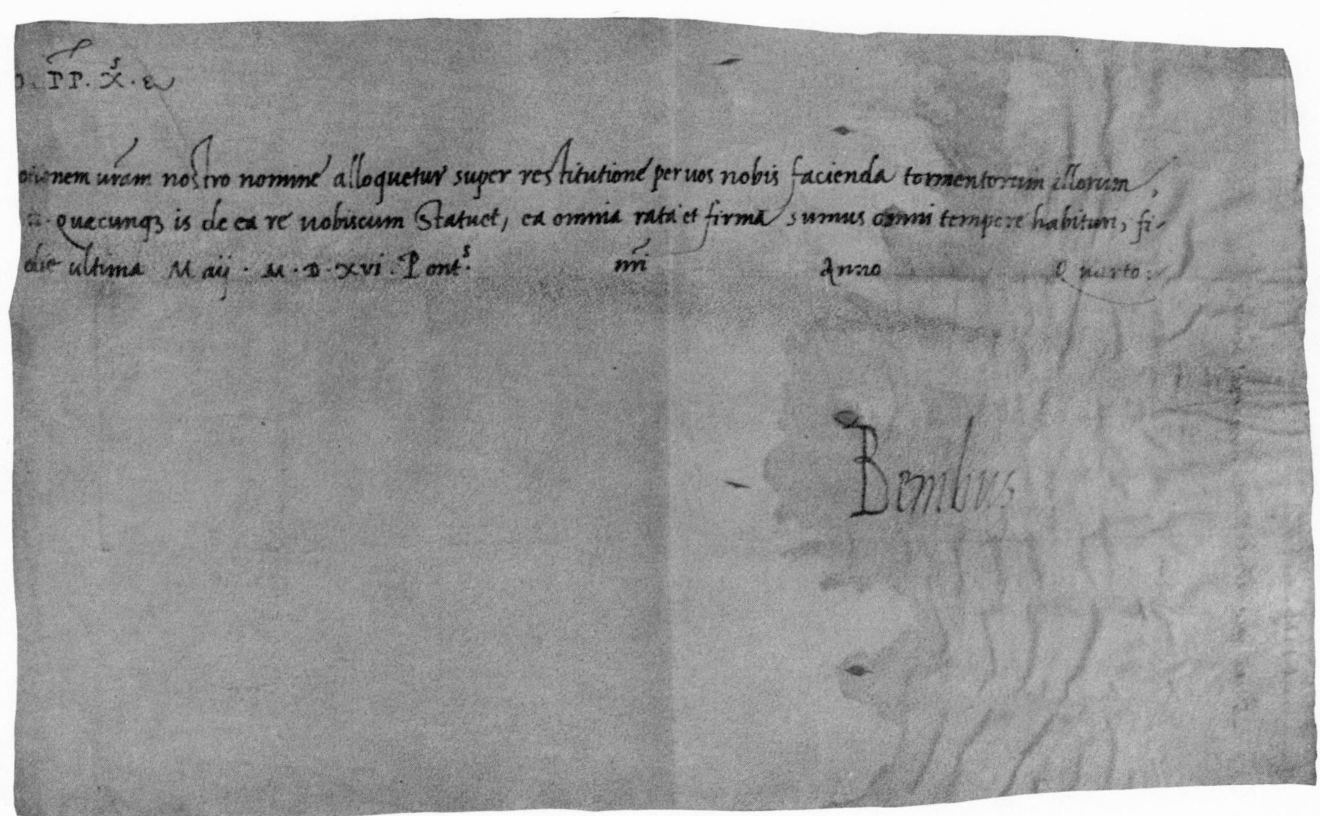

D. PP. X.

...onem uram nostro nomine alloquetur super restitutione per uos nobis facienda tormentorum illorum,
...quecunque is de ea re nobiscum statuet, ea omnia rata et firma sumus omni tempore habituri, ...
die ultima Maij · M · D · XVI · Pont^s nri Anno quarto.

Bembus

61 Attributed to Ludovico Arrighi, *Letter From Cardinal Pietro Bembo*, Rome, 1516

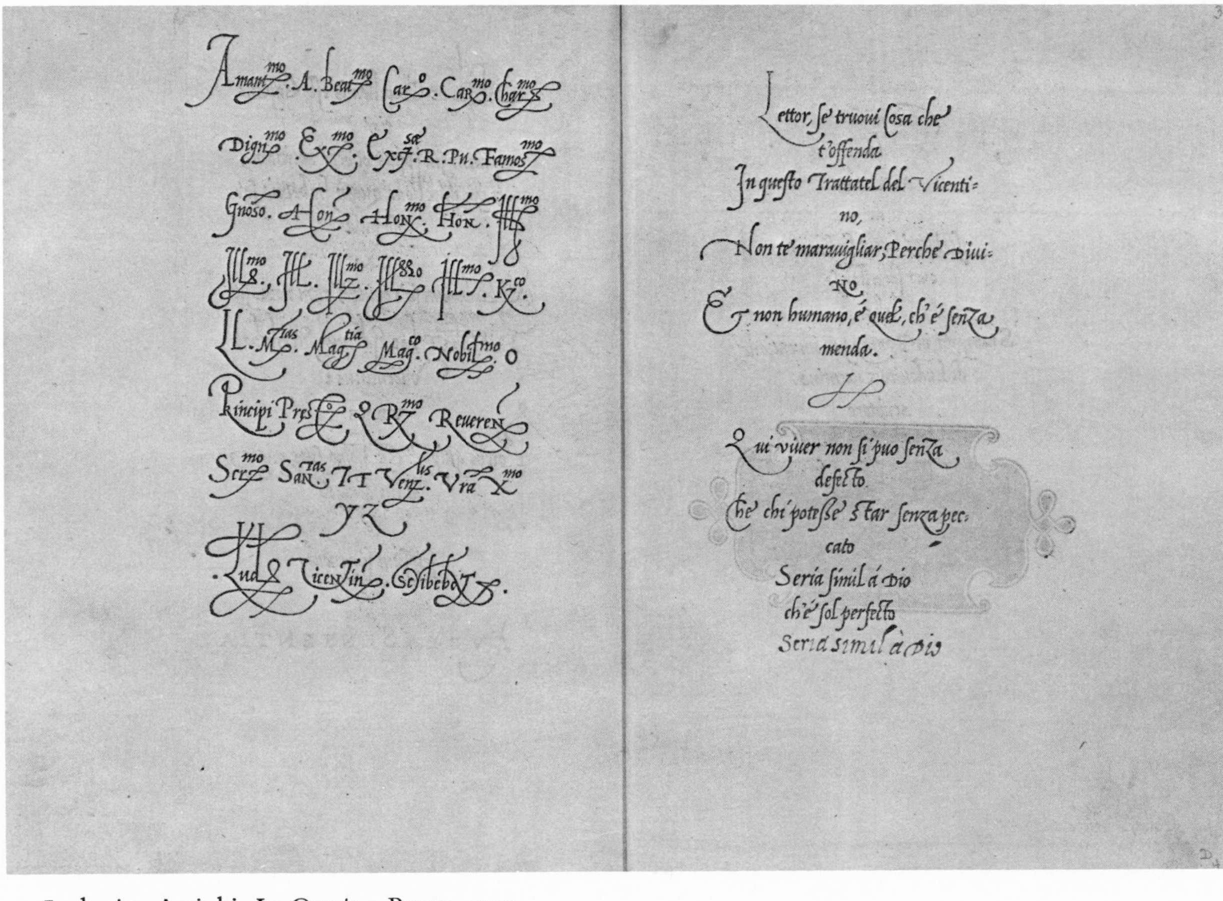

Lettor, se' truoui cosa che
t'offenda
In questo Trattatel del Vicentino,
Non te marauigliar, Perche' diuino
E non humano, e' quel, ch'e' senza
menda.

Qui viuer non si puo senza
defetto.
Che chi potesse star senza pec-
cato
Seria simil á Dio
ch'e' sol perfetto
Seria simil á Dio

59 Ludovico Arrighi, *La Operina*, Rome, 1522

*15*

So, my Reader, you must know that of the small letters of the Alphabet, some may be tied with those that follow, some may not: Those that may be tied with their followers are here written, namely, a c d f i k l m

n ſ s t u

Of which a d i k l m n u are tied with any that follow: But c f ſ s t tie only with some: The rest of the Alphabet, to wit, b e g h o p q r x y z ought not to be tied to the letter following. But to tie or not to tie, I leave to your judgment provided that the letters be equal.

62 John Howard Benson, *Translation of "La Operina"*

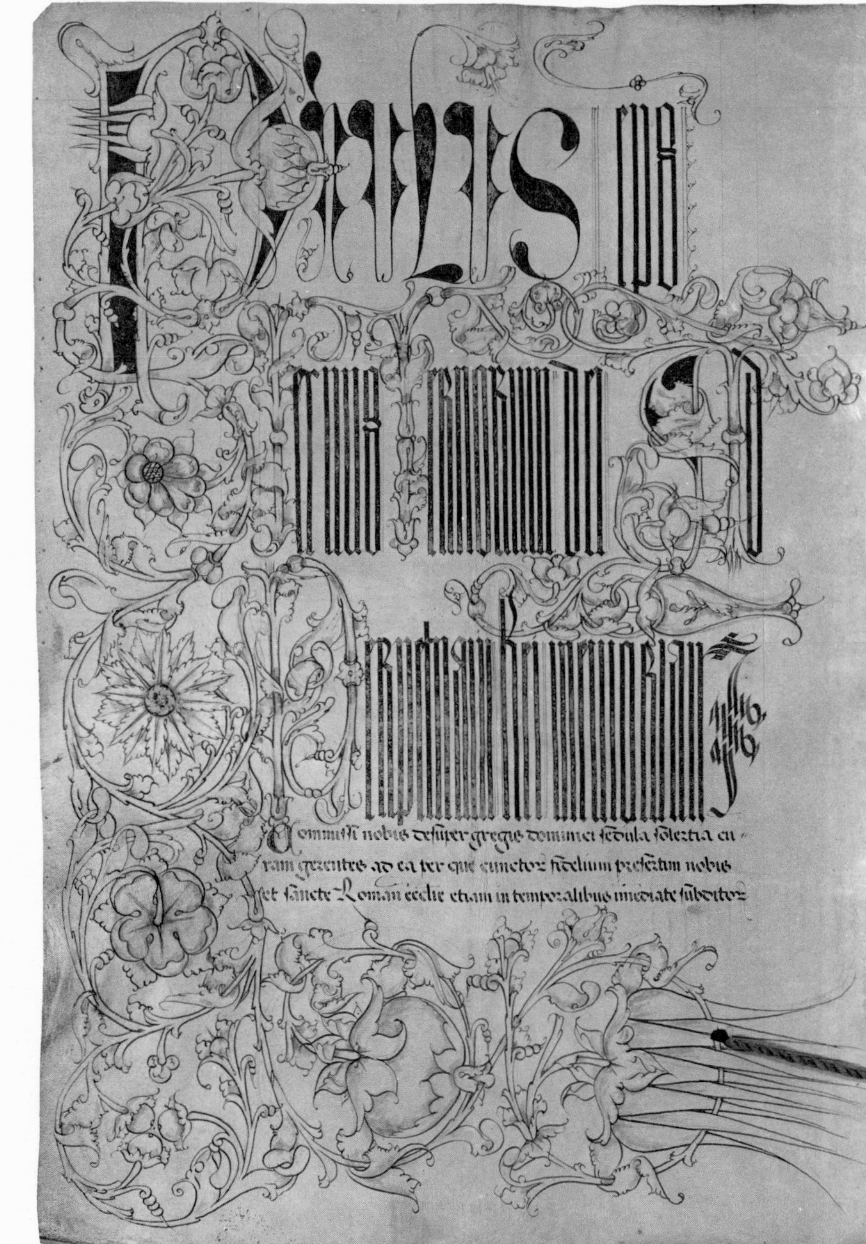


64 *Papal Bull*, Rome, 1537

In Italian. Various scripts. 52 paper leaves, 8¼×5½ inches. Woodcuts. Binding: vellum on boards.
Provenance: "Ascarli phavorini (?) et amicorum" (inscribed in an early hand); C. L. Ricketts.
*Lent by The John M. Wing Foundation of The Newberry Library; Esther Fisher Benson*

The last of the three major Italian copy-books of the sixteenth century is Palatino's volume of 1540. In extent, Palatino's manual was a more ambitious effort than Arrighi's or Tagliente's, containing models of "ancient and modern letters of all nations." Palatino's models of chancery script are among the handsomest, but are nearly impossible to execute if the writer is a person of modest ability.

Almost nothing is known of the scribe's early life. Born at Rossano, in Calabria, Palatino's known activities all took place in Rome. By 1538 he was a citizen of that city. The few contemporary documents which mention him indicate that the scribe was a part of the leading intellectual circles of the time. A lasting mark of Palatino's presence in Rome is the inscription he cut on the Porta del Popolo.

Bibliography: Henry K. Pierce, *The Instruments of Writing* (translated from the writing book of Giovanbattista Palatino, Rome, 1553), Newport, 1948; A. F. Johnson, "A Catalogue of Italian Writing-Books of the Sixteenth Century," *Signature*, n.s. 10, pp. 31–33; James Wardrop, "Civis Romanvs Svm: Giovanbattista Palatino and His Circle," *Signature*, n.s. 14, 1952, pp. 3–40; Bonacini, 1328.

## *Bernardino Cataneo*

ITALY ACTIVE 1544–BEFORE 1564

66 MS WRITING BOOK
Siena, February 4, 1545.
Ms. Typ 246 H. In Italian. Italic script. 20 vellum leaves, 5½×8 inches. Binding: contemporary brown morocco, gilt.
Provenance: Edward Raleigh; Sir Posthumous Hoby; Sir Philip Sydenham; Stephen Penny to Charles Joseph Hartford (1779); sale (London, 1933, no. 359).
*Lent by Mr. and Mrs. Philip Hofer*

Written in an exquisite and refined cursive italic script, this calligraphic specimen-book contains verses from *Orlando Furioso*. An Englishman, "Signor Odoardo Ralyg," (Edward Raleigh) acquired the volume in Siena according to an inscription in the manuscript. An Edward Raleigh is known to have been in Siena in 1543 and he is surely the purchaser. Little is known of the scribe, whose name occurs in the archives of the University at Siena, where he was employed. This manuscript is the only surviving example by a scribe who here demonstrates consummate ability in his art.

Bibliography: De Ricci, II, p. 1698, no. 29; James Wardrop, "Six Italian Manuscripts," *Harvard Library Bulletin*, 7, 1953, pp. 223–224 and pl. III; Walters *Cat.*, 1949, no. 231; Harvard *Cat.*, 1955, no. 124 and pl. 68; Portland *Cat.*, 1958, no. 34 and pl. 19; Alfred Fairbank and Berthold Wolpe, *Renaissance Handwriting*, Cleveland, 1960, p. 72 and pl. 36.

## *Vespasiano Amphiareo*

ITALY DIED 1563

67 UN MODO D'INSEGNAR A SCRIVERE...
Venice, 1548, C. T. di Navo.
In Italian. Various scripts and constructed letters. 48 paper leaves, 5½×8⅝ inches. Woodcuts and type.
Provenance: C. L. Ricketts.
*Lent by The John M. Wing Foundation of The Newberry Library*

His only printed work, Amphiareo's manual is an important document in the development of the chancery cursive hand. Amphiareo's use of loops and the joins connecting letters, commonly used in the mercantile scripts, anticipates Cresci's models (no. 70) and the latter's claims to having originated a more speedy, flowing hand.

Although he was an important scribe, little is known about Amphiareo. A Franciscan friar, born in Ferrara, he recorded in the dedication of the 1554 edition of this book that he had been teaching writing for thirty years.

Bibliography: A. F. Johnson, "A Catalogue of Italian Writing-Books of the Sixteenth Century," *Signature*, n.s. 10, 1959, pp. 34–36.

68 MS WRITING MANUAL
Probably Ferrara, ca. 1548.
In Italian. Various scripts. 20 vellum leaves, 7×10 inches.
*Lent by Mr. and Mrs. Philip Hofer*

The manuscript is signed "fr. Vespasianus Amphyareus Ferrarese," and probably was executed at about the same time as his printed writing book (no. 67) since on fol. 5v of the manuscript he mentions that he was then supervising the printing of a manual.

Bibliography: James Wardrop, "Six Italian Manuscripts in The Department of Graphic Arts," *Harvard Library Bulletin*, 7, no. 2, 1953, p. 24 and pl. IV; Portland *Cat.*, 1958, no. 36; Arnold Fairbank and Berthold Wolpe, *Renaissance Handwriting*, Cleveland, 1960, p. 92 and pl. 75.

## *Michelangelo Buonarroti*

ITALY 1475–1564

69 LETTER TO BENVENUTO ULIVERTI
Rome, April 19, 1549.
In Italian. Chancery cursive script. 1 paper leaf, folio.
Provenance: Azzolini Collection.
*Lent by The Pierpont Morgan Library*

In a bold chancery hand, Michelangelo requests of Benvenuto Uliverti and Partners in Rome payment of the monthly revenues granted to him by Pope Paul III. The latter, in 1548, had granted to the artist income from the office of Civil Notary in the Chancellery of Rimini.

Bibliography: De Ricci, II, p. 1528; Portland *Cat.*, no. 23; E. H. Ramsden, *The Letters of Michelangelo*, Stanford, 1963, vol. 2, p. 106, no. 328.

## *Giovanni Francesco Cresci*

ITALY ACTIVE 1552–1572

70 ESSEMPLARE DI PIU SORTI LETTERE...
Rome, 1560, A. Blado.
In Italian. Various scripts. 42 (of 44) paper leaves, 6⅝× 8⅝ inches. Woodcuts.
Provenance: C. L. Ricketts.
*Lent by The John M. Wing Foundation of The Newberry Library*

On the basis of this volume, Cresci has been called the first calligrapher of the Baroque. In it he criticized Palatino's models as being too slow and too heavy. These defects Cresci proposed to remedy by a more rounded script which makes greater use of the joins connecting letters. The resultant hand is more flowing in character, has a pronounced slope, and is quicker to write. Its heavily clubbed ascenders are also characteristic.

A manuscript by Cresci from 1572 states that he had been in Rome for twenty years. By 1556 he was employed as a scribe in the Vatican Library. Various documents trace his existence until 1572, after which nothing is heard of him.

Bibliography: Bonacini, 415; James Wardrop, "The Vatican Scriptors, Documents for Ruano and Cresci," *Signature*, n.s. 5, 1948, pp. 13–20; A. F. Johnson, "A Catalogue of Italian Writing-Books of the Sixteenth Century," *Signature*, n.s. 10, 1950, pp. 37–40.

71 IL PERFETTO SCRITTORE...
Rome, 1570, F. Aurei.
In Italian. Various scripts. 2 parts in one volume. 8⅛× 11 inches. Woodcuts and engravings.
Provenance: Prince of Liechtenstein.
*Lent by The Library of Congress (Lessing J. Rosenwald Collection)*

This is the second of Cresci's printed works and is more copious than his earlier copy-book (no. 70). However it does not greatly enlarge our knowledge of his scripts. In the introduction the scribe notes that he has striven for years to discover a manner of writing the chancery cursive hand with greater speed and style.

Bibliography: Library of Congress, *The Rosenwald Collection. A Catalogue of Illustrated Books . . .*, Washington, D. C., 1954, p. 113, no. 587.

## *Agnolo Bronzino*

ITALY 1503–1572

72 LETTER TO COSIMO I DE'MEDICI
Florence, signed April 15, 1564.
In Italian. Roman chancery script. 1 paper leaf, 11⅜ ×10⅝ inches. In ink.
Provenance: C. Fairfax Murray Collection of European Autographs. Acquired 1950.
*Lent by The Pierpont Morgan Library*

Bronzino demonstrates a clear and legible hand in this letter thanking Cosimo for his *salario*. The sheet was written at the time when the artist was at work in the Palazzo Vecchio and S. Stefano in Pisa.

Bibliography: Bond and Faye, *Supplement*, p. 376.

## *Giulantonio Hercolani*

ITALY ACTIVE 1571–1577

73 ESSEMPLARE UTILE DI TUTTE LE SORTI DE L'RE CANCELLARESCHE CORRENTISSIME...
Bologna, 1571.
Copperplate engravings. 34 paper leaves, 7⅞×11 inches.
Binding: modern vellum on boards.
Provenance: Stanley Morison; C. L. Ricketts.
*Lent by The John M. Wing Foundation of The Newberry Library*

With this volume Hercolani initiated a new way of printing copy-books in Italy. Using copperplate engravings rather than woodcuts, the scribe could reproduce, or have reproduced, his calligraphic designs in a medium with closer af-

La lettera Imperiale e simile alla
lettera Bollatica quale ciascun vo-
lendo imparar, Prima Bisogna sap
ben formar Tutte le Lettere dello sotto
scritto Alphabeto a Una per Una

.a.b.c.d.d.e.f.g.h.i.k.l.m.m.n.
n.o.p.p.p.q.r.r.s.s.t.u.v.x.x.y.z.

63 Giovanantonio Tagliente, *Lo Presente Libro*, Venicè, 1524

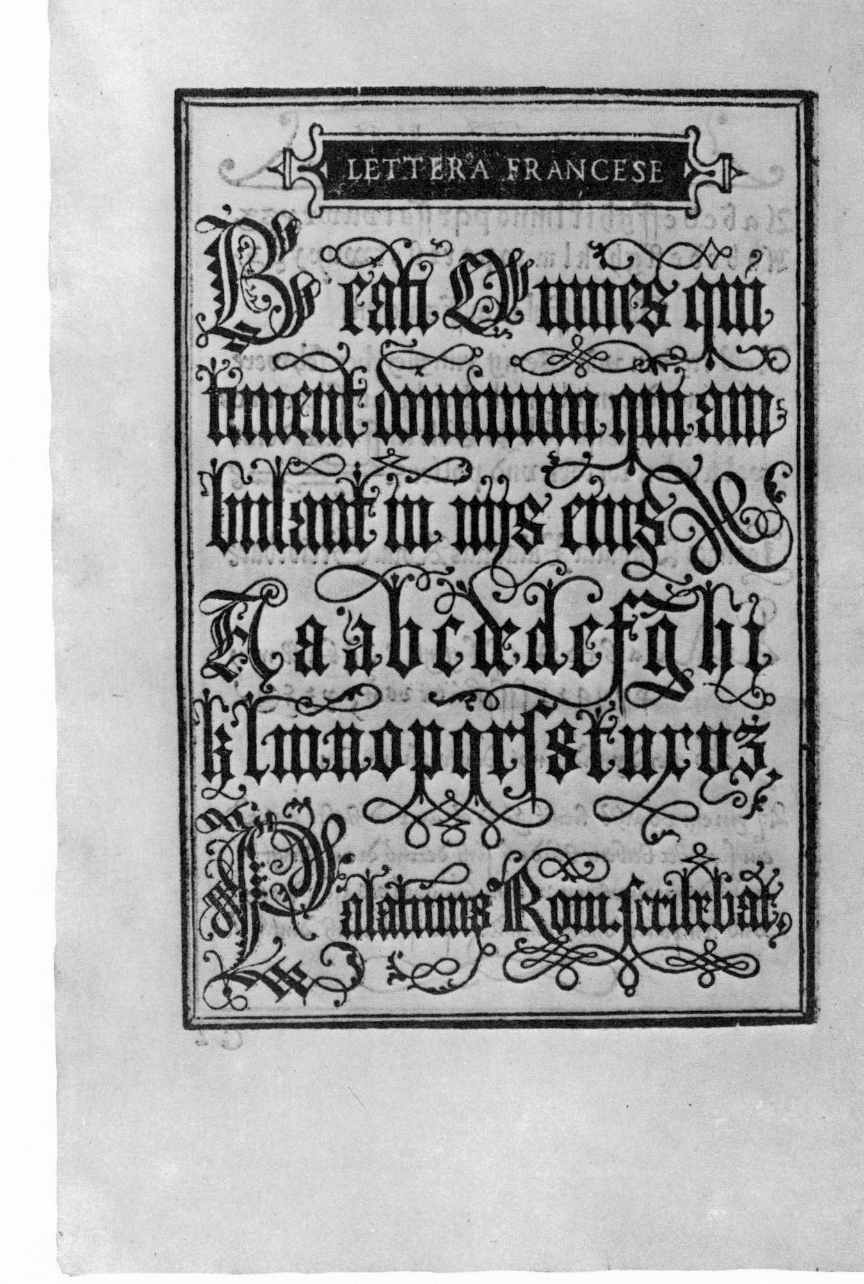


65 Giovanni Battista Palatino, *Libro Nuovo . . .*, Rome, 1540

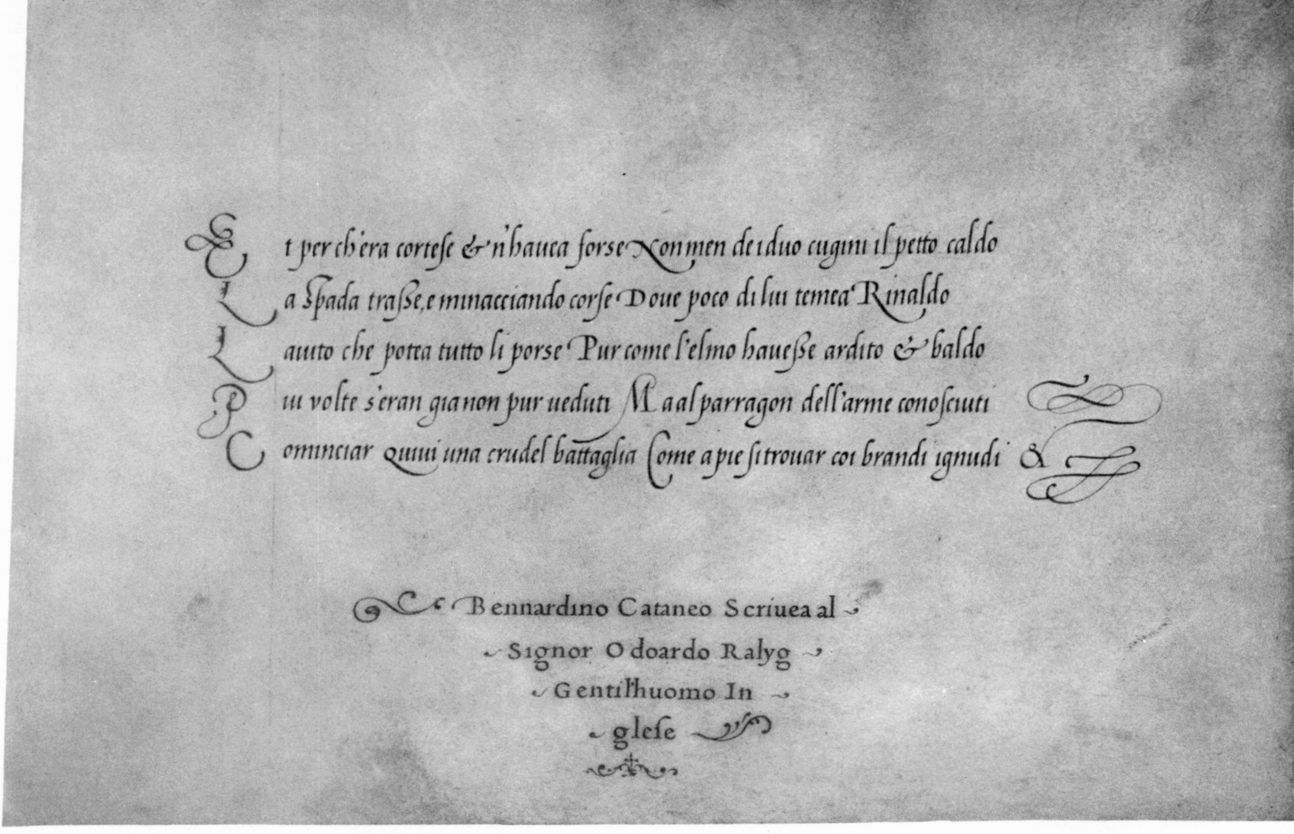
Et per ch'era cortese & n'hauea forse Non men dei duo cugini il petto caldo
La spada trasse, e minacciando corse Doue poco di lui temea Rinaldo
Lauito che potta tutto li porse Pur come l'elmo hauesse ardito & baldo
Piu volte s'eran gia non pur ueduti Ma al parragon dell'arme conosciuti
Cominciar quiui una crudel battaglia Come a pie si trouar coi brandi ignudi &

Bennardino Cataneo Scriuea al
Signor Odoardo Ralyg
Gentilhuomo In
glese

66 Bernardino Cataneo, *Writing Book*, Siena, 1545

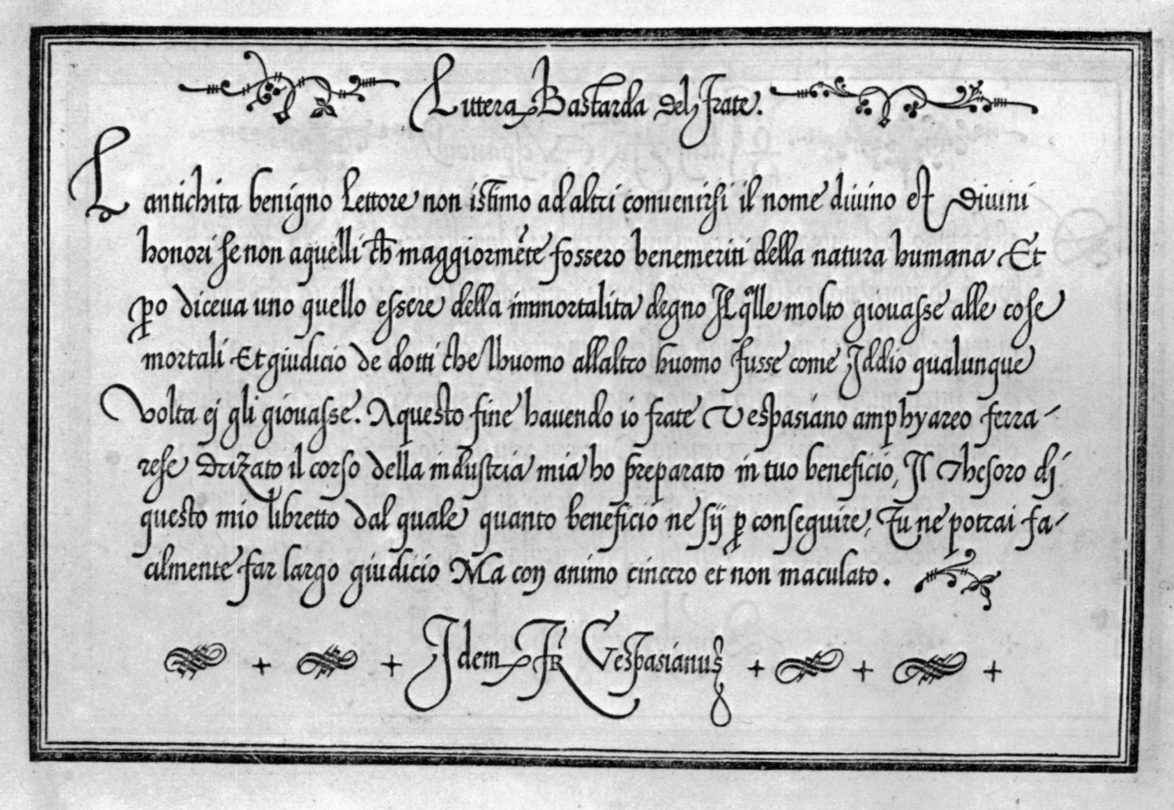
Littera Bastarda del frate.

L'antichita benigno Lettore non istimo ad altri conuenirsi il nome diuino et diuini
honori se non aquelli che maggiormēte fossero benemeriti della natura humana Et
po diceua uno quello essere della immortalita degno il q̄lle molto giouasse alle cose
mortali Et giudicio de dotti che l'huomo allaltro huomo fusse come Iddio qualunque
volta ei gli giouasse. A questo fine hauendo io frate Vespasiano amphyareo ferrarese drizato il corso della industria mia ho preparato in tuo beneficio il thesoro di
questo mio libretto dal quale quanto beneficio ne sij p conseguire, Tu ne potrai facilmente far largo giudicio Ma con animo sincero et non maculato.

Idem Fr Vespasianus

67 Vespasiano Amphiareo, *Un Modo d'Insegnar a Scrivere . . .*, Venice, 1548

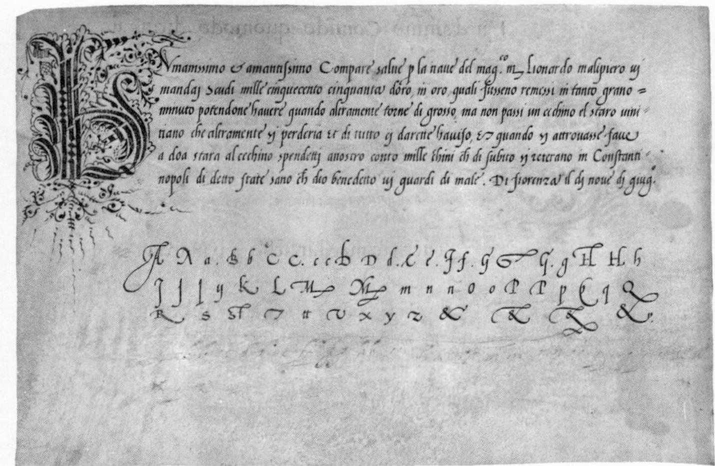

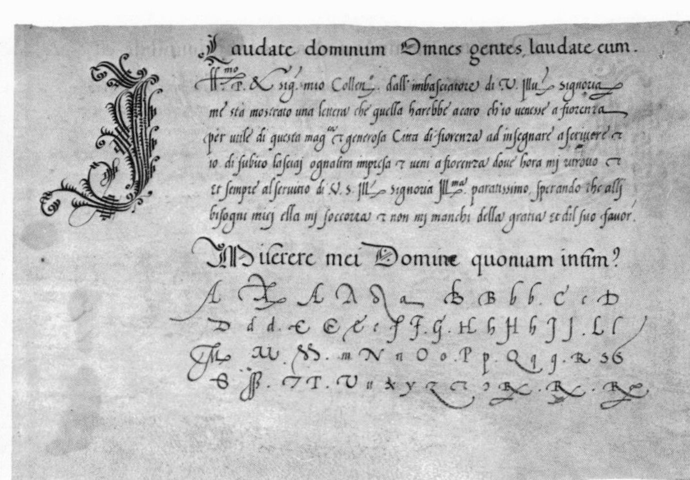

68 Vespasiano Amphiareo, *Writing Manual*, ca. 1548

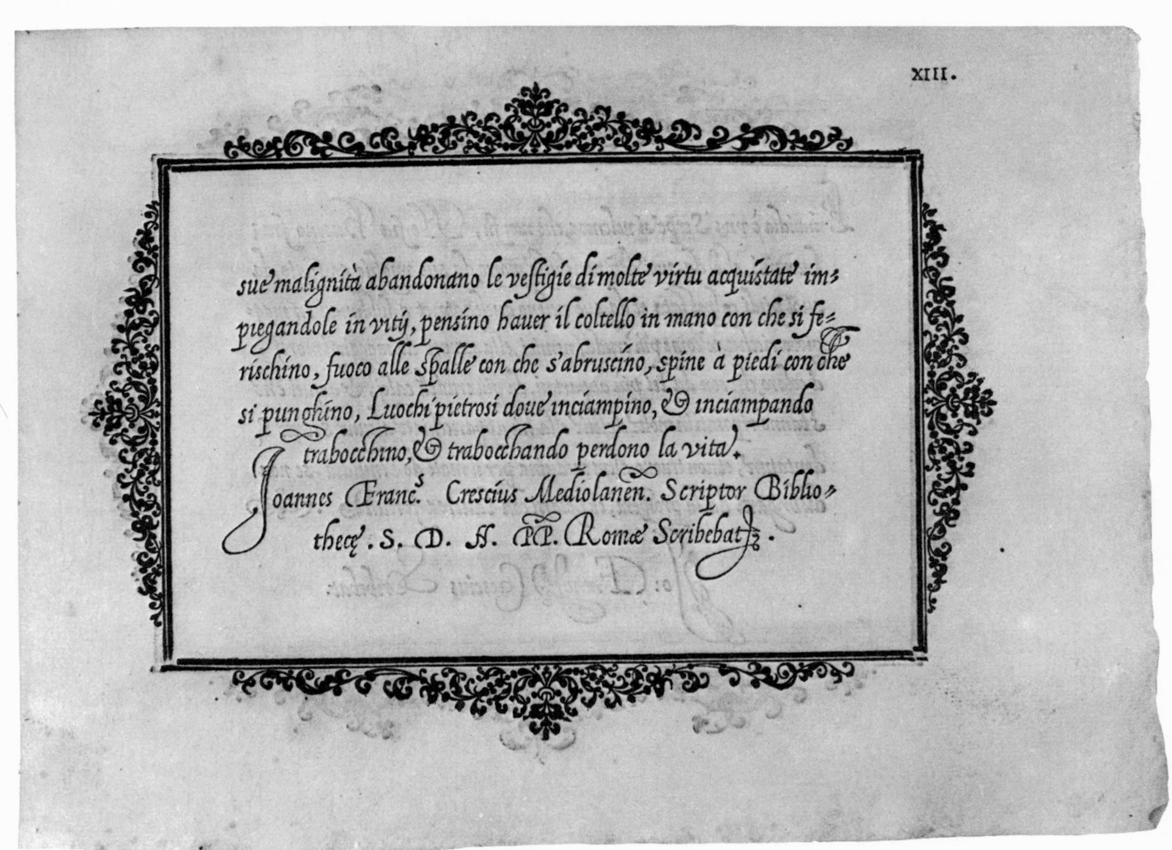

XIII.

sue malignità abandonano le vestigie di molte virtu acquistate im-
piegandole in vitij, pensino hauer il coltello in mano con che si fe-
rischino, fuoco alle spalle con che s'abruscino, spine à piedi con che
si punghino, Luochi pietrosi doue inciampino, & inciampando
trabocchino, & trabocchando perdono la vita.
Joannes Franc.s Crescius Mediolanen. Scriptor Biblio-
thecę. S. D. N. PP. Romæ Scribebat.

70 Giovanni Francesco Cresci, *Essemplare di Piu Sorti Lettere*, Rome, 1560

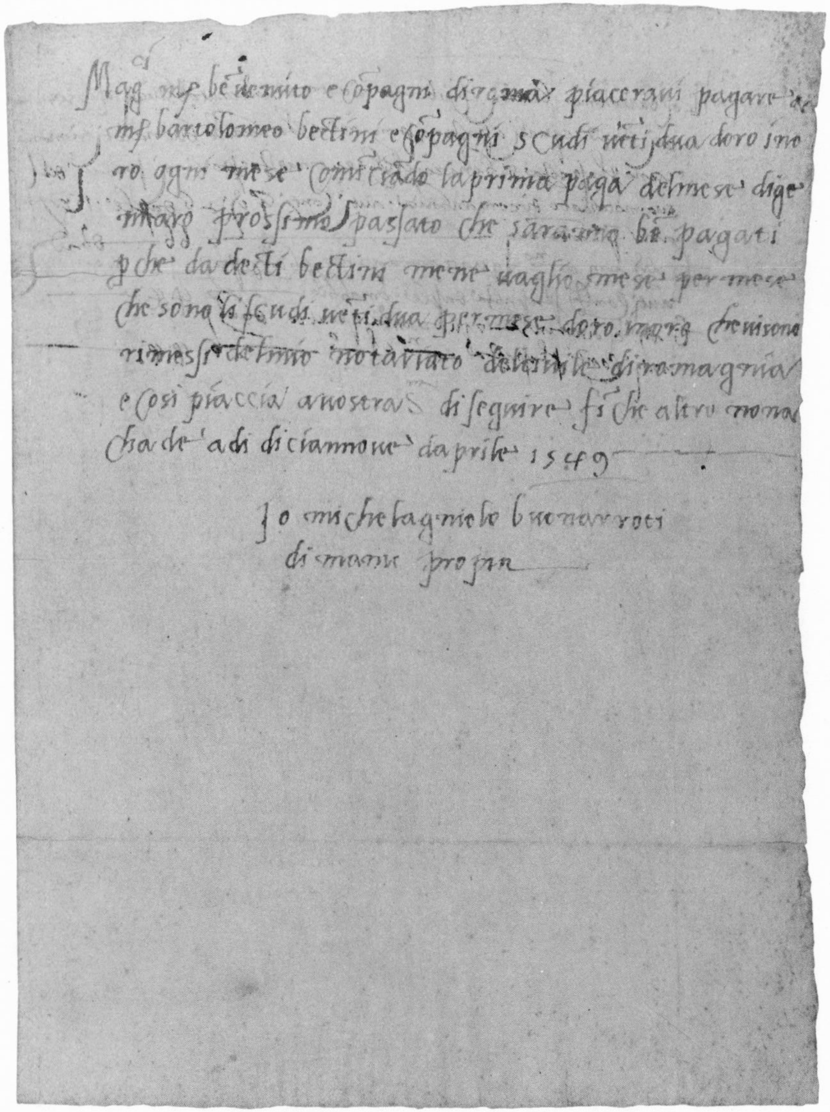

69 Michelangelo Buonarroti, *Letter to Benvenuto Uliverti*, Rome, 1549

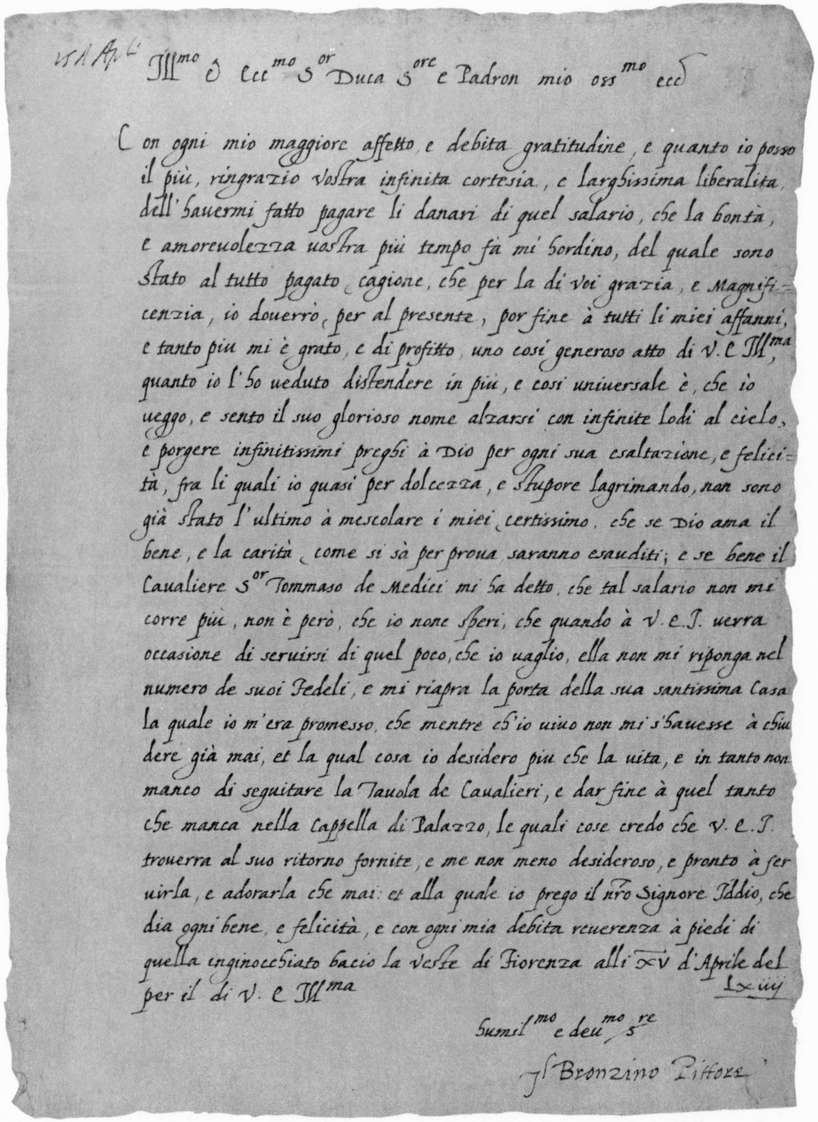

72 Agnolo Bronzino, *Letter to Cosimo I de' Medici*, Florence, 1564

finities to the pen's stroke. The swelling lines possible in the engraving process are more suitable than woodcuts for reproducing the pen's action as the instrument is manipulated with varying pressure. Hercolani used the qualities of engraving with discretion and clarity, foregoing the grandiose flourishes which so many later calligraphers found irresistible. Almost nothing is known of Hercolani's life other than the fact that he was also a Doctor of Law and Prior of the Church of La Maddalena in Bologna. The last record of the scribe is dated 1577.

Bibliography: Bonacini, 768; A. F. Johnson, "A Catalogue of Italian Writing-Books of the Sixteenth Century," *Signature*, n.s. 10, 1950, p. 41.

## *Anonymous*

74 DOGALE GRANTED BY NICOLÒ DA PONTE TO ZAUNE BADOER AS POVEDITOR OF CIVIDALE

Venice, May 11, 1580.

Ms.W.487. In Italian. Venetian chancery script. 190 vellum leaves, 8¾×6⅜ inches. In ink with rubrication, one miniature. Binding: original Venetian red morocco, gilt.

Provenance: Edward Quaile (sale, London, May 10, 1901, no. 49).

*Lent by The Walters Art Gallery*

Written in a handsome flowing chancery hand, this grant of privileges by Doge Nicolò da Ponte names Zaune Badoer as Governor of Cividale. The miniature and binding carry the arms of Badoer.

Bibliography: De Ricci, I, p. 855, no. 549.

## *Anonymous*

75 MS WRITING SPECIMEN BOOK

Italy, ca. 1580–1590.

Various scripts. 36 paper leaves, 8×11¼ inches (11 ff. of alphabet designs, 20 ff. of capital letters, 1 f. of 4 drawings imitating etchings, and 4 blank leaves). Brown, gold, and colored inks.

*Lent by Mr. and Mrs. Philip Hofer*

A series of elaborately flourished capitals, each filling a page, is the outstanding feature of this manuscript. Written with great verve and using a pen cut so as to produce a swelling line, the capitals look forward to the *traits de plume* of the seventeenth century and later. The flourished capitals anticipate Ruinetti's copperplate engravings (no. 77), the latter being more fully developed products of the Baroque.

Bibliography: James Wardrop, "Six Italian Manuscripts in the Department of Graphic Arts," *Harvard Library Bulletin*, 7, no. 2, 1953, p. 225 and pl. VI.

## *Anonymous*

76 MUTIUS RICCERIUS. *SACELLUM EXQUILINUM*

Rome, ca. 1610.

Ms.W.473. In Latin. Late Roman chancery script. 16 vellum leaves, 9½×6¾ inches. Ink with gold. Binding: contemporary red morocco, gold tooled with arms and imprese of Cardinal Borghese.

Provenance: Cardinal Scipione Borghese (1576–1632).

*Lent by The Walters Art Gallery*

This poem, dedicated to Pope Paul V (Camillo Borghese, Pope 1605–1621), praises the newly erected Borghese Chapel in Sta. Maria Maggiore, which had been designed for Paul by Ponzio in 1611. The rich binding is characteristic of the library of Cardinal Scipione Borghese, adopted nephew of Paul.

Bibliography: De Ricci, I, p. 842, no. 489.

## *Tomaso Ruinetti*

ITALY ACTIVE 1619

77 IDEA DEL BUON SCRITTORE

Rome (?), 1619.

In Italian. Various scripts. 44 paper leaves, 8⅝×11¾ inches.

Copperplate engravings.

Provenance: C. L. Ricketts.

*Lent by The John M. Wing Foundation of The Newberry Library*

Ruinetti's *Idea* is the first book to demonstrate the art of calligraphic flourishes and figures, using copperplate engravings. The earlier treatise by Hercolani (no. 73), illustrated with engravings, used the medium only for the reproduction of script. But in this volume elaborate figures and flourishes enhance the borders of each plate and dominate the script. Calligraphic virtuosity has here gained the upper hand; many later calligraphers found it impossible to resist the opportunity to display their inventive powers and skillful control of the pen.

Bibliography: Bonacini, 1585.

## *Amadeo Mazzoli da Forli*

ITALY ACTIVE 1762

78 MS OF PIETRO ARETINO'S *IL FILOSOFO*

North Italy, 1762.

In Italian. Script imitating italic and erect roman type. 48 paper leaves, 7¼×5 inches. Pen and black ink.

*Lent by Mr. and Mrs. Philip Hofer*

This written facsimile of a book printed at Venice ca. 1546 is an amazing tour-de-force. Even the breaks which would inevitably occur using wooden type are imitated. Because Aretino's comedies were on the Papal Index, original editions were rarities even in the eighteenth century. The manuscript is signed by Mazzoli and dated on the last page.

## *Juan de Ycíar (or Icíar)*

SPAIN 1522/23—PROBABLY AFTER 1572/73

79 RECOPILACION SUBTILISSIMA INTITULADA ORTHOGRAPHICA PRATICA
Saragossa, 1548.
In Spanish. Various scripts and constructed letters. 70 paper leaves, 7½×5¼ inches. Woodcuts and type.
Provenance: D. Felix Bois, Madrid.
*Lent by Mr. and Mrs. Philip Hofer*

Inspired by the copy-books of Arrighi, Tagliente, and Palatino, all mentioned in Ycíar's preface, in 1548 he published the volume described above, one of the earliest Spanish copy-books to illustrate the chancery hand. A second, enlarged edition appeared in 1550, retitled *Arte Subtilissima*... The work is notable for the exceptionally rich decoration of the woodcut plates, many of which are handsome examples of white on black ground printing. Only rarely is the identity of the early woodblock cutters known. In Ycíar's book each plate or group of plates is signed by the cutter, Jean de Vingle or Juan de Vingles. His uncommon prominence has led to the suggestion that de Vingles had a part in designing the plates.

In some laudatory verses about Ycíar prefacing this edition of his book, the author is said to be twenty-five years old and born at Durango. The seventeenth century writer and calligrapher, Pedro Díaz Morante, noted that Ycíar practised as a calligrapher until he was fifty (about 1572–1573) and then was ordained a priest. No further mention of the scribe is known.

Bibliography: Cotarelo y Mori, pp. 353–356; Juan de Ycíar, *A Facsimile of the 1550 Edition of ARTE SUBTILISSIMA*. Translated by Evelyn Shuckburgh, introduction by Reynolds Stone, London, 1960; Henry Thomas, "Juan de Vingles (Jean de Vingle) A Sixteenth-Century Book Illustrator," *The Library*, 4th ser., 18, no. 2, 1937, pp. 121–176.

## *Francisco Lucas*

SPAIN CA. 1530–AFTER 1580

80 ARTE DE ESCREVIR...
Madrid, 1580, F. Sanchez.
In Spanish and Latin. 117 paper leaves, 8×5½ inches. Woodcuts and type.
Provenance: M. D. Moya (inscribed in an early hand); Biblioteca de Salva (super-libris); C. L. Ricketts.
*Lent by The John M. Wing Foundation of The Newberry Library; The Library of Congress (Lessing J. Rosenwald Collection), 1608 edition*

Lucas' book is of exceptional importance in the development of Spanish calligraphy as it brought to that country a combination of italic chancery and local mercantile scripts. For more than two centuries Lucas' models of the *redondilla* and *bastarda* scripts remained in use, eventually giving way to a version of the English round hand.

Born in Seville, about 1530 Lucas went to Madrid, where he opened a writing school. His known activities there span only a decade, after which nothing more is known of his life. Bibliography: Cotarelo y Mori, 611; Portland *Cat.*, no. 40.

## *José de Casanova*

SPAIN 1613–1692

81 PRIMERA PARTE DEL ARTE DE ESCRIVIR...
Madrid, 1650.
In Spanish. Various scripts. 3 unnumbered leaves, plus 29 numbered leaves, including 30 plates, 11¾×7⅞ inches. Copperplate engravings.
*Lent by The Library of Congress (Lessing J. Rosenwald Collection)*

A number of seventeenth century copy-books contain examples of the *lettera bastarda*, a letter form of the greatest importance in the evolution of the round hand script. In Spain, this volume by Casanova was one of the principal copy-books to introduce the *lettera bastarda*. Casanova's script is slightly inclined and engraved with a light, elegant hand. In his preface the scribe noted that, being dissatisfied with the available engravers, he learnt the art and himself engraved the plates of this book. Born in Aragon, at Mallagón, in 1613 the scribe came to Valladolid where he was an official in the Secretariat of the Chancery.

Bibliography: Cotarelo y Mori, 203.

## *Francisco Xavier Santiago y Palomares*

SPAIN 1728–1796

82 HISTORIA DEL RUIDOS O DE SAFIO...
Spain, 1754–1761.
In Spanish and Latin. Various scripts. 68 paper leaves, 14⅜×10¼ inches, plus 15 paper leaves of various sizes. Ink and watercolor.
*Lent by Mr. and Mrs. Philip Hofer*

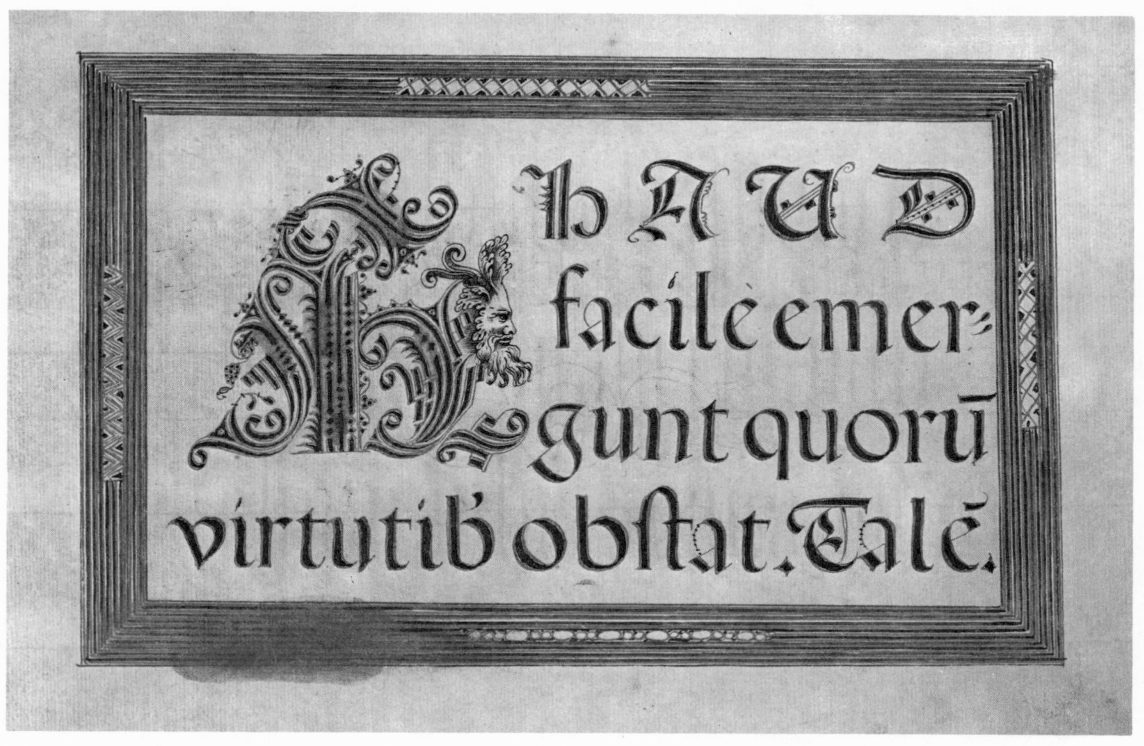


75 *Writing Specimen Book*, Italy, ca. 1580–1590

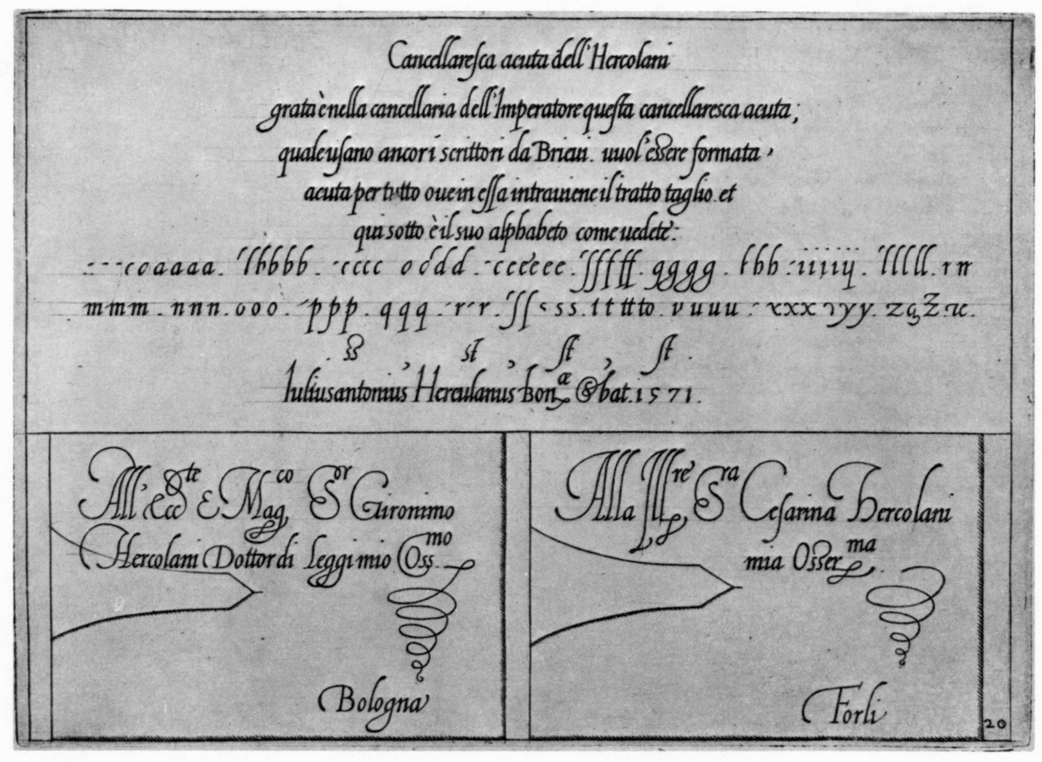


73 Giulantonio Hercolani, *Essemplare Utile . . .*, Bologna, 1571

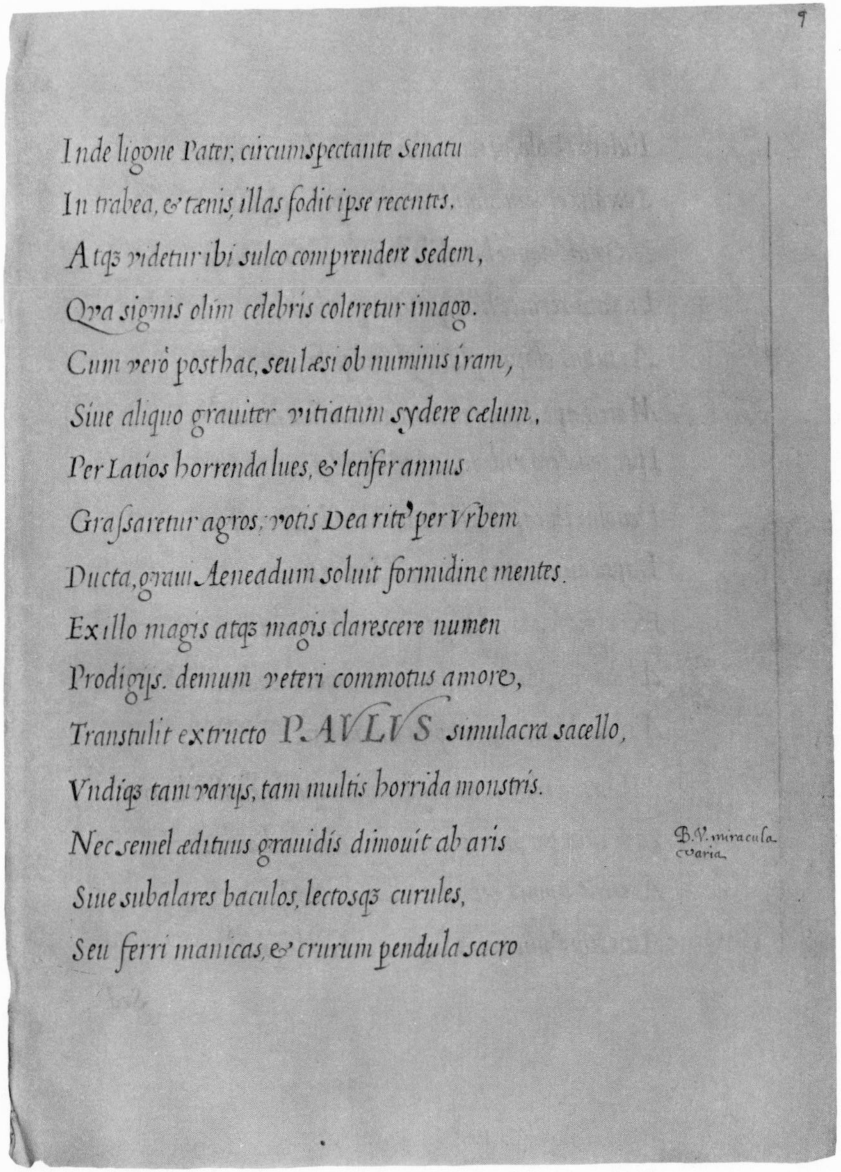

9

Inde ligone Pater, circumspectante Senatu
In trabea, & tænis, illas fodit ipse recentes.
Atq; videtur ibi sulco comprendere sedem,
Qua signis olim celebris coleretur imago.
Cum verò posthac, seu læsi ob numinis iram,
Siue aliquo grauiter vitiatum sydere cælum,
Per Latios horrenda lues, & letifer annus
Grassaretur agros; votis Dea rite per Vrbem
Ducta, graui Aeneadum soluit formidine mentes.
Ex illo magis atq; magis clarescere numen
Prodigijs. demum veteri commotus amore,
Transtulit extructo PAVLVS simulacra sacello,
Vndiq; tam varijs, tam multis horrida monstris.
Nec semel æditiuus grauidis dimouit ab aris
Siue subalares baculos, lectosq; curules,
Seu ferri manicas, & crurum pendula sacro

B.V. miracula varia

76 Mutius Riccerius: *Sacellum Exquilinum*, Rome, ca. 1610

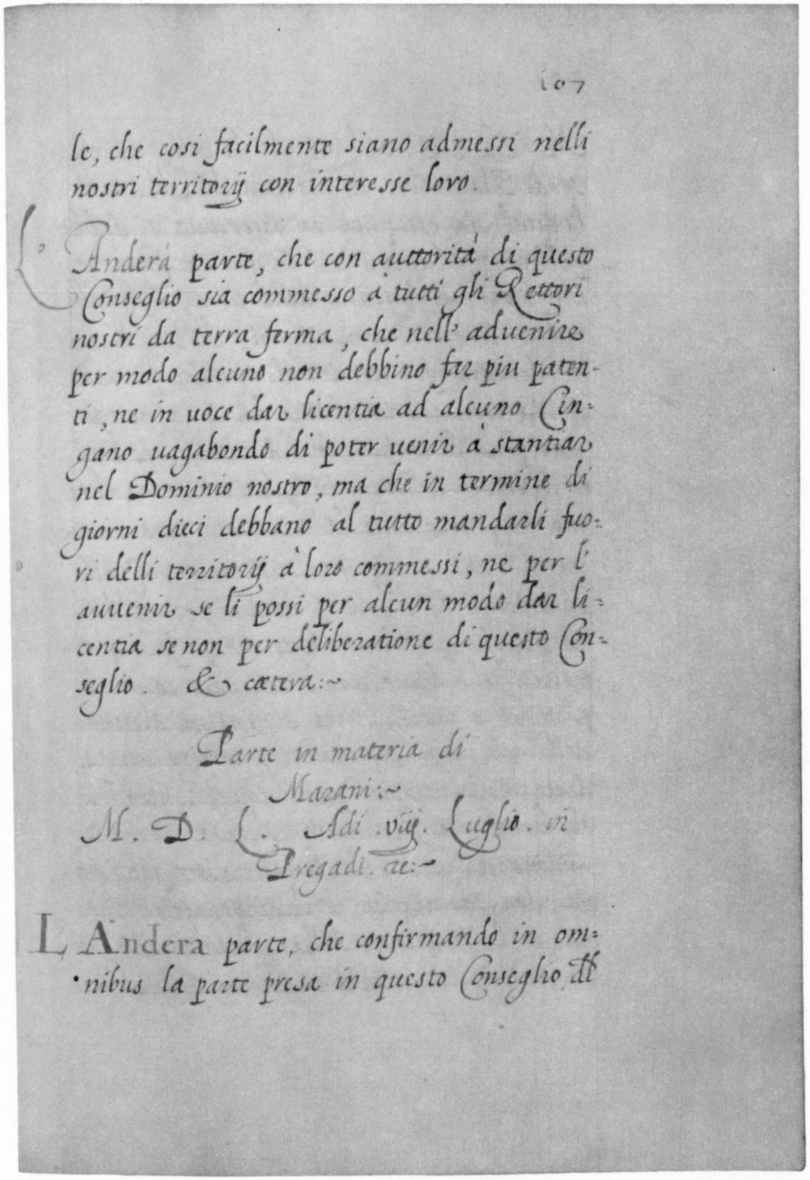

107

le, che così facilmente siano admessi nelli nostri territorij con interesse loro.

L'Anderà parte, che con auttorità di questo Conseglio sia commesso à tutti gli Rettori nostri da terra ferma, che nell'aduenire per modo alcuno non debbino far più patenti, ne in uoce dar licentia ad alcuno Cingano uagabondo di poter uenir à stantiar nel Dominio nostro, ma che in termine di giorni dieci debbano al tutto mandarli fuori delli territorij à loro commessi, ne per l'auuenir se li possi per alcun modo dar licentia se non per deliberatione di questo Conseglio. & cætera:~

Parte in materia di Marani:~
M. D. L. Adi. viij. Luglio. in Pregadi. &c:~

L'Andera parte, che confirmando in omnibus la parte presa in questo Conseglio di

74 *Dogale Granted by Nicolò da Ponte . . .*, Venice, 1580

PRIMO. 10

cheʼ la cerca. e giorneando col giuracchiare le uir= tu, che mai non hebbe, isforzano a credere, che non giuoca, che non tauerneggia, che non bestem= mia, che non iscialacqua, ch'è limosiniere, diuoto, una herba tagliata, fa del fango oro: sano come un pesce; che terria in festa un morto, che da del uoi a ognuno, & piu anchora.

Pap. Ciurmatori.

Dru. Cõsumato il piacere d'una stomana o due: ecco che la donna nouella il uede giocarsi le brache; lo sente attaccarla al Calendario imbriaco di quegli, con= sumator d'ogni cosa, non credente in nulla, fanta= stico, dadouero, & isfranciosato, da buon senno.

Pap. Che ti pare?

Dru. Quella storia di leggenda in dispregio de le mogli doueua al dirimpetto del suo dire, che subito ui= sto una foggia nuoua in dosso a le uicine, tengono la fauella a i mariti; e mai non gli fan motto infino attanto, che sono intese per discretione. doueua di co iscampanare, il come i lupi arrabiati fingano la gelosia persino a tanto, che le non ci fusser mai nate: si aueggono che gli bisogna trouar bertoni per lo intertenimento de le lor tauerne, de le loro

78 Pietro Aretino: *Il Filosofo*, by Amadeo Mazzoli da Forli, North Italy, 1762

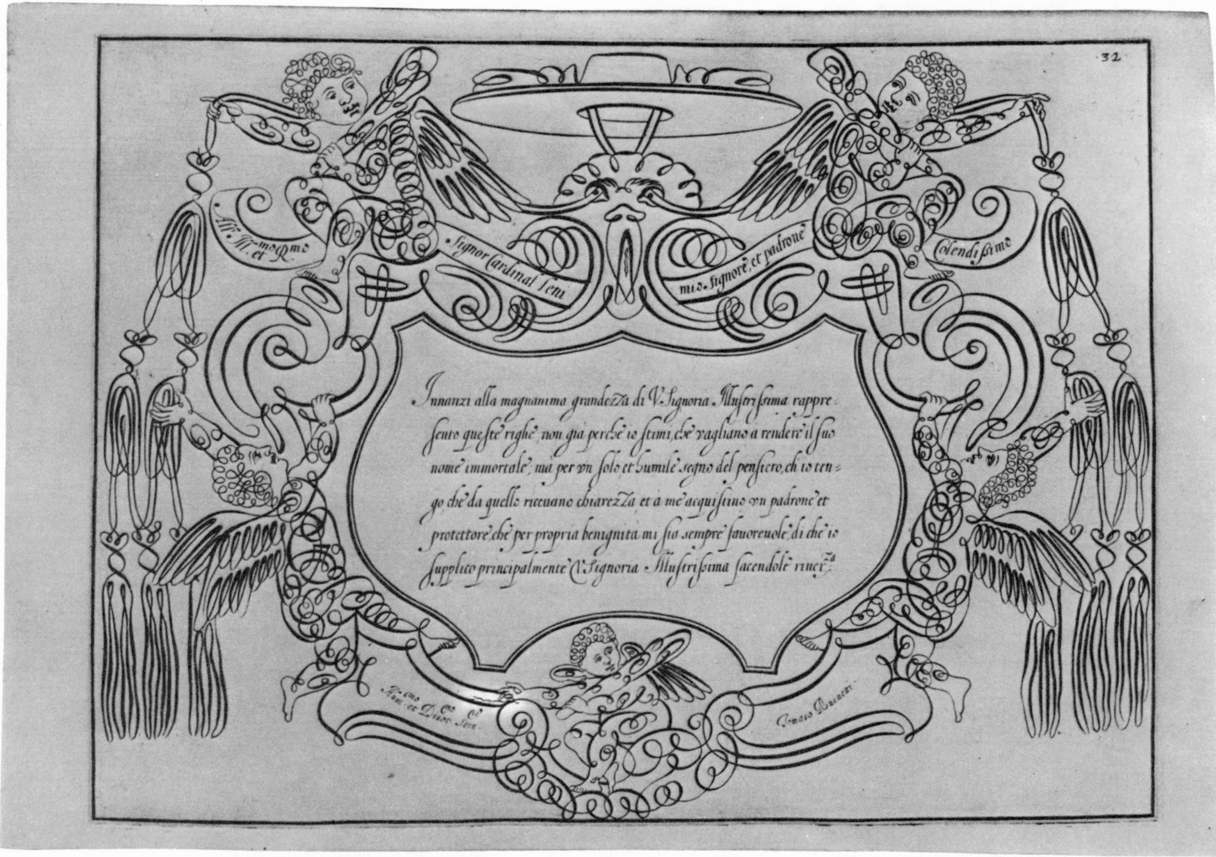


77 Tomaso Ruinetti, *Ideal del Buon Scrittore*, Rome (?), 1619

REDONDILLA. 57

abc, con sus principi-
os

[illegible]

Fr.co Lucas lo escreuia
en Madrid año de 1570

80 Francisco Lucas, *Arte de Escrevir . . .*, Madrid, 1580

Trata delos casos/y otras cosas necessarias a vn escriptor de libros.

Para ser vno buen artista de libros de yglesias: requiere tener muchas particularidades: entre las quales dire algunas delas mas necessarias. La primera que sea buen escriuano/y buen puntante: y que sepa hazer vna letra caudinal / y vn caso quadrado y de mediarle y illuminarle. Que sepa hazer vn caso peon: y vna letra q̃brada / porq̃ todas estas letras siruen cada vna para lo que es. Las letras caudinales siruẽ para que en poniendo vn caso prolõgado/o quadrado qualquiera que sea en vn officio o responso/o comunicãda luego la primera letra sea caudinal. Los casos quadrados siruẽ para principio de vn libro/o de vn officio sumptuoso que por mas adornalle se pone vna letra grande quadrada / y illuminada: y estas son las mas principales: y sabiendo hazerlas sabran hazer todas las otras y a este fin quise poner la geometria dellas y mas quatro tablas illuminadas con sus demediaduras las quales siruen para partir la color vna de otra. Porq̃ estos casos para ser biẽ hechos hã de ser de dos colores que son tornasol/y bermellon/y lo de fuera del caso ha de ser la vna color: y lo d̃ dẽtro ha d̃ ser otra lo q̃ no tienẽ ninguno delos otros casos porq̃ hã d̃ ser illuminados d̃ vna color: excepto q̃ el mesmo caso ha de ser de otra. Los casos prolongados siruen para poner en vn responso/o antiphona comunes o en semejãtes partes/y los casos peones siruen para poner en los versos de psalterios/por ser muy apropiados para este efecto. Y las letras quebradas siruen para los versos que vienen despues delos oficios/o responsos y assi yo puse de cada cosa vn abecedario lo mejor que me parescio/y puse los blancos porque se podrã contrahazer mejor que si fueran negros por los quales cada vno podra aprender a hazer los con toda perficion y arte.

79 Juan de Yciar, *Recopilacion Subtilissima . . .*, Saragossa, 1548

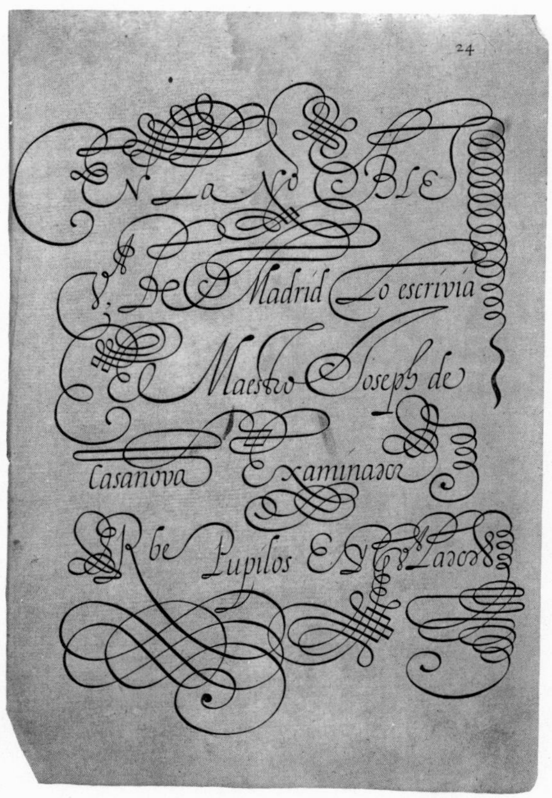


81 José de Casanova, *Primera Parte del Arte de Escrivir . . .*, Madrid, 1650

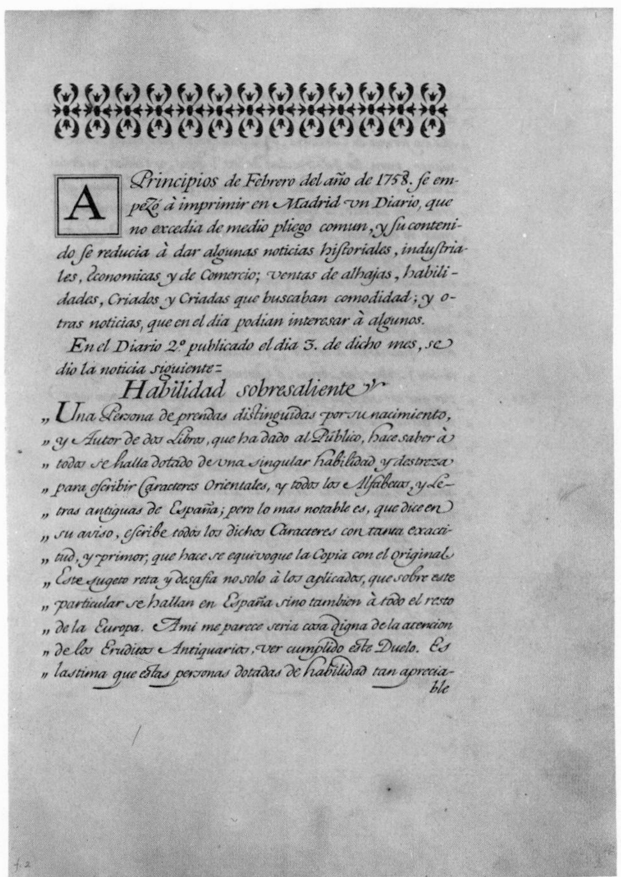

A Principios de Febrero del año de 1758. se empezó à imprimir en Madrid un Diario, que no excedia de medio pliego comun, y su contenido se reducia à dar algunas noticias historiales, industriales, economicas y de Comercio; ventas de alhajas, habilidades, Criados y Criadas que buscaban comodidad; y otras noticias, que en el dia podian interesar à algunos.

En el Diario 2.º publicado el dia 3. de dicho mes, se dio la noticia siguiente=

Habilidad sobresaliente

„ Una Persona de prendas distinguidas por su nacimiento,
„ y Autor de dos Libros, que ha dado al Público, hace saber à
„ todos se halla dotado de una singular habilidad y destreza
„ para escribir Caracteres Orientales, y todos los Alfabetos, y Le-
„ tras antiguas de España; pero lo mas notable es, que dice en
„ su aviso, escribe todos los dichos Caracteres con tanta exacti-
„ tud, y primor; que hace se equivoque la Copia con el original.
„ Este sugeto reta y desafia no solo à los aplicados, que sobre este
„ particular se hallan en España sino tambien à todo el resto
„ de la Europa. A mi me parece seria cosa digna de la atencion
„ de los Eruditos Antiquarios, ver cumplido este Duelo. Es
„ lastima que estas personas dotadas de habilidad tan aprecia-
ble

82 Francisco Xavier Santiago y Palomares, *Historia del Ruidos o de Safio*, Spain, 1754–1761

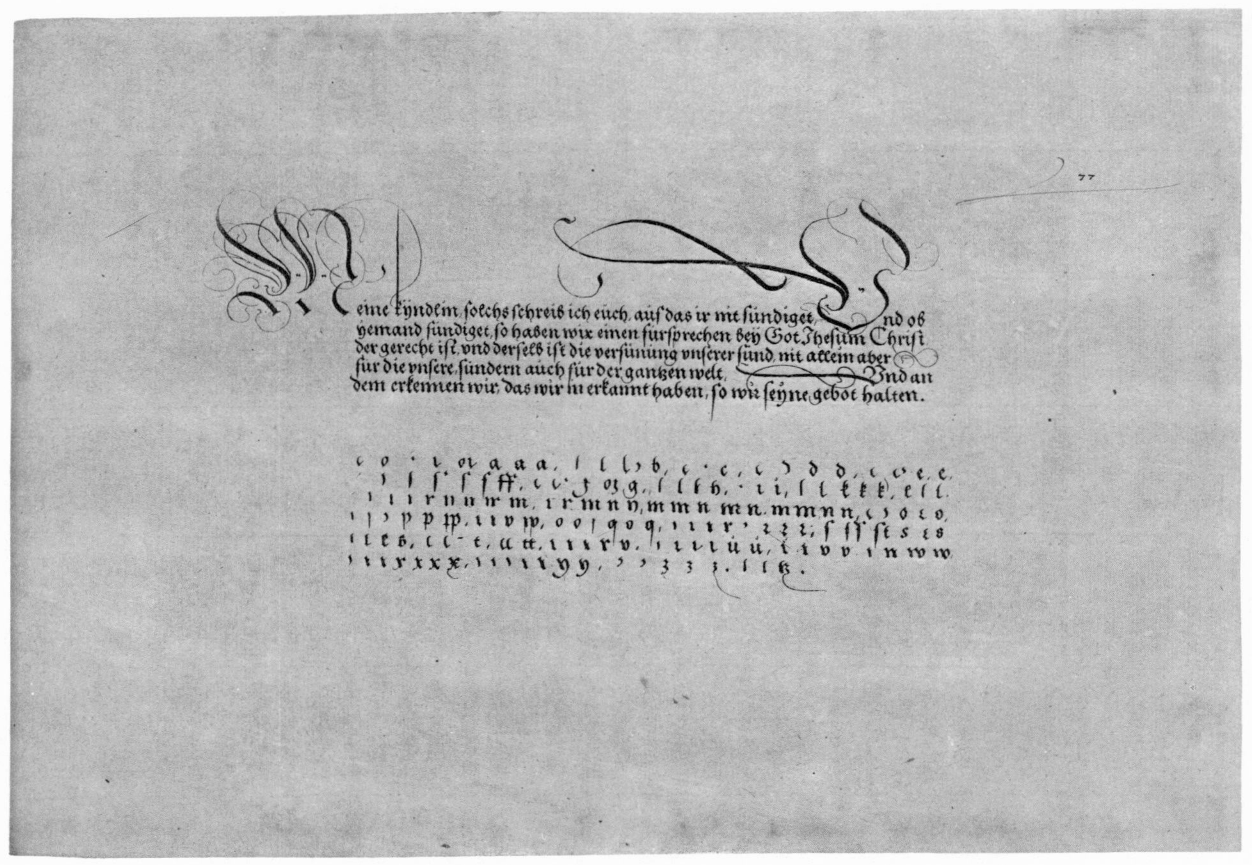

77

eine kyndelm, solchs schreib ich euch, auff das ir nit sündiget, nd ob
yemand sündiget, so haben wir einen fürsprechen bey Got Jhesum Christ
der gerecht ist, vnd derselb ist die versünung vnserer sünd, nit allein aber
für die vnsere, sündern auch für der gantzen welt, Und an
dem erkennen wir, das wir in erkannt haben, so wir seyne gebot halten.

83 Johann Neudörffer, the Elder, *Ein Gute Ordnung* . . . , Nuremburg, 1543 (?)

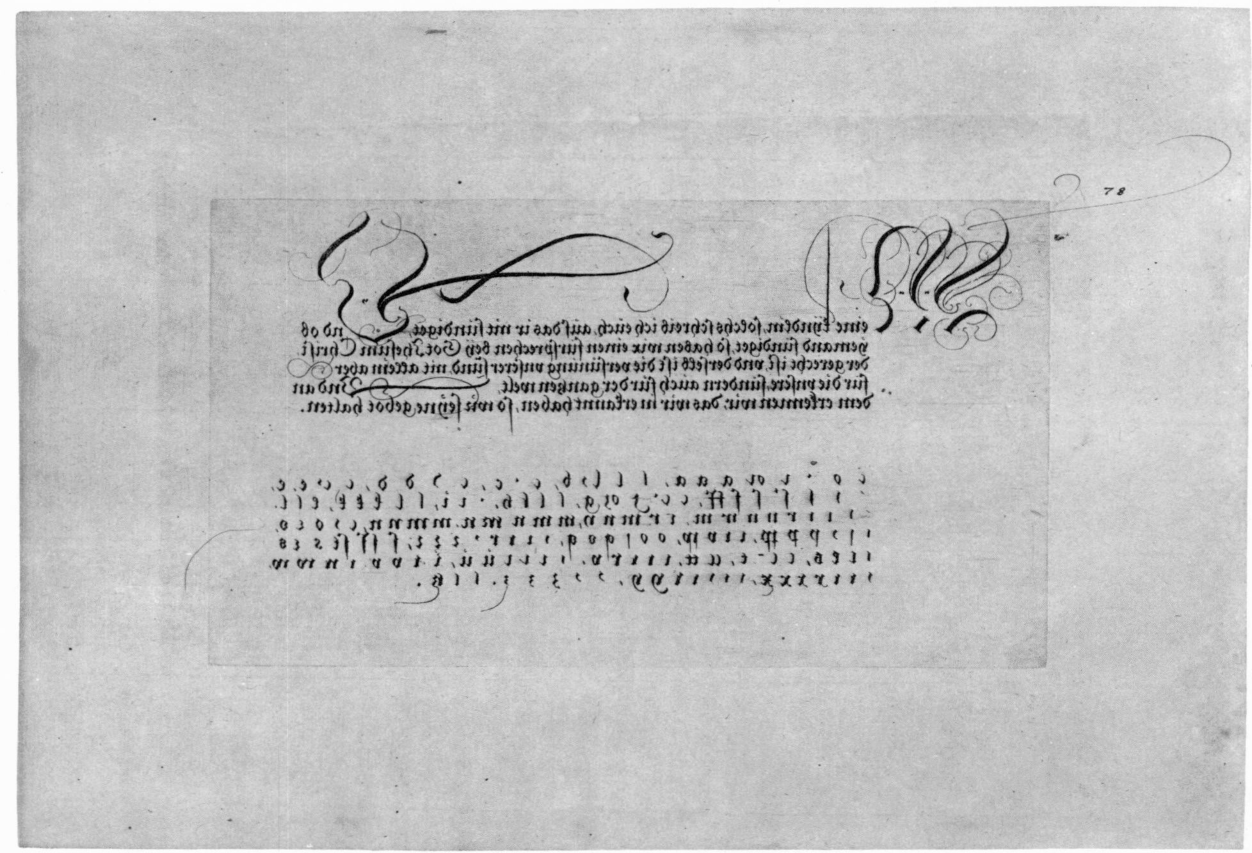

83 Johann Neudörffer, the Elder, *Ein Gute Ordnung* . . . , Nuremburg, 1543 (?)

Inspired by the copy-books of the seventeenth century Spanish calligrapher, Pedro Díaz Morante, Palomares initiated a revival of fine handwriting in eighteenth century Spain. Appalled by the decline of Spanish calligraphy, Palomares sympathized with Morante's ideal of writing well-formed letters with ease and speed. This manuscript shows Palomares' mastery of a variety of hands including Arabic scripts. Many of the leaves are written in earlier scripts and occasionally pages are finished with watercolor imitating the appearance of documents or printed leaves.

Born at Toledo, the scribe spent his early years in a cultivated household. His early classical education was surely responsible for the scribe's interest in paleography, a subject which attracted the interest of several contemporary Spanish scribes, notably Servidori. Later, at Madrid, where Palomares spent his mature years, the scribe published several books on antique scripts and documents.

## *Johann Neudörffer, the Elder*

GERMANY 1497–1563

83 EIN GUTE ORDNUNG...
Nuremburg, 1543 (?).
In German and Latin. 111 paper leaves (8 folding plates) with 14 leaves of MS calligraphic specimens bound in at the end, 8¼×11⅜ inches. Copperplate engravings.
*Lent by The Library of Congress (Lessing J. Rosenwald Collection)*

First published in 1538, this copy of *Ein Gute Ordnung* . . . is a somewhat later edition as it contains plates dated 1538, 1539, 1541, and 1543. The number of plates in the copies listed by Doede varies widely, some volumes containing up to 147 leaves.

In the study of German calligraphy, Neudörffer, the Elder, occupies a position of basic importance. The creation of a definitive fraktur script is credited in large part to the designs in his several copy-books. The 1538 book is his earliest important publication, and is one of, if not the, earliest writing manuals to be illustrated with engravings rather than woodcuts. In the book are some plates of script written in the normal manner and then repeated in reverse, presumably to aid printers who must engrave their plates in reverse script. Sheets printed from such plates appear in the normal direction when run through the press. A manuscript by Neudörffer entitled *Ein Gute Ordnung*, of twenty vellum leaves, is preserved in the Nuremburg Stadtsbibliotek (Hertel MS. 23).

Famed in Nuremburg as a writing master of the greatest skill, Neudörffer, the Elder, founded a family, several members of which were prominent calligraphers. Works by his son Johann, the Younger, and his grandson Anton are in this exhibition (nos. 84, 86–87).

Bibliography: Library of Congress, *The Rosenwald Collection. A Catalogue of Illustrated Books* . . . , Washington, D. C., 1954, p. 97, no. 484; Werner Doede, *Schön Schreiben, eine Kunst; Johann Neudörffer und Seine Schule im 16 und 17 Jahrhundert*, Munich, 1957; *idem., Bibliographie Deutscher Schreibmeisterbücher von Neudörffer bis 1800*, Hamburg, 1958, pp. 38–39; Albert Kapr, *Johann Neudörffer der Älte, der Grösse Schreibmeister der Deutschen Renaissance*, Leipzig, 1956.

## *Johann Neudörffer, the Younger*

GERMANY 1543–1581

84 MS COPY-BOOK SPECIMENS. PART I
Nuremburg, 1575 and 1584.
In Italian, German, and French. 10 vellum leaves, 6$\frac{5}{16}$× 9⅛ inches. Brown ink with flourished initials ornamented with gold; in five places polychrome initials from another MS have been attached over the original pen and ink initials. Binding: S. Cockerell.
*Lent by Mr. Mark Lansburgh*

This and the following entry (no. 85) at one time formed an album of calligraphic specimens by four German scribes: J. Neudörffer, the Younger, Christopher Balthasar, Georg Peschell, and Ryverding. As re-bound, the first part contains leaves by Neudörffer, the Younger (ff. 1r–10r), with a page by Balthasar (f. 10v), dated 1584, nine years later than the dated Neudörffer leaf.

Originally a single volume, it is known from the dated leaves that the four scribes worked on the album at different times over a period of at least sixty-three years. Consequently the manuscript illustrates principal examples of German renaissance calligraphy as the fraktur script evolved, based on earlier designs by scribes such as Neudörffer, the Elder (no. 83).

## *Georg Peschell*

GERMANY ACTIVE 1571–1586

85 MS COPY-BOOK SPECIMENS. PART II
Nuremburg, 1584–1637.
In Italian, German, and French-Dutch. 8 vellum leaves, 6$\frac{15}{16}$×9⅛ inches. In brown ink with flourished initials ornamented with gold. Binding: S. Cockerell.
*Lent by Mr. Mark Lansburgh*

The second part of the album consists of leaves by Christopher Balthasar (ff. 1r, 1v, 2r, 2v, 3r), Georg Peschell (ff. 3r,

4v, 5r, 5v, 6r), and Ryverding (ff. 6v, 7r, 7v, 8r, 8v). In each case the scribe has dated his work: Balthasar, 1584; Peschell, 1586; and Ryverding, 1637. Ff. 3 and 6 each contain writing by two different calligraphers, indicating that the album was worked on by various masters over the course of the sixty-three years of its known use.

## *Anton Neudörffer*

GERMANY DIED 1628

86 SCHREIBKUNST...
Nuremburg, 1601 and 1631 editions in one volume, Paul Kauffman (Erster Teil), Simon Halbmeyer, and Johan Pfann (Das Ander Theil), printers and engravers.
In German. Various scripts. 144 paper leaves, 7¾×6¼ inches. Woodcuts (Parts I and II) and engravings (Part III). Binding: contemporary vellum.
Provenance: presented by Johann Neudörffer to an ecclesiastical library in April 1632.
*Lent by The Walters Art Gallery*

The first two parts (46ff. with two folding plates, and 62ff.) illustrate writing tools, hand positions, and a number of alphabets of increasing elaboration. The third part (36ff.), an appendix published by Anton's son Johann, has engraved models of various current formal hands. The second section seems to be a collection of models in part by Anton and in part taken over from examples by his grandfather, Johann, the Elder.

Bibliography: Werner Doede, *Bibliographie Deutscher Schreibmeisterbücher von Neudörffer bis 1800*, Hamburg, 1958, pp. 52–53, 61.

87 MS COPY-BOOK
Nuremburg, 1598.
In Italian and German. 26 vellum leaves, 5¾×7¼ inches.
In dark brown ink with flourished initials in crimson, purple, or brown ink with gold heightening. Grotesques, putti, animals, floral garlands, and other decoration throughout. Binding: 17th century leather.
*Lent by Mr. Mark Lansburgh*

The manuscript is inscribed: "Antonius Neudörffer, Rechenmeister und Modist, A° 1598." Flourished initials of exceptional richness are a virtuoso display of the scribe's mastery in his art.

Bibliography: Mark Lansburgh, *An Illustrated Checklist of Ms. Leaves in The Collection of Mark Lansburgh*, Santa Barbara, 1962 (privately printed), pls. 13, 14.

## *E. F. F. von Glandorff*

GERMANY ACTIVE 1738

88 LETTERS PATENT GRANTING TITLE OF GRAF TO JOHN, ADOLF, AND FREDERICK VON BRÜHL
Berlin, 1738.
In German. Gothic script. 14 vellum leaves, 13½×9½ inches. Brown ink. Binding: crimson velvet.
*Lent by Mr. and Mrs. Harry A. Walton*

At the end of the manuscript is the signature of Charles VI of Germany, who, the previous year, had ennobled Heinrich von Brühl, brother to John, Adolf, and Frederick. The script is written with a light touch and generous spacing, each page being framed by an elaborate border

## *Cornelius Grapheus*

HOLLAND 1482–1558

89 LETTER TO ALBRECHT DÜRER
Antwerp, 1524.
Ms. Typ 1344. In Latin. Italic script. 1 paper leaf, 12½×8¾ inches.
Provenance: Willibald Pirckheimer.
*Lent by Mr. and Mrs. Philip Hofer*

The scribe, also Town Secretary of Antwerp, no doubt met Dürer while the artist was there in 1520–1521. In content the letter suggests that both men were secretly interested in the Protestant Reformation. Calligraphy may well have been a further bond between them, since in 1525 Dürer was to publish a treatise on constructed letter forms.

Bibliography: William Martin Conway, *Literary Remains of Albrecht Dürer*, Cambridge, England, 1889; Walters *Cat.*, 1949, no. 230; Harvard *Cat.*, 1955, no. 120 and pl. 59; Portland *Cat.*, 1958, no. 24.

## *Gerard Mercator*

HOLLAND 1512–1594

90 LITERARUM LATINARUM...
Antwerp, 1540, I. Richard.
In Latin. Italic script, with woodcut illustrations. 28 paper leaves, 7⅞×6¼ inches. Woodcuts.
*Lent by The Library of Congress (Lessing J. Rosenwald Collection)*

Chronologically Mercator's volume is the third treatise on italic script, being preceded by Arrighi in 1522 (no. 59) and Tagliente in 1524 (no. 63). Of the three manuals, Mercator's is the only one to be written entirely in Latin.

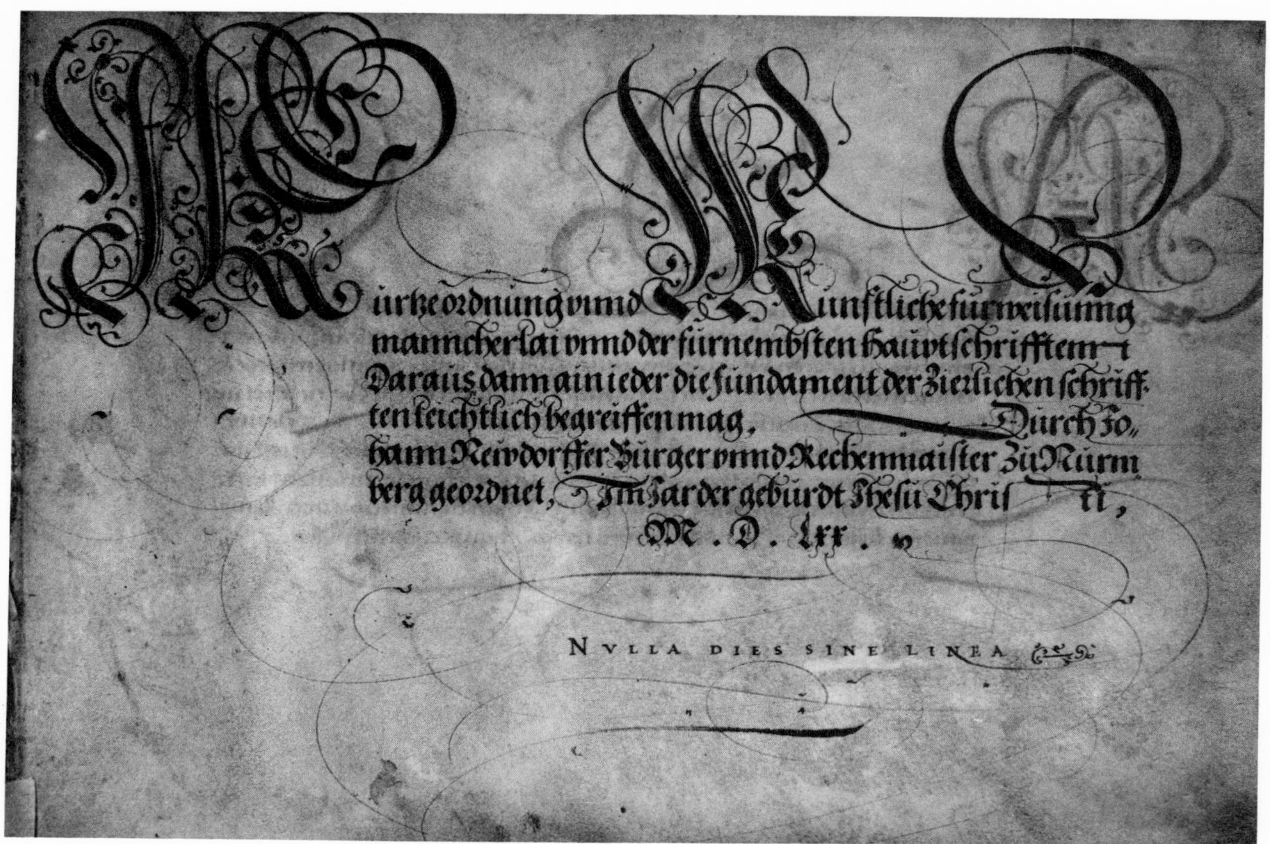


84 Johann Neudörffer, the Younger, *Copy-book Specimens. Part I*, Nuremburg, 1575 and 1584

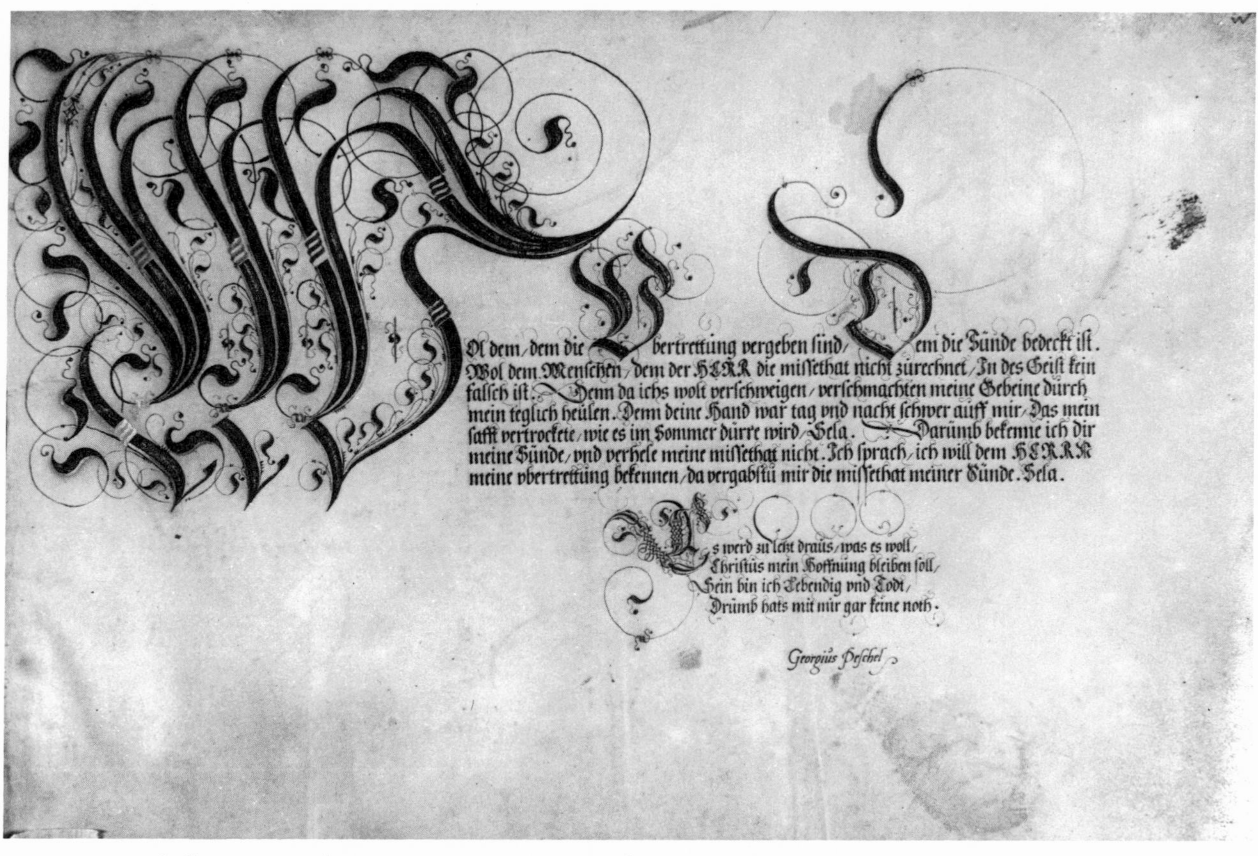


85 Georg Peschell, *Copy-Book Specimens. Part II*, Nuremburg, 1584–1637

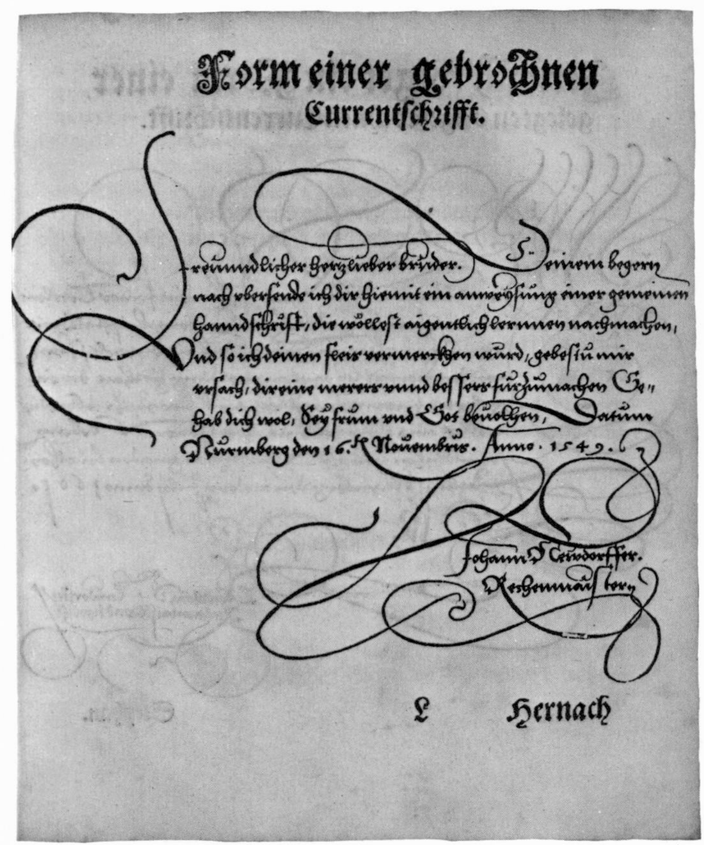


86 Anton Neudörffer, *Schreibkunst* . . . , Nuremburg, 1601 and 1631

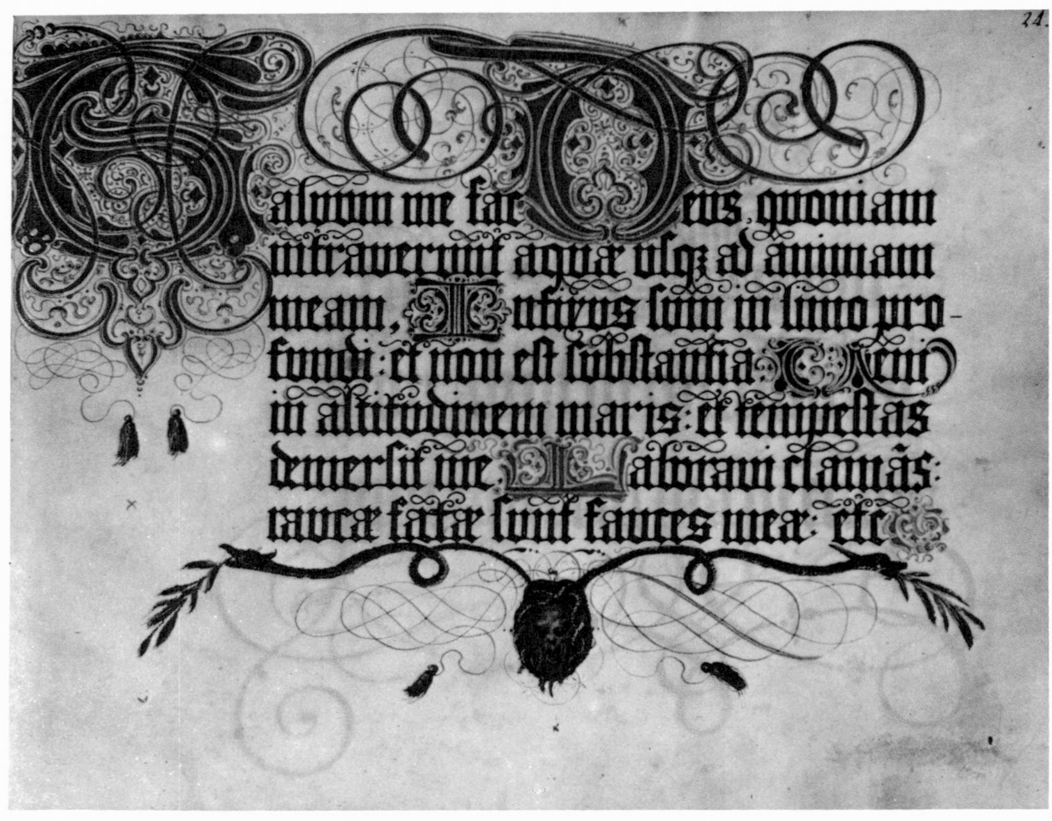


87 Anton Neudörffer, *Copy-Book*, Nuremburg, 1598

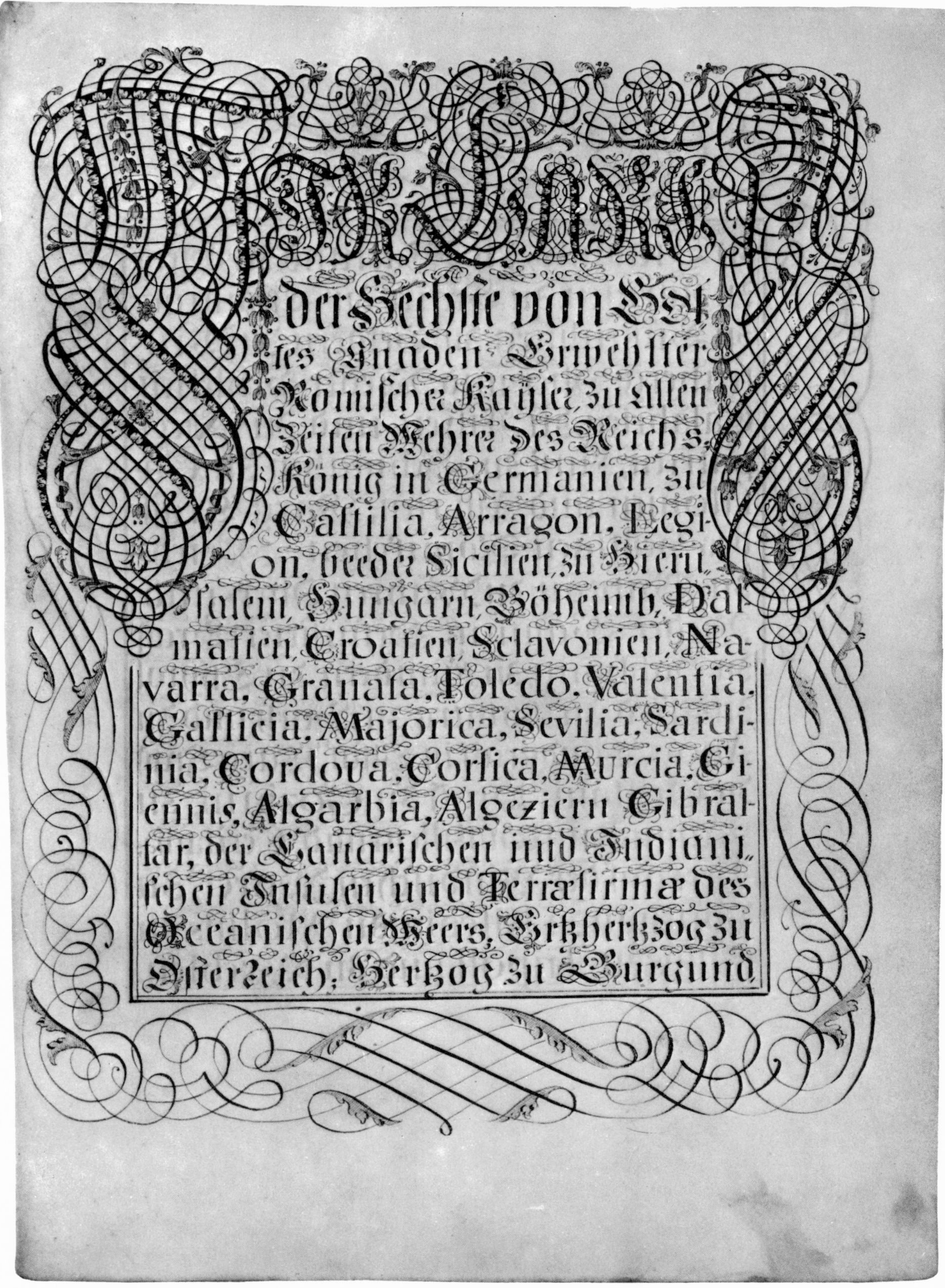
der Sechste von Got-
tes Gnaden Erwehlter
Römischer Kayser, zu Allen
Zeiten Mehrer des Reichs,
König in Germanien, zu
Castilia, Arragon, Legi-
on, beeder Sicilien, zu Hieru-
salem, Hungarn, Böheimb, Dal-
matien, Croatien, Sclavonien, Na-
varra, Granata, Toledo, Valentia,
Gallicia, Majorica, Sevilia, Sardi-
nia, Cordova, Corsica, Murcia, Gi-
ennis, Algarbia, Algeziern Gibral-
tar, der Canarischen und Indiani-
schen Insulen und Terræfirmæ des
Oceanischen Meers, Ertzhertzog zu
Osterreich, Hertzog zu Burgund

88 E. F. F. von Glandorff, *Letters Patent*, Berlin, 1738

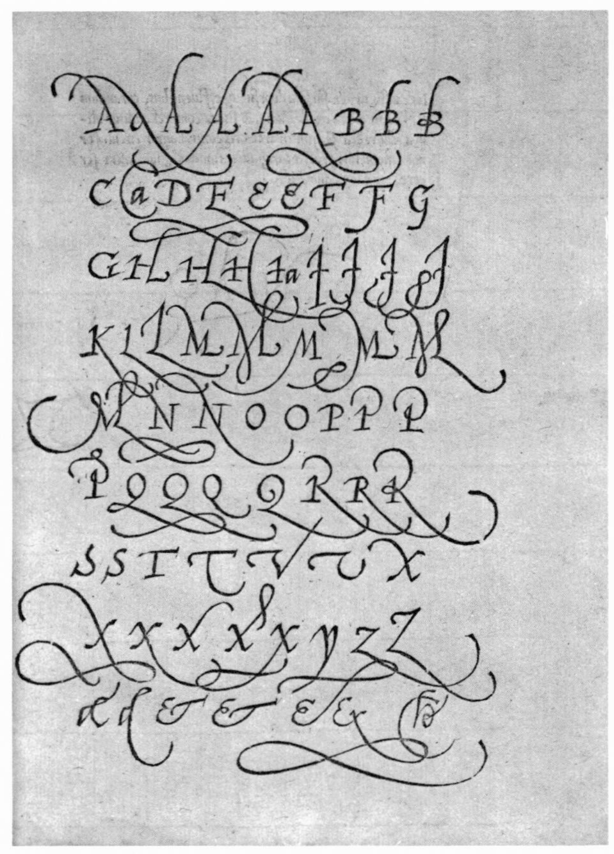

90 Gerard Mercator, *Literarum Latinarum . . .*, Antwerp, 1540

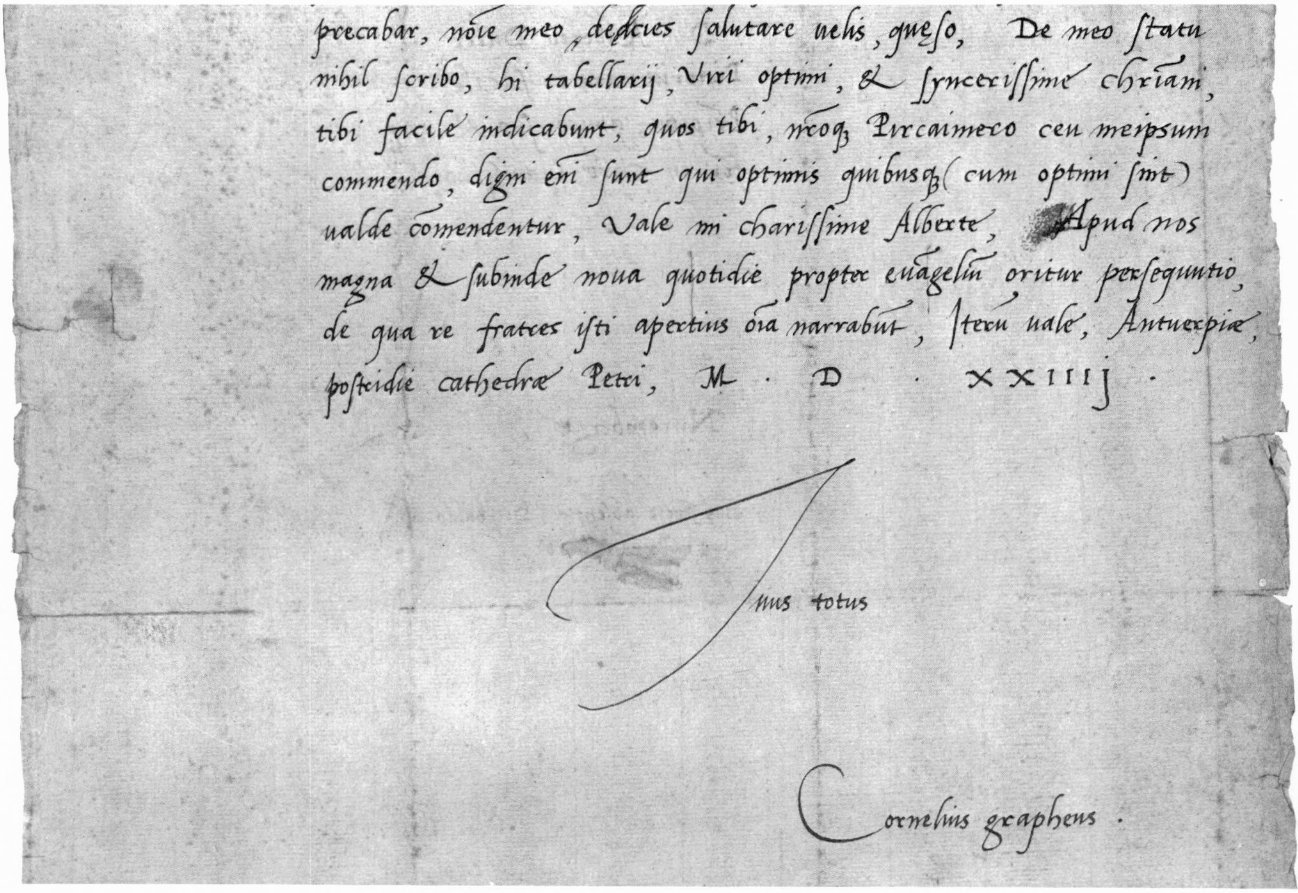

precabar, nõie meo, decies salutare uelis, queso, De meo statu
nihil scribo, hi tabellarij, viri optimi, & syncerissime christiani,
tibi facile indicabunt, quos tibi, meoq; Pircaimero ceu meipsum
commendo, digni eni sunt qui optimis quibusq; (cum optimi sint)
ualde comendentur, Vale mi charissime Alberte, Apud nos
magna & subinde noua quotidie propter euãgeliũ oritur persequutio,
de qua re fratres isti apertius oia narrabũt, Iterũ uale, Antuerpiæ,
postridie cathedræ Petri, M · D · XXIIIJ ·

Tuus totus

Cornelius grapheus .

89 Cornelius Grapheus, *Letter to Albrecht Dürer*, Antwerp, 1524

Famed as a cartographer and globe maker, Mercator also had to be a skilled calligrapher in order to engrave on his maps topographic names. The compressed character of italic script was ideally suited to the often confined spaces in which the cartographer worked.

Bibliography: *The Treatise of Gerard Mercator, LITERARUM LATINARUM . . .*, edited in facsimile with an introduction by Jan Denucé . . . and a note by Stanley Morison, Antwerp and Paris, 1930.

## *Jan I van de Velde*

HOLLAND 1568–1623

91 SPIEGHEL DER SCHRIJFKONSTE
Rotterdam, 1605.
In Dutch. Various scripts. 90 paper leaves, 8½×13¼ inches. Copperplate engravings and type. Binding: old stamped vellum.
Provenance: George A. Plimpton.
*Lent by The Columbia University Libraries*

Following Mercator's treatise (no. 90), van de Velde's copybook, described above, is usually considered the most important work on calligraphy to be printed in Holland. Van de Velde's scripts are a link between the *Italienne-bastarde* letters as seen in the Frenchmen Materot and Barbedor and the eighteenth century English round hand. Van de Velde enjoyed considerable fame as a calligrapher; one of his sons was the renowned artist Jan II.

Bibliography: Bonacini, 1931; Portland *Cat.*, no. 57.

## *David Roelands*

HOLLAND 1572–PROBABLY AFTER 1616

92 T'MAGAZIN OFT-PAC-HUYS...
Antwerp, 1616.
Paper leaves, 9½×14 inches. Copperplate engravings.
Binding: limp vellum.
Provenance: J. W. Six.
*Lent by The Library of Congress (Lessing J. Rosenwald Collection)*

In its lavish format, with handsomely engraved plates, this Dutch seventeenth century copy-book bears comparison to van de Velde's more famous manual (no. 91). Roelands' book is little known today, although one may assume that the work was a major publication since it rivals the best surviving calligraphy manuals of its time and place. The present copy comes from the library of the Six family, one of whose ancestors, Jan Six, befriended Rembrandt.

Almost nothing is known of Roelands' life other than his activity as a writing master in Antwerp and Vlissingen.

Bibliography: Bonacini, 1545.

## *Attributed to Geoffroy Tory*

FRANCE ABOUT 1480–1533

93 BOOK OF HOURS FOR USE OF BOURGES
France (Bourges), ca. 1510.
Ms.W.446. In Latin. Italic script. 93 vellum leaves, 6×3⅝ inches. 14 large and 4 small miniatures. Written in pen and brown ink with captions and liturgical indications in blue and red. The initials and line fillers are in matte gold on a brown ground. Binding: citron morocco, by Simier, early 19th century French.
Provenance: Jean Lallement, the Younger (d.1548); Cochran (1837), no. 46.
*Lent by The Walters Art Gallery*

The book was executed for Jean Lallement, the Younger, Seigneur de Marmagnac, who was Mayor of Bourges in 1510. In format the manuscript is close to a Book of Hours, also owned by Jean Lallement, the Younger, now in The Library of Congress (Lessing J. Rosenwald Collection). The Rosenwald manuscript has been attributed to the famous calligrapher and type-designer Geoffroy Tory. Both manuscripts are characterized by a beautiful script of great evenness and clarity.

Bibliography: De Ricci, I, p. 816, no. 341; Walters *Cat.*, 1949, no. 220.

## *Oronce Fine*

FRANCE 1494–1555

94 LA SPHERE DU MONDE
France, 1549.
Ms. Typ 57. In French. *Lettres bâtardes.* 70 paper leaves, 10×6¾ inches. Ink and watercolor, with maps, drawings, diagrams, and tables. Binding: modern black morocco, by Lortic, *fils.*
Provenance: Henri II; gift of Christian A. Zabriskie and Philip Hofer.
*Lent by Harvard College Library, Department of Printing and Graphic Arts*

The text is a translation in French of Finé's earlier *De Mundi*

*Sphaera*. The richly decorated manuscript was written for presentation to Henri II in an attempt to win the favor of the new monarch. In his time Finé's reputation among intellectuals was great, although his fame seems never to have brought him material rewards. In 1530 he became the first French Royal Mathematician, a position held until his death.

Bibliography: Harvard *Cat.*, 1955, no. 126 and pl. 65.

## *Pierre Hamon*

FRANCE ACTIVE BEFORE 1567

95 ALPHABET DE PLUSIERS SORTES DE LETTRES...

Paris, 1567, Robert Estienne.

In French. 39 paper leaves, plus 1 leaf of MS, 6¼×8⅝ inches. Copperplate engravings. Binding: 19th century quarter leather.

Provenance: Jost Creder of Solleure (1578); J. P. Poujade; H. Destailleur.

*Lent by The John M. Wing Foundation of The Newberry Library*

Although incomplete, this copy of Hamon's alphabet is of exceptional interest since it contains a manuscript leaf, probably by Hamon, used as copy for the engraver. The leaf is bound opposite the plate engraved from it. Hamon, the royal writing master and secretary to Charles IX, was accused of forging the monarch's signature and hung. His books were ordered destroyed and in consequence are extremely rare.

Bibliography: Bonacini 730 (variant?).

## *Lucas Materot*

FRANCE ACTIVE CA. 1608

96 LES OEUVRES

Avignon, 1608, I. Brameray.

Various scripts. 54 paper leaves, 7½×9⅞ inches. Type and copperplate engraving. Binding: contemporary limp vellum.

*Lent by Mr. James M. Wells*

Materot's *lettre bastarde* or *lettre Italienne-bastarde*, examples of which are in this book, is the source for the eighteenth-century English round hand and round text scripts as seen in books by Ayres (no. 113) and Snell (no. 115). The latter scripts have continued to influence handwriting into our own day.

Bibliography: Bonacini, 1138.

## *Jean I de Beaugrand*

FRANCE ACTIVE 1586–1601

97 PANCHRESTOGRAPHIE. EXEMPLES DE TOUTES LES SORTES D'ESCRITURES...

Paris, 1604.

In French. Various scripts. 67 paper leaves plus an additional dedicatory leaf, 7⅝×11¼ inches. Copperplate engravings and type. Binding: vellum on boards, stamped in gold with French royal arms.

Provenance: Louis XIII.

*Lent by Mr. and Mrs. Philip Hofer*

The author's son, Jean II de Beaugrand, presented this copy of his father's book to Louis XIII. An additional dedicatory page is bound between the second and third plates. Probably written ca. 1610–1615, Jean II hoped for a profitable commission. He seems to have inherited much of his father's skill, as shown by this sumptuous page, penned in gold on purple-tinted paper.

The dedicatory page mentions that for several years Jean I had worked in the service of Henry IV (1589–1610). The elder Beaugrand's several copy-books survive as evidence of his activity and great reputation.

## *Frère Didace*

FRANCE ACTIVE 1647

98 WRITING BOOK

Paris, 1647.

Ms. Typ 248 H. In Latin and French. Various scripts. 100 paper leaves, 6×4¼ inches. Written in gold and colors. Binding: contemporary citron morocco.

*Lent by Mr. and Mrs. Philip Hofer*

A prayer, *Litanie a l'Honore Beatissimae Virginis Mariae*, is written in an elaborate, large display script, with only a few words to each page. The composition of letters on the page is quite decorative, and seems to be uncommon for the time.

Little is known of the scribe aside from the inscription on this manuscript: "Par son Tres obeisant & Tres Obligé Serviteur Frere Didace de Paris pauvre petit Capucin tres Indigne. En nostre Convent de s Maretz a Vingt-huitiesme Decemb' 1647."

Bibliography: Walters *Cat.*, 1949, no. 233; Harvard *Cat.*, 1955, no. 145 and pl. 80.

## *Nicolas Jarry*

FRANCE ABOUT 1620–1674 (?)

99 OFFICE OF THE VIRGIN MARY

Paris, 1655.

In French and Latin. Erect and sloping roman script. 22

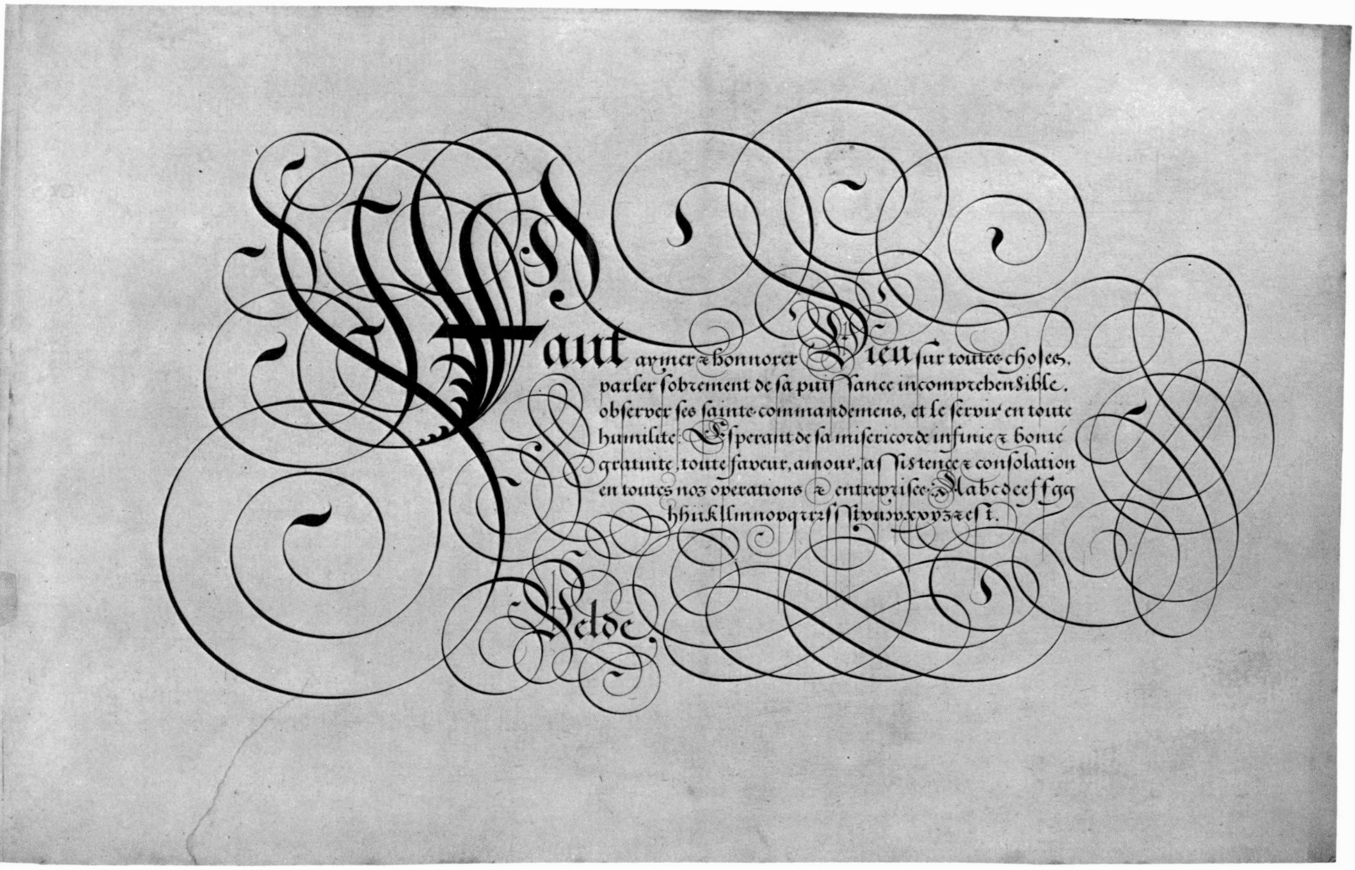

92 David Roelands, *T'Magazin Oft-Pac-Huys . . .*, Antwerp, 1616

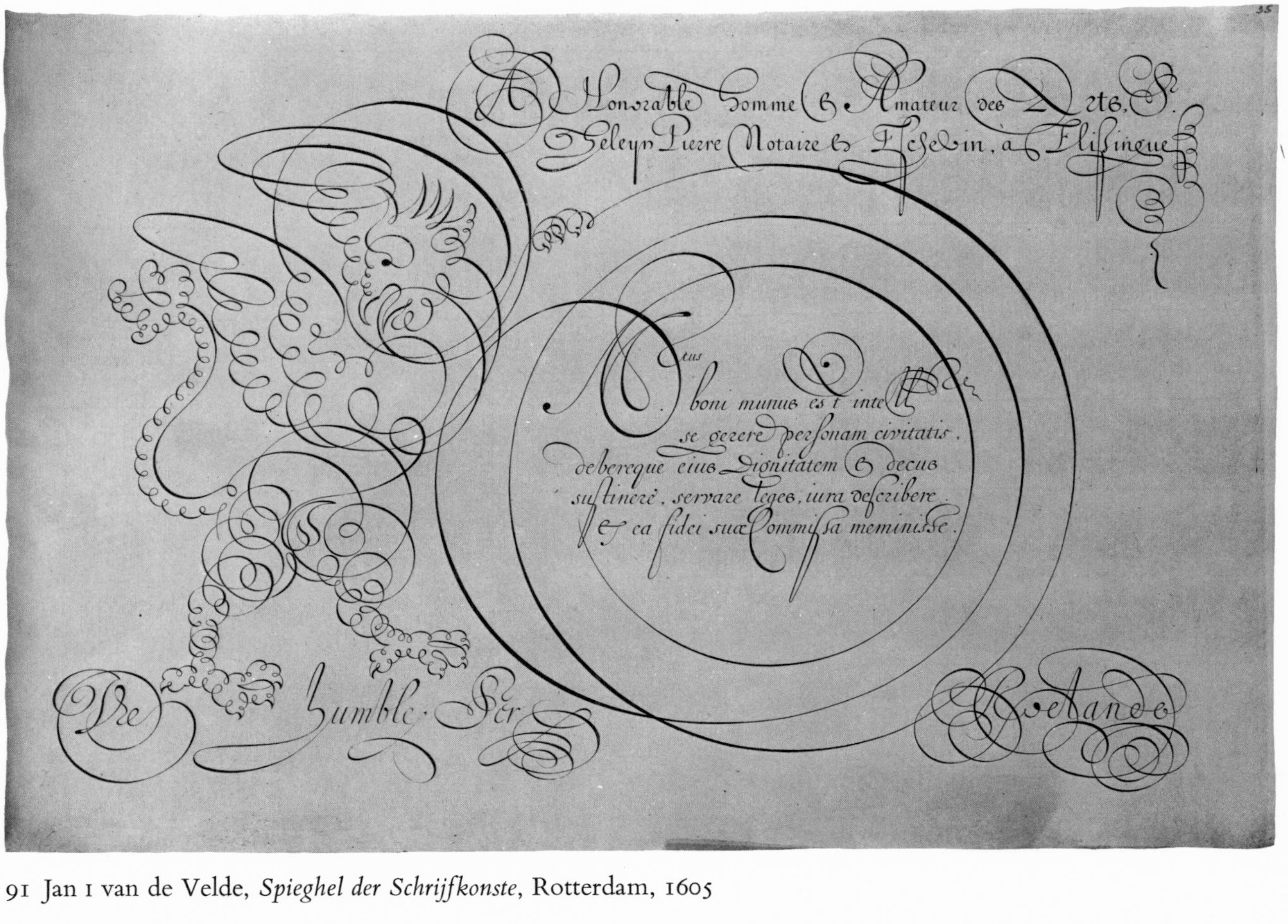

91 Jan I van de Velde, *Spieghel der Schrijfkonste*, Rotterdam, 1605

94 Oronce Finé, *La Sphere du Monde*, France, 1549

93 Attributed to Geoffroy Tory, *Book of Hours*, Bourges, ca. 1510

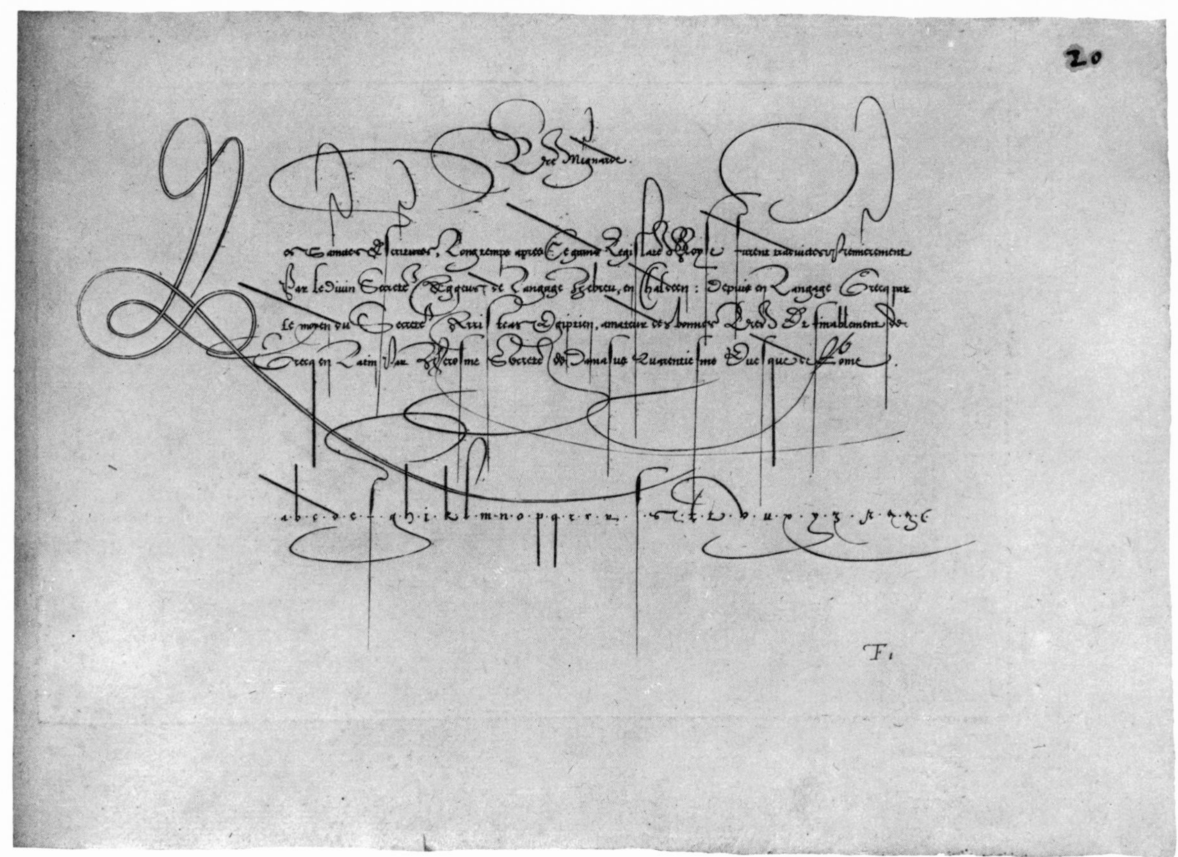

95 Pierre Hamon, *Alphabet . . .*, Paris, 1567

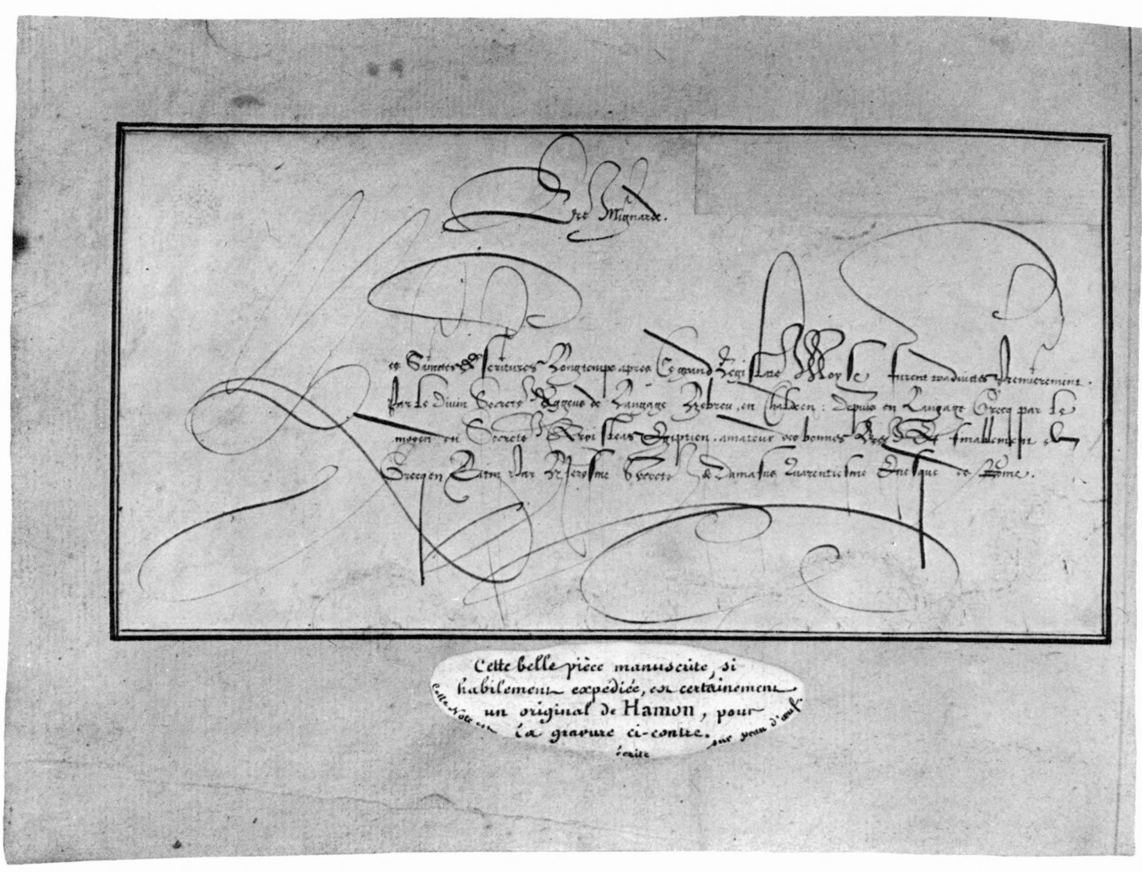


95 Pierre Hamon, *Alphabet . . .*, Paris, 1567

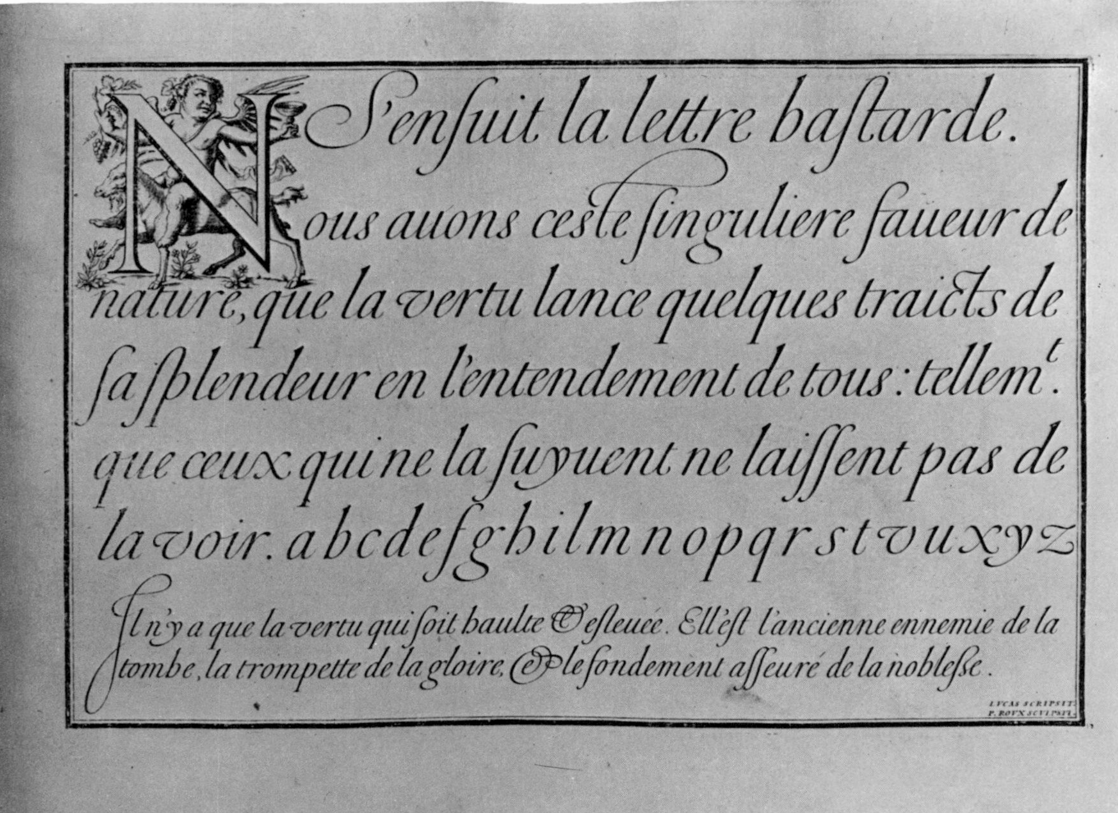

S'enſuit la lettre baſtarde.
Nous auons ceſte ſinguliere faueur de nature, que la vertu lance quelques traicts de ſa ſplendeur en l'entendement de tous: tellem^t. que ceux qui ne la ſuyuent ne laiſſent pas de la voir. a b c d e f g h i l m n o p q r s t v u x y z

Il n'y a que la vertu qui ſoit haulte & eſleuée. Ell'eſt l'ancienne ennemie de la tombe, la trompette de la gloire, & le fondement aſſeuré de la nobleſſe.

LVCAS SCRIPSIT.
P. ROVX SCVLPSIT.

96 Lucas Materot, *Les Oeuvres*, Avignon, 1608

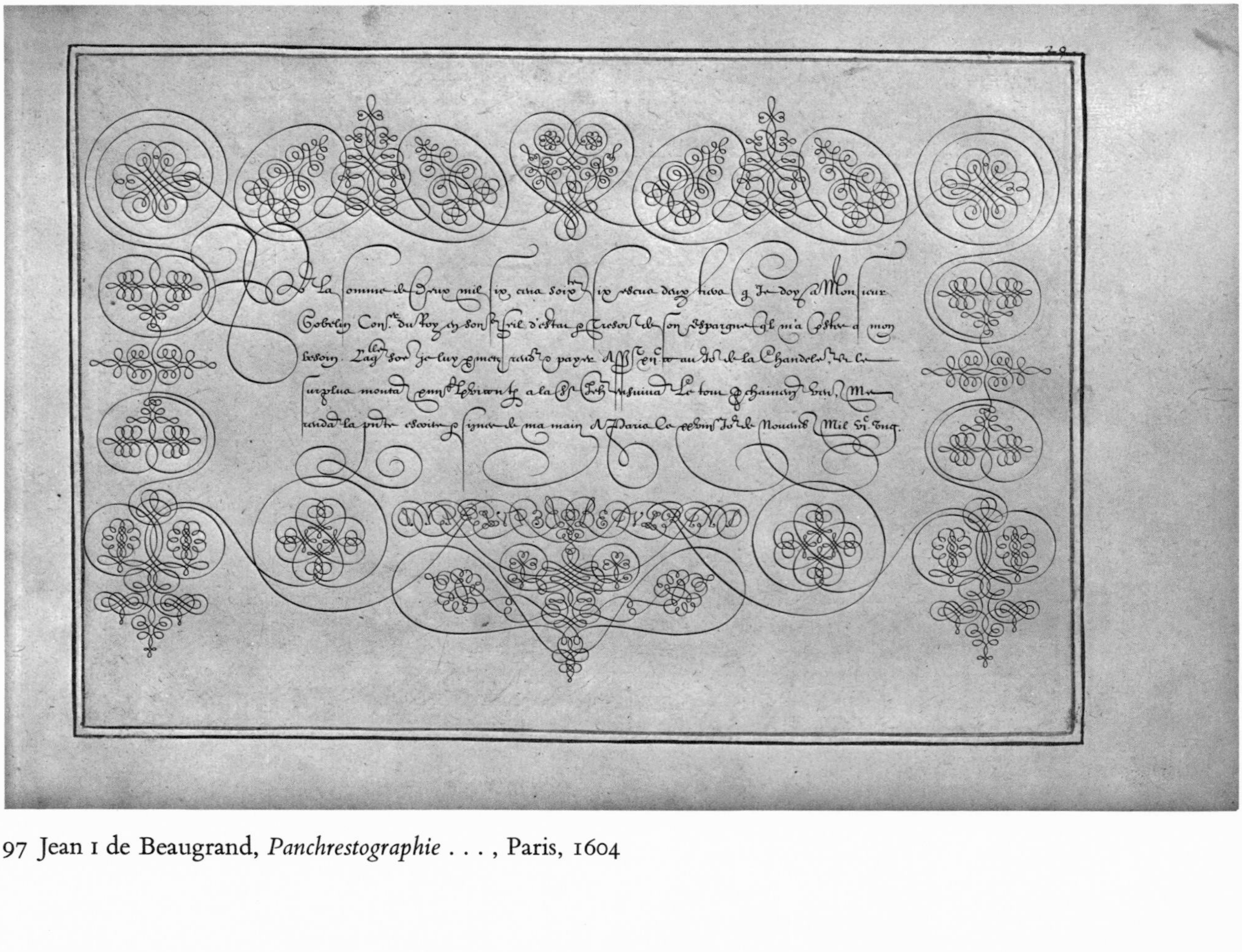

97 Jean I de Beaugrand, *Panchrestographie . . .*, Paris, 1604

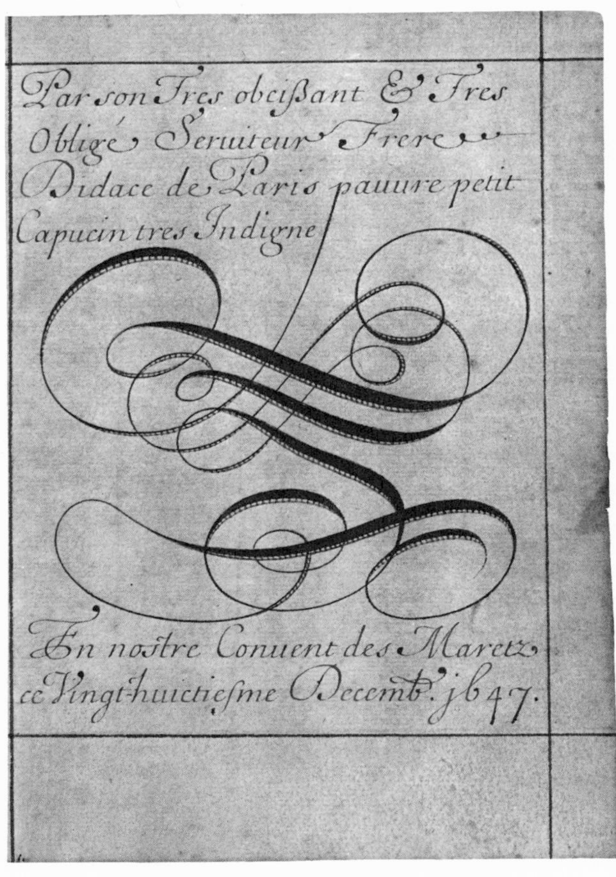

Par son Tres obeißant & Tres
Obligé Seruiteur Frere
Didace de Paris pauure petit
Capucin tres Indigne

En nostre Conuent des Maretz
ce Vingt-huictiesme Decemb. 1647.

98 Frère Didace, *Writing Book*, Paris, 1647

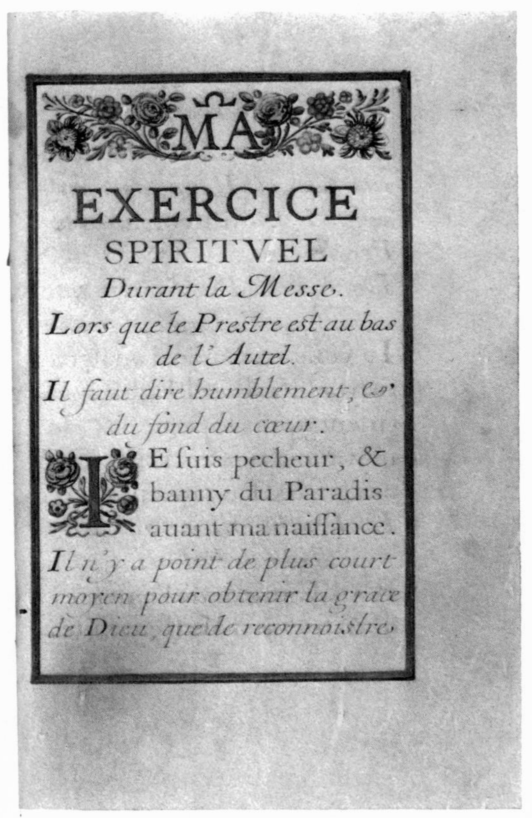

MA
EXERCICE
SPIRITVEL
Durant la Messe.
Lors que le Prestre est au bas
de l'Autel.
Il faut dire humblement, &
du fond du cœur.
IE suis pecheur, &
banny du Paradis
auant ma naissance.
Il n'y a point de plus court
moyen pour obtenir la grace
de Dieu, que de reconnoistre

99 Nicolas Jarry, *Office of The Virgin Mary*, Paris, 1655

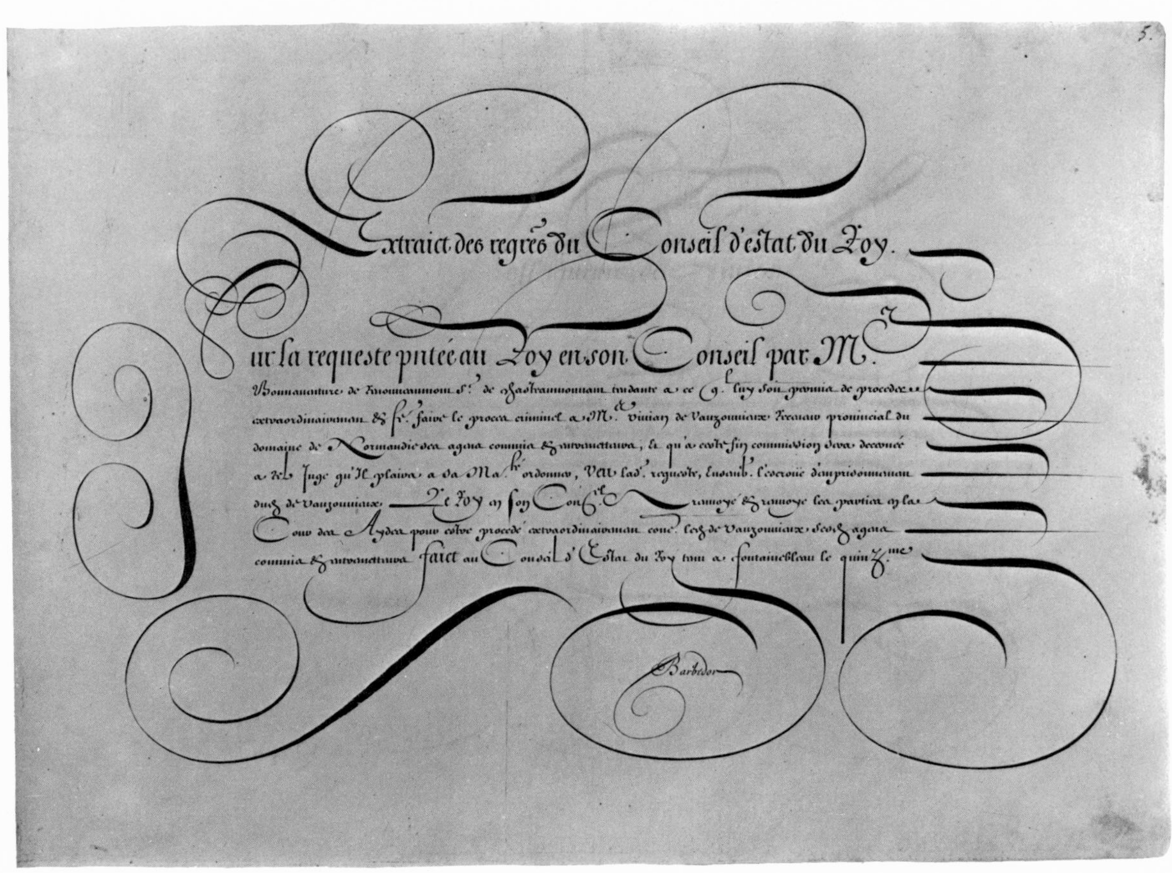

5.

Extraict des regres du Conseil d'estat du Roy.

Sur la requeste pntée au Roy en son Conseil par M.

Barbedor

100 Louis Barbedor, *Les Ecritures . . .*, Paris, ca. 1660

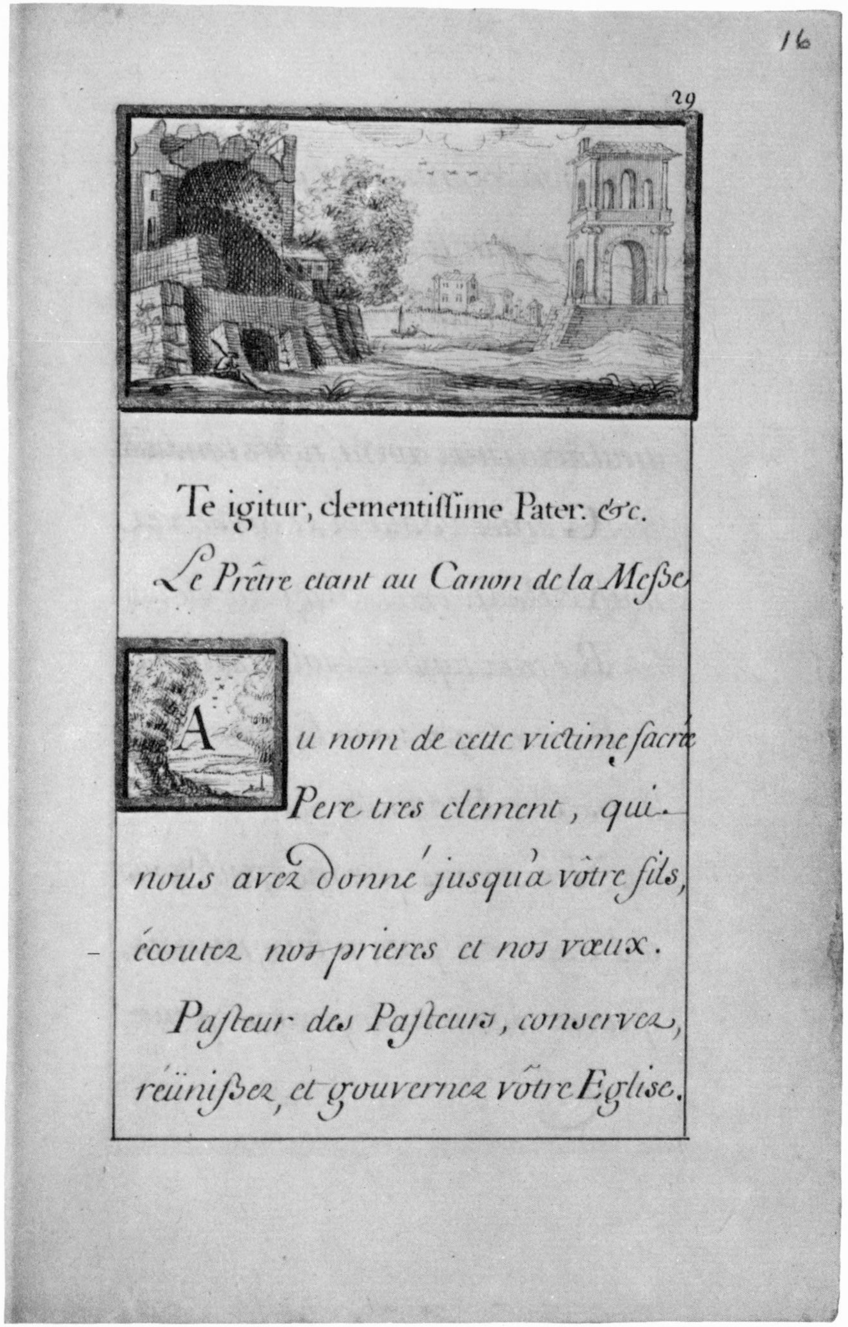

16

29

Te igitur, clementissime Pater. &c.

Le Prêtre etant au Canon de la Messe

Au nom de cette victime sacrée

Pere tres clement, qui

nous avez donné jusqu'à vôtre fils,

écoutez nos prieres et nos vœux.

Pasteur des Pasteurs, conservez,

réünissez, et gouvernez vôtre Eglise.

102 *Élévations de l'Âme* . . . , France (probably Paris), ca. 1700–1720

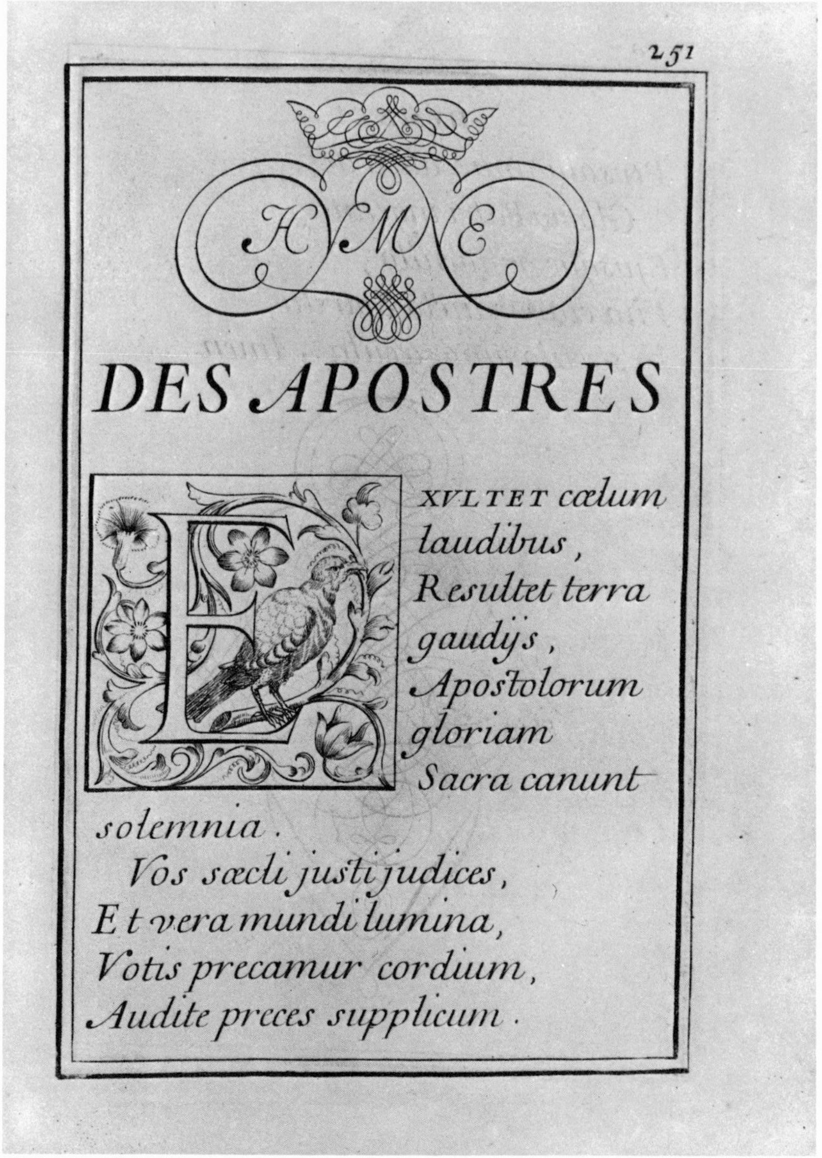

251

DES APOSTRES

EXULTET cœlum
laudibus,
Resultet terra
gaudijs,
Apostolorum
gloriam
Sacra canunt
solemnia.
Vos sæcli justi judices,
Et vera mundi lumina,
Votis precamur cordium,
Audite preces supplicum.

101 Louis Senault, *Heures Nouvelles* . . . , Paris

vellum leaves, 4 5/16×2 5/8 inches. Brown ink with colored inks and gold.
*Lent by Mr. and Mrs. Philip Hofer*

Using a delicate script of great refinement, Jarry has beautifully proportioned his letters to the limited space of the page, with no sense of crowding or loss of legibility. Typically, manuscripts by this calligrapher are small in format, although works in larger sizes are known.

Although little information about the scribe has survived, Jarry was the most renowned French calligrapher of his day. He worked for Louis XIV as "écrivain et noteur de sa musique."

Bibliography: Baron Roger Portalis, "Nicolas Jarry et la Calligraphie au XVIIe Siècle," *Bulletin du Bibliophile et du Bibliothécaire*, 1896.

## *Louis Barbedor*

FRANCE CA. 1589–1670

100 LES ECRITURES FINANCIERES ET ITALIENNE BASTARDE DANS LEUR NAIVITE...
Paris, ca. 1660, Nicolas Langlois.
In French and Latin. Various scripts. 52 paper leaves, 11¾×15¾ inches. Copperplate engraving and type.
Binding: modern.
Provenance: Alfred E. Hamill.
*Lent by The John M. Wing Foundation of The Newberry Library*

As one of the most important French calligraphers of the seventeenth century, Barbedor was given by Colbert, Louis XIV's financial secretary, the task of revising the scripts used in official documents and publications. Barbedor's scripts provide a link between the obsolete gothic cursives and the later development of the English round hand. His most famous book is *Les Ecritures . . .* , first published ca. 1647, in which the basis for the round hand is illustrated.

## *Louis Senault*

FRANCE ACTIVE 1669–1680

101 HEURES NOUVELLES DÉDIÉES A MADAME LA DAUPHINE...
Paris, no date.
In Latin and French. Sloping roman script with erect roman capitals, numerous engraved vignettes and culs-de-lampe. 132 paper leaves, 7⅜×4⅝ inches. Copperplate engravings.
Provenance: Marguerite Daniel, St. Cloud; Madame Charlet, 1697 (both old inscriptions).
*Lent by Miss Lilian Greif*

The elegant roman script of this book is ornamented with capitals framed by vignette landscapes or designs of birds or flowers. Calligraphic flourishes or floral designs frequently fill empty spaces at the bottom of a page. Prints by artists such as Israel Silvestre surely inspired the landscape vignettes which ornament the book and no. 102, a manuscript imitating a printed book of this style.

## *Anonymous*

102 ÉLÉVATIONS DE L'AME A DIEU DURANT LE SACRIFICE DE LA SAINTE MESSE
France (probably Paris, ca. 1700–1720).
Ms.W.507. In French. Sloping roman script with capitals in erect roman. 40 paper leaves, 6⅞×4⅝ inches. Pen and ink with gold on frames and initials. Binding: early 18th century French dark blue morocco with gilt tooling.
*Lent by The Walters Art Gallery*

The sixteen illustrations, numerous culs-de-lampe, historiated initials, and the script imitate engraved books by or in the style of Senault (no. 101). Another eighteenth century tour-de-force of writing in imitation of printing is in this exhibition (no. 78).

Bibliography: De Ricci, I, p. 817, no. 368.

## *Elizabeth I*

ENGLAND 1522–1603

103 LETTER TO KING EDWARD VI
Hatfield, ca. 1552–1553.
In English. Italic script. 1 paper leaf, 12½×17 inches.
Brown ink.
Provenance: Major F. A. V. Parker
*Lent by Mr. and Mrs. Philip Hofer*

Because Princess Elizabeth expresses anxiety for the health of her brother, King Edward VI, her letter is thought to date from 1552 or 1553, when Edward had been seriously ill. The letter was written April 21st, but is undated. Elizabeth would then have been about twenty years old when she wrote this letter. Her accomplished hand was formed under the tutorship of Roger Ascham, one of the foremost scribes of his time.

## *Jean de Beauchesne*

FRANCE 1538 (?)–AFTER 1610

and

## *John Baildon*

ENGLAND ACTIVE 1570

### 104 A BOOKE CONTAINING DIVERS SORTES OF HANDS

London, 1570, Thomas Vautrouiller.
In English. Various scripts. 37 paper leaves, $5\frac{3}{16}\times7\frac{1}{2}$ inches (lacks 9 leaves, dedication, and letter press). Woodcuts. Binding: modern green morocco.
Provenance: George A. Plimpton.
*Lent by The Columbia University Libraries*

Beauchesne, a Huguenot immigrant, has the honor of authoring the first copy-book to be printed in English. This book, described above, first appeared in 1570, edited and translated into English by John Baildon or Basildon, who otherwise is unknown. The copy here exhibited is the only surviving example of the first edition.

Bibliography: Heal, p. 127.

### 105 CALLIGRAPHIC SPECIMENS

England, 1575.
Ms. Typ 232 H. In Latin and French. 7 different scripts. 1 paper leaf, $18\frac{3}{4}\times12\frac{5}{8}$ inches.
*Lent by Mr. and Mrs. Philip Hofer*

This specimen of Beauchesne's mastery of various hands is on a blank leaf near the end of a copy of Schedel's *Nuremburg Chronicle* of 1493. The manuscript leaf is signed in reverse, or mirror image, writing and dated December 7, 1575.

Bibliography: Harvard *Cat.*, 1955, no. 135 and pl. 68; Portland *Cat.*, 1958, no. 39.

### 106 MS COPY-BOOK

England, ca. 1610.
In French and Italian. Various scripts. 28 vellum and paper leaves, $4\frac{5}{16}\times6\frac{5}{8}$ inches. Ink with gold. Binding: 18th century (?) calf.
Provenance: probably H. Sykes, Manchester; Thomas Herbert Noyes; C. L. Ricketts.
*Lent by The John M. Wing Foundation of The Newberry Library*

This copy-book was written for Elizabeth of Bohemia, daughter of James I. Beauchesne, her writing master, proudly notes on the colophon that he was in his seventy-third year when he wrote the book. Beauchesne was co-author, with John Baildon, of the first writing-book printed in England, *A Booke Containing Divers Sortes of Hands . . .* (no. 104).
Bibliography: probably the MS referred to in Heal, p. 128; National Book League, *In Praise of Italic*, 1954, no. 158.

## *John Scottowe*

ENGLAND ACTIVE LATE 16TH CENTURY

### 107 MS COPY-BOOK

England (probably Norfolk), 1592.
In English. Various scripts. 23 paper leaves, brown ink, $5\frac{7}{8}\times7\frac{7}{8}$ inches. Binding: modern.
Provenance: C. L. Ricketts.
*Lent by The John M. Wing Foundation of The Newberry Library*

The manuscript consists of a set of maxims, alphabetically arranged, each beginning with an ornamental capital. Signed and dated by Scottowe, the book illustrates a variety of hands. To judge from the capitals, the scribe was an accomplished draftsman with, at times, a lively sense of humor.

Little is known of Scottowe's life other than his activity as a schoolmaster, most probably at Norwich, attached to the Parish of St. Michael at Plea. In 1597 he was excommunicated for teaching without a license.

Bibliography: Bond and Faye, *Supplement*, p. 156, Wing no. 7.

## *Esther Inglis*

ENGLAND 1571–1624

### 108 ARGUMENTA IN LIBRUM PSALMORUM

England, 1606.
Ms. Typ 212 H. In Latin. Various scripts. 101 paper leaves, $4\times5\frac{3}{4}$ inches. Ink, numerous watercolor drawings, Egerton crest, and self-portrait of Esther Inglis. Binding: contemporary English brown calf, gilt.
Provenance: Sir Thomas Egerton; W. L. Boyne (1850); W. A. White (1915).
*Lent by Mr. and Mrs. Philip Hofer*

The manuscript is dedicated to Sir Thomas Egerton, Lord Chancellor of England, for whom it was evidently written. The minute but perfectly formed script ornamented with watercolor drawings is typical of the diminutive books in which this scribe specialized.

Bibliography: De Ricci, II, 1699, no. 30; Dorothy J. Jack-

What cause I had of sory when I harde first of your Maiesties siknes
al men migth gesse, but none but my selfe coulde fele, wiche to declare
wer or migth seme a point of flatery and therfore to write it I omit.
But as the sorow coulde not be litel, bicause the occasions wer many
so is the ioy gret to hire of the good escape out of the perillous disea=
ses. And that I am fully satisfied and wel assured of the same
by your graces owne hande I must nides giue you my most hūble
thankes assuring your Maiestie that a precious iewel at a nother
time could not so wel haue contented as your lettar in this case hathe
comforted me. For nowe do I say with Saint Austin that a dis=
ease is to be counted no siknes that shal cause a bettar helthe whan
it is past than was assured afore it came. for afore you had the
euery man thogth that that shulde not be eschued of you that was
not scaped of many. but sins you haue had the dout of the it is past
and hope is giuen to al men that it was apurgation by thes
menes for other wors diseases wiche migth happe this year.
Moreouer I cōsidar that as a good father that loues his childe derely
dothe punis him scharpely, So God fauoring your Maiestie gretly
hathe chastened you straitly, and as a father dothe it for the further good of
his childe, so hathe God prepared this for the bettar helthe of your grace.
And in this hope I commit your Maiestie to his handes most hūbly
crauing pardō of your grace that I did write no soner desiring
you to attribute the faute to my ill hed and not to my slothful
hande. Frō Hatfilde this 21 of April.

Your Maiesties most hūble
sistar to comande. Elizabeth

103 Elizabeth I, *Letter to King Edward VI*, Hatfield, ca. 1552–1553

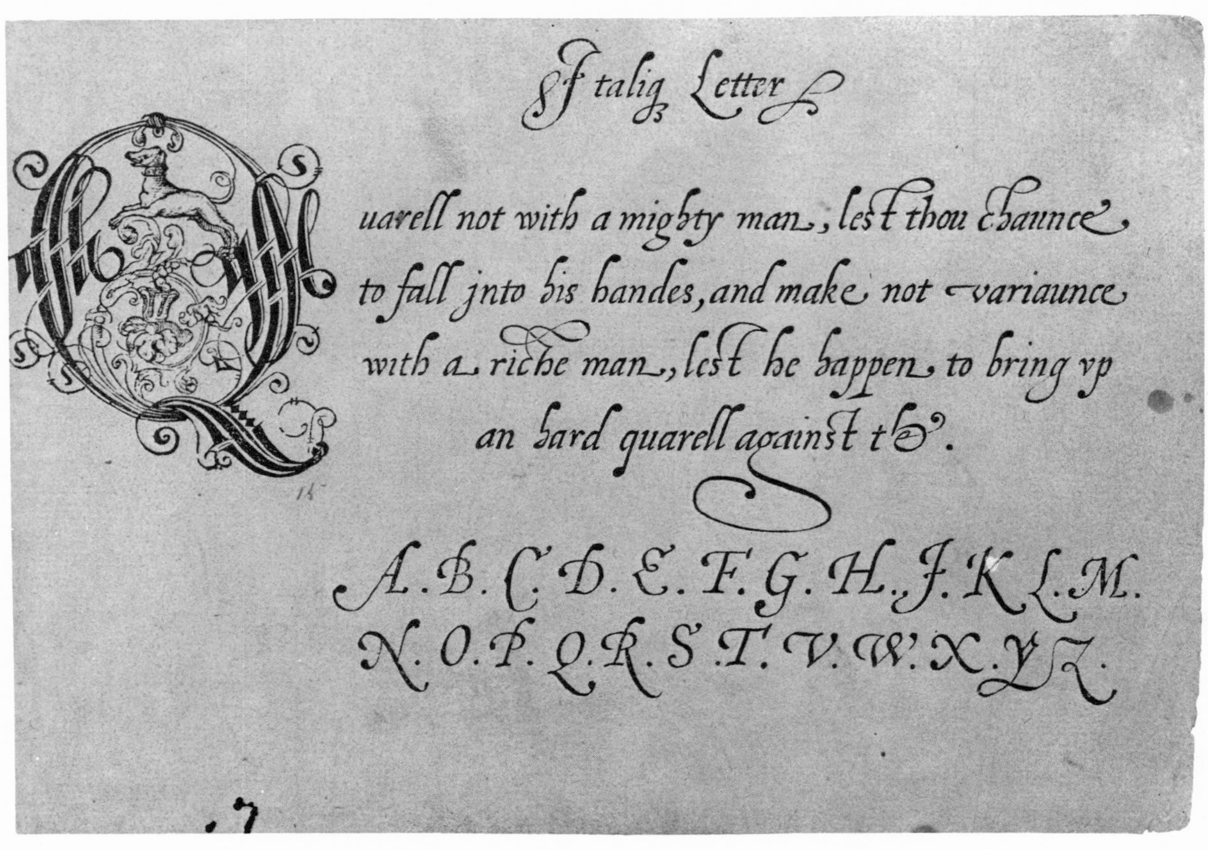

Italiq Letter

Quarell not with a mighty man, lest thou chaunce to fall jnto his handes, and make not variaunce with a riche man, lest he happen to bring vp an hard quarell against the.

A. B. C. D. E. F. G. H. J. K. L. M.
N. O. P. Q. R. S. T. V. W. X. Y. Z.

104 Jean de Beauchesne, *A Booke . . .*, London, 1570

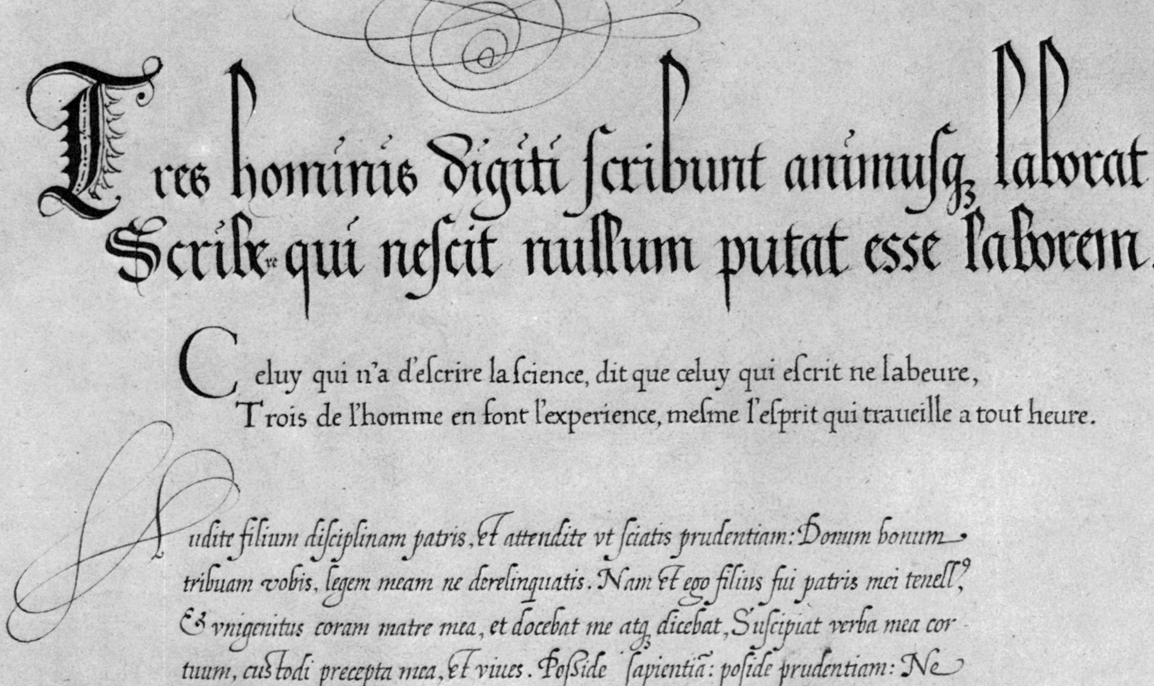

Tres hominis digiti scribunt animusq; laborat,
Scribere qui nescit nullum putat esse laborem.

Celuy qui n'a d'escrire la science, dit que celuy qui escrit ne labeure,
Trois de l'homme en font l'experience, mesme l'esprit qui traueille a tout heure.

Audite filium disciplinam patris, et attendite vt sciatis prudentiam: Donum bonum tribuam vobis, legem meam ne derelinquatis. Nam et ego filius fui patris mei tenell?, et vnigenitus coram matre mea, et docebat me atq; dicebat, Suscipiat verba mea cor tuum, custodi precepta mea, et viues. Posside sapientiā: poside prudentiam: Ne obliuiscaris neq; declines a verbis oris mei. Ne dimittas eam et custodiet te. Sal. Pro.

105 Jean de Beauchesne, *Calligraphic Specimens*, England, 1575

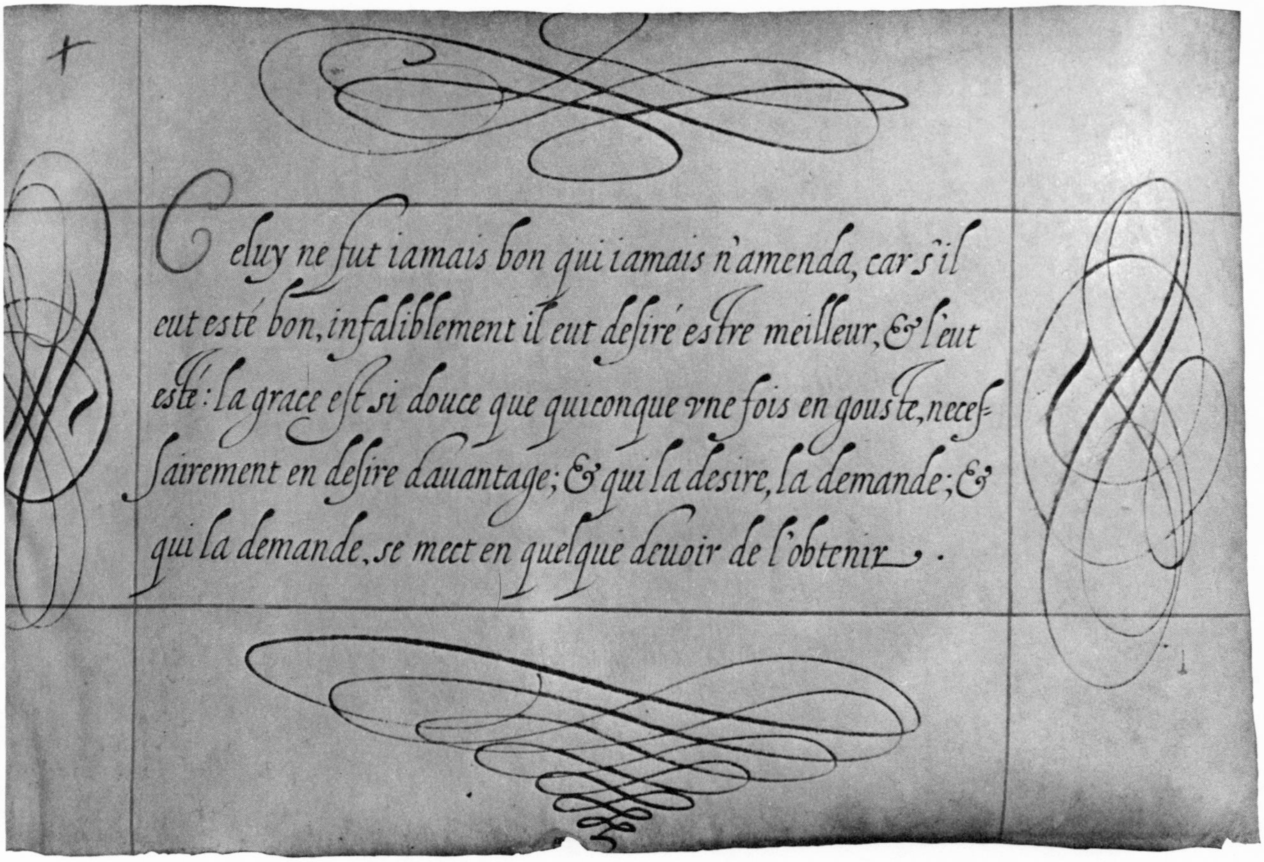

Celuy ne fut iamais bon qui iamais n'amenda, car s'il eut esté bon, infaliblement il eut desiré estre meilleur, & l'eut esté: la grace est si douce que quiconque vne fois en gouste, neces-sairement en desire dauantage; & qui la desire, la demande; & qui la demande, se meet en quelque deuoir de l'obtenir.

106 Jean de Beauchesne, *Copy-Book*, England, ca. 1610

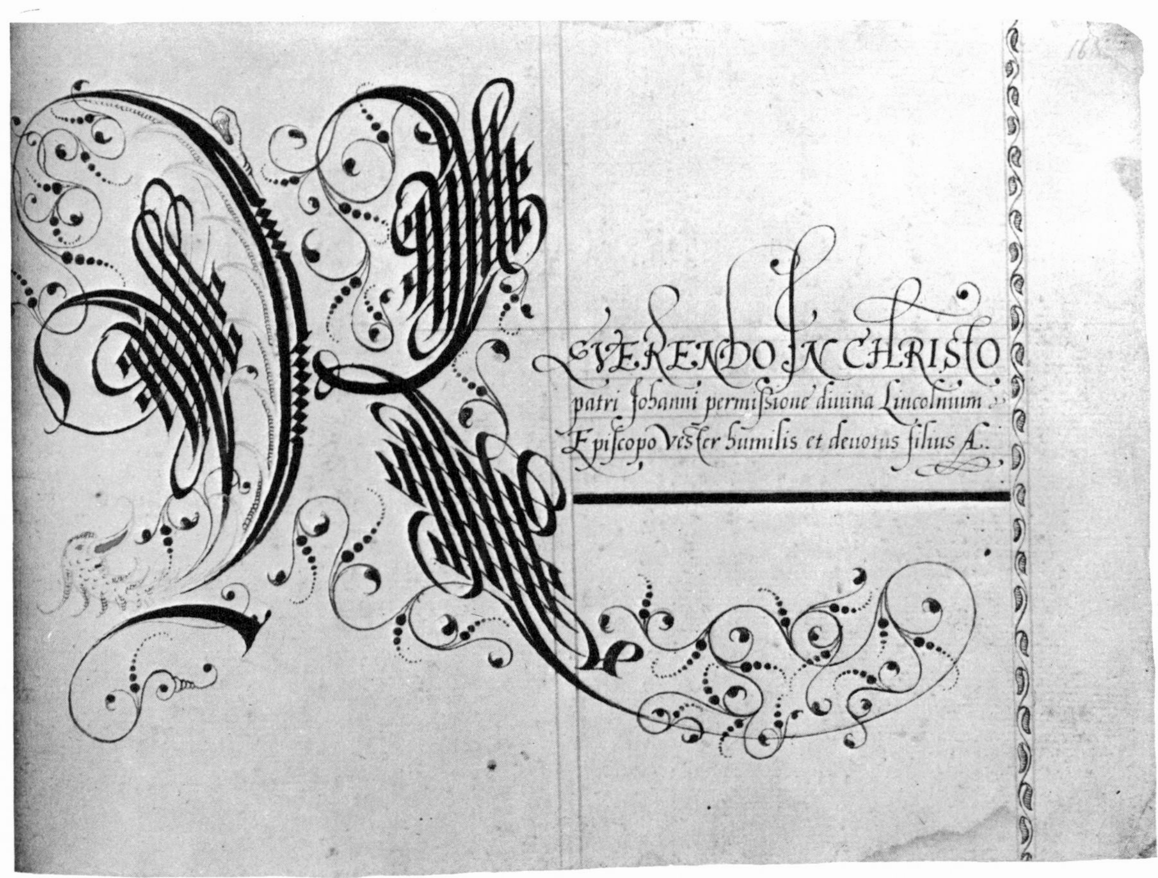


107 John Scottowe, *Copy-Book*, England, ca. 1592

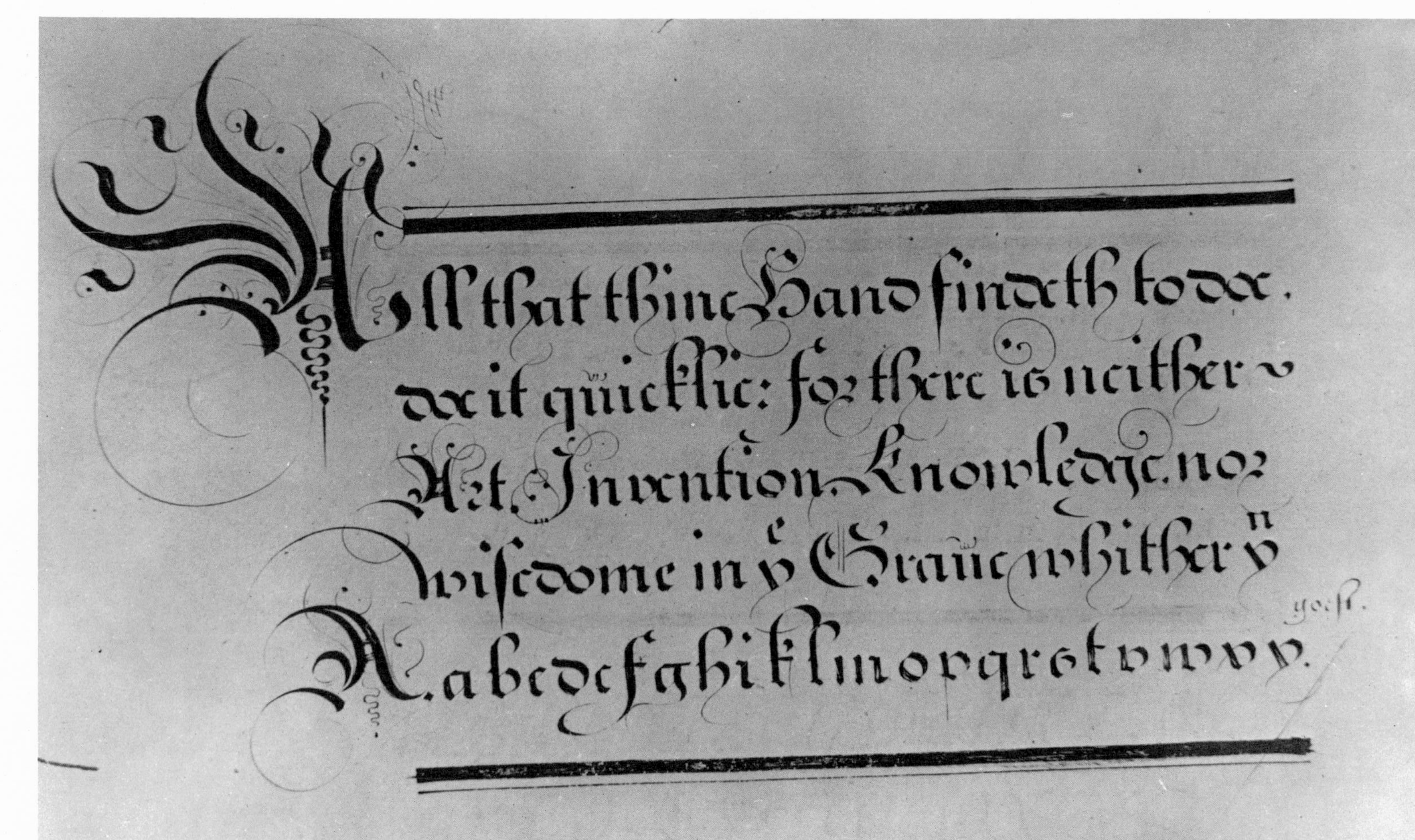


109 Martin Billingsley, *The Pen's Excellencie . . .*, London, 1618

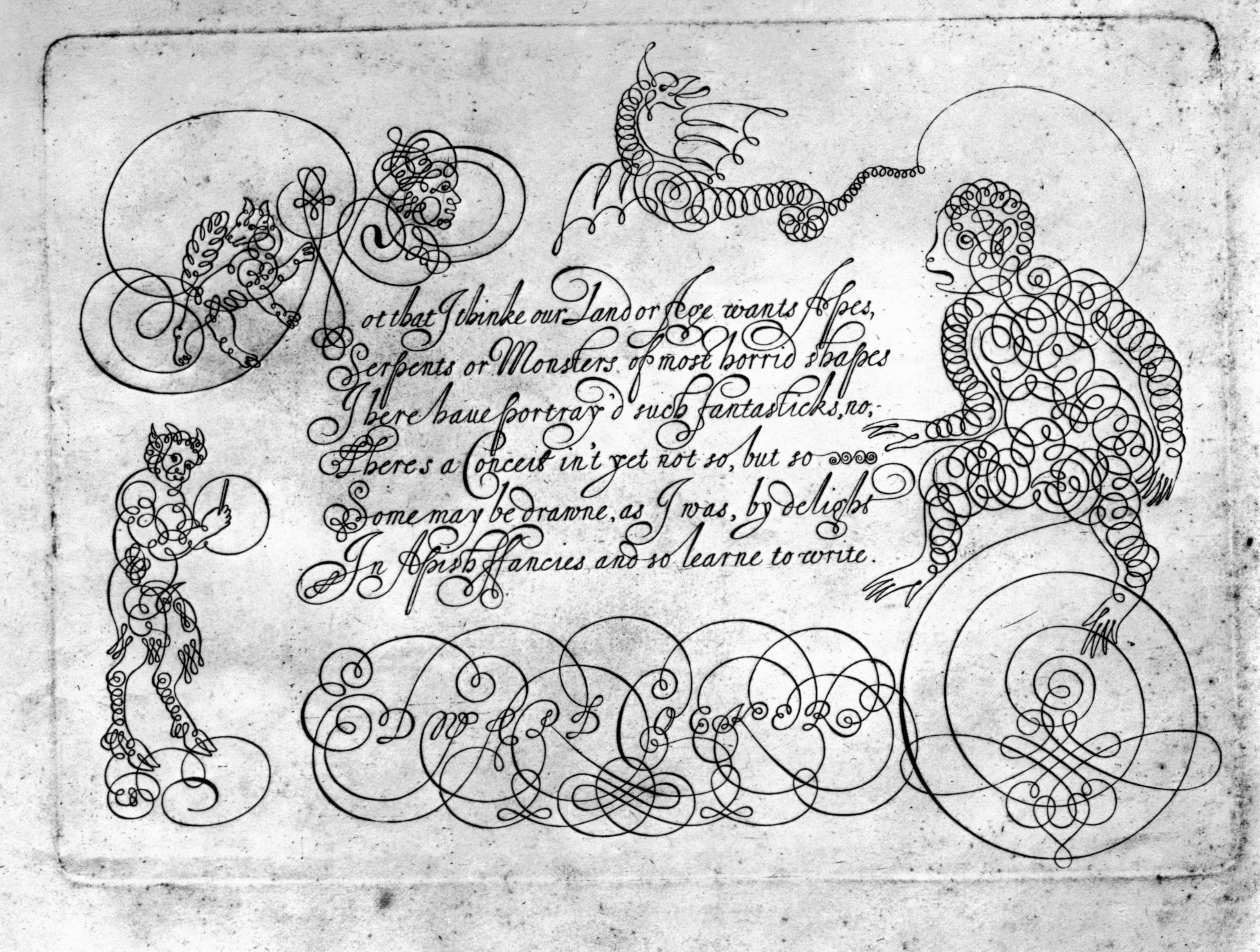


110 Edward Cocker, *The Pen's Transcendencie . . .*, London, 1657

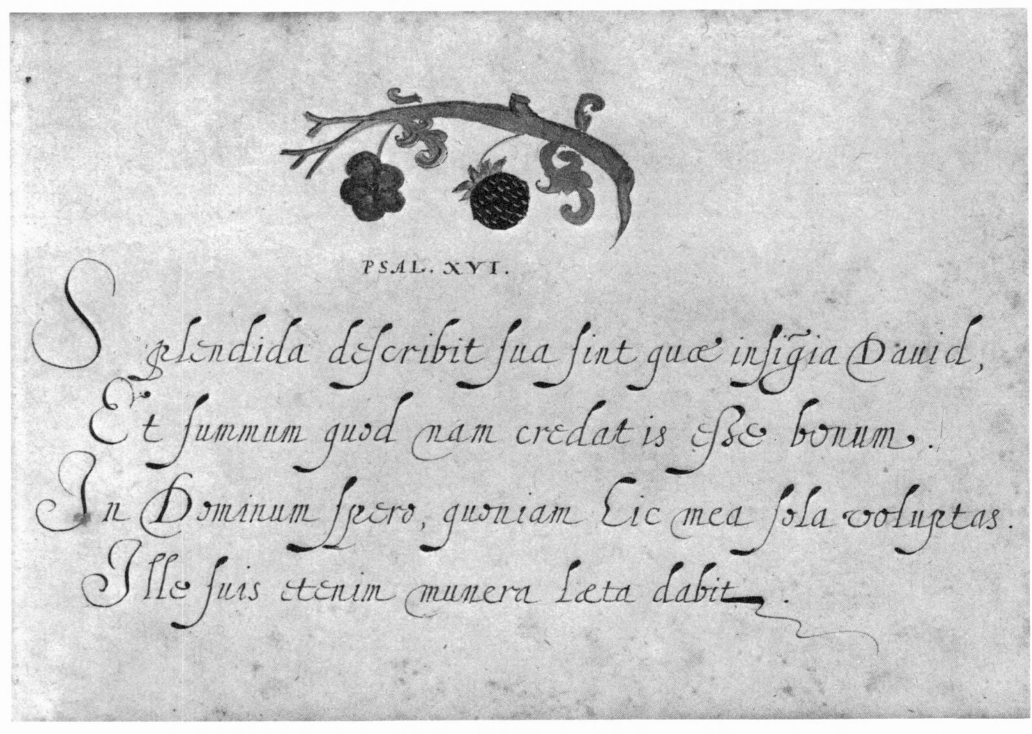


108 Esther Inglis, *Argumenta In Librum Psalmorum*, England, 1606

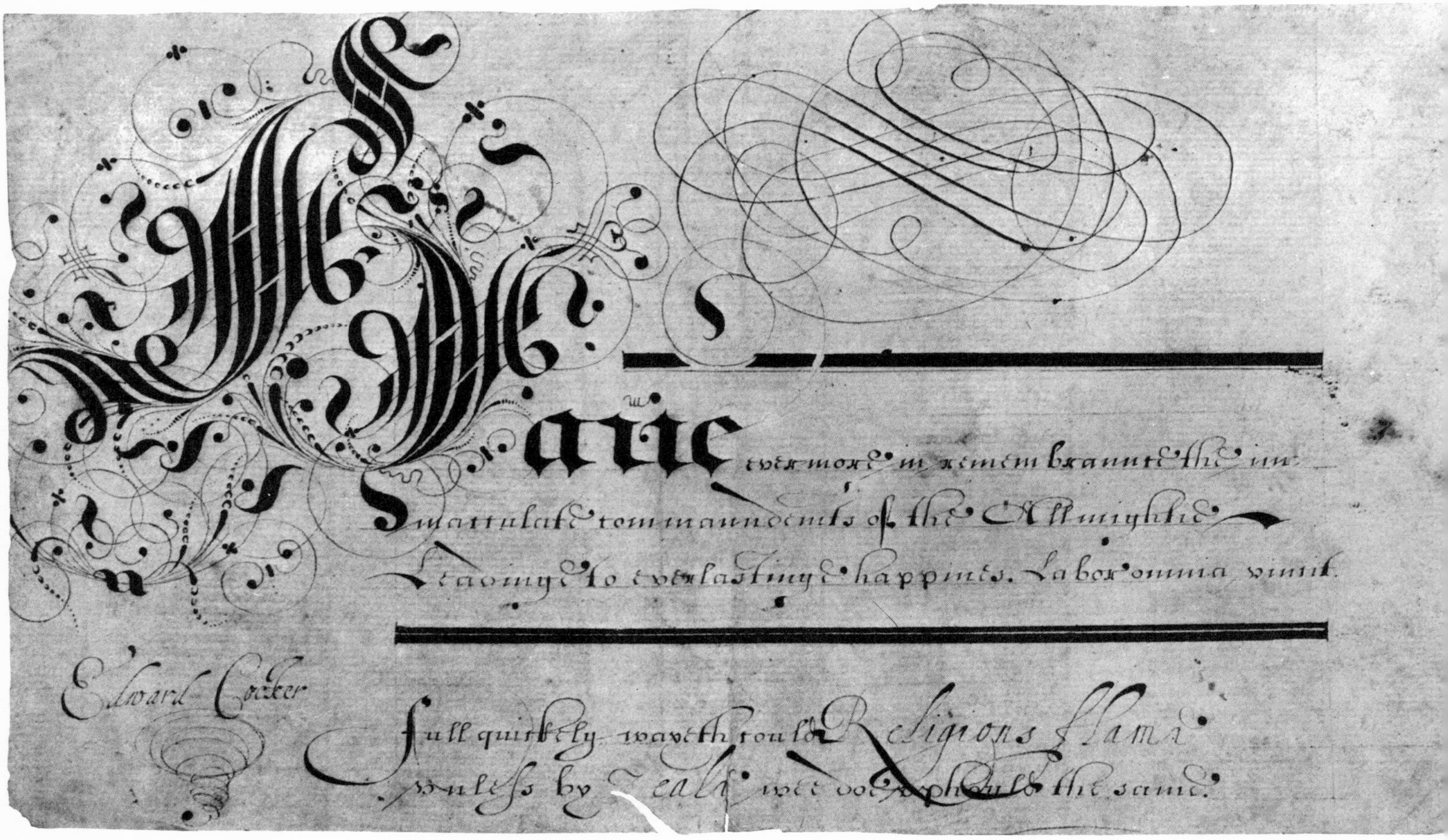

111 Edward Cocker, *Copy-Slip*, England

son, *Esther Inglis . . .*, 1937, no. 18; Walters *Cat.*, 1949, no. 232; Harvard *Cat.*, 1955, no. 143 and pl. 69.

## *Martin Billingsley*

ENGLAND 1591–1622

109 THE PEN'S EXCELLENCIE OR THE SECRETARIES DELIGHT...
London, 1618, George Humble.
In English. Various scripts. 41 paper leaves including 28 plates, 5½×7¼ inches. Copperplate engravings. Binding: half morocco.
*Lent by The Metropolitan Museum of Art (Gift of Felix Warburg, 1928)*

If one considers that Beauchesne (no. 104) was actually a Frenchman, then Billingsley's treatise described above may be regarded as the first English copy-book of any extent. The volume, Billingsley's first published work, is dedicated to King Charles I, whom the scribe tutored in calligraphy.

In his short life Billingsley composed three calligraphy manuals. He is one of the outstanding penmen of his day, and had justifiable pride in his skill. Few London scribes could match his performance, which led Billingsley to preface this volume with a virulent attack against his contemporary rivals.

Bibliography: Heal, p. 131.

## *Edward Cocker*

ENGLAND 1631–1676

110 THE PEN'S TRANSCENDENCIE; OR, FAIRE WRITINGS LABYRINTH
London, 1657.
In English. Various scripts. 31 paper leaves including one folding plate, 7½×10¼ inches. Copperplate engravings. Binding: marbled boards and calf spine.
Provenance: Sir Ambrose Heal.
*Lent by The Victoria and Albert Museum*

This is the most richly ornamented of the over two dozen copy-books produced by Cocker. The number of his publications alone would draw attention to their author, who was famed for his writing and widely admired for the complex calligraphic designs which ornament his copy-books.

The better part of Cocker's life was spent as a schoolmaster. Among his colleagues he was well known as the author of a highly popular textbook of arithmetic. So many editions of Cocker's text were printed that an unscrupulous publisher attached the scribe's name to a number of textbooks, hoping to enhance their sale.

Bibliography: Heal, p. 136, no. 3 a.

111 MS LEAF, "HAVE EVERMORE IN REMEMBRANCE"
England, undated.
In English. 1 paper leaf, 4¾×8¼ inches. Brown ink.
*Lent by The John M. Wing Foundation of The Newberry Library*

This elaborately flourished copy-slip is one of two by Cocker in The Newberry Library, both of which were most likely once part of a copy-book. The example exhibited is signed.

## *John Seddon*

ENGLAND 1644–1700

112 PENMAN'S PARADISE
London, 1695 (?).
In English. Various scripts. 34 paper leaves, 8¾×14 inches. Copperplate engravings.
Provenance: George A. Plimpton.
*Lent by The Columbia University Libraries*

Seddon's fame rests, at least in part, on his great facility in "striking"—the production of figures and flourishes by elaborate interlacing pen strokes, using no underdrawing as a guide. The swelling line possible in engraving led to the corresponding use of a pen cut so as to produce lines of greatly varying width. By the seventeenth century such virtuoso displays of penmanship are commonplace. The mastership of Sir John Johnson's Free Writing School, held by Seddon until his death, thereupon passed to Charles Snell (no. 115), the leader of a reaction against elaborately flourished writing.

Bibliography: Heal, p. 157.

## *John Ayres*

ENGLAND ACTIVE 1680–1705

113 A TUTOR TO PENMANSHIP
London, 1698 (?).
In English. Various scripts. 52 paper leaves, 9⅞×16⅛ inches. Copperplate engravings.
Provenance: George A. Plimpton.
*Lent by The Columbia University Libraries*

Ayres, the most eminent writing master of his day, in this,

his major work, argues that the use of copperplate engravings has been a stimulus to the calligrapher, since script may be easily reproduced by engraving. One of Ayres' best known champions was Samuel Pepys, an ardent collector of calligraphy. The latter's three folio volumes, now in the Pepysian Library of Magdalene College, Cambridge, contain plates from the copy-books of celebrated writing masters down to Pepys' day. The folios are a major early source for our knowledge of both English and continental calligraphy manuals.

Bibliography: Heal, pp. 151–152.

## *George Shelley*

ENGLAND 1666 (?)–1736 (?)

114 THE PENMAN'S MAGAZINE
London, 1705, Thomas Read.
In English. Various scripts. 20 paper leaves, 15⅞×10⅜ inches. Copperplate engravings. Binding: stitched, without covers.
Provenance: George A. Plimpton.
*Lent by The Columbia University Libraries*

Shelley's first published essay on penmanship is this volume of 1705. In style it is based on Seddon, who, according to the preface, began the designs for *The Penman's Magazine* but died before finishing them. Although famed in his time, little is known of Shelley's early career. He may have been interested in mathematics as well; later he won the important appointment as Master of the Writing School in Christ's Hospital.

Bibliography: Heal, p. 166.

## *Charles Snell*

ENGLAND 1667–1733

115 THE ART OF WRITING IN ITS THEORY AND PRACTICE
London, 1712, Henry Overton.
In English. 70 paper leaves, 8⅞×14¼ inches. Copperplate engravings and type.
Provenance: George A. Plimpton.
*Lent by The Columbia University Libraries*

Snell led a reaction against the elaborate "strikings" exemplified by the works of Seddon and Shelley (nos. 112, 114). This book is his first printed attack and plea for greater purity in writing. Two years later Snell published a treatise on the proportions and formation of letters.

Bibliography: Heal, p. 161.

## *George Bickham, Senior*

ENGLAND 1684–1758 (?)

116 THE UNIVERSAL PENMAN...
London, 1743, H. Overton.
In English. Various scripts. 212 paper leaves, 16½×10½ inches. Copperplate engravings. Binding: contemporary calf, rebacked.
*Lent by Mr. Wilmarth S. Lewis*

Issued in fifty-two parts between 1733 and 1741, this volume contains calligraphic designs by twenty-five contemporary scribes, all the plates being engraved by Bickham. Eighteen of the 212 plates seem to have been engraved by Bickham from his own designs. A scribe of considerable talent, he was also famed as an engraver of calligraphy. This is his monumental work, a compendium of all scripts then in current use in England. Bickham's publication came at a time when English handwriting was universally recognized. The round hand, ideal for commercial use, spread throughout Europe as England's expanding trade brought her into communication with other nations.

Little is known of Bickham's early life. He had a son, George Bickham, Junior, who was also a calligrapher. Bickham, Senior, was active as an engraver, but also gave drawing lessons.

Bibliography: Heal, pp. 171–172; George Bickham, Sr., *The Universal Penman*, Foreword by Philip Hofer, New York, 1941.

## *Abiah Holbrook, Junior*

AMERICAN COLONIES 1718–1769

117 THE WRITING MASTER'S AMUSEMENT
Boston, 1767.
Ms. in English. Various scripts. 25 paper leaves, 10½×16 inches. In ink and watercolor.
Provenance: bequest of Mrs. Rebecca Holbrook, 1795.
*Lent by the Harvard College Library, Department of Printing and Graphic Arts*

A petition of 1741 to open a school to teach writing and arithmetic contains the first mention of Holbrook, Jr. in the Boston town records. Soon after his petition was granted he was appointed master of the South Writing School, Boston. Calligraphy was a major concern of Holbrook's, and a number of examples by him exist to prove his skill. None is more splendid than the present volume, a collection of Scriptural quotations written, in Holbrook's words, to demonstrate his knowledge of ". . . all the Hands of Great

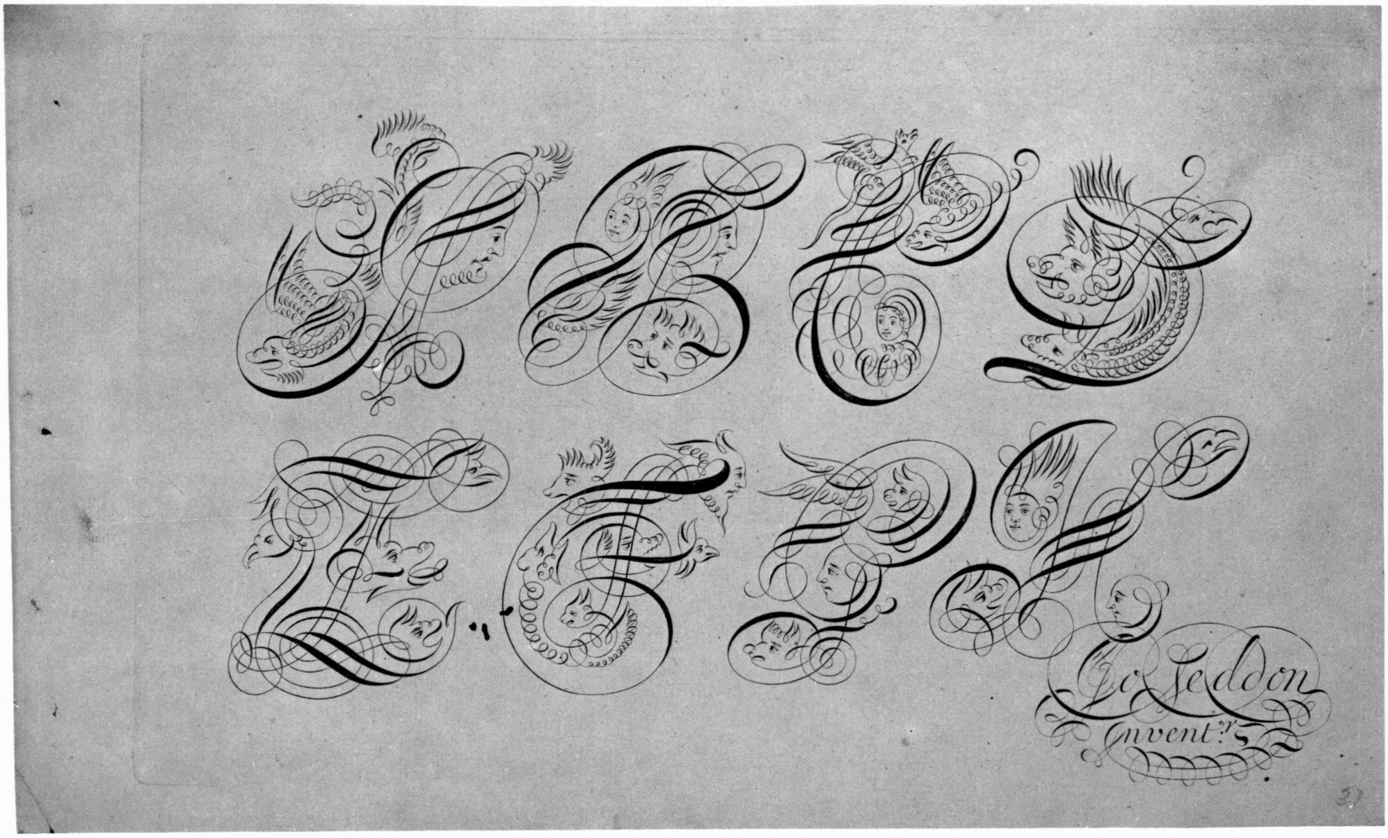

112 John Seddon, *Penman's Paradise*, London, 1695 (?)

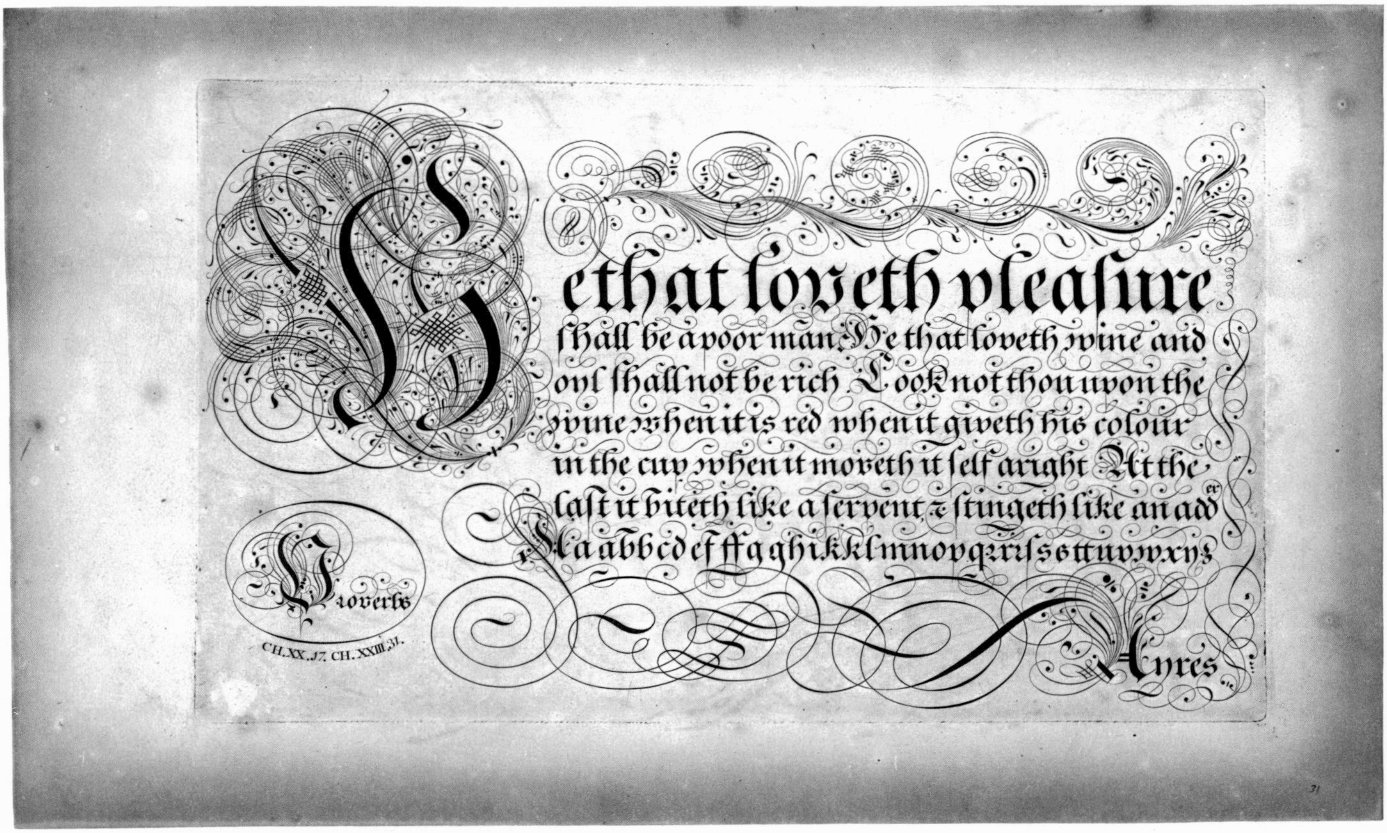

113 John Ayres, *A Tutor to Penmanship*, London, 1698 (?)

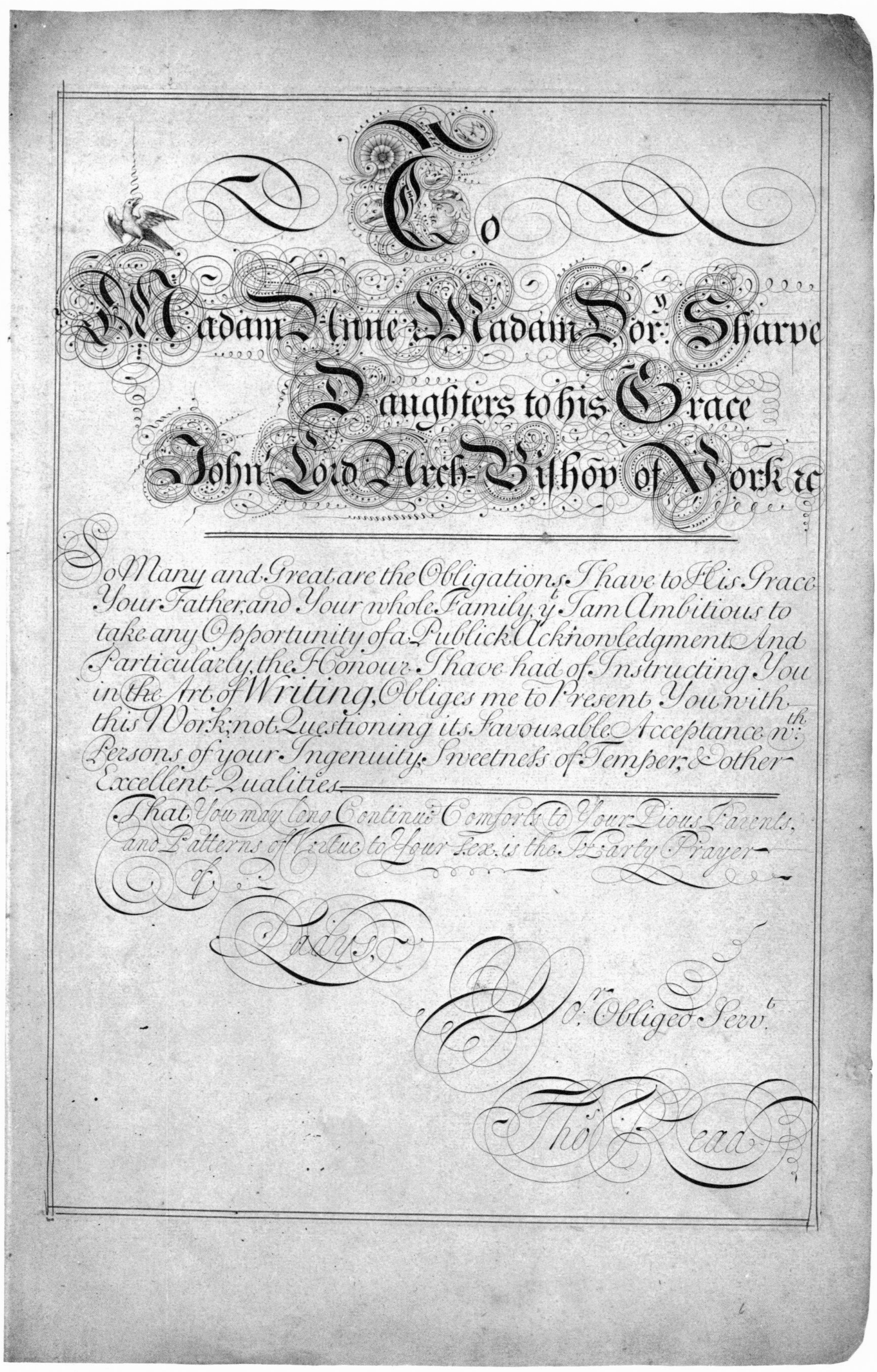

To
Madam Anne & Madam Dor:y Sharpe
Daughters to his Grace
John Lord Arch-Bishop of York &c

So Many and Great are the Obligations I have to His Grace Your Father, and Your whole Family, yt I am Ambitious to take any Opportunity of a Publick Acknowledgment. And Particularly the Honour I have had of Instructing You in the Art of Writing, Obliges me to Present You with this Work; not Questioning its Favourable Acceptance wth Persons of your Ingenuity, Sweetness of Temper, & other Excellent Qualities.

That You may long Continue Comforts to Your Pious Parents, and Patterns of Vertue to Your Sex, is the Hearty Prayer of

Ladys,

Yor: Obliged Servt.

Tho: Read

114 George Shelley, *The Penman's Magazine*, London, 1705

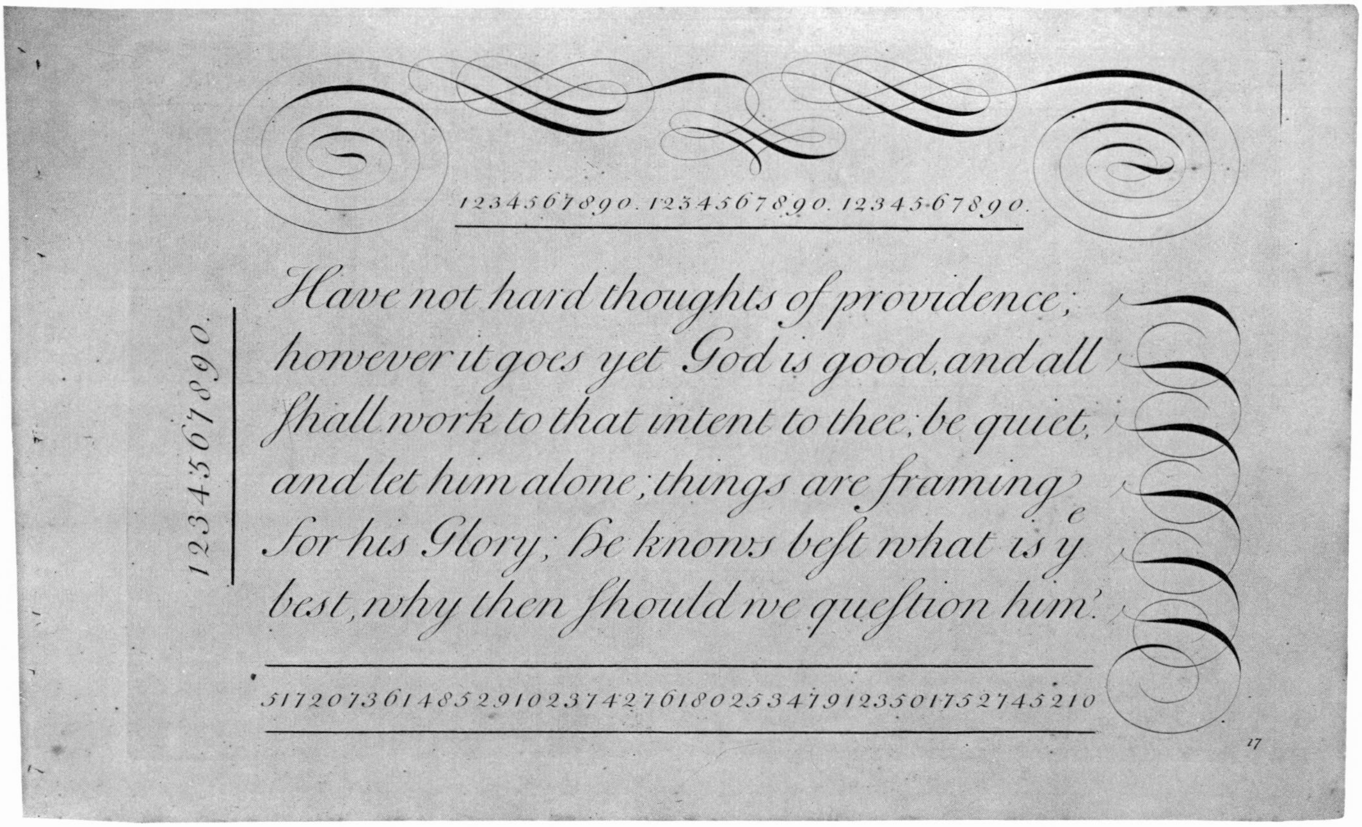

1234567890. 1234567890. 12345-67890.

1234567890.

*Have not hard thoughts of providence;*
*however it goes yet God is good, and all*
*ſhall work to that intent to thee; be quiet,*
*and let him alone; things are framing*
*For his Glory; He knows beſt what is yͤ*
*best, why then ſhould we queſtion him?*

5172073614852910237427618025347912350175274 5210

17

115 Charles Snell, *The Art of Writing* . . . , London, 1712

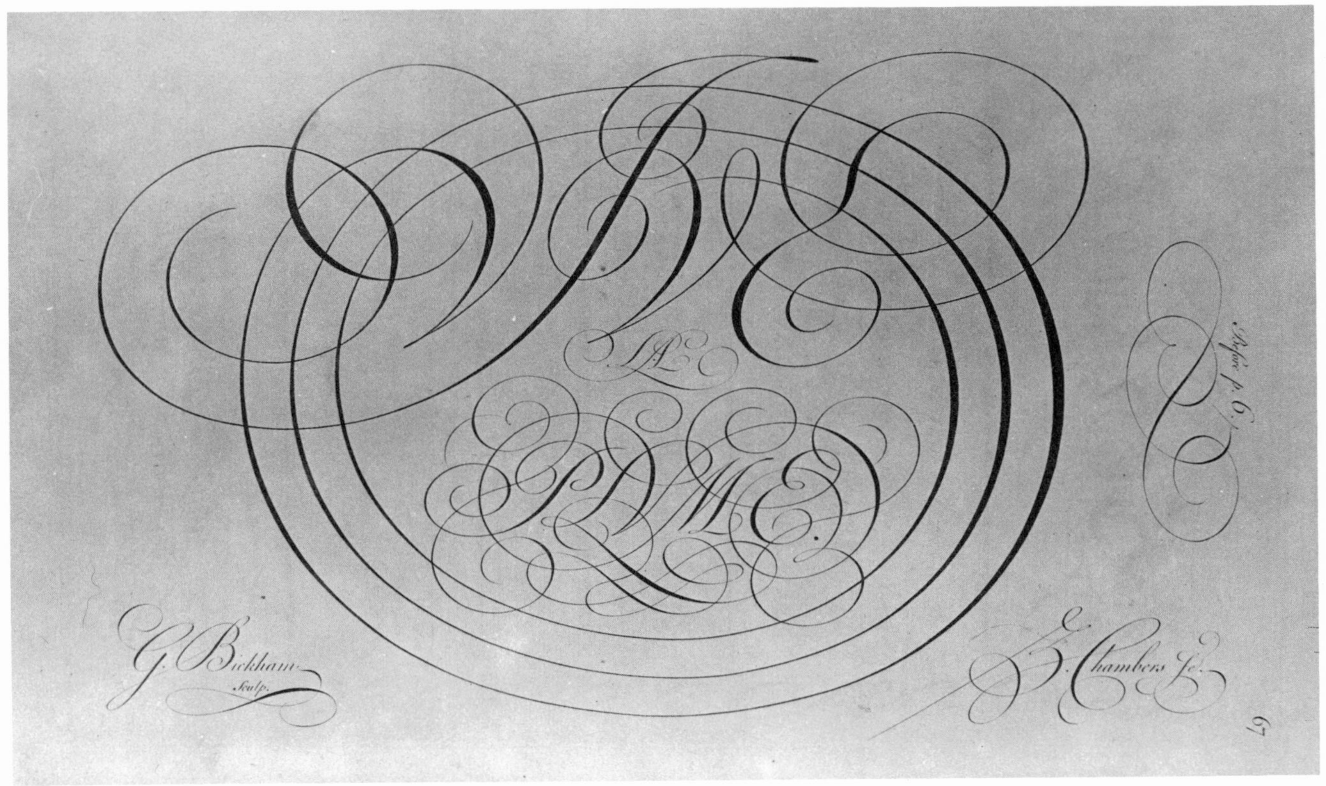


116 George Bickham, Senior, *The Universal Penman* . . . , London, 1743

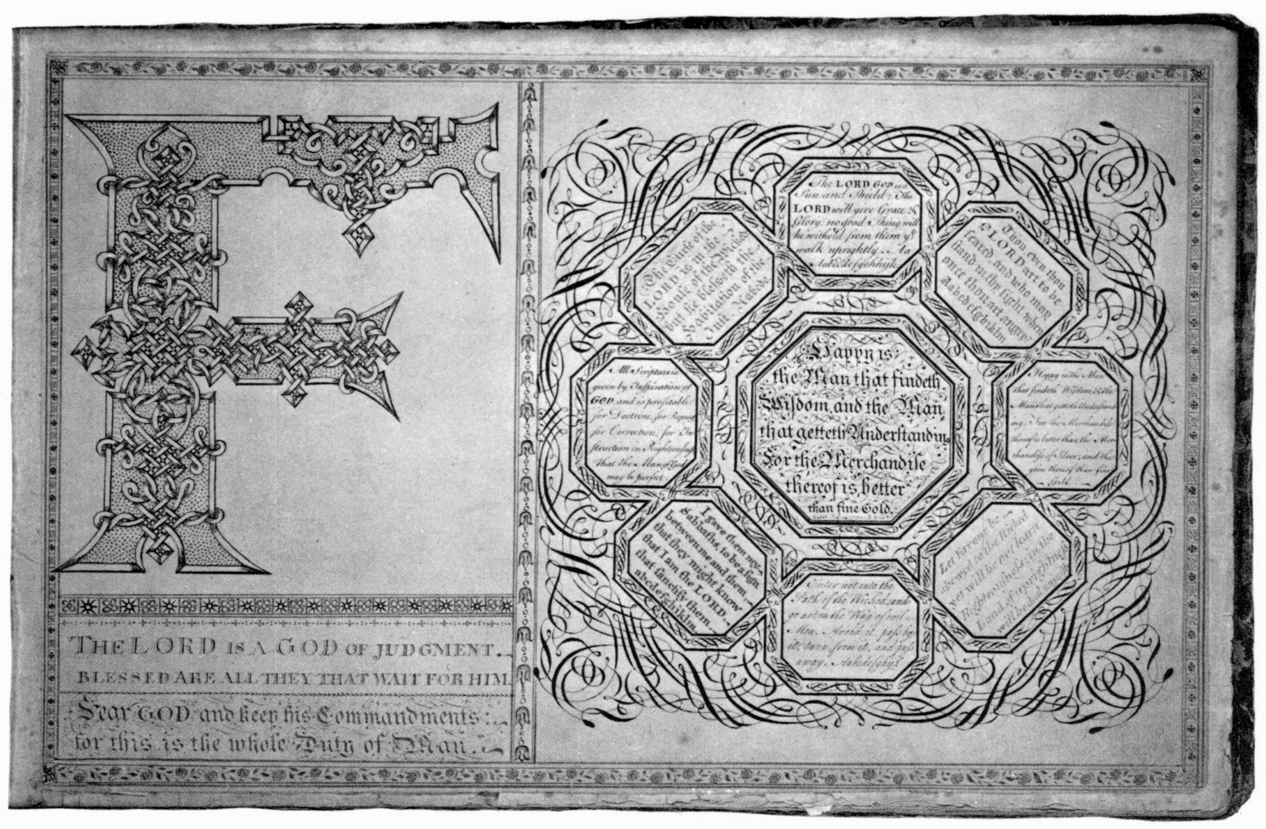


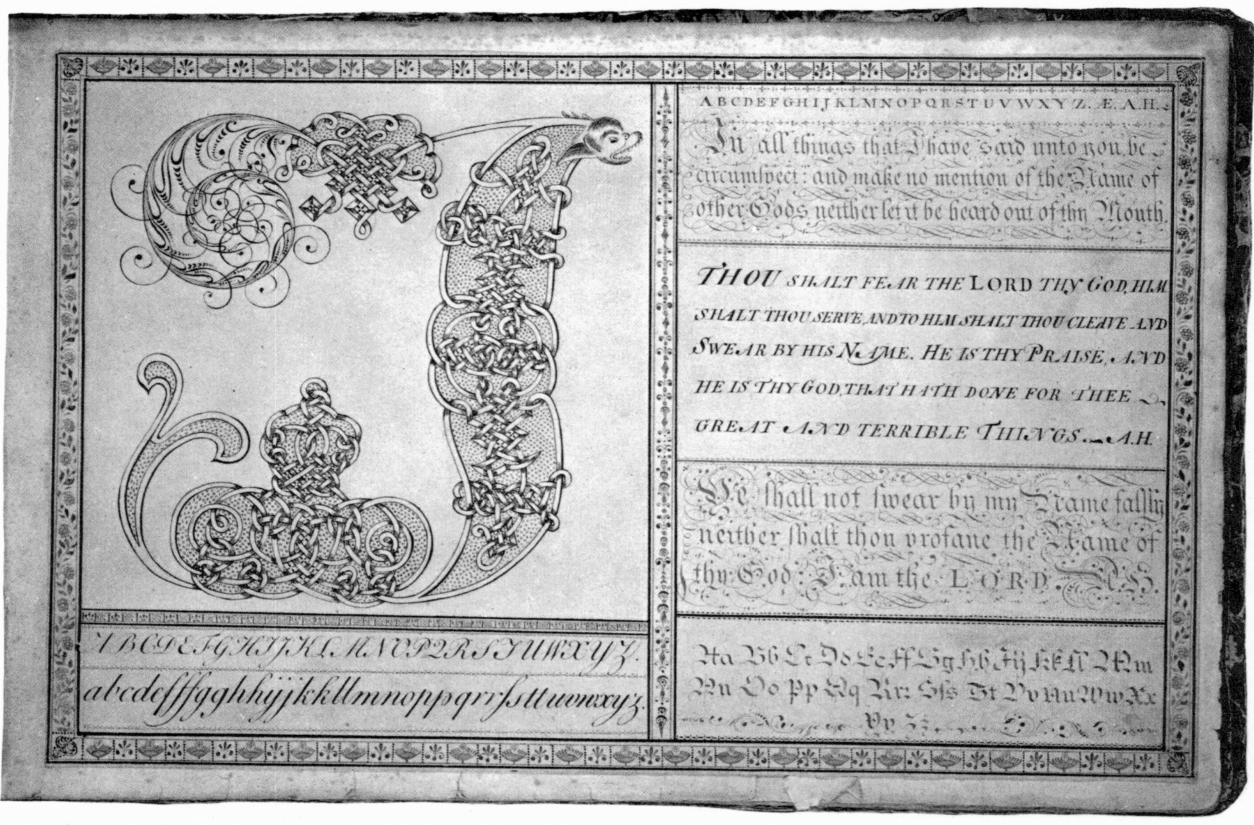


117 Abiah Holbrook, Junior, *The Writing Master's Amusement*, Boston, 1767

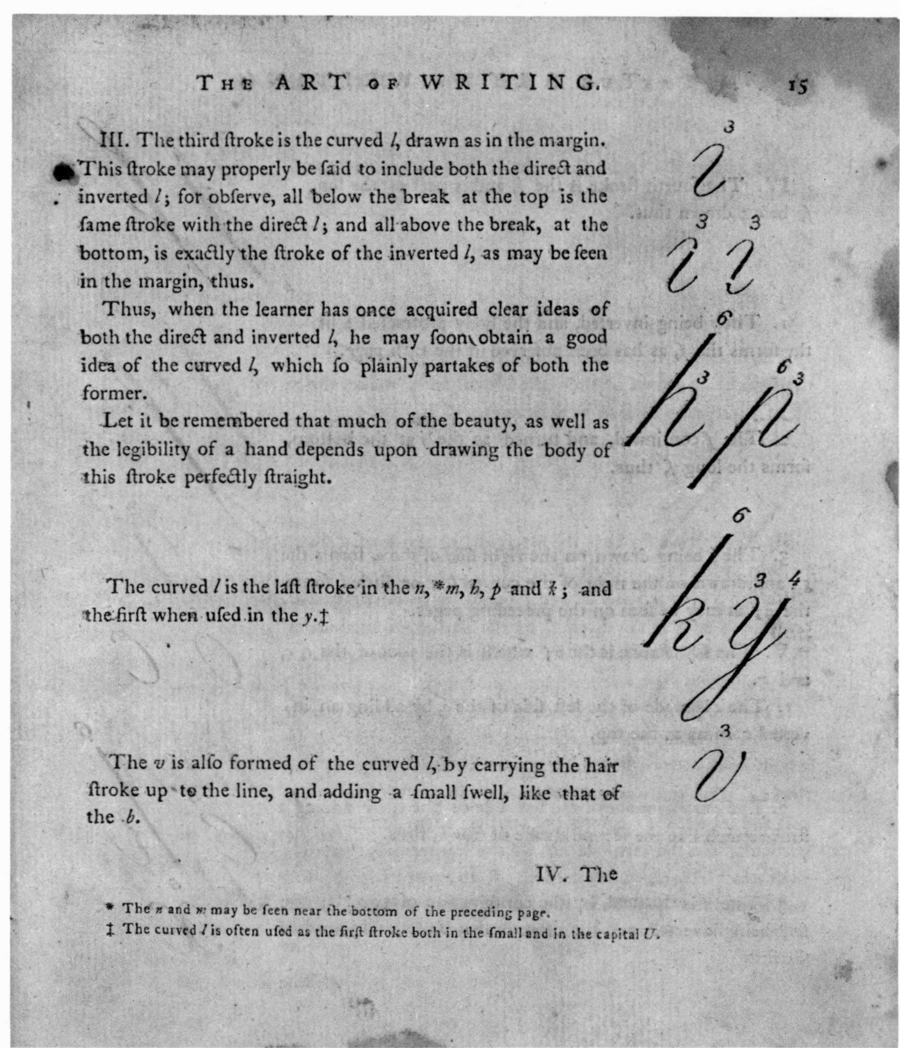

THE ART OF WRITING. 15

III. The third ſtroke is the curved *l*, drawn as in the margin. This ſtroke may properly be ſaid to include both the direct and inverted *l*; for obſerve, all below the break at the top is the ſame ſtroke with the direct *l*; and all above the break, at the bottom, is exactly the ſtroke of the inverted *l*, as may be ſeen in the margin, thus.

Thus, when the learner has once acquired clear ideas of both the direct and inverted *l*, he may ſoon obtain a good idea of the curved *l*, which ſo plainly partakes of both the former.

Let it be remembered that much of the beauty, as well as the legibility of a hand depends upon drawing the body of this ſtroke perfectly ſtraight.

The curved *l* is the laſt ſtroke in the *n*, **m*, *h*, *p* and *k*; and the firſt when uſed in the *y*.‡

The *v* is alſo formed of the curved *l*, by carrying the hair ſtroke up to the line, and adding a ſmall ſwell, like that of the *b*.

IV. The

* The *n* and *m* may be ſeen near the bottom of the preceding page.

‡ The curved *l* is often uſed as the firſt ſtroke both in the ſmall and in the capital *U*.

118 John Jenkins, *The Art of Writing. Book I*, Boston, 1791

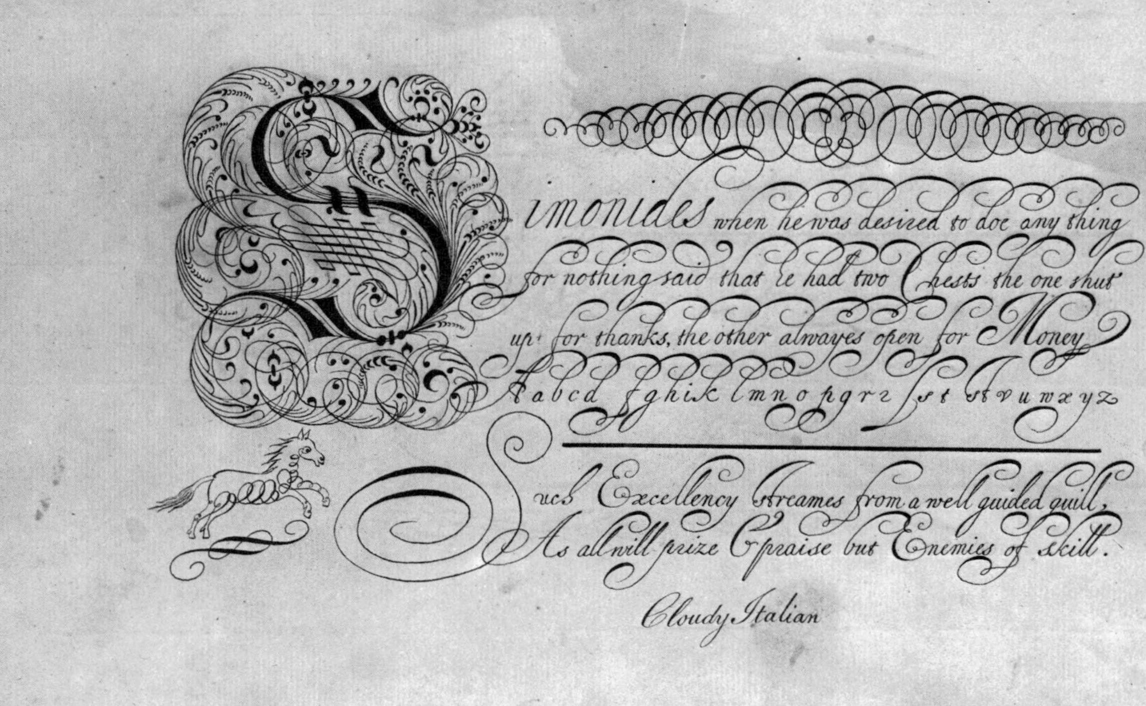



119 Phoebe Coleman Folger, *Drawing and Writing Book*, Nantucket, 1797–1806

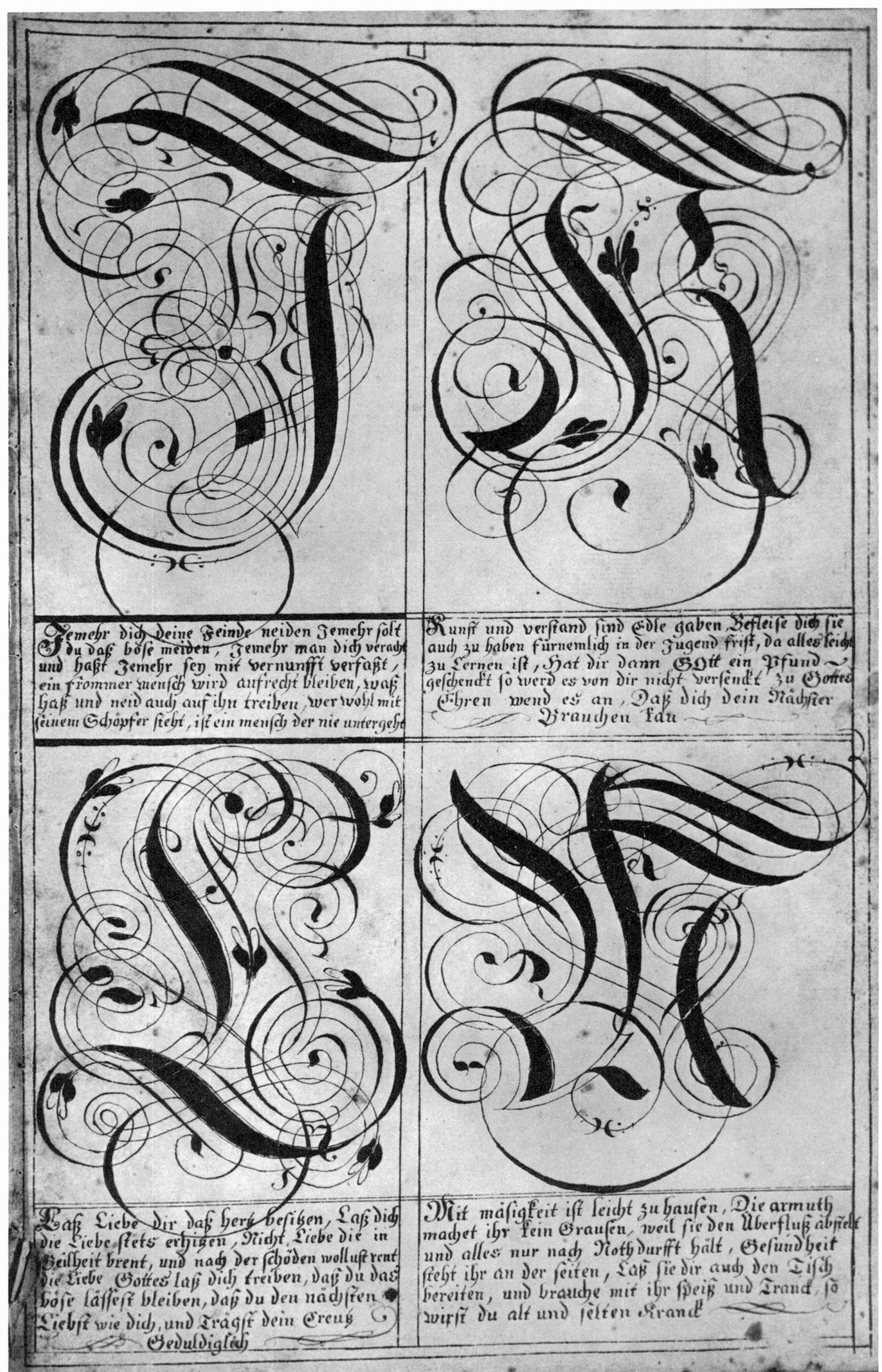


120 Yelles or Herbert Cassell, *Mennonite Alphabet Book*, Pennsylvania, ca. 1775–1800

Britain . . ." Dominating the manuscript is an alphabet of twenty-four letters (J and U omitted) drawn in an intricate strapwork pattern. According to the scribe he worked on the manuscript over a period of seven years. There is no question but that the alphabet is the most elaborate example of American calligraphy to have survived from the eighteenth century.

Bibliography: Ray Nash, *American Writing Masters and Copybooks*, Boston, 1959, p. 17f.; *idem*, "Abiah Holbrook and His 'Writing Master's Amusement,'" *Harvard Library Bulletin*, 7, no. 1, Winter, 1953, pp. 88–104; Peabody Institute Library, Baltimore, *Calligraphy and Handwriting in America*, Nov.–Dec. 1961, cat. no. 7.

## *John Jenkins*

UNITED STATES ABOUT 1755–1822

118 THE ART OF WRITING. BOOK I
Boston, 1791, Thomas and Andrews.
In English. Round hand script. 16 leaves, 7¾×6¼ inches. Copperplate engraving and wood engraving. Binding: grey wrapper.
*Lent by The Essex Institute*

Throughout the two and one-half centuries preceding Jenkins' 1791 publication, many scribes had analyzed letter forms in a search for methods of teaching calligraphy. Nash has pointed out that Jenkins' system differs basically from older sets of instructions. Previous copy-books had presented examples of correctly formed letters as models to be imitated. Instead, Jenkins here attempted to demonstrate that the round hand script might be formed on the basis of six motions of the pen. Hence, he claimed, if one learnt the six strokes, the letter forms would follow of accord, since Jenkins theorized that all letters could be created from a command of his six examples of the pen's motion. However, *s* and *k* could not comfortably find a place in his system, and *z* was omitted as "unnecessary." Originally the author planned to extend *The Art of Writing* to seven books, but the enterprise seems never to have gone beyond the third volume.

As a young man, Jenkins was asked to teach in a country school. Ashamed of his lack of calligraphic skill, he set about improving his hand. From the scribe's self-taught experiences he evolved his system, which occupied the better part of Jenkins' known activity. The third, and last, of the published books in the set appeared in 1817, five years before his death.

Bibliography: Ray Nash, *American Writing Masters and Copybooks*, Boston, 1959, pp. 26–34, 52–53.

## *Phoebe Coleman Folger*

UNITED STATES 1771–1857

119 DRAWING AND WRITING BOOK
Nantucket, 1797–1806.
Ms Typ 245 H. In English. Various scripts. 155 paper leaves, 12¾×8 inches. Pen and ink, with numerous watercolor drawings and diagrams. Binding: early suede calf, rebacked.
Provenance: purchased from a descendant of the Folger family.
*Lent by Mr. and Mrs. Philip Hofer*

This album is, in effect, a record of the interests of a young New England lady at the turn of the eighteenth century. Filled with watercolor drawings, quotations from a wide variety of texts, arithmetic lessons, and diagrams, she was also interested in calligraphy. A series of calligraphic pages were copied from Edward Cocker's *England's Penman* (1668).

Bibliography: Harvard *Cat.*, no. 159.

## *Yelles or Herbert Cassell*

UNITED STATES DATES UNKNOWN

120 MENNONITE ALPHABET BOOK
Pennsylvania (possibly Chester County), ca. 1775–1800.
In German. Fraktur script. 10 paper leaves, 8×13 inches. Pen and watercolor. Unbound.
Provenance: acquired in 1962 from a private Mennonite owner.
*Lent by The Free Library of Philadelphia*

This example of Pennsylvania Dutch fraktur script is an ornamental alphabet with four letters to the page, the last several pages being unfinished. The work is characteristic of Mennonite calligraphy and has, accompanying each letter, a short rhyme which is hortatory or pious in content.

# PART III: *The Nineteenth and Twentieth Centuries*

IF we accept the definition of calligraphy as "beautiful handwriting" or as "handwriting as an art" we must exclude most of the writing of the nineteenth century. Though present-day practitioners of the Spencerian style may cavil at the exclusion, no place could be found in the exhibition for this imitation of engraved letters. To quote from Lloyd Reynolds, "Compared with Arrighi, the Spencerian systems seem coldly mechanical in nature, quite illegible, and thoroughly lacking in character. The writing is in hair lines that are almost invisible, and when pen pressure is used to widen the stroke, it is distracting and adds nothing to the legibility of the script . . . Although Spencerian elegance finally gave way to the vapid commercial cursives of the Palmer variety, the reaction to this decadence had begun earlier . . ."[1] Those who are interested in nineteenth-century copybooks and Spencerian examples can find them in the Peabody Institute catalogue of the 1961–1962 exhibition.[2]

In England in the period 1870–1875, when public taste and craftsmanship had reached a nadir, William Morris led a vigorous fight for drastic changes in all aspects of culture. He revived interest in all the crafts, including printing and calligraphy. As he was the pioneer in this field, it is appropriate to start this section of the exhibition with one of his manuscripts, dated 1871.

Sydney Cockerell, who had been Morris's secretary, carried his influence to the second great pioneer of the early period, Edward Johnston. "Johnston carried out his enquiries with the perception of a craftsman, scientist and philosopher. He rediscovered the principles on which formal writing had been developed, the tools and materials used and the correct preparation of them. He discovered that the nature and form of a letter was determined by the nature and form of the pen that made it, that an edged-pen makes thick and thin strokes according to direction and not pressure and that the size of the letter is in direct ratio to the breadth of the edged-pen making it. He found out how to cut and sharpen reeds and quills, the angle at which to trim the chisel edge of the pen and how to hold the pen in relation to the horizontal line, in order that it should make the desired shapes of the letters when writing. He experimented with preparing the surface of skins on which to write and also the inks and pigments."[3]

Johnston's classes in the early 1900's included several of the scribes whose work is shown in this exhibition. They in turn taught others, many of whom still continue the Johnstonian tradition. Of all Johnston's styles the slanted pen hand, adapted from a tenth-century Winchester Psalter, which he called his Foundational Hand, became the style most used and is much in evidence in this catalogue.

In 1906 Johnston published his *Writing & Illuminating, & Lettering*, reprinted many times and still the *vade mecum* of scribes today. A sheet of the original manuscript is illustrated in the catalogue. Soon afterwards he gathered a class of devotees and formed a Society of Calligraphy for the advancement of lettering. A membership list for the

1. *Calligraphy: the Golden Age & Its Revival*. Portland Art Museum, Ore., 1958.
2. *Calligraphy & Handwriting in America, 1710–1962*. Italimuse Inc., Caledonia, N. Y., 1963.
3. Heather Child: *Calligraphy Today*. Watson Guptill, N. Y., 1964.

year 1908 includes the names of several of those represented here, besides the master: Jessie Bayes, Eric Gill, Graily Hewitt, Mervyn Oliver, Louise Powell and Anna Simons.

As printing had developed, handwriting and calligraphy had deteriorated, and illuminating had become imitative of medieval examples, but just as Johnston revived calligraphy, his pupil Graily Hewitt did much to revive the design of illuminating and to restore the difficult craft of gilding. Unlike Johnston, Hewitt and his several willing assistants produced many manuscripts book, memorials and documents. Florence Kingsford (later Lady Cockerell) and Louise Powell were superb illuminators. Along with others, Vera Law and Irene Base have carried on the tradition of gilding splendidly in recent years.

The Society of Calligraphers did not last many years, but in 1921 a number of Johnston's and Hewitt's pupils formed the Society of Scribes and Illuminators (S.S.I.). The importance of this Society to twentieth-century calligraphy cannot be overestimated. For over forty years its chief aim, "the re-establishment of a tradition of craftsmanship in the production of manuscripts, books and documents," has been scrupulously maintained. Candidates for membership must submit at least three original pieces of work, one on skin and showing raised gilding, and no candidate is elected unless three-quarters of the votes cast are in favor. The introduction of ingenious methods of reproduction and the change in taste in advertising and in other fields has led to a desire on the part of some younger members to relax the Society's rules, but the rigid entrance standards are still maintained.

Recently the Society of Scribes has been criticized in America for following the master too closely. Some would prefer to see more of Johnston's spirit and less of his substance. Rigid adherence to tradition and superficial resemblance to Johnston's work have been questioned on the grounds that he would not have approved. Be that as it may, the majority of pieces from S.S.I. members have their own authority and are works of art, and the material and media chosen are of the highest quality. Because they are essentially unique and permanent records they are appropriately restrained and formal. The burnished gold must be seen in the original for a complete appreciation of its beauty.

Scripts can be classified as formal book hands and cursive everyday correspondence hands. The cursive hands may be "set" or free. Johnston taught a formal (book) italic script of his own invention. Graily Hewitt taught an italic which was derived from Palatino and Lucas, but did not provide for joins. In the 1920's Alfred Fairbank, a pupil of Hewitt, was attracted by the italic hand, but found that the joinless italic was not fluent enough for his use as a government employe. He began research and experiments to produce a model which would stand up to everyday use. Fellow scribes evinced little interest, and even Johnston was discouraging. Nevertheless, Fairbank developed a set cursive italic as a book hand, undoubtedly the first scribe to do so, and in 1932 he published his pioneer work, *A Handwriting Manual*. Twenty years later, while President of the S.S.I., he proposed the formation of a Society for Italic Handwriting. This Society enlivened the schools and interested the amateurs. It has had the greatest effect on present day handwriting, for many schools in England, America and elsewhere have adopted italic.

Sporadic pioneer attempts to reform handwriting in America were successful in the early 1920's. In 1922 Marjorie Wise was teaching at Lincoln School, and in 1924 she produced *The Technique of Manuscript Writing*, which had sold 19,000 copies by 1942. She noted that "when Palmer Penmanship ran a campaign against me in 1924 I knew I was getting well known." Frances Moore taught spelling and writing at Miss Chapin's School in New York, and after working with Hewitt in England she introduced his italic, publishing *Handwriting for the Broad Pen* in 1926. Later, Paul Standard aspired to reform American penmanship on the basis of "the finest known running hand, Arrighi's Chancery Cursive." His article in *Woman's Day* in 1947 was the most influential step in this direction. A dozen schools in the East have been converted by him, and one, the Choir School of St. Thomas Church, New York City, advertises the teaching of italic script in its prospectus. In the West, Lloyd Reynolds has achieved considerable success in encouraging the teaching of italic.

Although the revival of calligraphy has been most widespread in England, it has been paralleled in continental Europe. Because there was no opportunity for women to study art in Prussia, Anna Simons went to study with Johnston, and later took his methods back to German pupils. Larisch and Koch, in Germany, were gifted teachers and, although they worked on different lines from Johnston's, their results were outstanding. Koch's influence at the Klingspor type foundry (in Offenbach, where he also taught lettering), produced a fine group of scribes and typographers.

Many other Europeans contributed to the rising standards of calligraphy in Europe. Ernst Schneidler, who attempted a reconstruction of the exemplary alphabet—a thoroughly Johnstonian method—and Jan van Krimpen, who combined typography and calligraphy so magnificently, left behind them many works of beauty and distinction. Present-day scribes include Imre Reiner, Walter Kaech, Hans Halbey, Hermann Zapf, Chris Brand, Erik Lindegren and others, many of whose scripts are based on classic models but are written with freedom and spontaneity. Unhappily, for reasons beyond the organizer's control, only a few are represented in this catalogue.

America, in the grip of Spencer, Palmer and Zaner-Bloser methods, did not begin the revival of calligraphy until Ernst Detterer returned from study under Johnston in 1913. In so large a country there could be no such general revival as occurred in England and elsewhere, but "pockets" of calligraphers tended to develop. Detterer's classes in Chicago constituted such a group, and many present-day calligraphers owe their skill to his teaching. Two of these stand out—Ray DaBoll and James Hayes, the latter carrying on where Detterer left off at his death in 1947.

In Massachusetts, W. A. Dwiggins became known for his calligraphy and design shortly after Johnston began his revival. Later, John Howard Benson in Rhode Island became an exponent of italic, cutting many beautiful inscriptions on stone. The Benson tradition is splendidly maintained by his son, John E. Benson.

In New York City teachers at Cooper Union Art School and at the Pratt Institute have inspired many calligraphers. The enthusiastic teaching of Lloyd Reynolds, Maury Nemoy, Byron Macdonald and Egdon Margo has stimulated much of the excellent work done in the West. Similar rewards have greeted the efforts of Arnold Bank in New York and Pittsburgh, and Alexander Nesbitt in Providence.

Current American styles of calligraphy are so different from the British as to make comparison difficult. The framed broadside, for example, and the manuscript book, have never caught on in the United States as they have in England. The American calligrapher is largely concerned, not with ceremonial work, but with commercial art, which is striking but ephemeral rather than unique and permanent. Thus, the American scribe tends to be inventive rather than traditional, fresh and dramatic in layout, as witness DaBoll's complexity and Macdonald's simplicity.

But despite the beautiful and influential work of the fine American calligraphers, public taste in such traditionally handwritten documents as diplomas and certificates remains unenlightened. Printed certificates pour out by the thousands, usually in hideous type, with names written in "gothic." Brilliant exceptions to this general mediocrity are those created by James Hayes, often in italic with distinguished pen-written roman majuscules. Engrossed certificates are also produced, done entirely by hand with gold and colored inks, sometimes with pleasing effect, but not to be compared with British examples, usually done on vellum with formal handwriting and raised and burnished gold. Two American scribes, Enid Perkins and Warren Ferris, practise this technique with results that measure up to British standards.

As the engraving of calligraphic forms and the chiselling of roman capitals are only indirect expressions of the art of the pen, the purist might exclude them from the field of calligraphy, holding that if an inscription is not made by the flow of ink down the slit of a pen it cannot properly be so described. The virtue and grace of calligraphy lie in the simple and *immediate* forming of letters by the pen. The stroke is made with skill in a fraction of a second and is followed by other such strokes to make a unity expressing not only the beauty of letters and words and their arrangement but also something of personality and individuality. "Handwriting is a system of movements involving touch, and in a sense, touch gives grace."[4] A few stonecutters, the finest of our day, have been strongly influenced by calligraphy, and have produced works that capture its grace and spontaneity. It has therefore seemed appropriate to show some examples of this welcome change from the static architectural inscription. The same consideration prompted the inclusion of the beautiful pieces of Steuben Glass, faithfully engraved from pen-written originals.

The method of selection in this part, generally successful, was decided months ago. The S.S.I. acted informally for Britain; Alexander Nesbitt, with his knowledge of Europe, suggested a number of calligraphers there; and several authorities in America provided the names of Americans to whom invitations should be sent. Unfortunately a few outstanding scribes, both American and European, failed to respond to repeated invitations, and are therefore not represented. The most remarkable feature of this part of the exhibition is the fact that no fewer than twenty-four pieces, or one-quarter, were done especially for the occasion, some of them commissioned by collectors. Deceased scribes' works were chosen from American sources because in most cases it was possible to make selections by personal visits to the owners.

This, the third part, is divided into two sections: in section A scribes up to 1940 are listed in chronological sequence; section B contains work done since 1948, and the calligraphers are listed in alphabetical sequence. The division at 1940 seemed logical: little teaching and work were done during World War II, but many changes took place. Thus the date of the work is the test, for scripts and styles change as scribes develop.

The compiler records his deep gratitude to a number of persons: Alfred Fairbank for unfailing help and advice over the last year, especially in the choice of the pre-1940 material and in the interpretation of the styles of writing; Mr. Fairbank and Lloyd Reynolds for pointing out the differences between British and American hands; Alexander Nesbitt for the selection of European scribes; John M. Cackett, the indefatigable secretary of S.S.I., and Heather Child, the Society's present chairman, for their kindness, courtesy and enthusiasm, which resolved most problems related to postwar British calligraphy.

Since recent books on calligraphy have provided little information about the scribes, it is hoped that the biographies in this catalogue will add value and interest. The unevenness in treatment of deceased scribes is due to limited information, although generous assistance in these was given when possible by Heather Child, Alfred Fairbank, John P. Harthan, James Hayes, Ida Henstock, Dorothy Mahoney, Mildred Ratcliffe, Paul Standard and James Wells. The living scribes provided their own biographical information, some with undue modesty. The biographies and text in this part of the catalogue were edited throughout by Dorothy Rolph, of New York City. The compiler records his thanks for her help and advice. Any errors are his.

The compiler is grateful also for Heather Child's permission to quote some opinions expressed in her *Calligraphy Today*. Although the break at 1940 and some of the theses advanced are similar, they were arrived at independently. That there is so much agreement is, however, not coincidental, since many opinions are shared generally in calligraphic circles.

4. Alfred Fairbank.

The compiler also records his thanks to two members of the Peabody Library staff: to Mrs. Sidney Painter, who performed the heavy task involving correspondence and registration, and to Miss Jeannette Markell, for her willing and capable assistance.

P. W. FILBY, Assistant Director
Peabody Institute Library

Note: 'S.S.I.' at the end of a scribe's biography denotes that the scribe is a craft member of the Society of Scribes and Illuminators.

# A: *to* 1940

## *William Morris*

121 SAGA OF KORMAK
England, 1871.
26 paper leaves, 16×10½ inches; ink with decoration. Binding: green levant morocco by Douglas Cockerell. An unpublished translation of the *Saga of Kormak Son of Ogmund*, with 4 pages of *The Story of Frithiof the Bold*. Ink, color, gold. History: William Morris – Mrs. Morris – Sir Sydney Cockerell – John M. Crawford, Jr. —The Pierpont Morgan Library.
*Lent by the Pierpont Morgan Library*

William Morris, poet, artist, teacher, manufacturer, printer and Socialist, was born in 1834 at Walthamstow, England, and died in 1896. In 1870 he began to produce illuminated manuscripts on vellum and paper, executed in various styles, but all of considerable beauty. He translated many Icelandic Sagas and wrote some of them out in an impeccable hand. In 1890 he started the Kelmscott Press at Hammersmith, where, in the following eight years, fifty-three books were produced. The last work of the press and its crowning glory was the *Kelmscott Chaucer*, many years in the making, and the most remarkable book of its time.

He was the father of the whole Arts and Crafts Movement, and raised the standard of book production in particular to great heights. His influence on typography is well known, but the importance of his pioneering revival of calligraphy is not always realized. Mackail's *Life of Morris* (1901) covers every facet of the man and his work.

## *Florence Kingsford*

122 THE SONG OF SONGS WHICH IS SOLOMON'S
Shelley House, Chelsea, 1902.
iv, 24 vellum leaves, 6½×4¾ inches; Ashendene Press, decorated by Florence Kingsford. Binding: morocco by Florence Paget.
*Lent by John M. Crawford, Jr.*

Florence Kingsford was born in 1871 at Canterbury, and died in 1949. She was one of Edward Johnston's earliest pupils, and in the first decade of the nineteenth century she illuminated about sixty books. In 1907 she married Sir Sydney Cockerell, but ill health for many years prevented her from producing further works.

This example is from C. H. St. John Hornby's Ashendene Press at Shelley House, Chelsea. Usually his finely printed books were innocent of any kind of decoration or ornament. The one exception is *The Song of Songs*, illuminated with supreme delicacy and grace by Florence Kingsford, and this therefore must surely rank as one of the most beautiful of all printed books. Forty copies, all on vellum, were printed in 1902. Wilfrid Blunt describes much of Florence Kate Cockerell's life in his *Cockerell* (1964).

## *Edward Johnston*

123 WRITING & ILLUMINATING, & LETTERING. Manuscript
England, c. 1903–1904.
Many paper leaves, various sizes, mainly 11×8 inches; typescript and broad pen, written by Edward Johnston and his wife, Greta. Unbound.
Acquired from Philip Duschnes, New York City, 1964.
*Lent by the Newberry Library*

124 AT MORNING by Robert Louis Stevenson
1926.
Vellum broadside, 10×6⅝ inches; black and red ink; roman and italic.
Purchased from Priscilla Johnston, 1956.
*Lent by the Newberry Library*

Edward Johnston was born in Uruguay in 1872. At the age of seventeen he evinced an interest in illuminating. Later, when his health broke down, he abandoned a medical career and, guided by Lethaby, Cockerell and Bridges, he devoted himself to the study and practice of calligraphy until his death at Ditchling, Sussex, in 1944.

From 1899 to 1912 he taught at the London County Council Central School of Arts and Crafts and from 1901 also at the Royal College of Art. His many pupils were inspired to perpetuate his influence, both in their work and in their own teaching. Shown in the present exhibition is work by no fewer than thirteen of his pupils: Detterer (127), Gill (137), Hewitt (132–3), Kingsford (122), Powell (135), Mahoney (181), Oliver (186), Raisbeck (191), Simons (131), Swindlehurst (202), Walker (130), Webb (128) and Wellington (209–10).

In 1906 he published his great manual, still the vade mecum for calligraphers, *Writing & Illuminating, & Lettering* (of which this exhibit is part of the original manuscript), and in 1909 he wrote *Manuscript and Inscription Letters*. He also designed type faces and all London admired his fine block letters for the Underground Railway.

He rediscovered the principles on which formal writing had been developed, the tools and materials and the correct preparation of them, and brought to the practice of a single craft as much genius as any craftsman who ever lived. Sir Sydney Cockerell wrote that "his development as a scribe followed rather closely that of professional handwriting from the eleventh to the fifteenth century. Starting with an open rounded hand inspired by the early Winchester School, his calligraphy tended to become more and more gothic and compressed. There are some who lament this . . . But no original artist can stand still and go on repeating himself . . ."

Although he spent much time teaching, his own work was eagerly sought, and many fine examples are extant. His influence on writing and illumination cannot be measured.

Two good works about him have been published: *Tributes to Edward Johnston, Calligrapher* (Society of Scribes and Illuminators, 1948), and *Edward Johnston*, by Priscilla Johnston (1959). He was the first honorary member of the Society of Scribes, and he was awarded the C.B.E. (Commander of the British Empire) in 1939.

## *Rudolf Koch*

125 DER KNABE UND DAS IMMLEIN by Eduard Friedrich Mörike
Germany, 1912.
5 paper leaves, 7⅝×6¼ inches; ink, with decoration in gold. Binding: vellum on boards.
Written as a birthday gift for Dr. Güggenheim.
*Lent by the Newberry Library*

Rudolf Koch was born in 1876 and died in 1934. He went to school in Nuremberg, and later worked in Hanau as an apprentice in metal engraving and chasing. He headed the newly organized lettering course at the School of Arts and Crafts in Offenbach. Later he taught with great success at the Werkstattgemeinschaft, where his pupils included Henri Friedlaender (no. 164) and Ernst Kellner.

For much of his life, Koch was interested in the handwritten book. He considered skill in lettering and impeccable craftsmanship to be of utmost importance, and these attributes are always evident in his work. Of his many pieces, *Herr erbarme Dich Meiner* is perhaps his best. His other interests included tapestry and type designing and woodcuts. Among his pupils and fellow workers were Fritz Kredel, Berthold Wolpe and Richard Bender. Outstanding is his work with Kredel on *Blumenbuch*, for which Kredel cut the flowers in wood during the period 1922–1929. Perhaps his most important contribution to graphic arts is his design of typefaces, which include *Koch Antiqua*, *Neuland*, *Marathon* and many others of great strength and beauty.

## *Ivy E. Harper*

126 ODE ON A GRECIAN URN by John Keats
England, 1915.
6 vellum leaves, 10¼×7¼ inches; pen and watercolor.
Binding: full green levant morocco, gilt, slipcase.
*Lent by Mr. and Mrs. Philip Hofer*

In spite of the beauty and fine execution of this piece, no other work by this scribe is to be found; and apart from the fact that she was British and worked in the Johnstonian tradition, nothing is known about her.

## *Ernst Frederick Detterer*

127 THE ART OF THE PEOPLE. Passage from an essay by William Morris
Chicago, Illinois, September 1917.
2 unbleached Arnold paper leaves, 11½×9 inches; red and black ink, watercolor; formal roman hand.
*Lent by James Hayes*

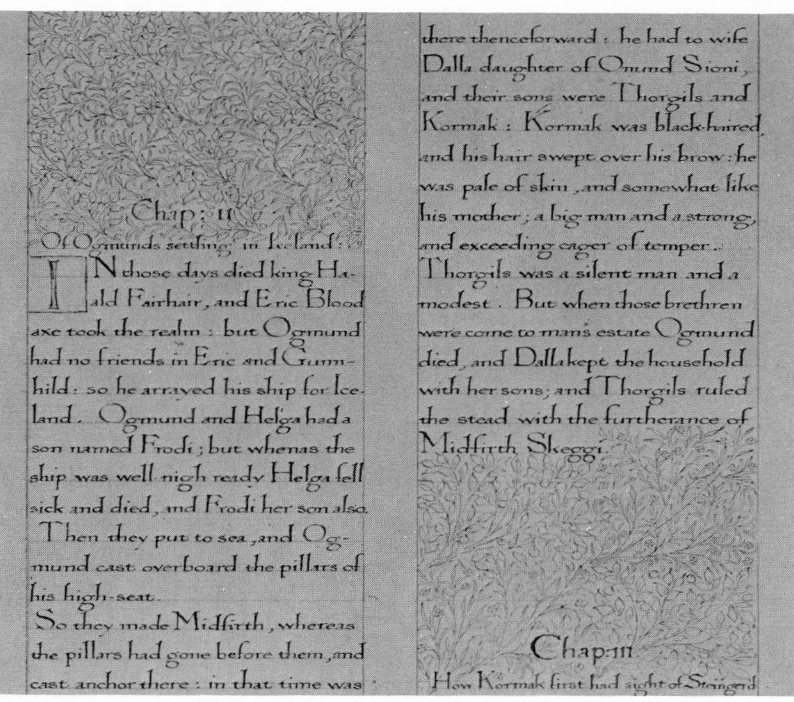

Chap: II
Of Ogmunds settling in Iceland:
IN those days died king Harald Fairhair, and Eric Blood axe took the realm: but Ogmund had no friends in Eric and Gunnhild: so he arrayed his ship for Iceland. Ogmund and Helga had a son named Frodi; but whenas the ship was well nigh ready Helga fell sick and died, and Frodi her son also. Then they put to sea, and Ogmund cast overboard the pillars of his high-seat. So they made Midfirth, whereas the pillars had gone before them, and cast anchor there: in that time was

there thenceforward: he had to wife Dalla daughter of Onund Sioni, and their sons were Thorgils and Kormak: Kormak was black-haired, and his hair swept over his brow: he was pale of skin, and somewhat like his mother; a big man and a strong, and exceeding eager of temper. Thorgils was a silent man and a modest. But when those brethren were come to man's estate Ogmund died, and Dalla kept the household with her sons; and Thorgils ruled the stead with the furtherance of Midfirth Skeggi.

Chap: III
How Kormak first had sight of Steingerd

121. Saga of Kormak. William Morris. 1871

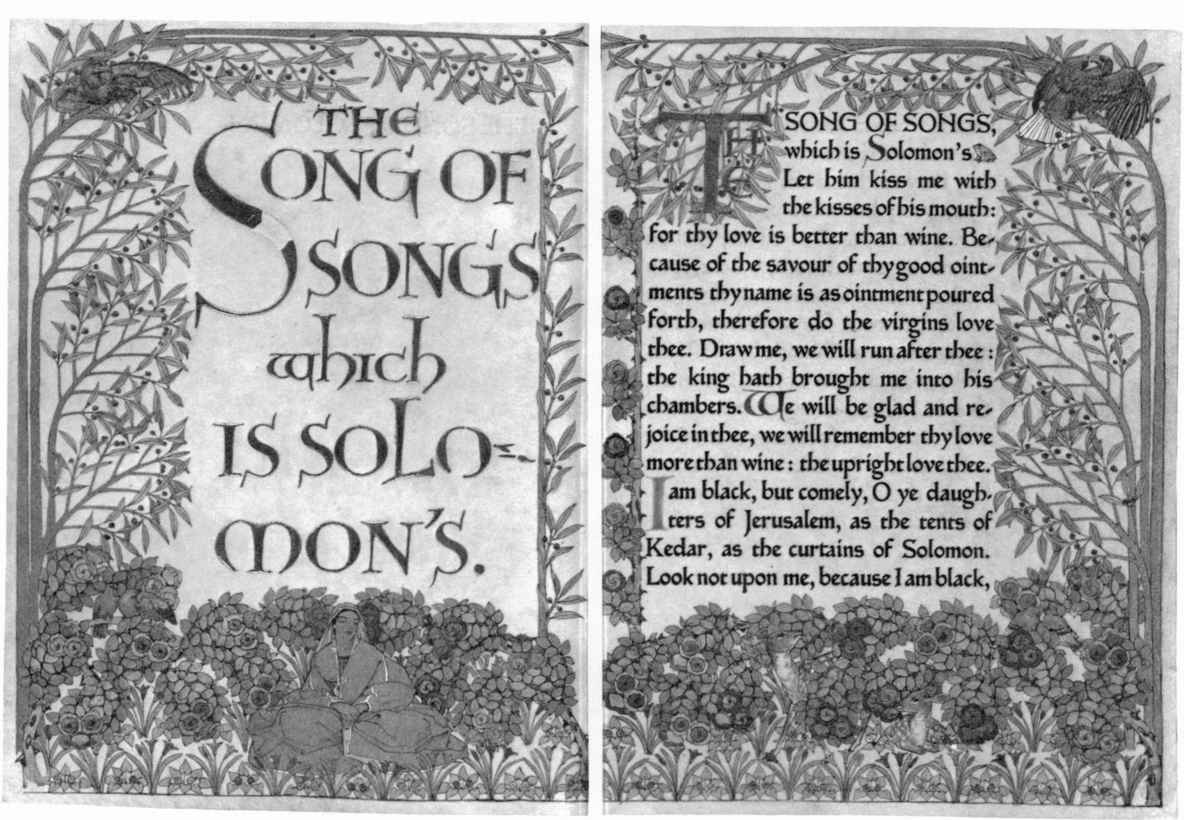

THE SONG OF SONGS which IS SOLOMON'S.

THE SONG OF SONGS, which is Solomon's. Let him kiss me with the kisses of his mouth: for thy love is better than wine. Because of the savour of thy good ointments thy name is as ointment poured forth, therefore do the virgins love thee. Draw me, we will run after thee: the king hath brought me into his chambers. We will be glad and rejoice in thee, we will remember thy love more than wine: the upright love thee. I am black, but comely, O ye daughters of Jerusalem, as the tents of Kedar, as the curtains of Solomon. Look not upon me, because I am black,

122. The Song of Songs Which is Solomon's. Florence Kingsford. 1902

"At Morning"

One of the Prayers written at Vailima by Robert Louis Stevenson (transcribed from "The Pocket R.L.S." 1902 Lond., by E.J. Oct. 1926).

The day returns & brings
us the petty round of irri-
tating concerns & duties.
Help us to play the man,
help us to perform them
with laughter & kind faces,
let cheerfulness abound
with industry. Give us to
go blithely on our business
all this day, bring us to our
resting beds weary & content
& undishonoured, & grant
us in the end the gift of
sleep.

124. At Morning. Edward Johnston. 1926

Chapter I.

The Student should have nothing to do with "Artistic Lettering" or "Quaint Lettering" or the novel misarrangements of "display" lettering, his concern is really with good lettering, and he should regard letters as definite characters, forms the parts of which written and inscribed words are made.

Letters are useful things. We must not degrade them from their high office of usefulness to serve the ends of ~~Artiness~~ Affectation or vulgarity: but we must choose good letters and build up fine inscriptions or books with them, precisely as ~~the~~ a Builder chooses good bricks and builds good walls or houses with them.

123. Writing & Illuminating, & Lettering. Edward Johnston. c. 1903–1904

he is at work at anything in which he specially excels. A most kind gift is this of— nature, since all men, nay, it seems all things too, must labor; so that not only does the dog take pleasure in hunting, and the horse in running, and the bird in fly-ing, but so natural does the idea seem to us, that we ima-gine to ourselves that the earth and the very elements rejoice in doing their appoint-ed work; and the poets have told us of the spring mead-ows smiling, of the exulta-tion of the fire, of the—

127. Morris: The Art of the People. Ernst Detterer. 1917

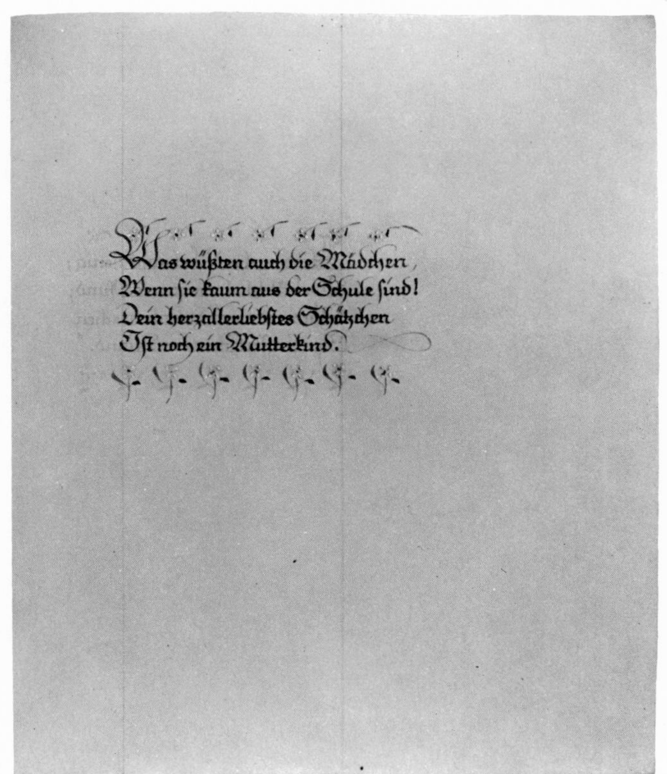
Was wüßten auch die Mädchen,
Wenn sie kaum aus der Schule sind!
Dein herzallerliebstes Schätzchen
Ist noch ein Mutterkind.

125. Mörike: Der Knabe und das Immlein. Rudolf Koch. 1912

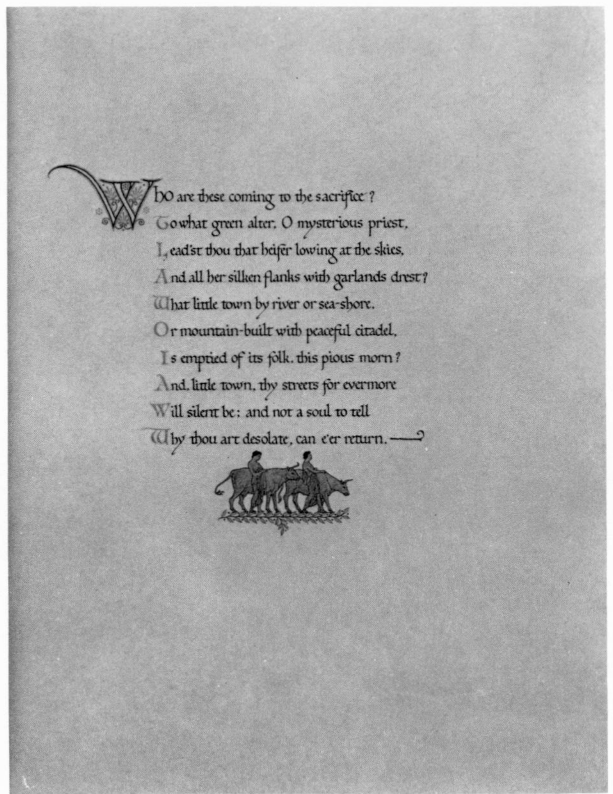
Who are these coming to the sacrifice?
To what green alter, O mysterious priest,
Lead'st thou that heifer lowing at the skies,
And all her silken flanks with garlands drest?
What little town by river or sea-shore,
Or mountain-built with peaceful citadel,
Is emptied of its folk, this pious morn?
And, little town, thy streets for evermore
Will silent be: and not a soul to tell
Why thou art desolate, can e'er return.—

126. Keats: Ode on a Grecian Urn. Ivy E. Harper. 1915

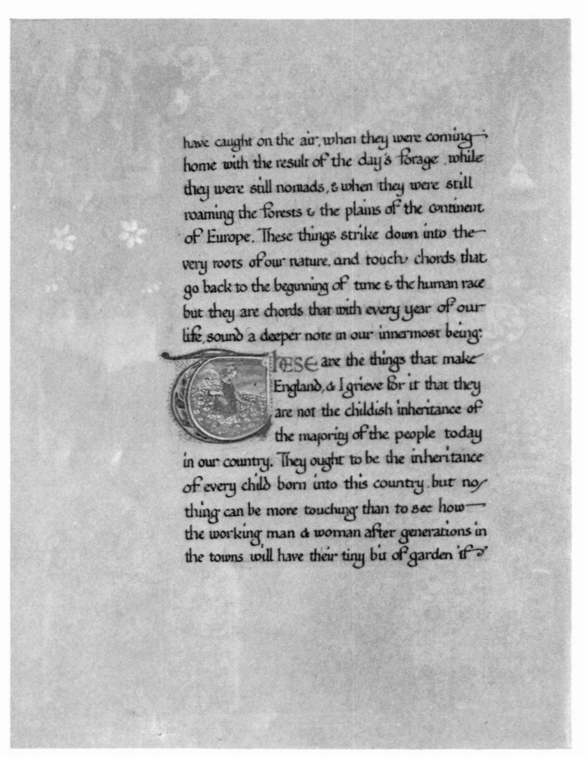

have caught on the air, when they were coming home with the result of the day's forage, while they were still nomads, & when they were still roaming the forests & the plains of the continent of Europe. These things strike down into the very roots of our nature, and touch chords that go back to the beginning of time & the human race but they are chords that with every year of our life, sound a deeper note in our innermost being: These are the things that make England, & I grieve for it that they are not the childish inheritance of the majority of the people today in our country. They ought to be the inheritance of every child born into this country, but nothing can be more touching than to see how the working man & woman after generations in the towns will have their tiny bit of garden if

134. Stanley Baldwin: England; Blake: Jerusalem. Jessie Bayes. c. 1930

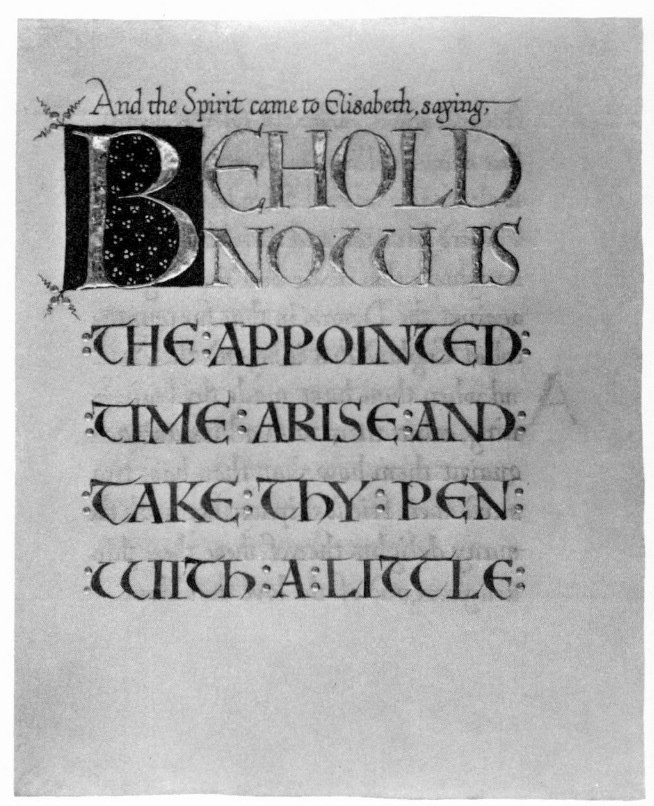

And the Spirit came to Elisabeth, saying,

BEHOLD NOW IS

:THE:APPOINTED:

:TIME:ARISE:AND:

:TAKE:THY:PEN:

:WITH:A:LITTLE:

128. Christmas Greeting to Mr. and Mrs. Edward Johnston. Elizabeth Webb. 1922–1926

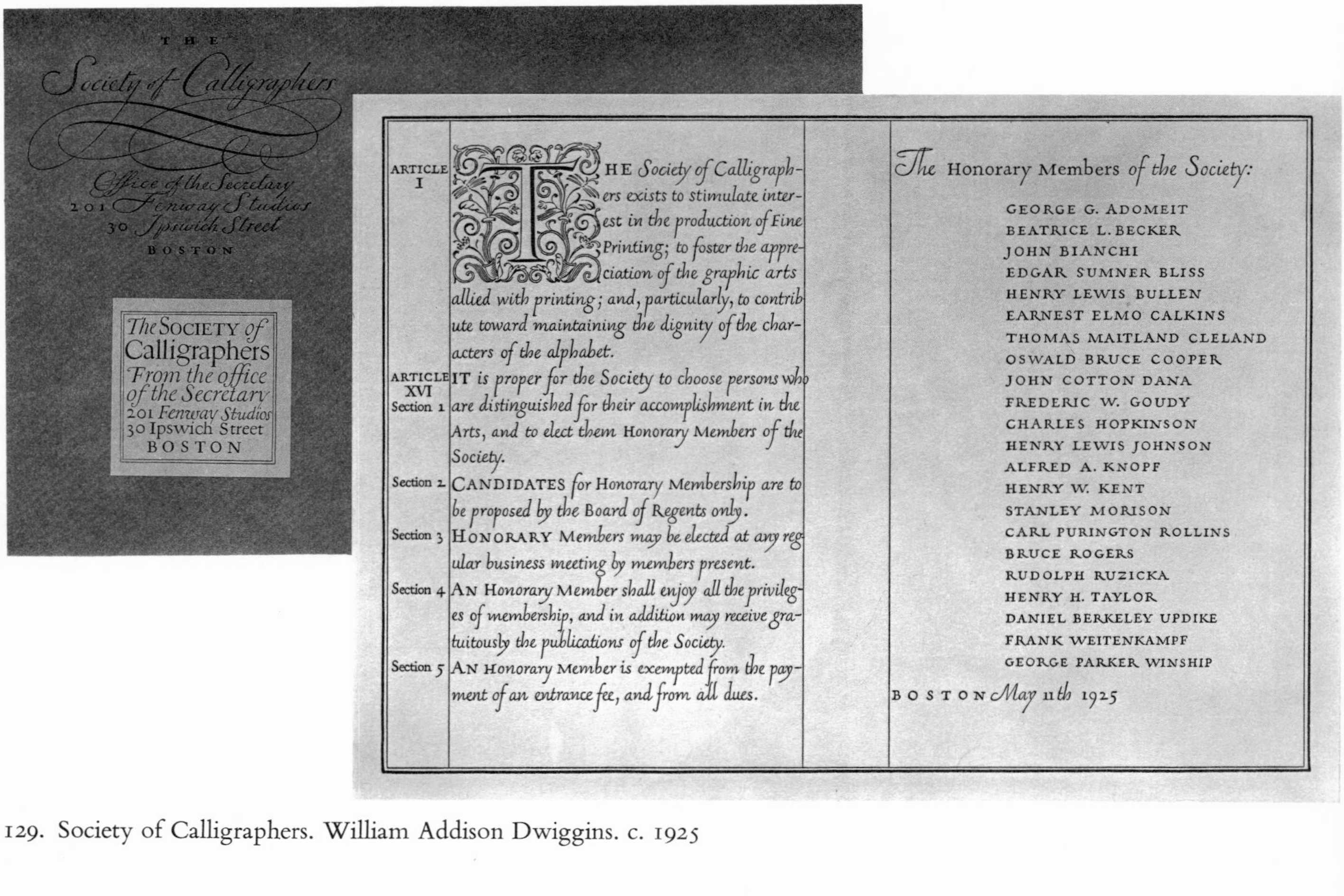

THE

*Society of Calligraphers*

*Office of the Secretary*
201 *Fenway Studios*
30 *Ipswich Street*
BOSTON

*The* SOCIETY *of* Calligraphers
*From the office of the Secretary*
201 *Fenway Studios*
30 Ipswich Street
BOSTON

ARTICLE I — THE *Society of Calligraphers exists to stimulate interest in the production of Fine Printing; to foster the appreciation of the graphic arts allied with printing; and, particularly, to contribute toward maintaining the dignity of the characters of the alphabet.*

ARTICLE XVI

Section 1 — IT *is proper for the Society to choose persons who are distinguished for their accomplishment in the Arts, and to elect them* Honorary *Members of the Society.*

Section 2 — CANDIDATES *for* Honorary *Membership are to be proposed by the Board of Regents only.*

Section 3 — HONORARY Members *may be elected at any regular business meeting by members present.*

Section 4 — AN Honorary Member *shall enjoy all the privileges of membership, and in addition may receive gratuitously the publications of the Society.*

Section 5 — AN Honorary Member *is exempted from the payment of an entrance fee, and from all dues.*

*The* Honorary Members *of the Society:*

GEORGE G. ADOMEIT
BEATRICE L. BECKER
JOHN BIANCHI
EDGAR SUMNER BLISS
HENRY LEWIS BULLEN
EARNEST ELMO CALKINS
THOMAS MAITLAND CLELAND
OSWALD BRUCE COOPER
JOHN COTTON DANA
FREDERIC W. GOUDY
CHARLES HOPKINSON
HENRY LEWIS JOHNSON
ALFRED A. KNOPF
HENRY W. KENT
STANLEY MORISON
CARL PURINGTON ROLLINS
BRUCE ROGERS
RUDOLPH RUZICKA
HENRY H. TAYLOR
DANIEL BERKELEY UPDIKE
FRANK WEITENKAMPF
GEORGE PARKER WINSHIP

BOSTON *May 11th* 1925

129. Society of Calligraphers. William Addison Dwiggins. c. 1925

Ernst Detterer is known as a designer of calligraphy and printing, but will be longer remembered as a teacher of these subjects.

He took private lessons from Edward Johnston (nos. 123–4) in 1913, and always regarded him as the greatest calligrapher of his time, and one of the greatest of all time. The skill that he developed under Edward Johnston advanced constantly until his death in 1947.

He was a pioneer of the Johnstonian calligraphic revival in America. As head of the Art Department of Chicago Normal College, and later as head of the Department of Printing Arts in the School of the Art Institute of Chicago (1921–1931), he directly communicated to hundreds of students a sound knowledge of letter forms. He was an exacting teacher with an uncompromising insistence on good taste, and those students who survived his discipline—and there were many—were able to proceed on their own, confident of their direction.

Later he became Custodian of the John M. Wing Foundation at the Newberry Library and formed its Calligraphy Study Group. Using the Library's rich collection of calligraphic material, he helped many students from many places in their quest for knowledge of the best in calligraphy.

## *Elizabeth Webb*

128 CHRISTMAS GREETING TO MR. AND MRS. EDWARD JOHNSTON
United States, started in 1922 and completed in 1926.
3 vellum leaves, 6×4⅝ inches; ink, color, gold.
Binding: vellum.
Acquired from Priscilla Gill, daughter of Edward Johnston.
*Lent by the Newberry Library*

Elizabeth Holden Webb was Edward Johnston's (nos. 123–4) first American pupil, and from Priscilla Johnston's book about her father we learn that the pupil became a friend of the family. She returned to the United States before World War I. She lived in New York City and took pupils, mainly from Park Avenue. She did a number of commissions, and at one point conducted a private press, called the Gramercy Park Press, in partnership with Margaret Zabriskie.

The Newberry Library has a number of letters from her to Edward Johnston from about 1916 to 1926.

## *William Addison Dwiggins*

129 SOCIETY OF CALLIGRAPHERS, articles and list of honorary members, envelope and label
Hingham, Massachusetts, c. 1925.
Paper, printed, 7⅝×10⅜; 9×6; 1⅞×1⅞ inches.
*Lent by Dorothy Abbe*

W. A. Dwiggins was born at Martinsville, Ohio, in 1880 and died in Hingham, Massachusetts, in 1956. He studied lettering under Frederic W. Goudy at the Frank Holme School of Illustration, Chicago, and moved to Hingham in 1904.

He became a free-lance designer, and had an unbroken commission for over thirty years to design the books of A. A. Knopf, Inc. He also designed books for the Limited Editions Club and others. He created types for Mergenthaler Linotype Co., including the *Metro Series*, *Electra*, *Caledonia*, *Eldorado* and *Falcon*, and also the *Caravan* series of typographic ornaments. He wrote books and pamphlets on printing and related subjects, and as an avocation did wood carving, particularly marionettes.

He had a number of exhibitions and in 1929 was a gold medallist of the American Institute of Graphic Arts. In 1947 Harvard awarded him an Honorary Master of Arts degree.

"The Society of Calligraphers" was the imprint under which Dwiggins issued a number of pamphlets related to calligraphy and printing. As a mark of respect he bestowed honorary membership in the Society upon twenty-two people in publishing and the graphic arts. The calligraphy shown is characteristic of his own style.

Dwiggins is commemorated in two volumes, Typophile Chap Books 35 and 36, *Postscripts on Dwiggins*, ed. by Paul A. Bennett (1960).

## *Madelyn Walker*

130 DREAM CHILDREN—a reverie by Charles Lamb
Petersfield, Hampshire, 1924; with colophon, 1926.
9 vellum leaves, 7×5⅜ inches; ink. Binding: full vellum.
Presented to Edward and Greta Johnston, 1926; acquired from Edward Johnston.
*Lent by the Pierpont Morgan Library*

Madelyn Walker was born at Ipswich, England. She studied at the Royal College of Art, London, under Edward Johnston (nos. 123–4), and later under Graily Hewitt (nos. 132–3) at the Central School of Arts and Crafts, London. She taught calligraphy, illuminating and embroidery at the Sheffield Technical School of Art, where Ida Henstock (no. 132) was one of her pupils.

She left Sheffield to work with Graily Hewitt in Hampshire; but after a short time there she retired to a convent, and now resides in a House of Prayer in Buckinghamshire.

She excelled in gilding, and beautiful examples of her work appear from time to time in exhibitions.

## *Anna Simons*

131 WOHER SIND WIR GEBOREN? by Goethe
N.p., n.d.
1 vellum leaf, 11½×8 inches; ink; gothic lettering. Mounted on board.
Acquired at a German auction in 1953.
*Lent by the Chiswick Book Shop, New York City*

Anna Simons was born at München-Gladbach in 1871 and died in 1951. In 1896 she went to London to study metal work at the Royal College of Art because Prussian art schools did not then admit women. When Edward Johnston (nos. 123–4) joined the staff in 1901, she became one of his pupils, and he often declared her to be one of his best. In 1905 Johnston was invited to Düsseldorf to teach a course in lettering for art teachers, the first of its kind. He could not go, but recommended his pupil instead, and in 1912, when he did go to Dresden to lecture, she stood beside him, translating his words while he gave his famous blackboard demonstrations.

Through her calligraphy, her teaching and her translation of *Writing & Illuminating, & Lettering*, a task that Johnston thought more difficult than writing the original, she influenced the whole current of German type design in its move away from the traditional gothic. During World War II her house was destroyed with all its calligraphic treasures.

## *William Graily Hewitt*

132 THE SONG OF THE THREE HOLY CHILDREN. *The Book of Daniel, III*
England, 1929.
6 vellum leaves, 10½×7½ inches; ink, watercolor, leaf gold; illuminated capitals and borders by Ida Henstock.
Binding: full red levant morocco.
Acquired from Graily Hewitt in 1948.
*Lent by Mr. and Mrs. Philip Hofer*

133 GEORGICS: Virgil
England, 1940–1946.
4 vols., handmade paper, 11×7 inches; ink, watercolor, leaf gold; decoration by Ida Henstock. Binding: boards.
*Lent by Mr. and Mrs. Philip Hofer*

Graily Hewitt was born in 1864 and died in 1952. He was called to the bar in 1889, but later turned to the study of manuscripts, and became one of Johnston's first pupils. In 1901 he succeeded Johnston (nos. 123–4) at the Central School of Arts and Crafts, London, and taught there for over thirty years. His pupils in this exhibition include: Fairbank (135), Hutton (170), Law (178), Mildred Ratcliffe (192) and Walker (130).

His painstaking experiments did much to revive the lost art of gilding with gesso and gold leaf, and his prolific work in this medium includes outstanding manuscript books, rolls of honour and patents of nobility. He collected a small group of artists around him to help with the drawing and decoration, executing most of the gilding himself, but after about two years the group split up, and Ida Henstock became his only assistant.

Among his published works are *Oxford Copy Books* (1916), *Lettering* (1930), *The Treyford Writing Cards* (1932) and *Handwriting: Everyman's Craft* (1938). He was a founder member of the S.S.I.

## *Ida Henstock*

Ida Henstock was born in Sheffield and was taught writing and illumination by Madelyn Walker (no. 130), who later was responsible for her joining a group of artists working for Graily Hewitt on the Royal Army Medical Corps Roll of Honour in Westminster Abbey. She collaborated with Graily Hewitt until his death in 1952, since when she has executed many complete works for clients public and private. S.S.I.

## *Jessie Bayes*

134 ENGLAND by Stanley Baldwin; JERUSALEM by William Blake
England, c. 1930.
5 vellum leaves, 11×8 inches; historiated initials, color, gilded. Binding: vellum.
*Lent by Mr. and Mrs. Harry A. Walton, Jr.*

Jessie Bayes was a painter, illuminator and mural decorator. She was a member of the Royal Society of Miniature Painters, and her work was exhibited in England, France and the United States. For some time she was the official purchaser of illuminated manuscripts for a Detroit gallery. One of her outstanding works was the Roll of Honour, King's Royal Rifles, for Winchester Cathedral, England. Although the lettering of the piece exhibited is not up to the standard of the gilding, this is an unusual example for its time. She was the sister of Gilbert Bayes, the sculptor.

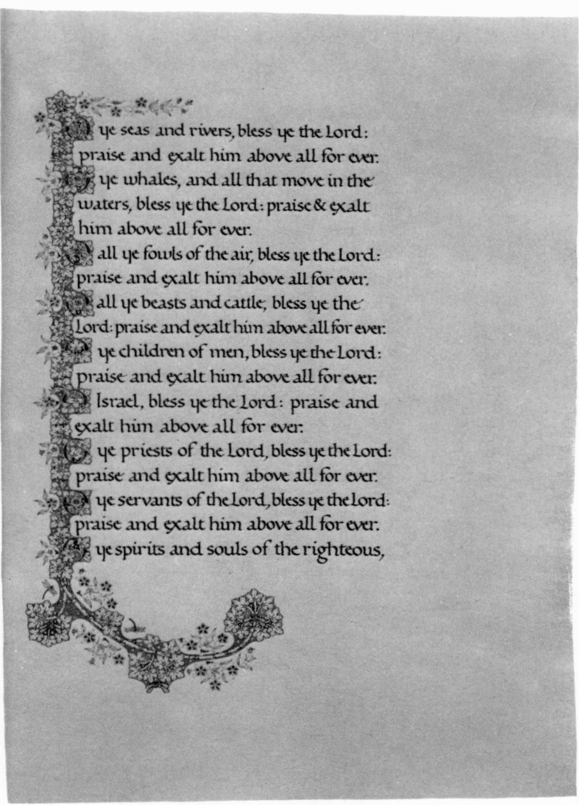

ye seas and rivers, bless ye the Lord:
praise and exalt him above all for ever.
ye whales, and all that move in the
waters, bless ye the Lord: praise & exalt
him above all for ever.
all ye fowls of the air, bless ye the Lord:
praise and exalt him above all for ever.
all ye beasts and cattle, bless ye the
Lord: praise and exalt him above all for ever.
ye children of men, bless ye the Lord:
praise and exalt him above all for ever.
Israel, bless ye the Lord: praise and
exalt him above all for ever.
ye priests of the Lord, bless ye the Lord:
praise and exalt him above all for ever.
ye servants of the Lord, bless ye the Lord:
praise and exalt him above all for ever.
ye spirits and souls of the righteous,

132. The Song of the Three Holy Children. William Graily Hewitt. 1929

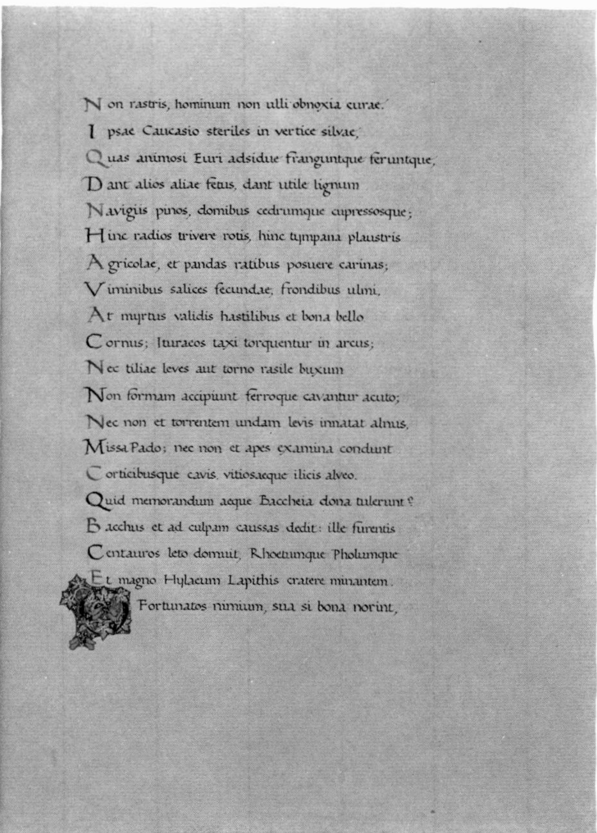

Non rastris, hominum non ulli obnoxia curae.
Ipsae Caucasio steriles in vertice silvae,
Quas animosi Euri adsidue franguntque feruntque,
Dant alios aliae fetus, dant utile lignum
Navigiis pinos, domibus cedrumque cupressosque;
Hinc radios trivere rotis, hinc tympana plaustris
Agricolae, et pandas ratibus posuere carinas;
Viminibus salices fecundae, frondibus ulmi,
At myrtus validis hastilibus et bona bello
Cornus; Ituraeos taxi torquentur in arcus;
Nec tiliae leves aut torno rasile buxum
Non formam accipiunt ferroque cavantur acuto;
Nec non et torrentem undam levis innatat alnus,
Missa Pado; nec non et apes examina condunt
Corticibusque cavis, vitiosaeque ilicis alveo.
Quid memorandum aeque Baccheia dona tulerunt?
Bacchus et ad culpam caussas dedit: ille furentis
Centauros leto domuit, Rhoetumque Pholumque
Et magno Hylaeum Lapithis cratere minantem.
Fortunatos nimium, sua si bona norint,

133. Virgil: Georgics. William Graily Hewitt. 1940–1946

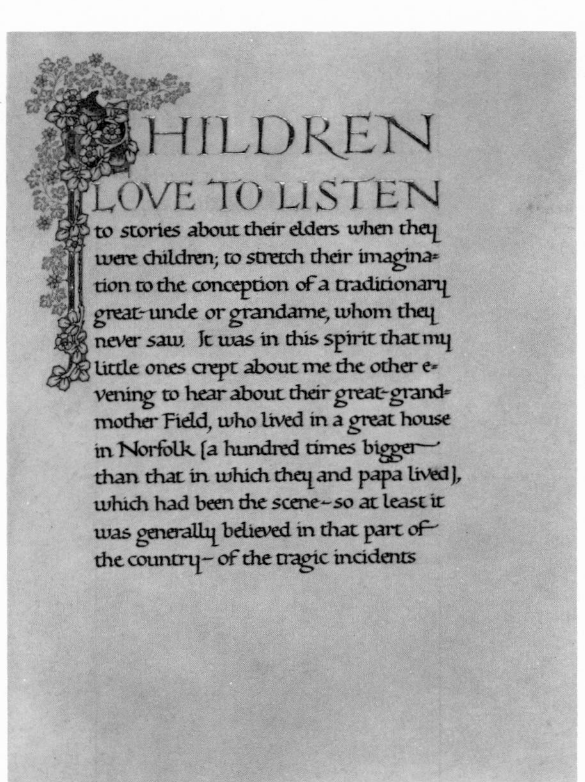

HILDREN
LOVE TO LISTEN
to stories about their elders when they were children; to stretch their imagination to the conception of a traditionary great-uncle or grandame, whom they never saw. It was in this spirit that my little ones crept about me the other evening to hear about their great-grandmother Field, who lived in a great house in Norfolk (a hundred times bigger than that in which they and papa lived), which had been the scene—so at least it was generally believed in that part of the country—of the tragic incidents

130. Lamb: Dream Children. Madelyn Walker. 1924–1926

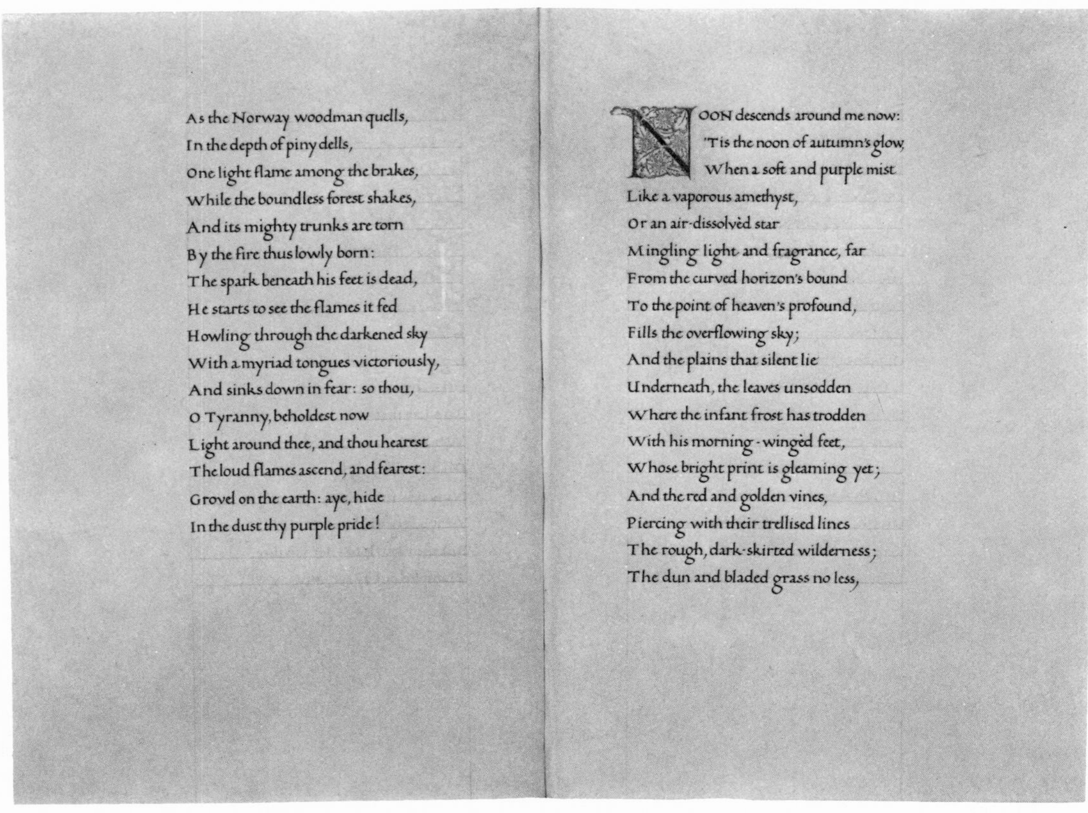
As the Norway woodman quells,
In the depth of piny dells,
One light flame among the brakes,
While the boundless forest shakes,
And its mighty trunks are torn
By the fire thus lowly born:
The spark beneath his feet is dead,
He starts to see the flames it fed
Howling through the darkened sky
With a myriad tongues victoriously,
And sinks down in fear: so thou,
O Tyranny, beholdest now
Light around thee, and thou hearest
The loud flames ascend, and fearest:
Grovel on the earth: aye, hide
In the dust thy purple pride!

NOON descends around me now:
'Tis the noon of autumn's glow,
When a soft and purple mist
Like a vaporous amethyst,
Or an air-dissolvèd star
Mingling light and fragrance, far
From the curved horizon's bound
To the point of heaven's profound,
Fills the overflowing sky;
And the plains that silent lie
Underneath, the leaves unsodden
Where the infant frost has trodden
With his morning-wingèd feet,
Whose bright print is gleaming yet;
And the red and golden vines,
Piercing with their trellised lines
The rough, dark-skirted wilderness;
The dun and bladed grass no less,

135. Shelley: Lines on the Euganean Hills. Alfred J. Fairbank. 1931

Woher sind wir geboren?
Aus Lieb.
Wie wären wir verloren?
Ohn Lieb.
Was hilft uns überwinden?
Die Lieb.
Kann man auch Liebe finden?
Durch Lieb.
Was läßt nicht lange weinen?
Die Lieb.
Was soll uns stets vereinen?
Die Lieb!

Goethe

131. Goethe: Woher sind wir geboren? Anna Simons. n.d.

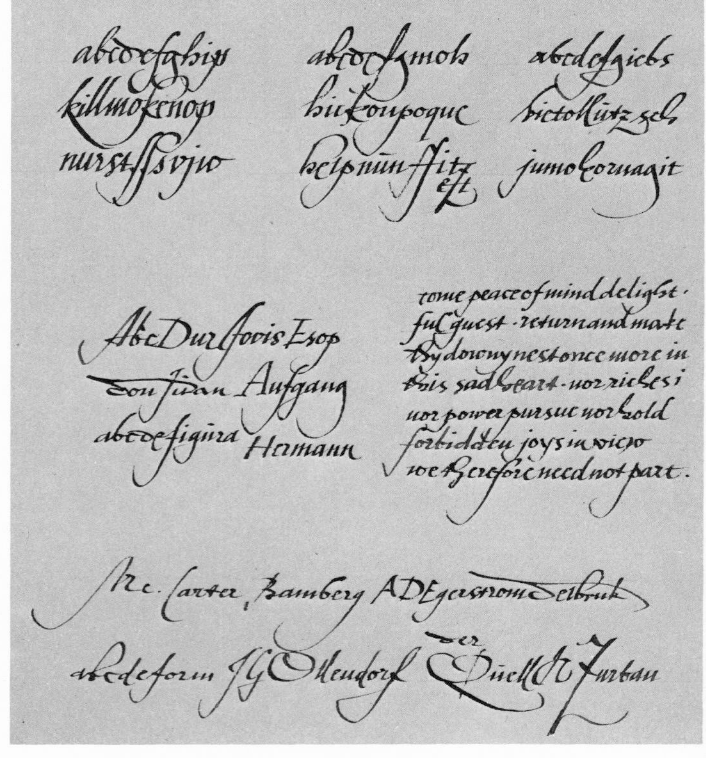


136. Alphabet. Ernst Schneidler. c. 1930–1940

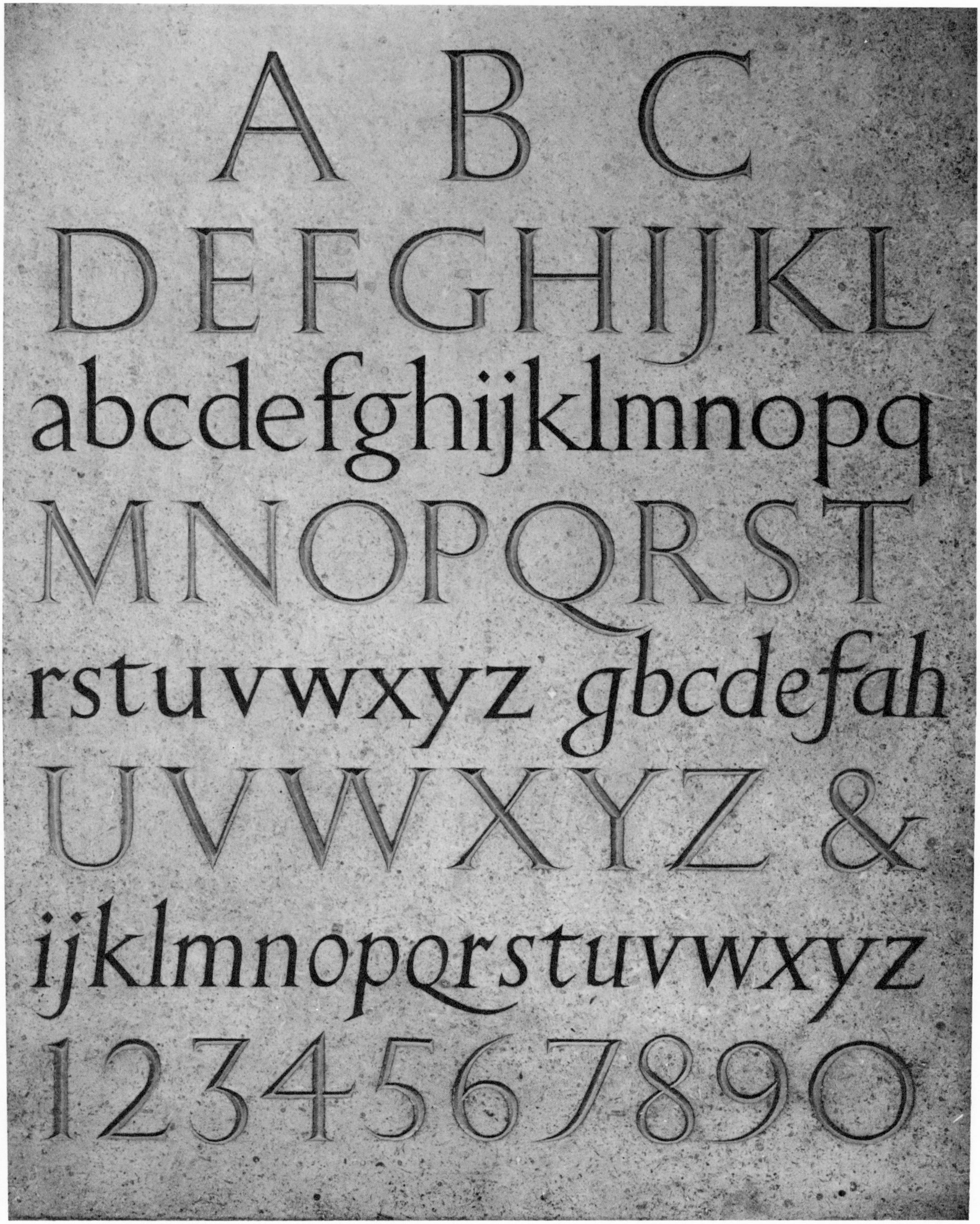

137. Alphabet Stone. Eric Gill. c. 1938

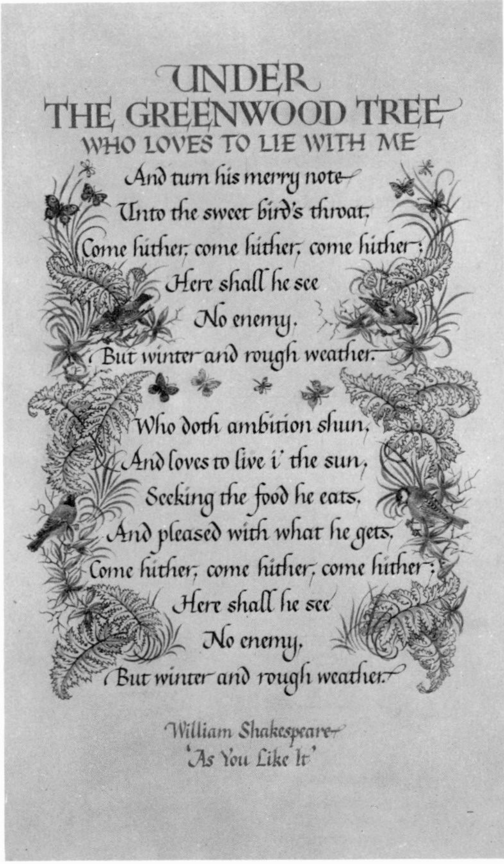


138. Shakespeare: Under the Greenwood Tree.
C. Harry Adams. 1964

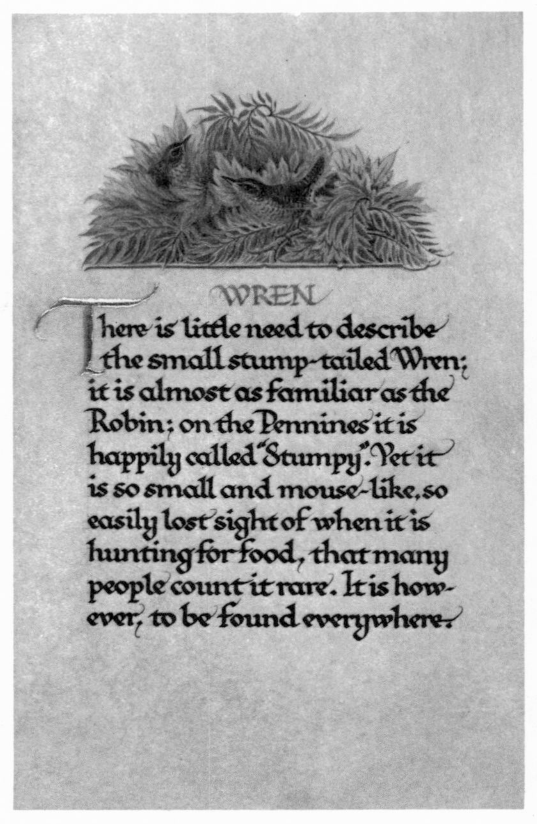


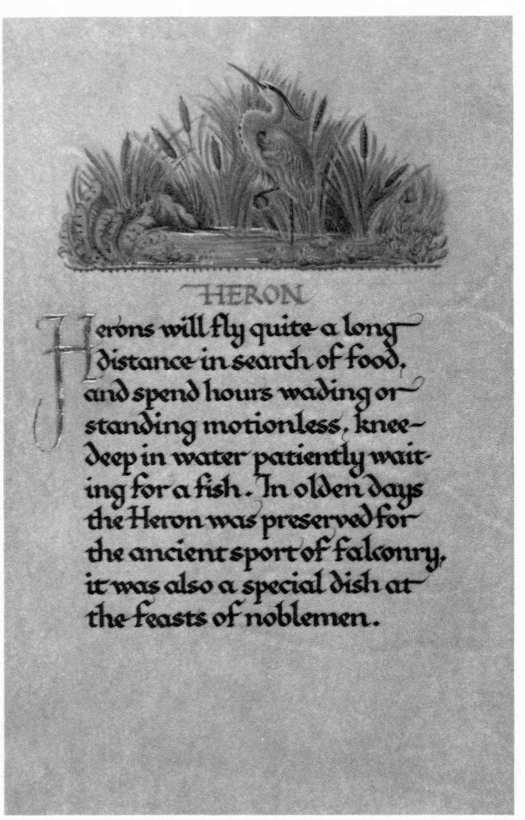


139. Birds of Britain. Margaret Adams. 1954

## *Alfred J. Fairbank*

135 LINES ON THE EUGANEAN HILLS by Percy Bysshe Shelley
Croydon, Surrey, 1931.
16 parchment leaves, 9⅝×6½ inches; ink, color; written in roman script and gilded by A. J. Fairbank; illuminated by Louise Powell. Binding: by Charles McLeish.
Acquired from Louise Powell, 1950.
*Lent by Mr. and Mrs. Philip Hofer*

Alfred Fairbank was born in 1895. From 1920 to 1922 he attended evening classes in calligraphy and illuminating at the Central School of Arts and Crafts, London, under Graily Hewitt (nos. 132–3) and Lawrence Christie. From 1925 to 1939 he collaborated with Louise Powell on many works such as the one shown. He designed and directed the production of the Royal Air Force Books of Remembrance and the relevant roll of the American Air Force, now in St. Clement Danes Church, London, ten volumes containing 150,000 names. He has exhibited in most of the important centers of the world, but he is best known as the foremost living proponent of the italic hand.

Edward Johnston inspired although he did not teach him, and his early interest in italic handwriting flowered in 1928 in his design of *Condensed Bembo Italic* type. Believing there was a need for standards in calligraphy, he was a founder member of the Society of Scribes and Illuminators in 1921 and served as its President from 1951 to 1963. He has taught at least a thousand teachers italic handwriting in short courses and for many years has been of indefatigable help in every aspect of its revival. He was awarded the C.B.E. (Commander of the British Empire) by the Queen in 1951 for his services to calligraphy. At his suggestion the Society for Italic Handwriting was founded in 1952.

Now retired from government service, he has had time to expand his researches into renaissance handwriting. His many articles, pamphlets and books include *A Handwriting Manual* and associated writing cards (1932), *A Book of Scripts* (1949, etc.) and *Renaissance Handwriting: an Anthology of Italic Scripts*, by Fairbank & Wolpe (1960). His series of *Beacon Writing Books* (1961, etc.) are influencing the teaching of writing in schools everywhere.

## *Louise Powell*

Louise (Lessore) Powell was born in 1882 and died in 1956. She belonged to a long line of painters and became an important figure in the Johnstonian School of illumination and writing. One of Johnston's early pupils, she also came under the influence of W. R. Lethaby and (Sir) Sydney Cockerell. For a short time she was an assistant to Graily Hewitt (nos. 132–3), and she and Hewitt were commissioned by Fairfax Murray to make additions to William Morris's incomplete manuscript, *The Aeneid of Virgil*, where she did the borders of floriate and foliate decoration. She also worked on another incomplete Morris manuscript, *Frithiof the Bold* (no. 121), and on the decorated initials and borders for the Ashendene Press edition of *Don Quixote*.

Later she collaborated on the production of *Comus*, *Horace*, *Ecclesiasticus* and other works with Alfred Fairbank (above), who considers her the greatest illuminator of this century. She lavished most of her skill and imagination on embellishing the writing of others, but the Victoria and Albert Museum Library possesses a manuscript book of *Psalms* entirely in her hand, written in 1905. She was the wife of Alfred Powell, architect, and was an early craft member of the S.S.I.

## *Ernst Schneidler*

136 ALPHABET
Southern Germany, c. 1930–1940.
1 paper leaf, 6½×5½ inches; ink.
This and other pieces by Schneidler were acquired from his son, Peter Schneidler, in 1960.
*Lent by the Pierpont Morgan Library*

Ernst Schneidler was born in 1882 and died in 1956. In 1920 he organized the Graphic Arts Department of the Stuttgart Akademie, retiring in 1949, after thirty years' teaching. During this time he sent forth a band of students who remade Germany's graphic arts. His many pupils, including Imre Reiner, Albert Knor and Georg Trump, have today virtually taken full command of the leading graphic art posts in Germany. His four-volume *Der Wassermann* portfolio of graphic and typographic problems is unique both in pedagogy and graphic art history. It was only after his death that Germany fully understood the range of his scribal powers; and through exhibitions arranged by his son Peter his work became known internationally.

In an appreciation of him, at the time the Pierpont Morgan Library acquired his pieces, Paul Standard wrote, "To his two American correspondents he confided his ideal as *Ritterlichkeit*—chivalry; and he felt that only in America could that vanishing virtue survive."

## *Eric Gill*

137 ALPHABET STONE
England, c. 1938.
Hopton Wood stone, 24×19½ inches.
*Lent by John M. Crawford, Jr.*

Eric Gill was born in Brighton in 1882 and died near Uxbridge in 1940. In 1897 he studied at the Chichester Art School, intending to become an architect, but found little to interest him in current architecture. In his leisure time he took up lettering and letter cutting under Edward Johnston (nos. 123–4), and after sharing rooms with Johnston he moved to Ditchling, Sussex. In 1913 he became a Roman Catholic and was commissioned to carve the Stations of the Cross in Westminster Cathedral. His interests had extended to engraving and typography, and works came from him at St. Dominic's Press, Ditchling. His engravings for the Golden Cockerel Press are outstanding, as are his types, *Perpetua* (1925) and *Gill Sans-serif* (1927).

Although never a teacher in the formal sense, he trained Reynolds Stone (no. 201) and David Kindersley (nos. 175–6), among others, in letter cutting. The *Dictionary of National Biography*'s statement, "His lettering in stone, with its impersonal grandeur and its finality, was the noblest that had been seen for centuries," is well demonstrated by the stone shown in this exhibition. Like William Morris, he was a great thinker and writer, and his *Autobiography* (1940) is regarded as a classic.

# B: 1948 *to* 1965

## *C. Harry Adams*

138 UNDER THE GREENWOOD TREE. From *As You Like It* by William Shakespeare
England, 1964.
1 handmade paper leaf, 18×11 inches; ink, watercolor. Decoration by C. Harry Adams; italic lettering by Margaret Adams.
One of a series carried out for the Shakespeare Quatercentenary Exhibition in April 1964, held at the Royal Birmingham School of Artists.
*Lent by Stuart B. Schimmel*

Harry Adams was born in 1894. He was a student at the Birmingham College of Art and was for many years on its staff. He retired from the headmastership of Moseley School of Art, Birmingham, in 1961. Besides the many commissioned works he has done alone, he has collaborated with his wife, Margaret Adams (no. 139), on much illustration and decoration for Stanbrook Abbey Press, Worcester. He decorated the two Books of Consecration for the new Coventry Cathedral. S.S.I.

## *Margaret Adams*

139 BIRDS OF BRITAIN
Birmingham, England, 1954.
13 vellum leaves, $7\frac{3}{4} \times 4\frac{5}{16}$ inches; ink, watercolor, gilding; Winchester foundational hand. Binding: green morocco, gold tooled.
*Lent by Stuart B. Schimmel*

Hilda Margaret Adams was born in Bridgnorth, Shropshire, in 1912. She studied at the Birmingham College of Art and was a pupil of Harry Adams (no. 138) and Daisy Alcock. Her main work now is for Stanbrook Abbey, Worcester, where she hand-decorates and gilds the fine printing of this press. One of the most successful examples of her work is on Siegfried Sassoon's *The Path of Peace* (1959), printed by Stanbrook Abbey. She has performed many notable commissions, including the gilding of the two Books of Consecration for the new Coventry Cathedral. S.S.I.

## *Margaret Alexander*

140 THE ROSE by Logan Pearsall Smith
England, 1961.
12 vellum leaves, 9×7 inches; ink, color, gold; foundational hand based on English tenth-century writing. Binding: white pigskin, gold tooled by Roger Powell.
*Lent by Richard Harrison*

Margaret Alexander was born in Hampstead, England, in 1902. She studied at the Slade School of Fine Art and taught calligraphy and illuminating there, 1928–1957. She was also a calligrapher to the House of Lords, 1926–1963. She has executed addresses to a long list of distinguished persons, including four sovereigns of her country. Her commissioned works have been exhibited internationally, and are to be found in many of the great institutions in Britain, continental Europe and the United States, as well as in the finest private collections. S.S.I.

## *Marie Angel*

141 A BESTIARY
England, 1960.
26 vellum leaves, 4×4 inches; watercolor drawings. Unbound.
*Lent by Mr. and Mrs. Philip Hofer*

Conte said proudly when they praised it, and he would tell the Signora about it. And as they sat there, drinking the wine he offered them, he alluded with the cheerful indifference of old age to his love affair, as though he took for granted that they had heard of it already.

THE LADY lived across the valley there beyond that hill. I was a young man then, for it was many years ago. I used to ride over to see her; it was a long way, but I rode fast, for young men, as no doubt the Signora knows, are impatient. But the lady was not kind, she would keep me waiting, oh, for hours; and one day when I had waited very long I grew very angry, and as I walked up and down

6

in the garden where she had told me she would see me, I broke one of her roses, broke a branch from it; and when I saw what I had done, I hid it inside my coat — so —; and when I came home I planted it, and the Signora sees how it has grown. If the Signora admires it, I must give her a cutting to plant also in her garden; I am told the English have beautiful gardens that are green, and not burnt with the sun like ours.'

The next day, when their mended carriage had come up to fetch them, and they were just starting to drive away from the inn, the Conte's old servant appeared with the rose-cutting neatly wrapped up, and the compliments and wishes for a buon

7

140. Logan Pearsall Smith: The Rose. Margaret Alexander. 1961

ABC abc
defghijklmnop
qrstuvwxyz
Scripta

144. Calligraphic Alphabet. Arthur Baker. 1964

Wilfrid Owen: Strange Meeting

It seemed that out of battle I escaped
Down some profound dull tunnel, long since scooped
Through granites which titanic wars had groined.
Yet also there encumbered sleepers groaned,
Too fast in thought or death to be bestirred.
Then, as I probed them, one sprang up, and stared
With piteous recognition in fixed eyes,
Lifting distressful hands as if to bless.
And by his smile, I knew that sullen hall,
By his dead smile I knew we stood in Hell.
With a thousand pains that vision's face was grained;
Yet no blood reached there from the upper ground,
And no guns thumped, or down the flues made moan.
'Strange friend,' I said, 'here is no cause to moan.'
'None,' said the other, 'save the undone years,
The hopelessness. Whatever hope is yours,
Was my life also; I went hunting wild
After the wildest beauty in the world,
Which lies not calm in eyes, or braided hair,
But mocks the steady running of the hour,
And if it grieves, grieves richlier than here.
For by my glee might many men have laughed,
And of my weeping something had been left,
Which must die now. I mean the truth untold,
The pity of war, the pity war distilled.
Now men will go content with what we spoiled.
Or, discontent, boil bloody, and be spilled.
They will be swift with swiftness of the tigress,
None will break ranks, though nations trek from progress.
Courage was mine, and I had mystery,
Wisdom was mine, and I had mastery;
To miss the march of this retreating world
Into vain citadels that are not walled.
Then, when much blood had clogged their chariot wheels
I would go up and wash them from sweet wells,
Even with truths that lie too deep for taint.
I would have poured my spirit without stint
But not through wounds; not on the cess of war.
Foreheads of men have bled where no wounds were.
I am the enemy you killed, my friend.
I knew you in this dark; for so you frowned
Yesterday through me as you jabbed and killed.
I parried; but my hands were loath and cold.
Let us sleep now....'

146. Wilfrid Owen: Strange Meeting. Stuart Barrie. 1964

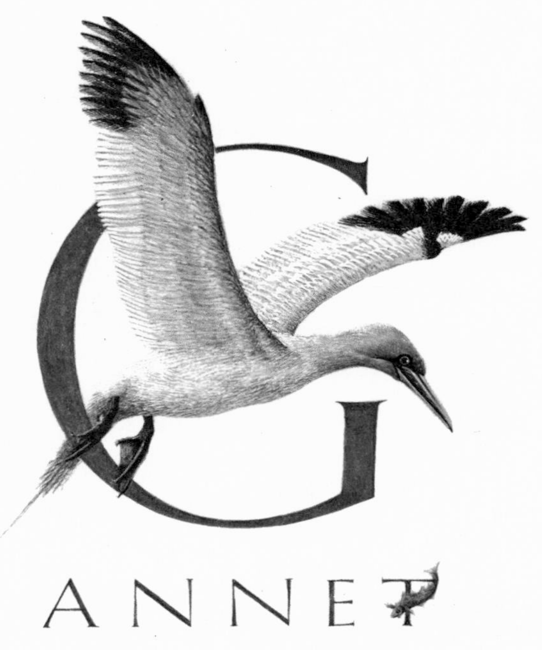


141. A Bestiary. Marie Angel. 1960

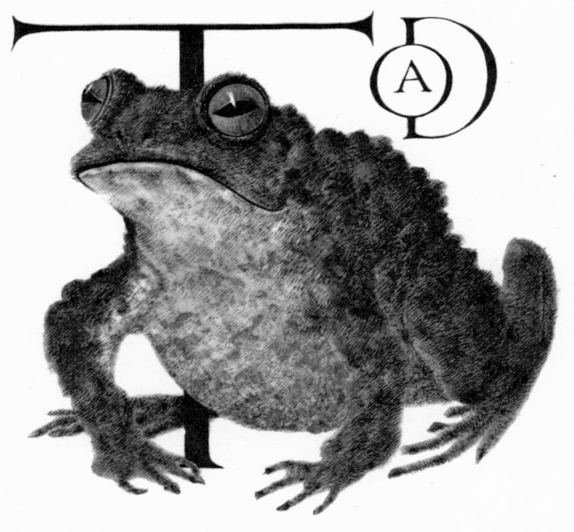


142. A New Bestiary. Marie Angel. 1964

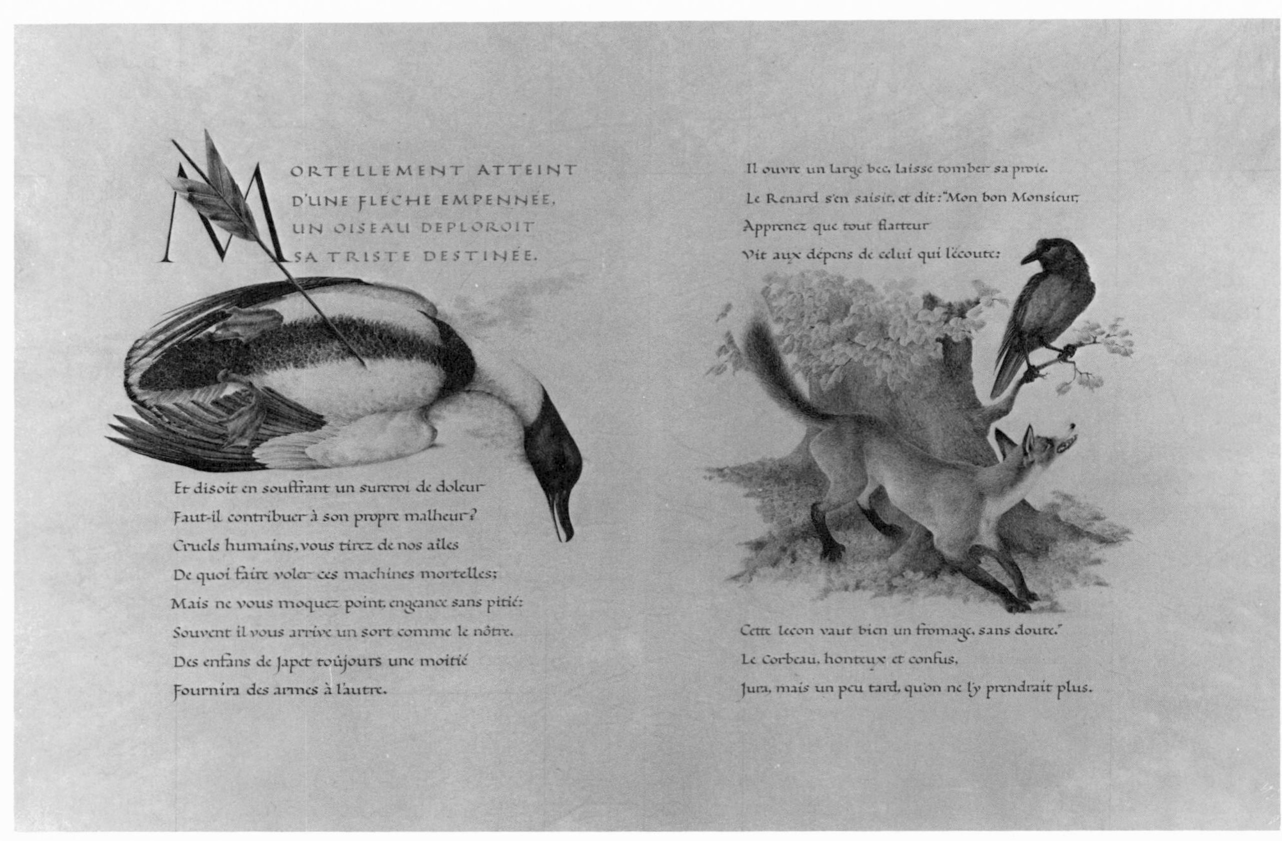

MORTELLEMENT ATTEINT
D'UNE FLECHE EMPENNÉE,
UN OISEAU DEPLOROIT
SA TRISTE DESTINÉE.

Et disoit en souffrant un surcroi de doleur
Faut-il contribuer à son propre malheur?
Cruels humains, vous tirez de nos ailes
De quoi faire voler ces machines mortelles;
Mais ne vous moquez point, engeance sans pitié:
Souvent il vous arrive un sort comme le nôtre.
Des enfans de Japet toûjours une moitié
Fournira des armes à l'autre.

Il ouvre un large bec, laisse tomber sa proie.
Le Renard s'en saisit, et dit: "Mon bon Monsieur,
Apprenez que tout flatteur
Vit aux dépens de celui qui l'écoute:

Cette lecon vaut bien un fromage, sans doute."
Le Corbeau, honteux et confus,
Jura, mais un peu tard, qu'on ne l'y prendrait plus.

143. Fables d'Esope. Marie Angel. 1960–1964

142 A NEW BESTIARY
England, 1964.
25 vellum leaves, 4×4 inches; watercolor drawings. Unbound.
*Lent by Mr. and Mrs. Philip Hofer*

143 FABLES D'ESOPE
England, 1960–1964.
34 vellum leaves, 18×24 inches; ink, watercolor; small roman hand. Unbound.
*Lent by Richard Harrison*

Marie Angel was born in London in 1923. She entered Croydon School of Art and Crafts, 1930, and in 1945 she passed into the School of Design at the Royal College of Art, Kensington, where she was a pupil of Professor E. W. Tristram and Dorothy Mahoney (no. 181). Much of her work has been done for the College of Arms; but she has achieved the greatest success with her miniature drawings of plants and animals, which exemplify the humor and delicacy of her calligraphy and illustrations. Most of her work is in the hands of private collectors in the United States. The *Bestiary* and *New Bestiary* were issued as books by the Department of Graphic Arts, Harvard College, in 1960 and 1964. The *Bestiary* had achieved three printings by 1963. S.S.I.

## *Arthur Baker*

144 CALLIGRAPHIC ALPHABET
Piedmont, California, 1964.
1 paper leaf, 22×17 inches; black ink; contemporary italic hand.
*Lent by the Artist*

Arthur Baker was born in the 1930's, and attended art schools and colleges in California and New York, including classes at Columbia University under Oscar Ogg (no. 185). He is now occupied in calligraphy and design for advertising and publishing, and has designed a number of calligraphic type styles. October House Inc. reports that it will publish the following books by him during 1965 and 1966: *Calligraphics—800 Alphabet Variations, Manual Calligraphicum, Abstract Calligraphy* and *Contemporary American Calligraphy*.

## *Arnold Bank*

145 TESTIMONIAL TO LLOYD REYNOLDS
given by the Portland Art Commission
Pittsburgh, Pennsylvania, 1963–1964.
1 vellum leaf, 13⅝×19¾ inches; india ink; cancelleresca corsiva, decorative alphabet in simple hand.
*Lent by Lloyd J. Reynolds*

Arnold Bank was born in New York City in 1908. He was trained in mural decoration and lettering at the Art Students League and at other New York City schools. He was for some years art director of *Time*, and has taught in a number of institutions, including the Art Students League and the Pratt Institute Art School in New York. He was particularly successful as a Fulbright Senior Fellow and Lecturer in typographic arts in England, 1954–1957, where his demonstrations on huge sheets of paper are still carefully preserved. He has been Associate Professor of Graphic Arts at Carnegie Institute of Technology, Pittsburgh, since 1960. His several one-man shows have attracted wide attention, and many of his works have been illustrated in contemporary books on lettering. He has also designed architectural inscriptions for the Institute of Fine Arts of New York University, the entrance to the Public Library of Dayton, Ohio, and the "Credo" monument in Rockefeller Center, New York.

## *Stuart Barrie*

146 STRANGE MEETING by Wilfrid Owen
Edinburgh, October 1964.
1 vellum leaf, 10½×13½ inches; ink; in a more current hand than normal italic, and heavier in contrast.
*Lent by the Artist*

Stuart Barrie was born in Edinburgh in 1925. After four years' service in the R.A.F. as draughtsman/cartographer, he studied at the Edinburgh College of Art under Nora Patterson. He acknowledges the influence of Rudolf Koch (no. 125) and Hermann Zapf (no. 218). He has been teaching lettering and calligraphy at the Edinburgh College of Art since 1957, and is book-jacket designer for Oliver & Boyd, Ltd., publishers. The exhibited work is a poem selected by Mr. Barrie from *The Collected Poems of Wilfrid Owen*, published by New Directions. S.S.I.

## *Irene Base*

147 QUOTATION FROM SHAKESPEARE
Shirehampton, Bristol, 1964.
1 vellum leaf, 7×5¼ inches; gilded; foundational majuscules with gold versals. Binding: by Sydney M. Cockerell.
*Lent by Stuart B. Schimmel*

Irene Base was born in Norwich, England. She studied at

Norwich School of Art and Chelsea School of Art, and was the pupil of Mervyn C. Oliver (no. 186) and C. W. Hobbis. Two of her outstanding pupils are Marjorie Tuson (no. 205) and Wendy Parnell (no. 187). Her work is to be found in many institutional and private collections and has been widely exhibited and reproduced. Her skill in illumination caused her to be chosen to write the chapter on gilding in *The Calligrapher's Handbook* (1956). S.S.I.

## *John E. Benson*

148 ALPHABET STONE
Newport, Rhode Island, December 1964.
Slate. 19⅞×15⅞ inches.
*Lent by E. Harold Hugo*

John E. Benson was born in Newport, Rhode Island, in 1939. He attended the Rhode Island School of Design for four years, taking his degree in sculpture and participating in the senior honors program, which sent him to Rome for his last year, 1960–1961.

He learned letter cutting at the John Stevens Shop, which belonged to his father, John Howard Benson (no. 149), and is now carried on by his mother. Starting in 1955 under his father's own guidance, he worked every afternoon after school and in the summers while an art student. Since 1961 he has given his full time to the work of the shop and is now, at twenty-five, a partner in the firm.

## *John Howard Benson*

149 ALPHABET STONE
Newport, Rhode Island, 1955.
Vermont slate, 18×23½ inches.
*Lent by John M. Crawford, Jr.*

John Howard Benson was born in Newport, Rhode Island, in 1901, and died there in 1956. He attended the National Academy of Design and the Art Students League in New York, where he studied with Joseph Pennell. In 1927 he bought the John Stevens Shop in Newport and returned there, to work for the rest of his life as a teacher, stone carver, calligrapher, wood engraver, sculptor, designer and maker of dies for medals.

For thirty-five years he was a serious student of letters, delving deeply into their origins, their underlying forms, their history, their adaptability to various materials and their ancient and modern use. At will he could write any of the great historic hands, and did so in his classes at the Rhode Island School of Design.

Among the best-known examples of his stone carving may be mentioned the inscription in italic capitals over the entrance to the Grace Rainey Rogers Auditorium at the Metropolitan Museum of Art in New York and the Second World War Memorial tablet in the chapel of The Phillips Exeter Academy in New Hampshire.

In 1950 he and Arthur G. Carey wrote a successful book, *The Elements of Lettering*, and in 1954 he translated and transcribed Arrighi's *Operina* (see no. 63), making this fundamental book available for the first time to English-speaking students.

In 1955 he received an Honorary Degree of Master of Arts from Yale.

Eloquent testimony was paid to him by Philip Hofer in Typophile Chap Book 31, *John Howard Benson & His Work* (1957).

## *H. J. Blackman*

150 PRESENTATION ADDRESS TO ARVID BERGVALL
Richmond, 1964.
1 vellum sheet, 18×14 inches; copperplate, names in roman, raised gold, other headings in blue and gold.
*Lent by the Artist*

H. J. Blackman was born in London in 1912. Except for instruction in lithography at Bolt Court School of Lithography before World War II, he is entirely self-taught. During the war he was with the Geographical Section, War Office, engaged on operational maps for the Armed Services. He is a professional copperplate writer, and is at present chief cartographer, calligrapher and heraldic artist to the Middlesex County Council. S.S.I.

## *Chris Brand*

151 BOOK JACKET *De Christen en der Arbeid*
Breda, Netherlands, 1961.
1 paper sheet, 7¾×4¾ inches; italic hand.
*Lent by the Artist*

Chris Brand was born in Utrecht in 1921. He is self-taught, and from 1948 to 1953 worked in Brussels, executing commissions for various government institutions. He now lives in the Netherlands and teaches at the Academy of Fine Arts and Crafts Sint Joost at Breda and at the Royal Academy for Arts and Crafts at 's-Hertogenbosch. His work, mainly commercial, includes charters, monograms, trademarks, book jackets and type. His most recent typeface is *Albertina*, for the Monotype Corporation. He has written widely on handwriting, and recently issued a book on italic handwriting for primary schools. He has exhibited in Europe, Great Britain and the United States.

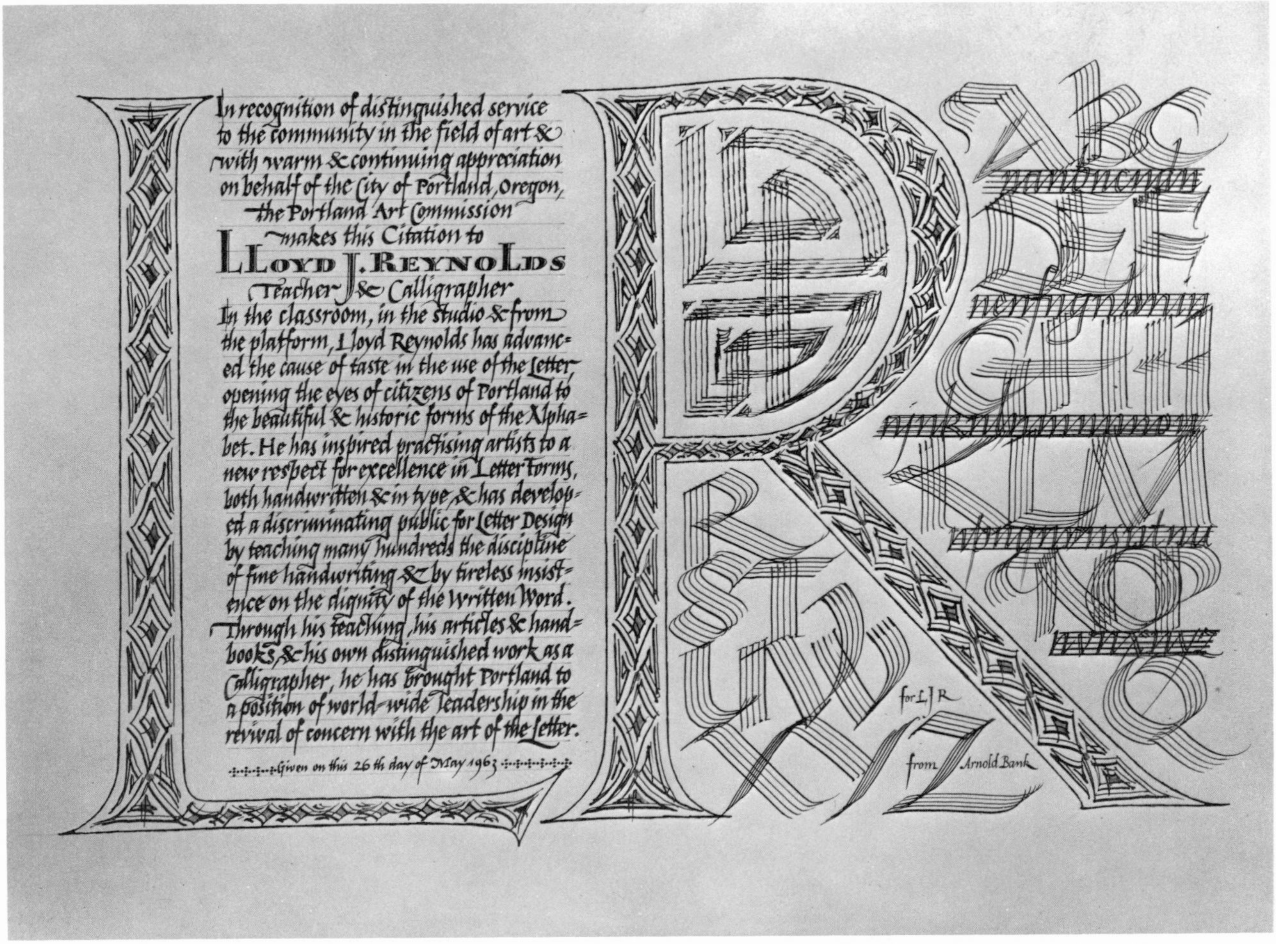

In recognition of distinguished service to the community in the field of art & with warm & continuing appreciation on behalf of the City of Portland, Oregon, the Portland Art Commission makes this Citation to

LLOYD J. REYNOLDS

Teacher & Calligrapher

In the classroom, in the studio & from the platform, Lloyd Reynolds has advanced the cause of taste in the use of the Letter, opening the eyes of citizens of Portland to the beautiful & historic forms of the Alphabet. He has inspired practising artists to a new respect for excellence in Letter Forms, both handwritten & in type, & has developed a discriminating public for Letter Design by teaching many hundreds the discipline of fine handwriting & by tireless insistence on the dignity of the Written Word. Through his teaching, his articles & handbooks, & his own distinguished work as a Calligrapher, he has brought Portland to a position of world-wide leadership in the revival of concern with the art of the Letter.

Given on this 26th day of May 1963

for L J R

from Arnold Bank

145. Testimonial to Lloyd Reynolds. Arnold Bank. 1963–1964

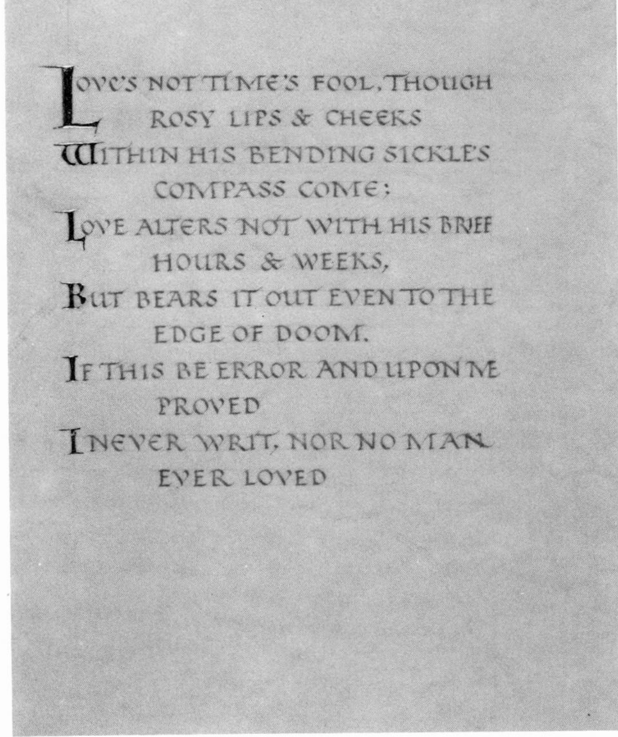

LOVE'S NOT TIME'S FOOL, THOUGH
ROSY LIPS & CHEEKS
WITHIN HIS BENDING SICKLE'S
COMPASS COME:
LOVE ALTERS NOT WITH HIS BRIEF
HOURS & WEEKS,
BUT BEARS IT OUT EVEN TO THE
EDGE OF DOOM.
IF THIS BE ERROR AND UPON ME
PROVED
I NEVER WRIT, NOR NO MAN
EVER LOVED

147. Quotation from Shakespeare. Irene Base. 1964

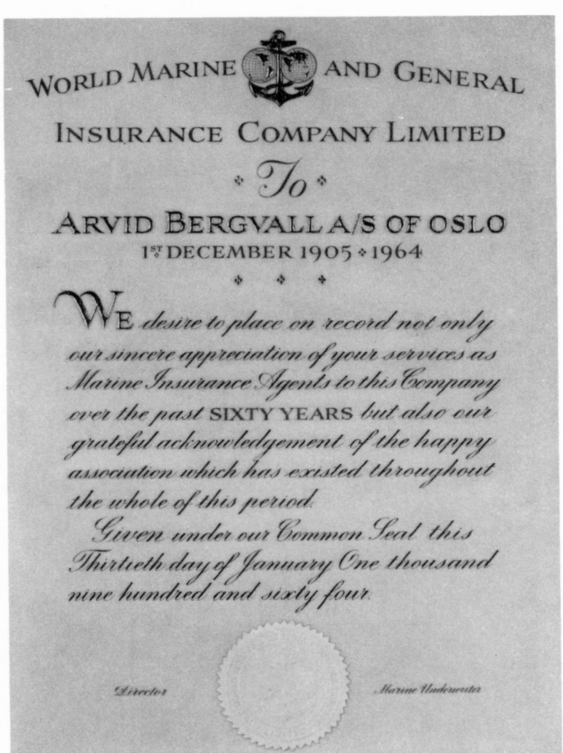

WORLD MARINE AND GENERAL
INSURANCE COMPANY LIMITED

To

ARVID BERGVALL A/S OF OSLO
1st DECEMBER 1905 • 1964

WE desire to place on record not only our sincere appreciation of your services as Marine Insurance Agents to this Company over the past SIXTY YEARS but also our grateful acknowledgement of the happy association which has existed throughout the whole of this period.

Given under our Common Seal this Thirtieth day of January One thousand nine hundred and sixty four.

Director

Marine Underwriter

150. Presentation Address to Arvid Bergvall. H. J. Blackman. 1964

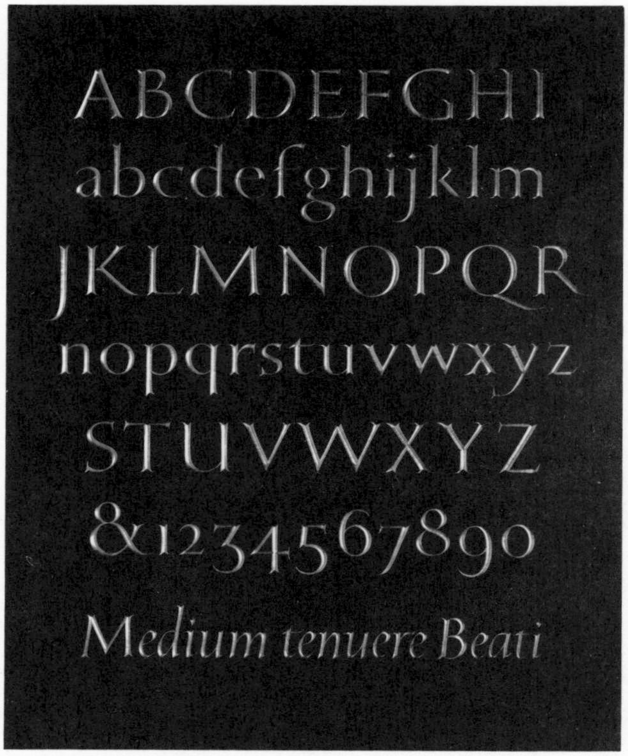

ABCDEFGHI
abcdefghijklm
JKLMNOPQR
nopqrstuvwxyz
STUVWXYZ
&1234567890
*Medium tenuere Beati*

148. Alphabet Stone. John E. Benson. 1964

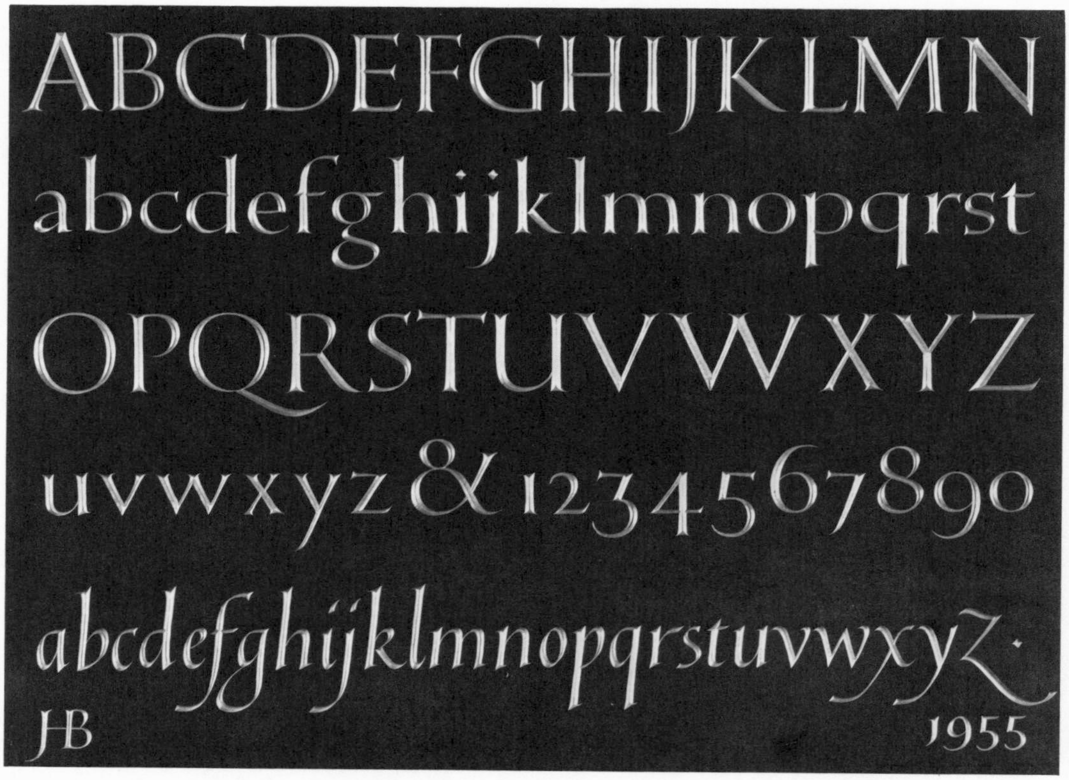

ABCDEFGHIJKLMN
abcdefghijklmnopqrst
OPQRSTUVWXYZ
uvwxyz&1234567890
*abcdefghijklmnopqrstuvwxyz·*
JHB 1955

149. Alphabet Stone. John Howard Benson. 1955

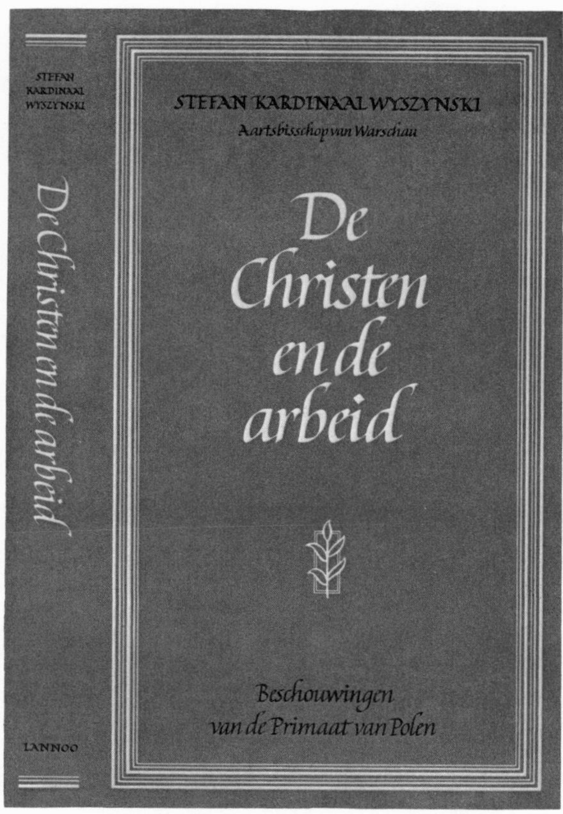


151. Book Jacket. Chris Brand. 1961

AND GOD SAID, LET US MAKE MAN IN OUR IMAGE, AFTER OUR LIKENESS: & LET THEM HAVE DOMINION OVER THE FISH OF THE SEA, & OVER THE FOWL OF THE AIR, & OVER THE CATTLE, & OVER ALL THE EARTH, AND OVER EVERY CREEPING THING THAT CREEPETH UPON THE EARTH.

So God created man in his own image, in the image of God created he him; male and female created he them.

And God blessed them, and God said unto them, Be fruitful, &

8

153. The Creation. Ann Camp. 1954

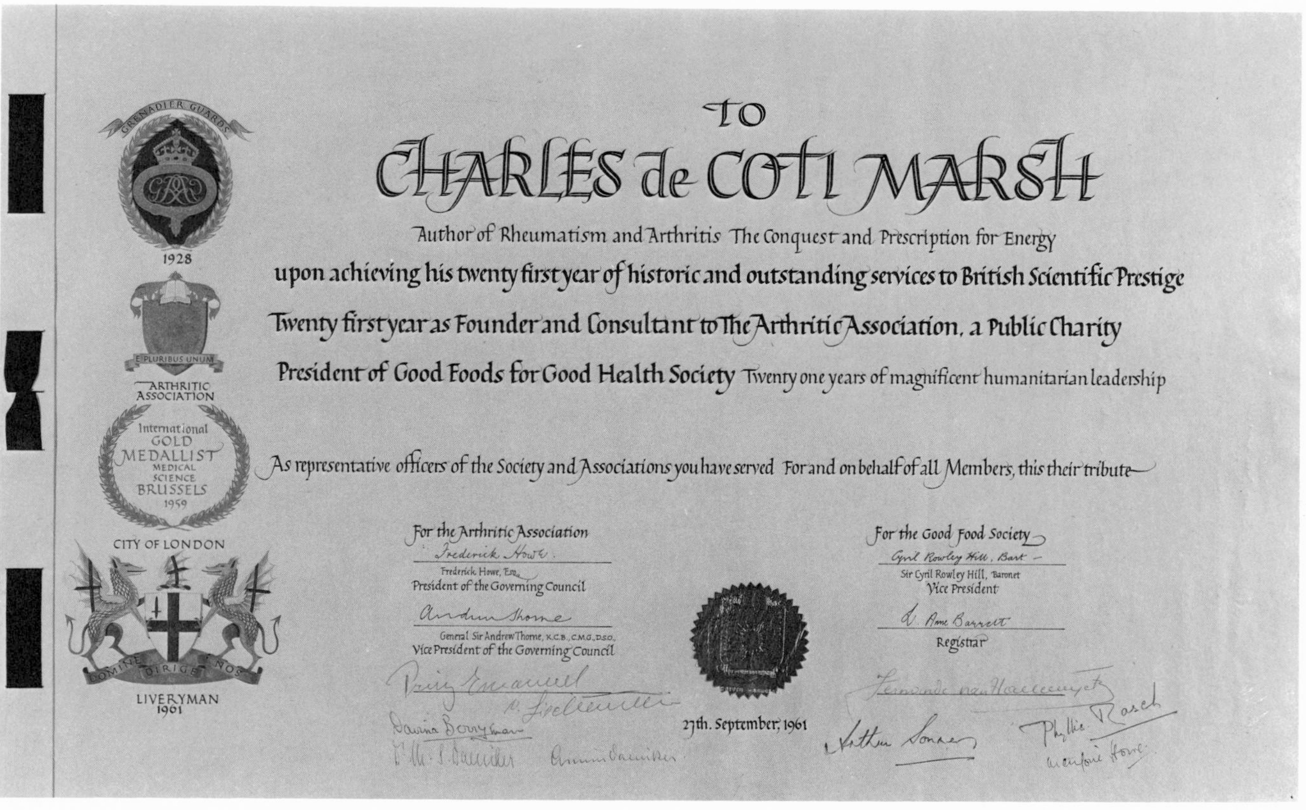


152. Award to Charles de Coti Marsh. John M. Cackett. 1961

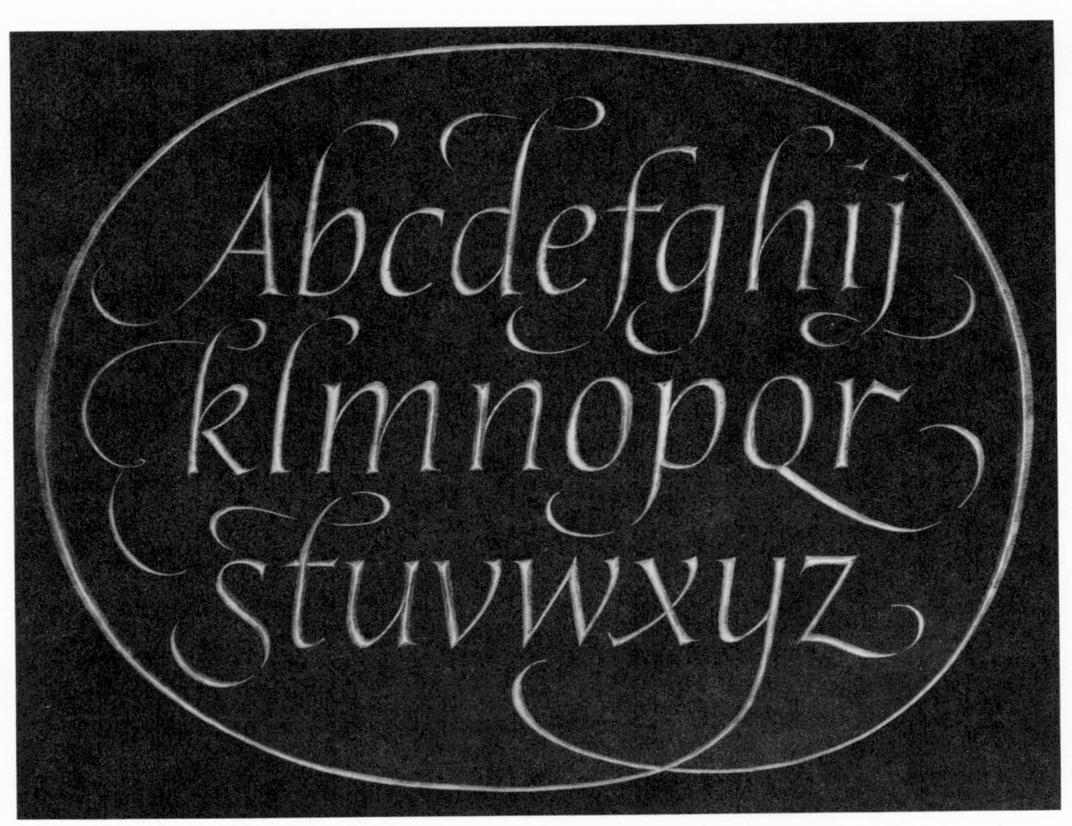


155. Alphabet Stone. Will Carter. 1963

. . . and I said to the man who stood
at the gate of the year, 'Give me a light
that I may tread safely into the unknown.'
And he replied, 'Go out into the darkness,
and put your hand into the hand of God.
That shall be to you better than light,
and safer than a known way.'

154. Anonymous Quotation. Will Carter. 1964

## *John M. Cackett*

152 AWARD TO CHARLES DE COTI MARSH
London, 1961.
1 handmade paper leaf, 13×21 inches; black stick ink, color, powder gold. (Decoration by Wendy Westover.)
*Lent by Charles de Coti Marsh*

John Cackett was born at Bedfont, Middlesex, in 1918. He has not at any time been engaged as a professional calligrapher; and although he accepts commissions in a private capacity, he is a lay member, not a craft member, of the Society of Scribes and Illuminators. He has studied at the Central School of Arts and Crafts, London, under the guidance of Ann Camp (no. 153). As the Secretary of the Society of Scribes he has worked unceasingly to further its ideas and objectives, and every exhibition with which he is associated is a model of courtesy, skill and efficiency.

## *Wendy Westover*

Wendy Westover was born in Epsom, Surrey, in 1928. She studied at the Wimbledon School of Art, Surrey, from 1944 to 1948 and at the Slade School of Fine Art, University of London, from 1948 to 1950, where Margaret Alexander (no. 140) instructed her in calligraphy. In 1950 and 1951 she studied lettering and letter cutting under David Kindersley (nos. 175–6) at his Barton workshop. She has many outstanding works in various institutions and in private collections. Her county maps have become internationally known. S.S.I.

## *Ann Camp*

153 THE CREATION
London, March 1954.
14 paper leaves; 8½×6 inches; red and black ink; foundational hand. Binding: handmade paper, decorated cover.
*Lent by the Artist*

Ann Camp was born in London in 1924 and has lived there all her life. She first studied calligraphy with Mervyn C. Oliver (no. 186) at Hampstead Garden Suburb Institute, and afterwards under Dorothy Mahoney (no. 181) at the Royal College of Art. She has written articles on the historic background and basic principles of calligraphy. In many of her commissions she uses a classic style adorned with heraldry—a happy harmony. S.S.I.

## *Will Carter*

154 ANONYMOUS QUOTATION
Cambridge, England, 1964.
Sandalwood and Nigerian walnut plaque, 22½×39 inches; incised lettering, colored.
*Lent by the Artist*

155 ALPHABET STONE
Cambridge, England, 1963.
Welsh slate, 12×15 inches; V-cut.
*Lent by Stuart B. Schimmel*

Will Carter was born in 1912. He has had no art school training, but taught himself to carve letters in wood, developing his own methods and individual style. He studied carving in stone and slate under David Kindersley (nos. 175–6). In addition to calligraphy and letter cutting, typography engages his attention; a lifelong interest that started when, as a boy of twelve, he was given a set of type. He runs the Rampant Lions Press in Cambridge, and designed the typeface *Klang* (Monotype Series 593) which was received with acclaim in 1955.

He had one-man exhibitions in five European capitals in 1956–1957 and a highly successful lecture tour of the United States and Canada in 1961. One of his best works is the series of teak panels made for the Hopkins Center at Dartmouth College, Hanover, New Hampshire, in 1962.

## *Edward M. Catich*

156 ALPHABET STONE & BRUSH KINETICS
Davenport, Iowa, 1964.
Black slate, 24×31½ inches. The letters SPQR are in the same height (4⅝ inches) and color as those on the Trajan Inscription in Rome. Line 2, in gold, contains letters 3¾ inches tall; line 3, in blue, contains the basic, written, unretouched, single strokes for the chief parts of the Trajan alphabet. From these elements every letter of the Trajan alphabet may be written.
*Lent by La Casa del Libro, San Juan, Puerto Rico*

Edward Catich was born in 1906. His prime interest in writing and lettering led him to studies at the art schools of Chicago and graduate work in the Art Department of the University of Iowa, but he feels that his most valuable training came from making signs, show cards and theater posters. His four years of study for the priesthood at the American College in Rome were avocationally given over to paleographic and epigraphic studies, which culminated in his scholarly research on the Trajan inscription. These studies are described and illustrated in his definitive book, *Letters Redrawn from the Trajan Inscription in Rome* (1961), which has won worldwide recognition and has gone into its second edition. His book on serifs is eagerly awaited.

## *Heather Child*

157 DECORATIVE MAP OF VENICE
London, 1961.
1 vellum leaf, 22½×28½ inches; ink, watercolor; roman and italic hands.
*Lent by William T. Brantman*

158 RUMFUSTION. One of a set of six recipes for festive drinks. [*Not illustrated.*]
London, 1964.
1 paper leaf, 14×10½ inches; ink, watercolor; formal italic hand with decorative border.
*Lent by the Artist*

Heather Child was born in Winchester, England. She studied calligraphy and heraldry at the Chelsea School of Art under Mervyn C. Oliver (no. 186). Since 1948 she has worked as a free-lance artist and designer, specializing in calligraphy, decorative maps, heraldry and botanical illustrations. She is the author of *Decorative Maps* (1956), *Calligraphy Today* (1963) and *Heraldic Design* (1965). She is the present Chairman of the Society of Scribes and Illuminators.

## *Raymond F. DaBoll*

159 DISCIPLINED FREEDOM
Hinsdale, Illinois, 1948.
Broadside, Eastern's Atlantic Antique Laid Bond paper, 22×17 inches.
*Lent by P. W. Filby*

Ray DaBoll was born in 1892 at Clyde, New York. He studied at the Rochester Institute of Technology, 1911–1913, and the Art Institute of Chicago, 1914. After some years of practical experience in an engraving house and agency art departments, he found his "most valuable experience as 'handy man' to Oswald Cooper, 1919–1922." In 1937, attracted by a Johnstonian exhibition, he began intensive study and practice of calligraphy in the Newberry Library classes led by Ernst Detterer (no. 127).

His work ever since has been chiefly calligraphic, and his calligraphy catches the spirit of each text that he writes, modifying his classic hand to modern use with grace and humor. The list of his accomplishments is long, varied and distinguished, and includes the title page and headings in this catalogue.

The broadside *Disciplined Freedom* was the only calligraphic piece in a series of twenty-four broadsides produced by the Sutherland-Abbott Advertising Agency of Boston, Massachusetts, for Eastern Corporation, Paper Manufacturers, at Bangor, Maine. The original is no longer fit for exhibition, but this offset litho is unique in that the calligrapher has corrected it, and has sharpened some of the letters.

## *Ernest R. Duncombe*

160 ADDRESS TO THE HONORABLE VINCENT THOMAS
Buckhurst Hill, Essex, September 1963.
1 vellum leaf, 17×11½ inches; black, red and blue ink, burnished gold; compressed roman hand.
*Lent by the Honorable Vincent Thomas*

Ernest R. Duncombe was born in 1906 in London, where he was trained at the Central School of Arts and Crafts, London, by Irene Wellington (nos. 209–10). He is noted for his ecclesiastical work, both in England and in other countries. His Imperial Majesty the Emperor of Ethiopia is among the royal personages who possess examples of his calligraphy. S.S.I.

## *Fritz Eberhardt*

161 THE LORD'S PRAYER in English, German and Swedish
Philadelphia, 1958.
10 paper leaves, 8×8½ inches; black, red and blue ink.
Binding: full blue Scottish goatskin, hand-tooled by Fritz Eberhardt.
Written and bound for the Klingspor Museum, Offenbach, Germany.
*Lent by the Klingspor Museum, Offenbach*

Fritz Eberhardt was born in Germany in 1917, and was a student of bookbinding in Leipzig when Rudo Speman came to the school as a young man to teach calligraphy. The sight of Speman's work struck him like lightning and for the first time he felt the full impact of writing as an art. He gave up bookbinding, in which he was well advanced, to become one of Speman's pupils.

After many years, and for various reasons, Eberhardt has gone back to bookbinding, never quite forgetting fine writing. The creation of a well-shaped black letter with a broad-nibbed pen on fine white paper gives him such excitement and delight that it can stand by itself without any application or purpose.

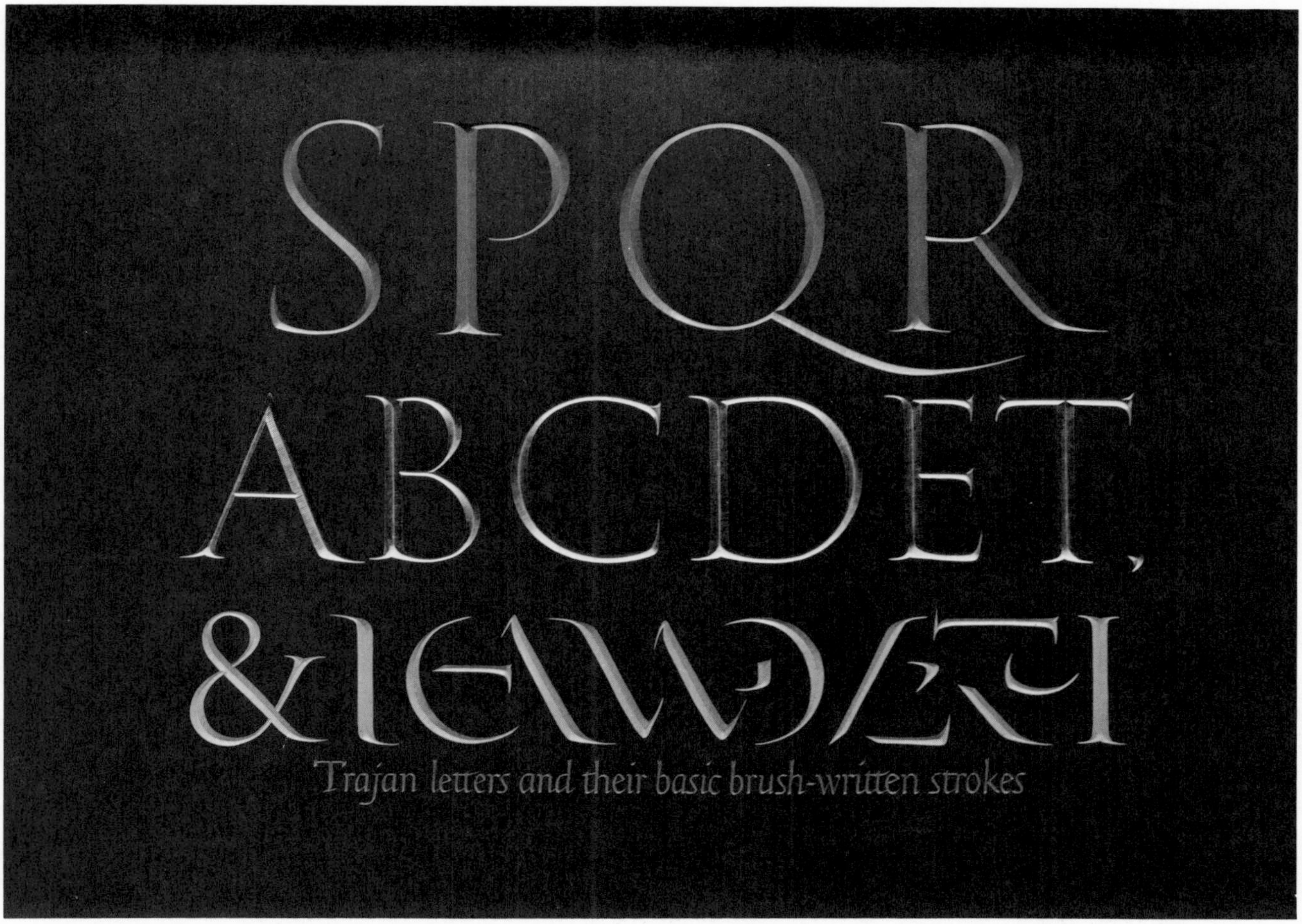

SPQR
ABCDET,

Trajan letters and their basic brush-written strokes

156. Alphabet Stone & Brush Kinetics. Edward M. Catich. 1964

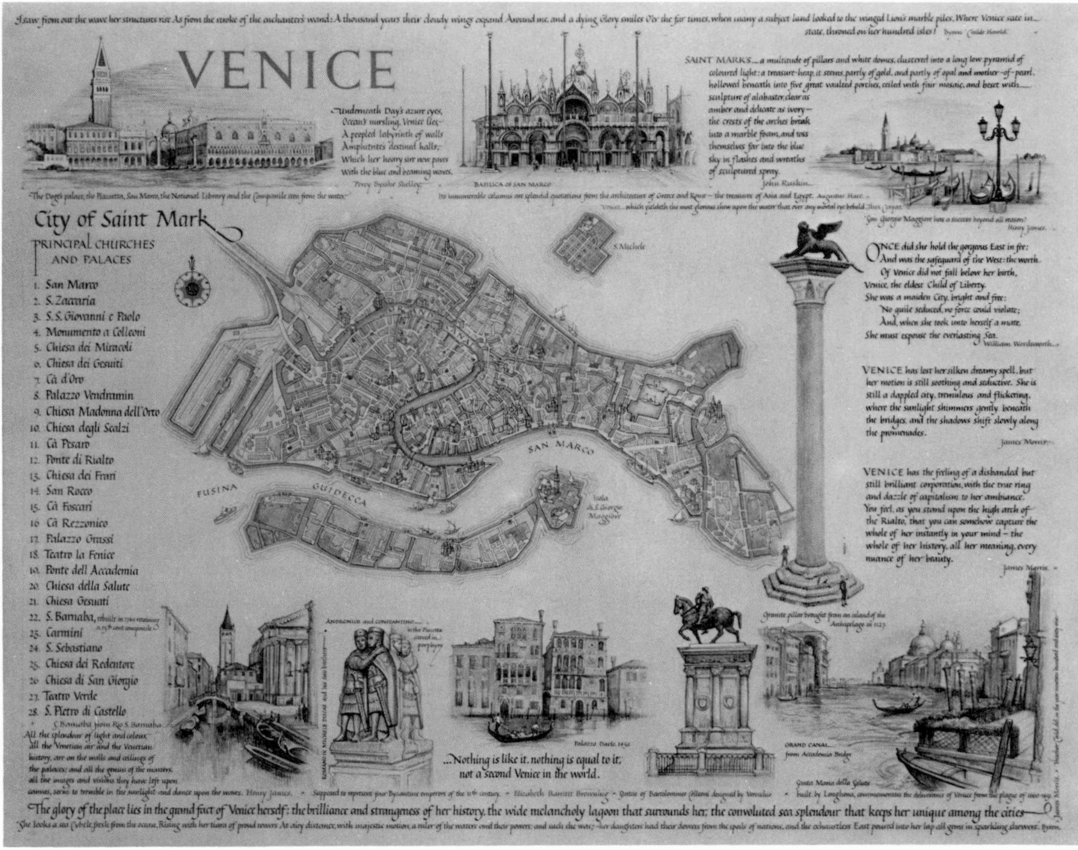


157. Decorative Map of Venice. Heather Child. 1961

THIS IS A SPECIMEN SHEET OF **Calligraphy;**

# Disciplined freedom is the Essence of it

[ AS OF ANY OTHER JUST FORM OF GOVERNMENT ]

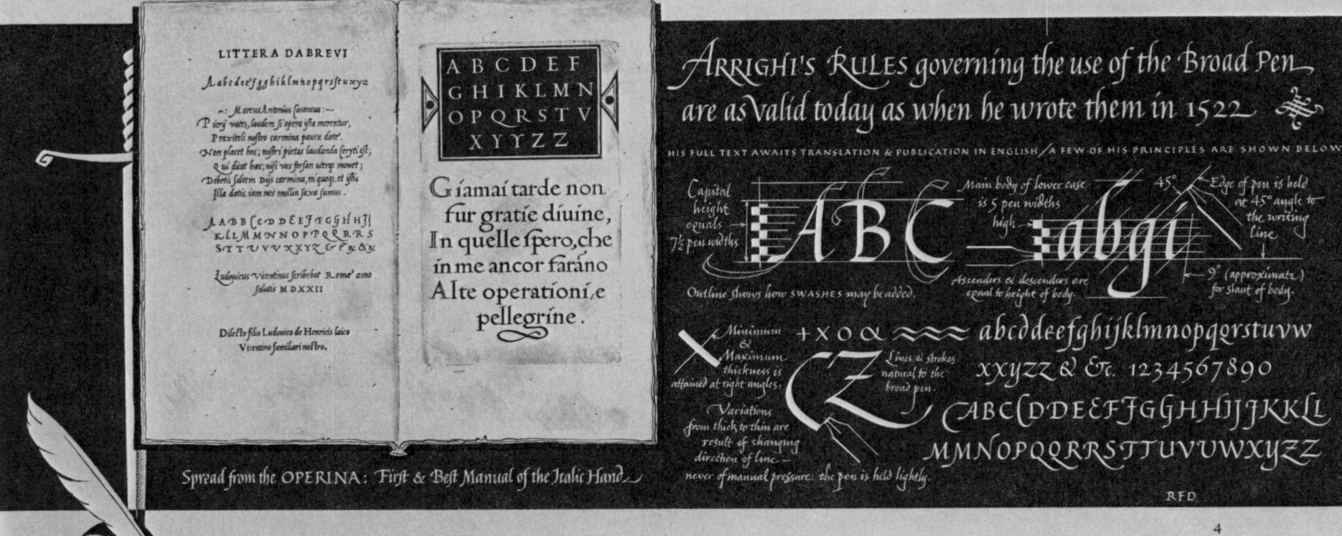


VARIOUS CALLIGRAPHICAL AUTHORITIES ARE AGREED that the best model for the instruction of handwriting is the Chancery Cursive, a style which attained its highest development in the early XVI century. Its leading exponent was LUDOVICO DEGLI ARRIGHI[1] of VICENZA. His work was widely imitated throughout Europe but by 1800 had given place to mercantile hands that could be written with greater speed.[2] When these, with later & still speedier methods gave way to the typewriter and the business machine, handwriting as an art, fell to its nadir. ¶ Within the past fifteen years, however, there have been signs that Calligraphy is coming back, chiefly by way of Book Publishers who were the first to sense that the freedom & warmth of Humanistic writing can supplement Type, and may even replace it in full pages of text on appropriate [but rare] occasions.

This lends support to J. COBDEN SANDERSON's contention that[3] *It is the function of the Calligrapher to revive and restore the craft of the Printer to its original purity of intention and accomplishment.* ¶ It is not suggested here that the earliest Types, which were naturally based on calligraphic forms, should be revived, nor that calligraphic mannerisms should be imitated in modern Types, for that, as pointed out by STANLEY MORISON,[4] *is artificial, and inconsistent with the nature of printing which is a branch of engraving.* Rather, the plea is for an *accordance* such as existed between the early Printer and his Calligrapher for whatever benefits may be derived now, as then, from shared knowledge. In this connection it may be mentioned that ARRIGHI, himself, in 1523, worked as a printer in partnership with LAUTIZIO BARTOLOMEO DEI ROTELLI, the greatest engraver of his time. ¶ Directness is mandatory in the use of the Broad Pen — the Scribe's task being to make good letters with the fewest possible strokes and to maintain an even texture and *temper* without retouching. White is a betrayer, a sneak, and an ever present help in time of trouble. A fairly constant rate of speed also helps to hold the necessary regularity of pattern throughout the mass, whether in a single line of text or in a full page. The faster the speed the more flowing and connected the letters become, hence the term *Cursive*; but whether the letters are made in the *Cursive* or in the slower style of roman *majuscule & minuscule* [caps & lower case] the operation, in calligraphic parlance, is still called writing.

*Eastern's Atlantic Antique Laid is a crisp, crackling, genuinely watermarked paper with the look & feel of exceptional quality. Uniform in every respect, its tub-sized surfaces take Offset, or Letterpress, or Pen equally well. Free from waves, wrinkles, or curl, and precision cut on all 4 edges, it runs easily on the press without trouble or fuss. — An impressive paper worthy of the finest printing, Eastern's Atlantic Antique Laid is ideal for special jobs & for outstanding letterheads, envelopes, brochures, and folders. Specify this distinguished sheet for your best customers. Its cost is much less than its quality would indicate.*

1 ARRIGHI was equally well known as VICENTINO, a surname derived from his native village, VICENZA.

2 Calligraphy's Flowering, Decay, & Restauration by PAUL STANDARD (Society of Typographic Arts) CHICAGO, 1947

3 Ecce Mundus — The Book Beautiful LONDON, 1902. The fuller Quotation is: "When printing was young the Printer carried into type the tradition of the Calligrapher and of the Calligrapher at his best. As this tradition died out in the distance, the craft of the printer declined. It is the function of the Calligrapher to revive" etc...

+ He added that the Printer "must at the same time be a Calligrapher, or in touch with him."

4 THE ART OF **Printing** (The Diamant Classics) NEW YORK, 1945. A small book (4½×3¼) of highly concentrated information on the relation of printing and Calligraphy, with a comprehensive Bibliography.

N.B. A definition of Calligraphy by STANLEY MORISON: Calligraphy is the art of fine writing communicated by agreed signs. If these signs or symbols are painted or are engraved on wood or on stone, we have that extension of writing known as LETTERING, ie., a large script generally formed with mechanical aids such as the rule, compass, & square. But it is the essence of handwriting that it be free from such, though not from all government, & of beautiful handwriting that it possess style... Calligraphy may be defined as free hand in which the freedom is so nicely reconciled with order that the understanding eye is pleased to contemplate it.

The above roman is based on ARRIGHI's writing, 1520, in the Colophon of the MISSALE ROMANUM

YOU MAY DEPEND ON ITS FINE PRINTING QUALITIES

THIS IS A SPECIMEN SHEET OF EASTERN'S ATLANTIC ANTIQUE LAID CREAM, SUBSTANCE 24, MADE BY

**Eastern Corporation · Bangor, Maine**

*Makers of ATLANTIC BOND and other Fine Business Papers*



159. Disciplined Freedom. Raymond F. DaBoll. 1948

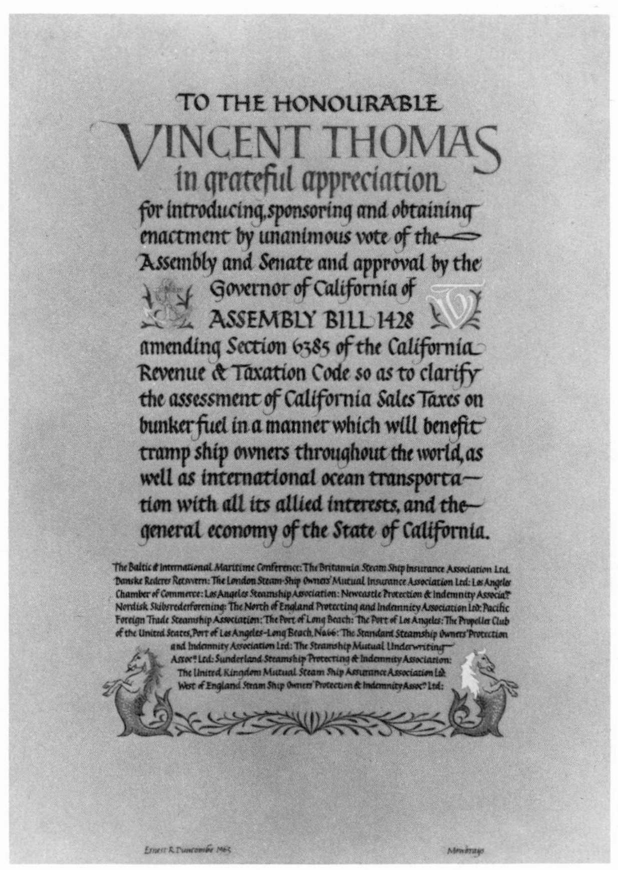


160. Address to the Honorable Vincent Thomas.
Ernest R. Duncombe. 1963

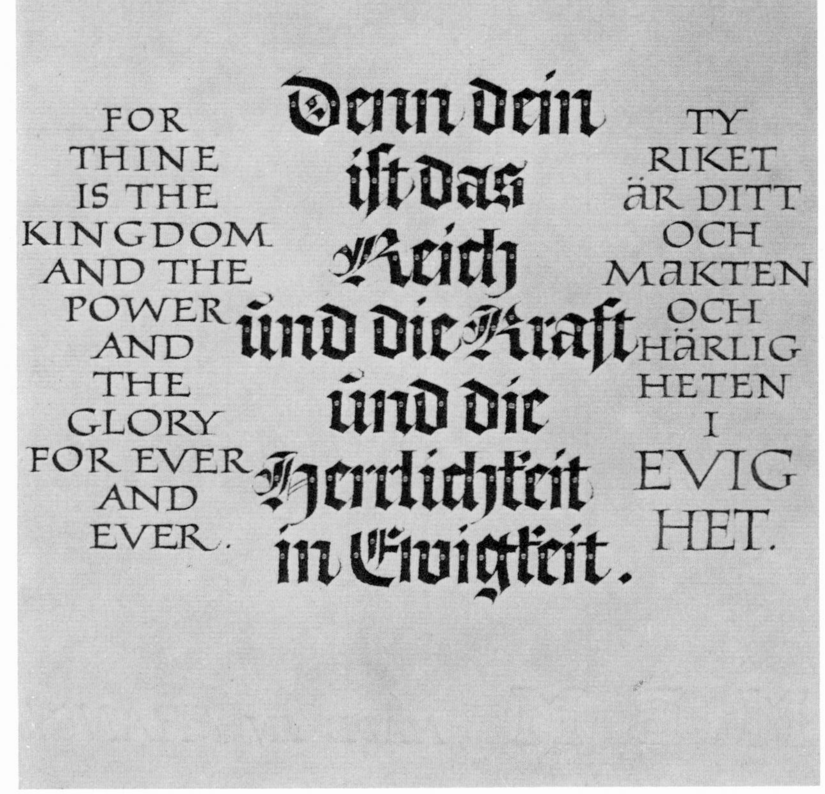


161. The Lord's Prayer. Fritz Eberhardt. 1958

THE EXECUTIVE COMMITTEE OF
THE CATHOLIC CHURCH EXTENSION SOCIETY
OF THE UNITED STATES OF AMERICA

A TESTIMONIAL TO THE HONORABLE

Charles C. Kerwin

Knight Commander of the Order of Pius IX

WHEREAS, The Honorable Charles C. Kerwin has been intimately connected with & zealously served The Catholic Church Extension Society for forty years under the Chancellorships of George William Cardinal Mundelein, Samuel Alphonsus Cardinal Stritch and Albert Gregory Cardinal Meyer and under the Presidencies of Archbishop William David O'Brien & Monsignor Joseph B. Lux, and since 1925 Mr. Kerwin has unselfishly devoted much of his time and ability in assisting the officers of the Society in the difficult office of Treasurer and subsequently Vice President, and

WHEREAS, during these many years, Mr. Kerwin's outstanding work on behalf of the Society and other charitable deeds has been recognized and honored by His Holiness Pope Pius XI with the medal Pro Ecclesia Pontifice and Knight of the Order of Pius IX, & by His Holiness Pope Pius XII by the Honor of Knight Commander of the Order of Pius IX and personally with a medal by Our Gloriously Reigning Pope Paul VI, and

WHEREAS, Mr. Kerwin, through reasons of advanced service above and beyond the call of duty and of family health, on January 8th asked to be relieved of the duties of Vice-President and Treasurer, be it therefore

RESOLVED: in this special meeting of the Executive Committee of The Catholic Church Extension Society called by the Chancellor, His Eminence Albert Cardinal Meyer and held in Chicago, January 20, 1964 that the retirement of Mr. Kerwin be accepted with deepest regret and the sincere appreciation & most grateful thanks of the Executive Committee in the name of the entire Board of Governors for all his years of faithful service to Extension Society, with the prayer that Almighty God will grant him many more years and abundant reward in His Heavenly Kingdom, be it further

RESOLVED: that the Honorable Charles C. Kerwin, K.C.O.P., is hereby appointed to the Board of Governors of the Society, & be it further

RESOLVED: that this resolution properly illuminated be presented to Mr. Kerwin at a testimonial dinner to be given by the Society on April 20th, 1964 & that it be spread on the minutes of the Committee to be read at the next annual meeting of the Board of Governors.

Warren W. Ferris scripsit

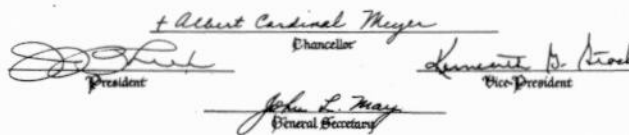


Most Reverend Edward F. Hoban
Most Reverend Ralph J. Hayes

Most Reverend Leo Binz
Most Reverend Stanislaus V. Bona

162. Testimonial Honoring Charles C. Kerwin. Warren Ferris. 1964

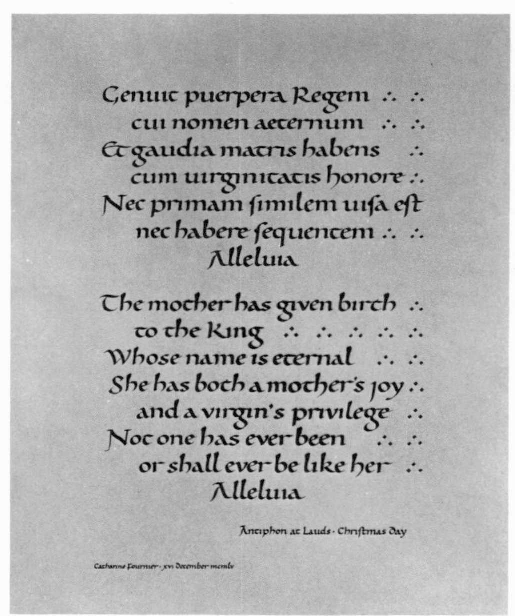

Genuit puerpera Regem ∴ ∴
cui nomen aeternum ∴ ∴
Et gaudia matris habens ∴
cum uirginitatis honore ∴
Nec primam similem uisa est
nec habere sequentem ∴ ∴
Alleluia

The mother has given birth ∴
to the King ∴ ∴ ∴ ∴ ∴
Whose name is eternal ∴ ∴
She has both a mother's joy ∴
and a virgin's privilege ∴
Not one has ever been ∴ ∴
or shall ever be like her ∴
Alleluia

Antiphon at Lauds · Christmas day

Catharine Fournier · xvi december mcmlv

163. Genuit Puerpera Regem.
Catharine Fournier. 1955

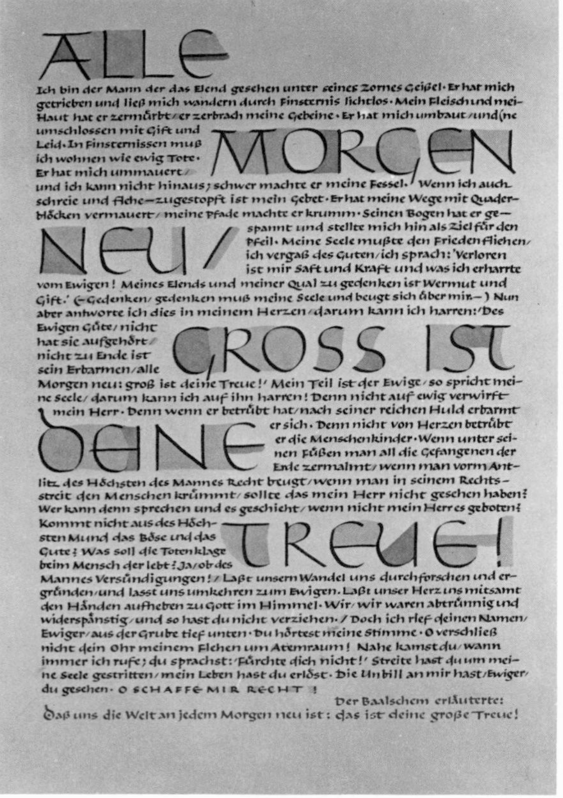

ALLE

Ich bin der Mann der das Elend gesehen unter seines Zornes Geißel · Er hat mich getrieben und ließ mich wandern durch Finsternis lichtlos · Mein Fleisch und mei- Haut hat er zermürbt / er zerbrach meine Gebeine · Er hat mich umbaut / und (ne umschlossen mit Gift und Leid · In Finsternissen muß ich wohnen wie ewig Tote · Er hat mich ummauert /

MORGEN

und ich kann nicht hinaus; schwer machte er meine Fessel · Wenn ich auch schreie und flehe – zugestopft ist mein Gebet · Er hat meine Wege mit Quaderblöcken vermauert / meine Pfade machte er krumm · Seinen Bogen hat er gespannt und stellte mich hin als Ziel für den Pfeil · Meine Seele mußte den Frieden fliehen / ich vergaß des Guten / ich sprach: 'Verloren ist mir Saft und Kraft und was ich erharrte vom Ewigen! Meines Elends und meiner Qual zu gedenken ist Wermut und Gift.' (– Gedenken / gedenken muß meine Seele und beugt sich über mir. –) Nun aber antworte ich dies in meinem Herzen / darum kann ich harren: 'Des Ewigen Güte / nicht hat sie aufgehört / nicht zu Ende ist sein Erbarmen / alle Morgen neu: groß ist deine Treue!' Mein Teil ist der Ewige / so spricht meine Seele / darum kann ich auf ihn harren! Denn nicht auf ewig verwirft mein Herr · Denn wenn er betrübt hat / nach seiner reichen Huld erbarmt er sich · Denn nicht von Herzen betrübt er die Menschenkinder · Wenn unter seinen Füßen man all die Gefangenen der Erde zermalmt / wenn man vorm Antlitz des Höchsten des Mannes Recht beugt / wenn man in seinem Rechtsstreit den Menschen krümmt / sollte das mein Herr nicht gesehen haben? Wer kann denn sprechen und es geschieht / wenn nicht mein Herr es geboten? Kommt nicht aus des Höchsten Mund das Böse und das Gute? Was soll die Totenklage beim Mensch der lebt? Ja / ob des Mannes Versündigungen! / Laßt unsern Wandel uns durchforschen und ergründen / und lasst uns umkehren zum Ewigen. Laßt unser Herz uns mitsamt den Händen aufheben zu Gott im Himmel · Wir / wir waren abtrünnig und widerspänstig / und so hast du nicht verziehen. / Doch ich rief deinen Namen / Ewiger / aus der Grube tief unten · Du hörtest meine Stimme · O verschließ nicht dein Ohr meinem Flehen um Atemraum! Nahe kamst du / wann immer ich rufe; du sprachst: 'Fürchte dich nicht!' Streite hast du um meine Seele gestritten / mein Leben hast du erlöst · Die Unbill an mir hast / Ewiger / du gesehen · O SCHAFFE MIR RECHT!

NEU / GROSS IST DEINE TREUE!

Der Baalschem erläuterte:
Daß uns die Welt an jedem Morgen neu ist: das ist deine große Treue!

164. Alle Morgen Neugross ist Deine Treue!
Henri Friedlaender. 1960

## *Warren Ferris*

162 TESTIMONIAL HONORING CHARLES C. KERWIN
Los Altos, California, April 1964.
1 Strathmore Rag Ledger paper leaf, 25×14 inches; ink, color, raised and burnished gold.
*Lent by Charles C. Kerwin*

Warren Ferris was born in Rochester, New York, in 1890, and has lived in California since 1954. He attended the school of the Art Institute of Chicago and worked there in advertising until World War I. After his military service he went to Washington. One day he "strolled through the back door" of the U. S. Government Printing Office, and stayed for twenty-two years, to become Chief of Printing and Design—the first full-time printing designer in the Federal service. He is now Honorary Consultant in Typography and Design to the Library of Congress, where a case of his works is on exhibition, including the first page of the 12,000-word Constitution of the State of Alaska, commissioned by the Governor of that state. Mr. Ferris is one of the very few Americans to have mastered the difficult art of illuminating in raised gold.

## *Catharine Fournier*

163 GENUIT PUERPERA REGEM. A Christmas antiphon
New York City, 1955.
1 paper leaf, 18½×15¼ inches; black ink with brown initials; caroline minuscules with uncial initials.
*Lent by the Artist*

Catharine Fournier was born in Brooklyn in 1908. She began to study calligraphy about ten years ago, first under Hollis Holland (no. 169) and later under Marvin Newman. Almost immediately, she felt the fascination of the craft and became a willing victim in the never-ending struggle between the wayward pen and the ideal in the mind's eye. As an executive of a large food corporation she is, of necessity, a "weekend" calligrapher—but unlike most weekend artists, now also a professional.

She believes that calligraphy offers superb satisfactions as a leisure-time cultural activity, and looks to the day when Westerners will recognize this, as the Chinese and Japanese have done for centuries.

She received the *New York Herald Tribune* Children's Spring Book Festival award, 1964, for her book *The Coconut Thieves.*

## *Henri Friedlaender*

164 ALLE MORGEN NEUGROSS IST DEINE TREUE! From *Lamentations, III*
Jerusalem, Israel, 1960.
1 paper leaf, 21×14¼ inches; ink, color.
*Lent by the Artist*

Henri Friedlaender was born in Germany. He was a pupil of Koch (no. 125), but the Nazi movement forced him to emigrate to Holland, where the Dutch kept him hidden from the Nazi invaders. The war over, he quickly became one of Holland's leading graphic artists. In the 1950's he accepted the Directorship of the Hadassah Apprentice School of Printing in Jerusalem, a post he now holds. Most of his writing is now done in Hebrew.

## *William M. Gardner*

165 UNFINISHED SONG OF SANDY THE SHEPHERD. Verse from *The Coming of Christ* by John Masefield
Wittersham, Kent, 1955.
1 vellum leaf, 20×27½ inches; ink, color and burnished gold; formal italic hand and basic lower case and capitals, with versals. The vellum is purposely framed unstretched in order that its undulations should scatter light from the gold impressions stamped by means of type metal border fleurons.
*Lent by the Artist*

William M. Gardner was born in Newcastle-on-Tyne in 1914. He studied under Dr. E. W. Tristram (a student of Johnston) at the Royal College of Art. At the Central School of Arts and Crafts, London, he was trained in calligraphy by Mervyn C. Oliver (no. 186) and in engraving by George T. Friend. He wrote the chapter on heraldry in illuminated manuscripts in *The Calligrapher's Handbook* (1956). He has lectured widely in England, and he served as Visiting Professor at Colorado State University in 1963. He is internationally known as a medallist as well as a calligrapher. S.S.I.

## *Tom Gourdie*

166 JOHN HOWARD BENSON CITATION
Kirkcaldy, Scotland, July 1959.
1 paper leaf, 13×15 inches; ink and color; modern half uncial, formal italic and foundation hand capitals. To mark the award (posthumously) of the Catholic Art Society Gold Medal.
*Lent by Esther Fisher Benson*

Tom Gourdie was born in Cowdenbeath, Scotland, in 1913, and studied at the Edinburgh College of Art under Irene Wellington (nos. 209–10). He is best known for his pioneer introduction of italic handwriting in Scotland by lecturing, organizing exhibitions and writing instructional books on the subject. His books have achieved international distribution.

Since 1947 he has been teaching art at Kirkcaldy High School in Scotland, and since 1962 he has served as Calligraphic Adviser to E. S. Perry, Ltd., manufacturers of Osmiroid pens.

He has found time to lecture in many parts of the world, including South Africa, New Zealand, New South Wales and Malaysia. In 1963 he was invited by the Swedish Board of Education to Stockholm to introduce his *Simple Modern Hand* to Swedish schools. Lectures in Oslo, Norway, followed this visit.

In 1959 he received the M.B.E. (Member of the Order of the British Empire) for services to calligraphy and education. S.S.I.

## *Freda Hands*

167 BAPTISM SERVICE
London, November 1948.
17 handmade paper leaves, 6¼×4¼ inches; black, blue and red ink, burnished gold; crushed foundational hand, rubrics in italic hand. Binding: blue morocco by Morrell.
Prepared for the baptism of Prince Charles, for the Queen's use.
*Lent by Her Majesty Queen Elizabeth II*

Freda Hands was born in London. She attended the Chelsea School of Art, where she was taught by Mervyn C. Oliver (no. 186). As a free-lance artist she has performed a variety of commissions, including book jackets and church work for Messrs. A. R. Mowbray & Co. She has made nearly one hundred memorial books and rolls of honour, including one particularly notable work, the Royal Army Service Corps Roll, with over 9,000 names. S.S.I.

## *James Hayes*

168 THE HIPPOCRATIC OATH
Evanston, Illinois, 1954.
Broadside, Whatman's paper, 22×16½ inches; ink, watercolor, gold; roman hand.
*Lent by the School of Medical Science, University of South Dakota, Vermillion, South Dakota*

James Hayes was born in Saginaw, Michigan, in 1907. His calligraphic studies began at the School of the Art Institute, Chicago, in 1926, under Ernst Detterer (no. 127). There followed work in commercial lettering and three years of study under Lazló Moholy-Nagy at the New Bauhaus, Chicago. Following service in World War II he turned to calligraphy as a full-time profession, and has produced for clients countless works of all description: commercial, ecclesiastical, educational and governmental. He extends the use of calligraphy to bookplates and inscriptions on wood panels, stone, metal and fixed wall positions.

The influence of his first teacher, Detterer, has pervaded his life and work. He led the Calligraphy Study Group at the Newberry Library from 1947, when Detterer, its founder, died, until 1960.

## *Hollis Holland*

169 THE BOOK OF BOOKS. Paragraphs from the King James Version of the English Bible (A. A. Knopf) New York City, c. 1950.
1 Harrison Elliot paper handmade leaf, 13¼×15½ inches; ink; uncial hand.
*Lent by Herbert Farrier*

Hollis Holland was born in 1908 in Memphis, Tennessee. During 1926–1936 he worked across the country and back again, doing theatrical posters for various motion picture companies. He has served as art director and typographic designer for several advertising agencies, notably for the J. Walter Thompson Company in Mexico and Brazil, as well as their New York office. He taught calligraphy and letter design for ten years at Columbia University. Since 1948 he has specialized in lettering and typographic design for publishers. Photo-Lettering, Inc., has introduced four of his alphabets, *Title*, *Beleze*, *Antiga* and *Seminar*. His favorite alphabets are uncial, which he likes to "float between the lines" as in the example shown.

## *Dorothy Hutton*

170 HERALDIC RECORD OF THE ORDERS, DECORATIONS AND MEDALS OF SIR WINSTON SPENCER CHURCHILL
London 1959, with the addition in 1964 of American citizenship.
1 vellum leaf; 17×11 inches; ink, color, burnished, raised and matt gold; italic and formal hands.
A gift to Sir Winston Churchill from the Marquess and Marchioness of Cholmondeley, 1959.
*Lent by Lady Churchill, G.B.E.*

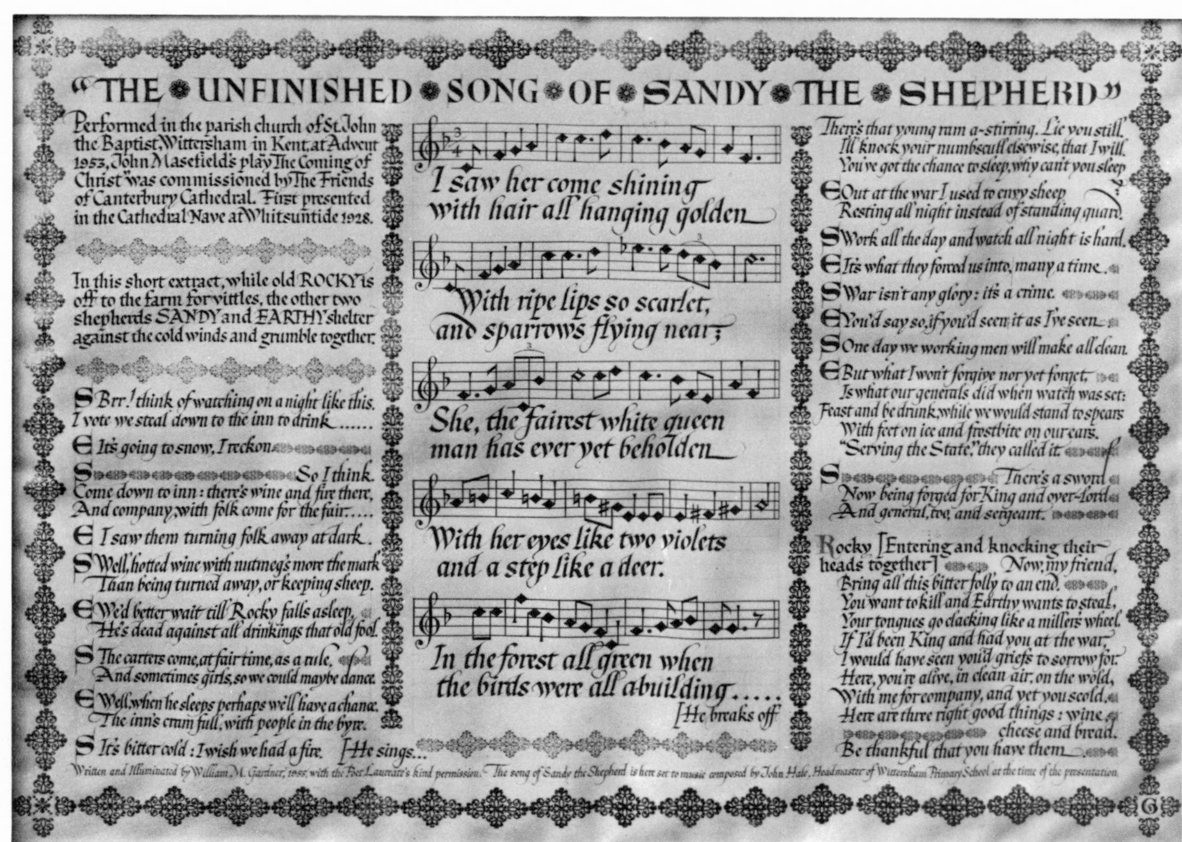

"THE UNFINISHED SONG OF SANDY THE SHEPHERD"

Performed in the parish church of St. John the Baptist, Wittersham in Kent, at Advent 1953, John Masefield's play The Coming of Christ was commissioned by The Friends of Canterbury Cathedral. First presented in the Cathedral Nave at Whitsuntide 1928.

In this short extract, while old ROCKY is off to the farm for vittles, the other two shepherds SANDY and EARTHY shelter against the cold winds and grumble together.

S Brr.! think of watching on a night like this.
I vote we steal down to the inn to drink......
E It's going to snow, I reckon.
S So I think.
Come down to inn: there's wine and fire there,
And company, with folk come for the fair.....
E I saw them turning folk away at dark.
S Well, hotted wine with nutmegs more the mark
Than being turned away, or keeping sheep.
E We'd better wait till Rocky falls asleep,
He's dead against all drinkings that old fool.
S The carters come, at fair time, as a rule,
And sometimes girls, so we could maybe dance.
E Well, when he sleeps perhaps we'll have a chance.
The inn's cram full, with people in the byre.
S It's bitter cold: I wish we had a fire. [He sings...

I saw her come shining
with hair all hanging golden
With ripe lips so scarlet,
and sparrows flying near;
She, the fairest white queen
man has ever yet beholden
With her eyes like two violets
and a step like a deer.
In the forest all green when
the birds were all abuilding.....
[He breaks off

There's that young rum a-stirring. Lie you still,
I'll knock your numbscull elsewise, that I will.
You've got the chance to sleep, why can't you sleep
E Out at the war I used to envy sheep
Resting all night instead of standing guard.
S Work all the day and watch all night is hard.
E It's what they forced us into, many a time.
S War isn't any glory: it's a crime.
E You'd say so, if you'd seen it as I've seen.
S One day we working men will make all clean.
E But what I won't forgive nor yet forget,
Is what our generals did when watch was set:
Feast and be drunk, while we would stand to spears
With feet on ice and frostbite on our ears.
"Serving the State," they called it.
S There's a sword
Now being forged for King and over-lord
And general, too, and sergeant.

Rocky [Entering and knocking their heads together] Now, my friend,
Bring all this bitter folly to an end.
You want to kill and Earthy wants to steal,
Your tongues go clacking like a miller's wheel.
If I'd been King and had you at the war,
I would have seen you'd griefs to sorrow for.
Here, you're alive, in clean air, on the wold,
With me for company, and yet you scold.
Here are three right good things: wine,
cheese and bread.
Be thankful that you have them.

Written and Illuminated by William M. Gardner, 1955, with the Poet Laureate's kind permission. The song of Sandy the Shepherd is here set to music composed by John Hale, Headmaster of Wittersham Primary School at the time of the presentation.

165. Masefield: Unfinished Song of Sandy the Shepherd. William M. Gardner. 1955

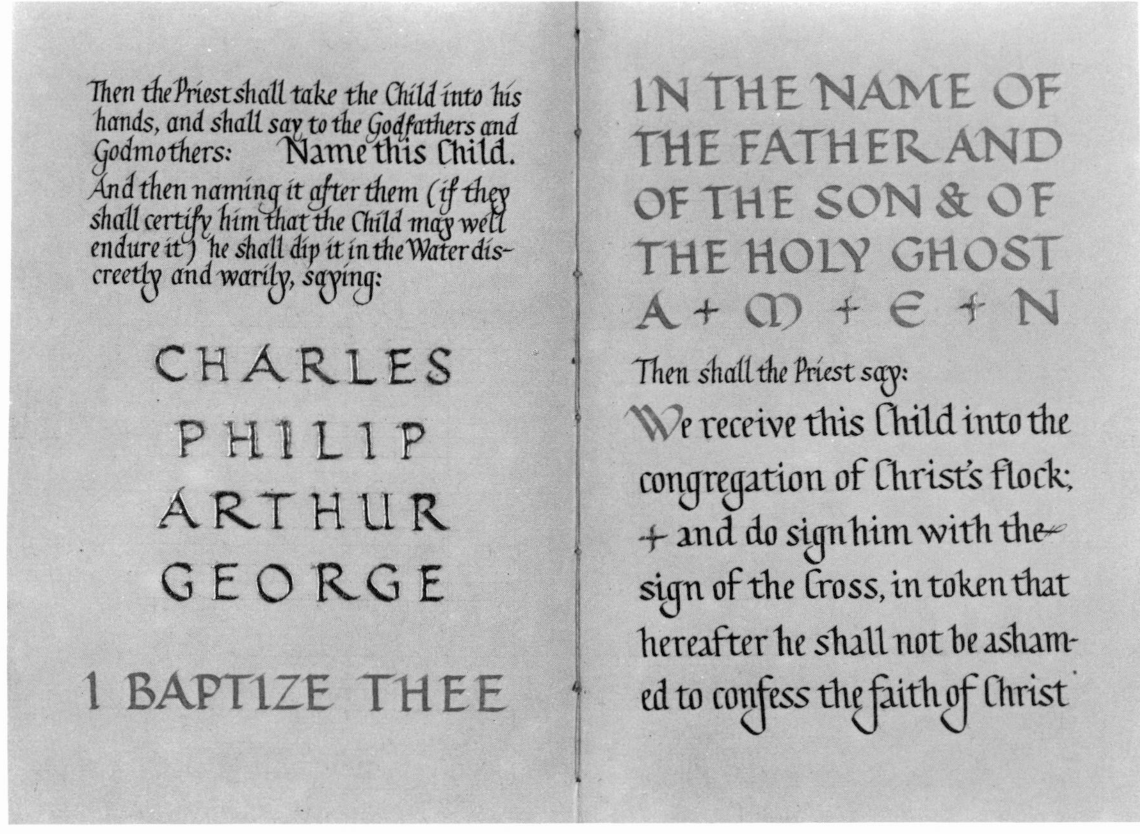

Then the Priest shall take the Child into his hands, and shall say to the Godfathers and Godmothers: Name this Child.
And then naming it after them (if they shall certify him that the Child may well endure it) he shall dip it in the Water discreetly and warily, saying:

CHARLES
PHILIP
ARTHUR
GEORGE

I BAPTIZE THEE

IN THE NAME OF THE FATHER AND OF THE SON & OF THE HOLY GHOST
A + M + E + N

Then shall the Priest say:

We receive this Child into the congregation of Christ's flock; + and do sign him with the sign of the Cross, in token that hereafter he shall not be ashamed to confess the faith of Christ

167. Baptism Service. Freda Hands. 1948

THE CATHOLIC ART ASSOCIATION holds to the classical view that a work of art is anything that is made well. It encourages a truer understanding of this view and a better practice of arts of all kinds.

JOHN HOWARD BENSON

devoted his life to the study of letters and to the restoration to common use of their best forms. He saw letters as things to be read and, therefore, necessarily legible; as things to be imagined and made and, therefore, necessarily works of art. He saw them historically, subject to the laws of time as well as of space.

*He was a master of lettering in many techniques but his greatest achievement was the restoration of carved lettering in stone to its proper dignity among the arts. Not only was his own work without rival during the thirty years of his working life, but he succeeded in establishing a glyptic tradition which has survived his death.*

*The Officers and Members of the Catholic Art Association ask his widow*

ESTHER FISHER BENSON

*to accept this medal on his behalf, as a token of the very real esteem and gratitude in which they hold her husband's memory*

AT SAINT ELIZABETH'S COLLEGE, NEW JERSEY, ON THE FEAST OF ST. HELEN, AUGUST EIGHTEENTH ANNO DOMINI 1959

*For the Association*

Thomas Phelan

*President*

*Tom Gourdie, Scribe*

166. John Howard Benson Citation. Tom Gourdie. 1959

the word bible comes from the greek word biblia the plural of the word meaning book / the plural form was used because the writings of what we recognize as a single book came into existence as entirely separate books and not until centuries later were combined to constitute what we now call the bible / the books of the old testament are the sacred books or writings or scriptures of the ancient hebrews and of modern jews / here are preserved the history the religion and the literature of the ancient hebrews a people who 2000 years ago created a great civilization / the books of the new testament constitute the literature of the christians of the first century of the new era / here is related the story of the rise and development of christianity under the leadership of christ / these books of the new testament were added to the writings of the old testament to form the christian bible which we read today / a third collection of writings called the apocrypha also appears in one or the other of two forms in the complete modern christian bible / the books of the apocrypha were written in the last three centuries in the era before christ / although these writings are quite similar to the writings of the old testament they have been differently evaluated by religious denominations / the hebrews have never regarded these books as part of their sacred scriptures / in the roman catholic bible they are printed in their appropriate places along with the other books of the old testament / in protestant bibles if they appear at all they are printed as a separate division between the two testaments / most of the books of the bible were written in palestine / the old testament was originally written in hebrew the new testament in greek or in part it may be in aramaic a semitic dialect which was the spoken language of palestine in the time of christ and presumably the language which christ and his disciples used / the whole bible has come down to us through two important languages greek and latin / the old testament was translated from the hebrew into greek in the closing centuries of the era before christ / the great latin translation of the whole bible was that made by bishop jerome at the end of the fourth century after christ / this is the so-called latin vulgate the official bible today of the roman catholic church / translations of the whole bible into the various languages of modern europe have been made from the early middle ages down to our own times / the wycliffe english bible appeared in the fourteenth century the famous luther german bible in the early sixteenth century the king james version and the douai translation (the roman catholic english bible) at the beginning of the seventeenth century / the english revised version appeared in 1885 the american revised edition in 1901 / both are based on the king james version / several interesting and important english translations have also been made in the present century / the king james version however still lives on as the bible classic of english literature / the king james version appeared in 1611 / before the middle of the seventeenth century it had practically superseded all other protestant english translations and for three hundred years it has remained the standard version of the bible for english readers / by the middle of the nineteenth century it had become recognized not only as a great book of religion but also as a masterpiece of english expression / the composition of the bible covered a period of about 1000 years approximately from 850 b.c. to a.d. 150 / some parts of the old testament in one form or another may have existed in writing long before 850 b.c. / but we have no reason to think that any of the books in the form in which they have been preserved were composed before the ninth century before christ that is about the time of the greek epics of homer / the books of the new testament may be dated much more definitely / none of them came into being before a.d. 50 and we are reasonably safe in saying that none of them was composed after a.d. 150 / we know very little about the authors of most of the books of the bible / in the early centuries of hebrew history authorship was by no means the important matter that it is today / the writing itself like the play in hamlet was the thing not the person who was responsible for the actual composition / it was not until the late centuries of the era before christ when the editor the compiler the preserver of records came into existence that a need for names of authors was felt / then the writings that had been handed down without names were ascribed to the famous men of earlier times / thus we have books that were attributed to such national heroes as moses joshua david solomon / but for most of the books of the old testament such as genesis exodus leviticus numbers deuteronomy joshua judges ruth samuel kings esther job the psalms proverbs ecclesiastes the song of songs we know no authors / we can say that moses may have been responsible for some of the writing of the first five books that david may have written some of the psalms and that solomon may have been responsible for some of the words of wisdom of the proverbs / and we have definite authors for some of the writings of the prophets amos hosea isaiah jeremiah and ezekiel and the rest / the authors of the other books are unknown / about the books of the new testament we have likewise very little information / to luke the physician are generally ascribed the gospel of that name and the acts of the apostles / paul is clearly recognized as the author of at least ten of the epistles / to john mark belongs the second gospel / the author of the gospel according to st. matthew is unknown / the three epistles bearing the name of john are connected with the fourth gospel in style and thought and were written either by the john who wrote that gospel or by another person of that same school of thought / much uncertainty prevails as to the identity of the men whose names are attached to the other books / the english bible like all other enduring classics is a book which appeals to people of all times / we are accustomed to say for example that shakespeares plays are not for one age the age in which they were written but for all time / indeed we think much more highly of shakespeare's plays today than his contemporaries did in the late sixteenth and early seventeenth centuries / so with the bible with its noble english rendering the king james version / it is a great human document a book of joys and sorrows loves and hates struggles of body and spirit heroic and unheroic adventures / and for english speaking people this book has been handed down in a version which has the characteristics of great english style harmonious rhythms natural picturesque and apt figurative expressions simple direct clear anglo-saxon diction / the humanness of the bible is in the final analysis the essential feature of this english classic / for english speaking people at least the bible has become almost a household word / it has become a part of their spiritual consciousness / the bible remains a book of living english literature / +

from the book of books / the king james version of the english bible abridged and arranged with editorial comments for younger readers / written out in an uncial hand as an experiment in achieving even color in massed writing / hollis holland / new york city / january 1951 /

169. The Book of Books. Hollis Holland. c. 1950

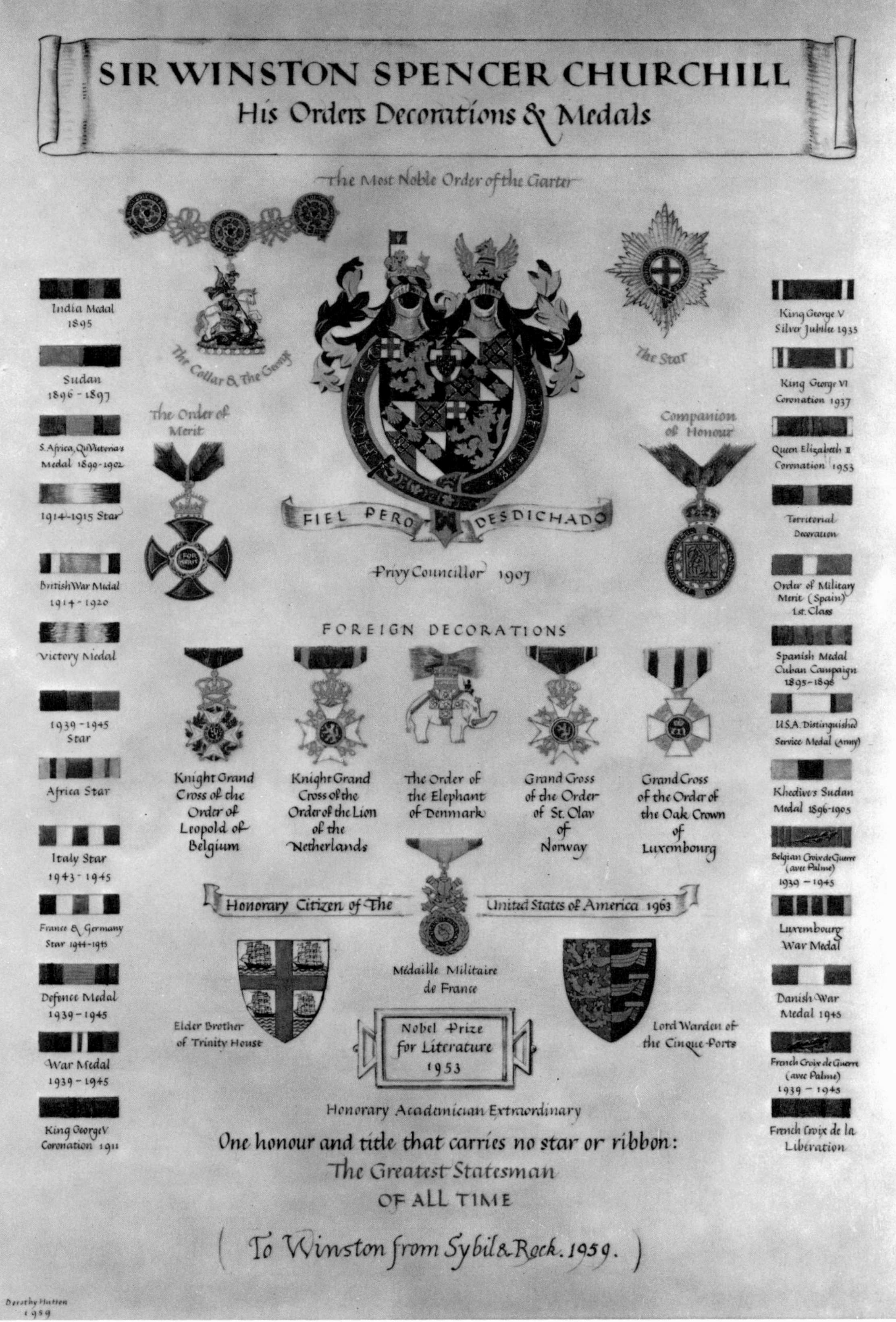


170. Heraldic Record of the Orders, Decorations & Medals of Sir Winston Spencer Churchill. Dorothy Hutton. 1959–1964

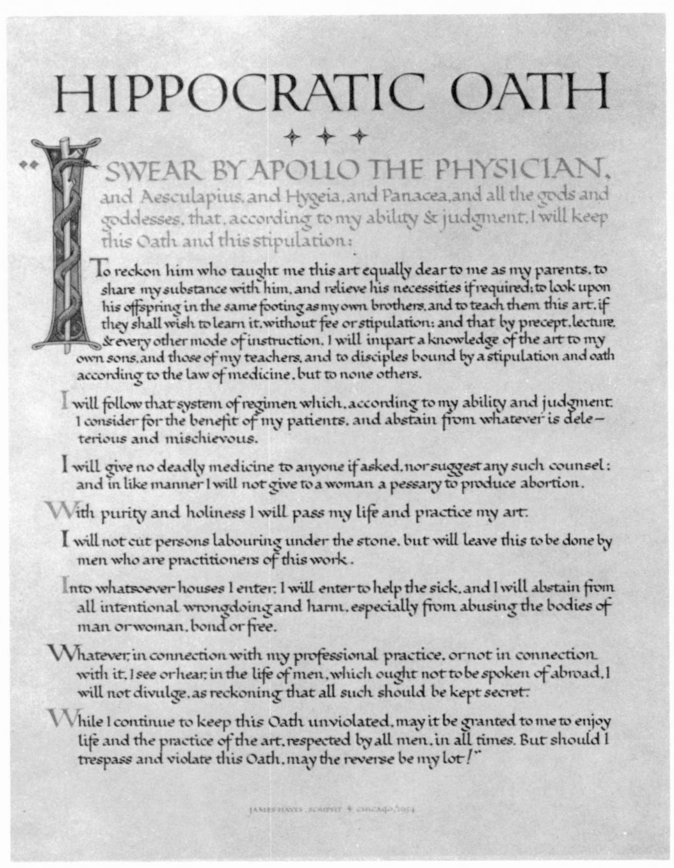

# HIPPOCRATIC OATH

I SWEAR BY APOLLO THE PHYSICIAN, and Aesculapius, and Hygeia, and Panacea, and all the gods and goddesses, that, according to my ability & judgment, I will keep this Oath and this stipulation:

To reckon him who taught me this art equally dear to me as my parents, to share my substance with him, and relieve his necessities if required; to look upon his offspring in the same footing as my own brothers, and to teach them this art, if they shall wish to learn it, without fee or stipulation; and that by precept, lecture, & every other mode of instruction, I will impart a knowledge of the art to my own sons, and those of my teachers, and to disciples bound by a stipulation and oath according to the law of medicine, but to none others.

I will follow that system of regimen which, according to my ability and judgment, I consider for the benefit of my patients, and abstain from whatever is deleterious and mischievous.

I will give no deadly medicine to anyone if asked, nor suggest any such counsel; and in like manner I will not give to a woman a pessary to produce abortion.

With purity and holiness I will pass my life and practice my art.

I will not cut persons labouring under the stone, but will leave this to be done by men who are practitioners of this work.

Into whatsoever houses I enter, I will enter to help the sick, and I will abstain from all intentional wrongdoing and harm, especially from abusing the bodies of man or woman, bond or free.

Whatever, in connection with my professional practice, or not in connection with it, I see or hear, in the life of men, which ought not to be spoken of abroad, I will not divulge, as reckoning that all such should be kept secret.

While I continue to keep this Oath unviolated, may it be granted to me to enjoy life and the practice of the art, respected by all men, in all times. But should I trespass and violate this Oath, may the reverse be my lot!"

168. The Hippocratic Oath. James Hayes. 1954

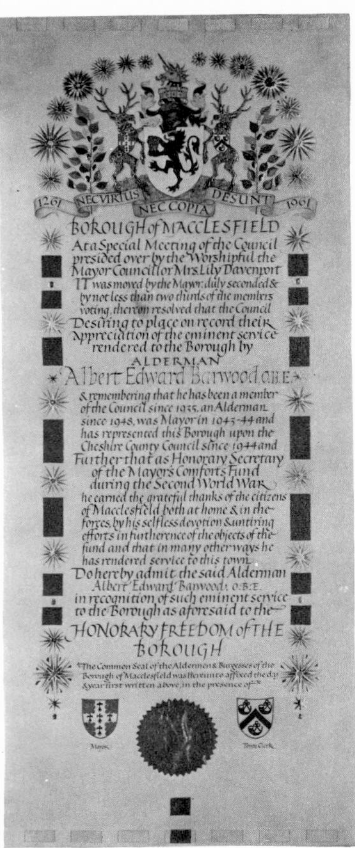

1261 NEC VIRTUS NEC COPIA DESUNT 1961

BOROUGH of MACCLESFIELD

At a Special Meeting of the Council presided over by the Worshipful the Mayor Councillor Mrs Lily Davenport IT was moved by the Mayor, duly seconded & by not less than two thirds of the members voting, thereon resolved that the Council Desiring to place on record their Appreciation of the eminent service rendered to the Borough by

ALDERMAN

Albert Edward Barwood O.B.E.

& remembering that he has been a member of the Council since 1935, an Alderman since 1948, was Mayor in 1943-44 and has represented this Borough upon the Cheshire County Council since 1944 and Further that as Honorary Secretary of the Mayor's Comforts Fund during the Second World War he earned the grateful thanks of the citizens of Macclesfield both at home & in the forces, by his selfless devotion & untiring efforts in furtherence of the objects of the fund and that in many other ways he has rendered service to this town

Do hereby admit the said Alderman Albert Edward Barwood, O.B.E. in recognition of such eminent service to the Borough as aforesaid to the

HONORARY FREEDOM of THE BOROUGH

"The Common Seal of the Aldermen & Burgesses of the Borough of Macclesfield was hereunto affixed the day & year first written above, in the presence of"

Mayor. Town Clerk.

171. Presentation Address. Donald Jackson. 1961

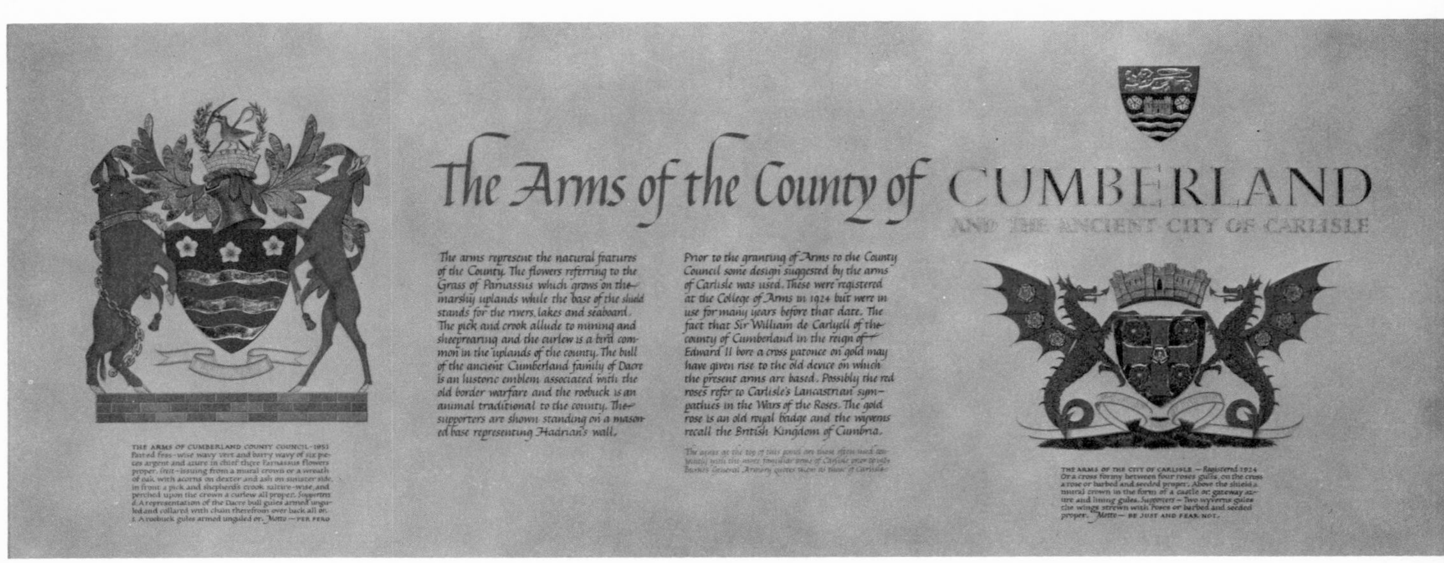

# The Arms of the County of CUMBERLAND

AND THE ANCIENT CITY OF CARLISLE

The arms represent the natural features of the County. The flowers referring to the Grass of Parnassus which grows on the marshy uplands while the base of the shield stands for the rivers, lakes and seaboard. The pick and crook allude to mining and sheeprearing and the curlew is a bird common in the uplands of the county. The bull of the ancient Cumberland family of Dacre is an historic emblem associated with the old border warfare and the roebuck is an animal traditional to the county. The supporters are shown standing on a masoned base representing Hadrian's wall.

Prior to the granting of Arms to the County Council some design suggested by the arms of Carlisle was used. These were registered at the College of Arms in 1924 but were in use for many years before that date. The fact that Sir William de Carlyell of the county of Cumberland in the reign of Edward II bore a cross patonce on gold may have given rise to the old device on which the present arms are based. Possibly the red roses refer to Carlisle's Lancastrian sympathies in the Wars of the Roses. The gold rose is an old royal badge and the wyverns recall the British Kingdom of Cumbria.

172. Panel Describing the Arms of the County of Cumberland. Margaret James. 1964

Dorothy Hutton was born at Bolton, Lancashire, and studied calligraphy for two years under Graily Hewitt (nos. 132–3), at the Central School of Arts and Crafts, London. A few of her works have been illuminated by others, including Irene Base (no. 147), and Vera Law (no. 178), but she has produced a long and splendid series of illuminated manuscripts of her own, including registers, rolls of honour and many patents of nobility for the Crown Office and the House of Lords. She wrote the chapters on pigments and media, and illumination and decoration in *The Calligrapher's Handbook* (1956). In 1959 she received the M.V.O. (Member of the Royal Victorian Order). She is a founder member of the S.S.I.

## *Donald Jackson*

171 PRESENTATION ADDRESS
London, 1961.
1 vellum leaf, 26×10½ inches; black ink, watercolor, burnished gold.
*Lent by the Artist*

Donald Jackson was born in 1938 in Lancashire. He studied at the Central School of Arts and Crafts, London, with Irene Wellington (nos. 209–10) and Mervyn C. Oliver (no. 186). He is now lecturing at Camberwell School of Art. He works privately, and has been engaged on numerous commissions for Her Majesty's Crown Office of the House of Lords.

The magnificent gilding of this address makes it hard to believe that it was only a sample. The Borough of Macclesfield presented four such addresses by Mr. Jackson to its most prominent citizens in commemoration of its 700 years of incorporation. The mulberry leaves symbolize the town's principal industry, silk weaving. S.S.I.

## *Margaret James*

172 PANEL DESCRIBING THE ARMS OF THE COUNTY OF CUMBERLAND
Sheffield, Yorkshire, 1964.
1 vellum leaf, 10½×26¼ inches; ink, color with gum gold, platinum and arabic aluminum leaf; Italian sixteenth-century cursive hand; captions in a round-hand variant of the same period. Stretched on board.
*Lent by the Artist*

Margaret James was born in Maryport, Cumberland, England, in 1932. She was trained at Leeds College of Art under T. W. Swindlehurst (no. 202), and later at the Royal College of Art, where she had the benefit of contact with Arnold Bank (no. 145), then visiting Fulbright Fellow. "Having the patience to create, but none to teach," she has worked as a free-lance letterer in many media. Her patience manifestly does extend to research, as witness this panel embodying the new arms of her county. S.S.I.

## *Fridolf Johnson*

173 GREETING TO THOMAS MAITLAND CLELAND ON HIS 80TH BIRTHDAY, FROM THE TYPOPHILES
New York City, August 1960.
2 paper leaves, 10½×7¾; red and gold ink; chancery cursive hand.
*Lent by the Artist*

Fridolf Johnson was born in Chicago in 1905. He studied at the Chicago Art Institute, and was an art director for some years in Chicago. While in California he handled advertising art and illustrated children's books. He moved to New York in 1952 and is at present Executive Editor and Art Director of *American Artist*, for which he has written many articles on calligraphy, typographic design and other subjects.

In his spare time he works professionally on calligraphy and runs a small press, *The Mermaid*, which produces felicitous works from time to time. In Los Angeles he was co-founder of the Society of Calligraphers.

The present work, given to Thomas Maitland Cleland, noted designer, is signed on page three by twenty-four members of The Typophiles, New York.

## *Edward Karr*

174 QUOTATION FROM ST. BENEDICT
Boston, Massachusetts, 1965.
1 paper leaf, 14×11 inches; ink, burnished gold; chancery hand.
*Lent by the Artist*

Edward Karr was born in Connecticut in 1909. He was self-taught, and has been a designer, letterer and calligrapher with a Boston studio since 1945. He has been instructor in lettering and calligraphy at the School of the Museum of Fine Arts, Boston, since 1947. He is a member and Past President of the Society of Printers, Boston. He was responsible for the television program in the "Museum Open House" series, "Words as Pictures," where he demonstrated the use of the broad-edged pen.

## *David Kindersley*

175 ALPHABET STONE
Barton, Cambridgeshire, 1965.
Welsh slate, 43×31 inches; cut freehand, roman letters.
*Lent by the Artist*

176 ELEGY WRITTEN IN A COUNTRY CHURCH YARD (excerpt) by Thomas Gray
Barton, Cambridgeshire, 1965.
Welsh slate, 12×23 inches.
*Lent by Stuart B. Schimmel*

David Kindersley was born in Codicote, Hertfordshire, in 1916. He was first apprenticed to Gilbert Ledward, and was Eric Gill's (no. 137) last pupil. His own pupils include Will Carter (nos. 154–5) and the letter cutter of Coventry Cathedral, Ralph Beyer. Besides his numerous inscriptions to be found in many countries, he has designed an alphabet for street signs which has been adopted by the Ministry of Transport. His other interest is in a new system of spacing, which has been used in the lettering throughout the New University Press building in Cambridge, England. His relief maps and heraldry at the American Military Cemetery near Cambridge represent one of his foremost achievements.

The alphabet shown was cut entirely freehand, with dummy and chisel, without guide lines or any drawing out on the slate or previous designing. It is the "3rd edition" of one cut in 1951, and embodies the letter cutter's present thoughts about roman letters.

## *Veronica Laing*

177 LIFE IN THE WOODS THROUGH THE SEASONS. Extracts from *Walden* by H. D. Thoreau
Boston, Massachusetts, 1953.
14 paper leaves, 10½×8⅜ inches; ink, watercolor; personal hand. Binding: half linen box case.
*Lent by Mr. and Mrs. Philip Hofer*

Veronica Laing was born in New York City and attended Barnard College, where she majored in mathematics. Her individual style of calligraphy was developed under the tutelage of her father, Rudolph Ruzicka. Her works include stencil prints, paste papers and maps for numerous books, such as *Jonathan Eagle*, by her husband, Alexander Laing, and *The Great Books of the Western World.*

## *Vera Law*

178 PSALM 122, part of Verse 7
London, January 1948.
1 vellum leaf, 2⅞×3½ inches; raised and burnished gold versals.
*Lent by the Artist*

Vera Law was born in Northampton, England, in 1900. When studying at the Central School of Arts and Crafts, London, she had as her teachers Graily Hewitt (nos. 132–3) and Lawrence Christie. She has done much gilding in collaboration with Dorothy Hutton (no. 170) and other calligraphers. One outstanding commission is the Metropolitan Police Roll of Honour in Westminster Abbey. She is a founder member of the S.S.I.

## *Byron J. Macdonald*

179 QUOTATION: FAIRBANK ON CALLIGRAPHY
San Francisco, California, December 1964.
1 paper leaf, 13¼×19¾ inches; ink, tempera; foundational italic and condensed version of bâtarde.
*Lent by the Artist*

180 CHRISTMAS CARD
San Francisco, California, 1963.
1 paper leaf, 14×9⅝ inches; red, black and gold ink; version of bold, condensed bâtarde.
*Lent by the Artist*

Byron Macdonald was born in San Francisco and attended evening classes at the California School of Fine Arts while earning his living by writing show cards. This occupation, he thinks, is an invaluable background for the calligrapher as "it gives one a sense of layout (being able to dramatize) and great manual dexterity with pen and brush." He did department-store lettering and theatre-lobby posters before progressing to advertising-agency reproduction lettering.

His study of the development of letters led him to calligraphy. His current favorite alphabets are the uncial and bâtarde, which he is developing in various weights for use in his commissions. Besides teaching at the California College of Arts and Crafts, he applies his calligraphic talents to a wide variety of uses, from liturgical literature to movie titles, and from architectural inscriptions to trademarks, letterheads, posters and books, including the cover of this catalogue.

All calligraphers are born old, but grow younger (says quinquagenarian Macdonald) as their interest and practice of the ancient craft develope.

His manual, *The Broad Pen*, will be published by Artone Color, New York City.

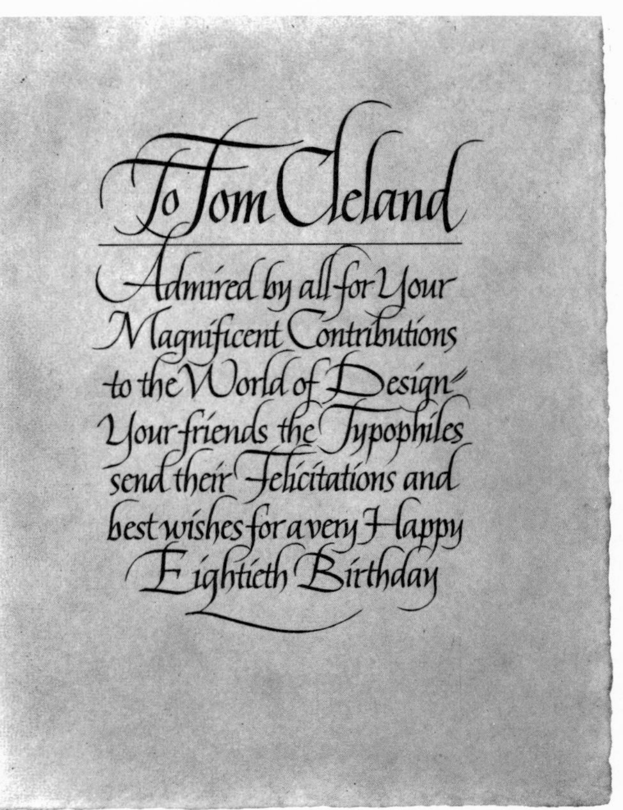


173. Greeting to Thomas Maitland Cleland on His 80th Birthday, from The Typhophiles. Fridolf Johnson. 1960

# Bene Dictum, Benedicte

IF ANY PILGRIM MONK come from distant parts, if with wish as a guest he dwell in the monastery, and will be content with the customs he finds in the place, and do not perchance by his lavishness disturb the monastery but is simply content with what he finds, he shall be received, for as long a time as he desires.

IF, indeed, he finds fault with anything, or expose it, reasonably, and with humility of charity, the Abbott shall discuss it prudently, lest perchance God had sent him for this very thing.

BUT if he shall have been found gossipy and contumacious in the time of his sojourn as guest, not only ought he not to be joined to the body of the monastery but also it shall be said to him honestly that he must depart. If he does not go, let two stout monks, in the name of God, explain the matter to him.

174. Quotation from St. Benedict. Edward Karr. 1965

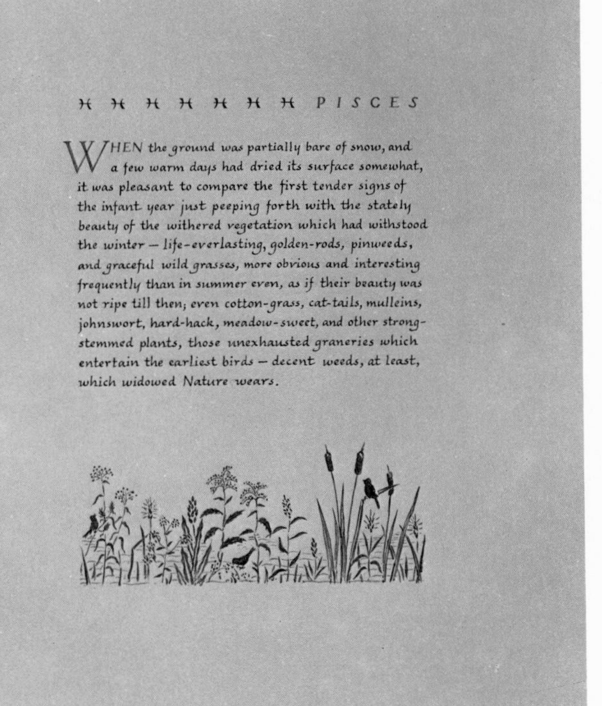


177. Thoreau: Life in the Woods Through the Seasons. Veronica Laing. 1953

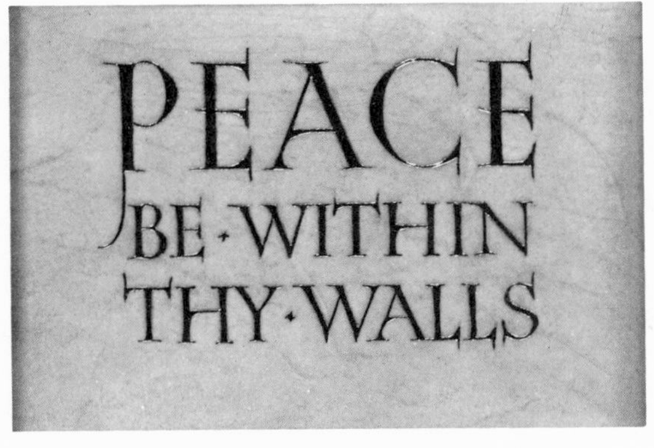


178. Psalm 122. Vera Law. 1948

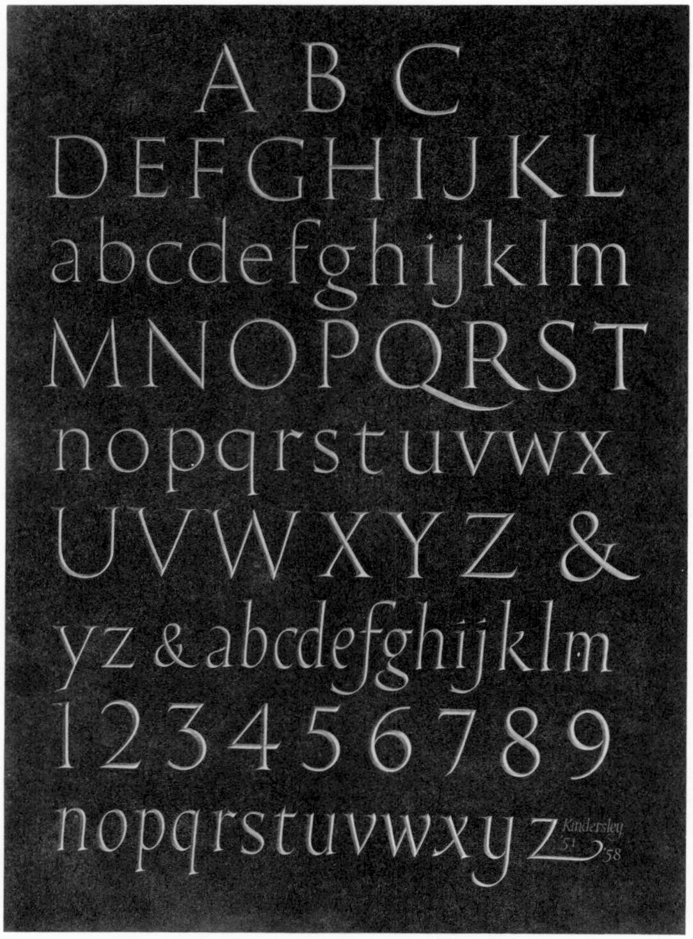

175. Alphabet Stone. David Kindersley. 1965

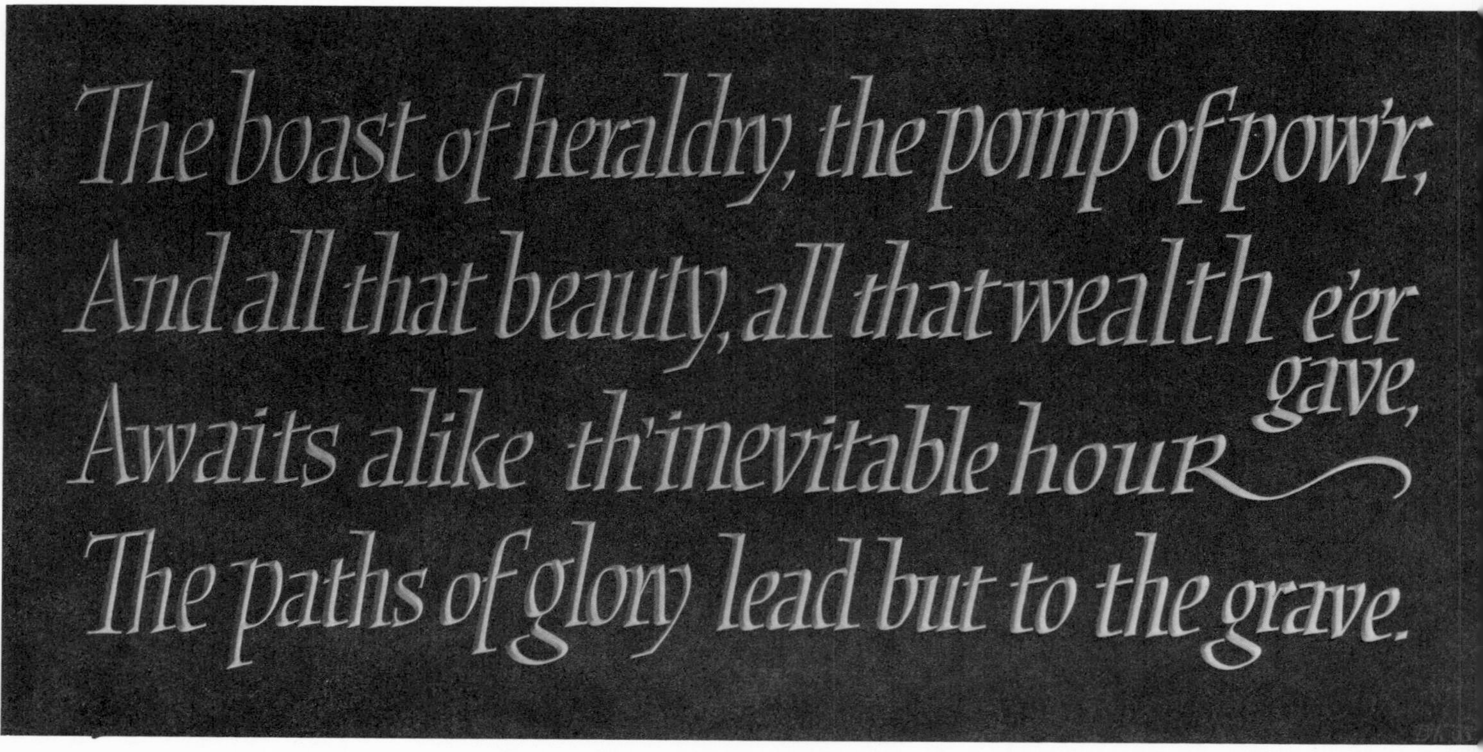

176. Gray: Elegy Written in a Country Church Yard. David Kindersley. 1965

CALLIGRAPHY is "handwriting as an art." To some, calligraphy will mean formal penmanship. It will suggest manuscript books, broadsides and scrolls, with precise scripts against which are set the vivid colours of illumination.

Others may think of calligraphy as the cursive handwriting used for correspondence and records which has legibility and beauty in spite of a swift pen. Calligraphy, then, may be considered as covering formal or informal handwriting, and to be found in the enduring and precious manuscript book preserved on the book-collector's shelf or on the envelope already lying in the waste-paper basket. Formal penmanship of today is a revival of the tradition of handwriting of pre-printing times. This revival in a machine age of a tradition associated with illuminated manuscripts is not a curious archaism, as it might seem at first. In our civilization a place is established for the products of the quill by the rightness of the old tradition and the virtues that arise from the work of the craftsman. While there is a clearly marked division between formal and cursive, due to a difference in approach or aim, yet the history of handwriting shows formal script merging into cursive or acquiring cursive characteristics, and cursive, because of its vitality, elevated to a book-script or becoming formalized. The tool of the craft is the edged pen which makes thick and thin strokes without resort to controlled pressures, and does so straightforwardly. It is essentially the letter-making tool... It may, therefore, be relied on largely to determine questions of form in letters. In fact a broad-nibbed pen actually controls the hand of the writer and will create alphabets out of their skeletons, giving harmony and proportion to the different letters. It was the edged pen that fashioned the early scripts, and it will be seen to be as suitable for making round letters of great clarity as for shaping elaborate richly patterned angular gothic letters. Sharpness of the pen, reed or quill is essential.

*Excerpts from opening chapter of "Lettering of Today" by Alfred Fairbank. Byron J. Macdonald, scribe 1964*

179. Quotation: Fairbank on Calligraphy. Byron Macdonald. 1964

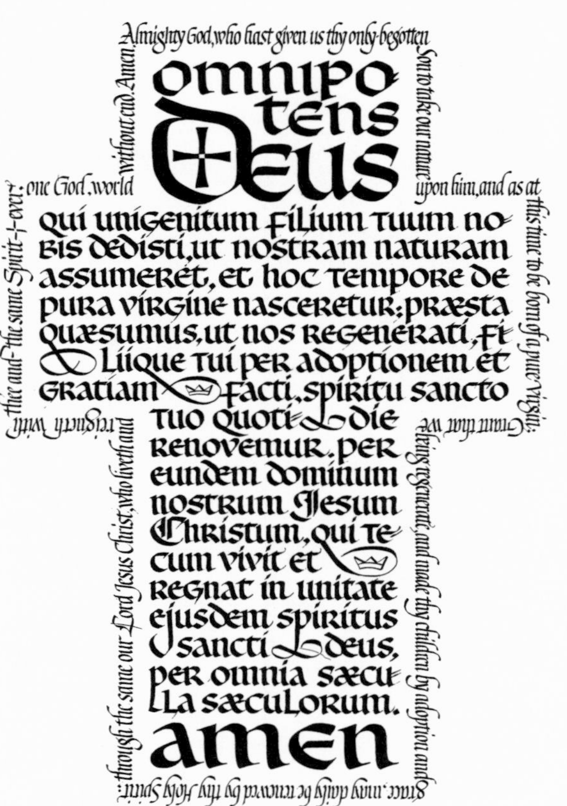


180. Christmas Card. Byron Macdonald. 1963

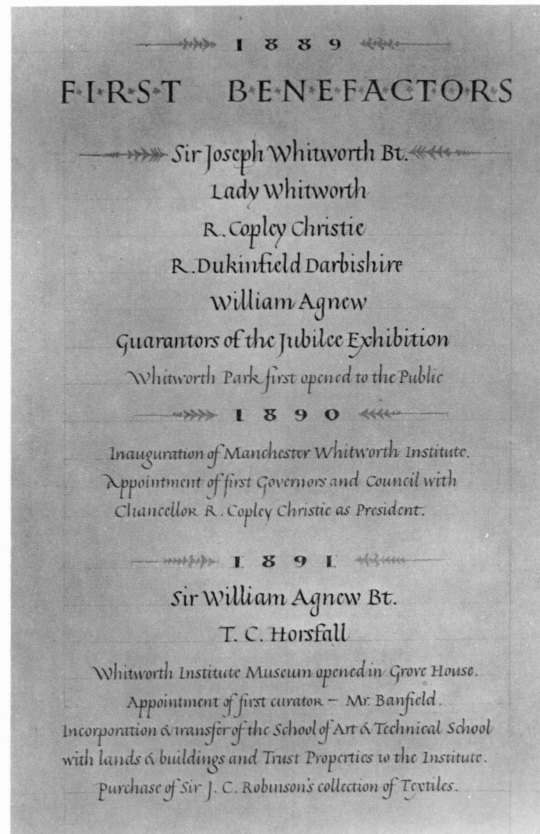

1 8 8 9

F·I·R·S·T B·E·N·E·F·A·C·T·O·R·S

Sir Joseph Whitworth Bt.
Lady Whitworth
R. Copley Christie
R. Dukinfield Darbishire
William Agnew
Guarantors of the Jubilee Exhibition
Whitworth Park first opened to the Public

1 8 9 0

Inauguration of Manchester Whitworth Institute.
Appointment of first Governors and Council with
Chancellor R. Copley Christie as President.

1 8 9 1

Sir William Agnew Bt.
T. C. Horsfall
Whitworth Institute Museum opened in Grove House.
Appointment of first curator – Mr. Banfield.
Incorporation & transfer of the School of Art & Technical School
with lands & buildings and Trust Properties to the Institute.
Purchase of Sir J. C. Robinson's collection of Textiles.

181. The Whitworth Benefactors Book. Dorothy Mahoney. 1954

Miniver Cheevy, child of scorn,
Grew lean while he assailed the seasons;
He wept that he was ever born,
And he had reasons.

Miniver loved the days of old
When swords were bright and steeds were prancing;
The vision of a warrior bold
Would set him dancing.

Miniver cursed the commonplace
And eyed a khaki suit with loathing;
He missed the medieval grace
Of iron clothing.

Miniver scorned the gold he sought,
But sore annoyed was he without it;
Miniver thought, and thought, and thought,
And thought about it.

Miniver Cheevy, born too late,
Scratched his head and kept on thinking;
Miniver coughed and called it fate,
And kept on drinking.

EDWIN ARLINGTON ROBINSON

182. Edwin Arlington Robinson: Miniver Cheevy. Egdon H. Margo. 1965

## *Dorothy Mahoney*

181 THE WHITWORTH BENEFACTORS BOOK, with notes compiled by Margaret Pilkington
Wrotham, Kent, 1954.
66 handmade laid paper leaves (30 blank), 15¼×10¾ inches; ink, watercolor, raised and powdered gold; Spanish sixteenth-century hand. Binding: blue morocco leather, gold tooled by Roger Powell and Peter Waters. Solander case by Roger Powell.
*Lent by the Whitworth Art Gallery, University of Manchester, England*

Dorothy Louise Mahoney was born in 1902 at Wednesbury, South Staffordshire. She studied art at the Ryland Memorial School, West Bromwich, and under Edward Johnston (nos. 123–4) at the Royal College of Art. Later she became his assistant, and from the time of his death in 1944 until 1953 she was responsible for the teaching of lettering and calligraphy at the College. She was lecturer in calligraphy at the Central School of Arts and Crafts, London, until the summer of 1964 when calligraphy was removed from the syllabus. She now teaches at the London County Council Stanhope Institute. She has had many distinguished pupils, including Marie Angel (141–3), Sheila and Peter Waters (207–8), Ann Camp (153) and John Woodcock (215). She is particularly known for her work in cathedrals and churches, but it is also to be found in many public and private collections, notably that of the Marquess of Cholmondeley. S.S.I.

## *Egdon H. Margo*

182 MINIVER CHEEVY by Edwin Arlington Robinson
Sherman Oaks, California, 1963.
1 Barcham-Green paper leaf, 13×18 inches; ink, color; personal hand.
*Lent by the Artist*

Egdon Margo was born in Boston in 1906. He moved to New York in 1923 and studied at the Art Students League under Warren Chappell and others. He studied lettering and worked with J. Albert Cavanagh. At the outbreak of World War II he was called to Washington to become Chief of Visual Information for the United States Public Health Service. He enlisted in the 8th Air Force, and, while in England, became interested in calligraphy after a chance meeting with a former student of Edward Johnston. Later he served as Art and Design Director for Military and Civilian Publications in Washington, D. C., where he also taught classes in design, typography and lettering. He went to California in 1949, teaching at the School for Allied Arts, The Kann Institute of Art and the University of California. He has lectured extensively on calligraphy and typographic design. His distinctive letterheads and religious texts are well known in the West.

Lately he has become interested in "private pressmanship" and is experimenting in typography on several historical hand presses. His aim in all his work is "to adapt the uses of the past to contemporary letter forms, making calligraphy vital, dashing and personal for our machine age."

## *Maury Nemoy*

183 SAMADHI. Quotation from the poem by Conrad Aiken
Los Angeles, California, January 1965.
1 "Elephant" gray-green paper leaf, 16¾×13¾ inches; ink, tempera; italic hand.
*Lent by the Artist*

Maury Nemoy was born in 1912 in Chicago and went to Los Angeles as a boy. He has attended the Art Center School, Chouinard Art Institute and San Fernando Valley State College, and has been a professional graphic designer, lettering artist and calligrapher since 1932. Since 1953 he has specialized in the entertainment field of motion pictures, television and records. He has been responsible for over one hundred and fifty album covers for Capitol Records and for work on the IBM World's Fair puppet shows for Charles Eames. Notable among his achievements are the thirteen plaques he devised for use with the unusual clock in the Midtown Plaza in Rochester, New York. His greatest reward has been teaching calligraphy at the University of California and at the Chouinard Art Institute, Los Angeles.

The piece exhibited is written in italic with free, sharp endings to maintain the rhythm and vitality of Conrad Aiken's thought. It exemplifies Maury Nemoy's special talent for conveying the mood and character of each text, which has earned him awards from the American Institute of Graphic Arts and the Los Angeles Art Directors' Club.

## *Alexander Nesbitt*

184 CITATION FOR ROBERT H. I. GODDARD, SR.
Providence, Rhode Island, 1958.
1 paper leaf, 17¾×11½ inches; ink, tempera; italic hand.
*Lent by Robert H. I. Goddard, Jr.*

Alexander Nesbitt was born in Paterson, New Jersey, in

1901. His formal art training was at the Art Students League in New York, but his main inspiration came from a visit to Germany in 1926, where he met Hadank and Beucke. For almost thirty years he worked in New York in the field of letters and type, and taught at the Traphagen School, the Cooper Union and New York University. Since 1957 he has served as Associate Professor at the Rhode Island School of Design, but in 1965 he is going to Southeastern Massachusetts Technological Institute to organize a graduate course in visual design.

He has had considerable success with his books, which include *The History and Technique of Lettering* (1957), *Decorative Alphabets and Initials* (1959) and *200 Decorative Title Pages* (1964). His translation of Renner's *Color: Order and Harmony* (Reinhold) will be published this year.

## *Oscar Ogg*

185 BOOK JACKET
New York City, 1949.
1 paper leaf, 13×11½ inches; ink.
*Lent by the Artist*

Oscar Ogg was born in Richmond, Virginia, in 1908. In his early years he worked as a typographer and as art director in an advertising agency. Until World War II he was a freelance designer, lettering artist and calligrapher. In 1946 he started his work with the Book-of-the-Month Club, producing announcements and books that became a standard of excellence.

He founded the School of Calligraphy at Columbia University, New York City, in 1946, and has lectured on calligraphy all over the United States.

His book and jacket designs have won many awards in the American Institute of Graphic Arts "Fifty Book" Exhibitions.

Among his own writings, *The 26 Letters* (1948, etc.) has remained a best seller, and his *Three Classics of Italian Calligraphy* (1953) has proved of great value to calligraphers.

## *Mervyn C. Oliver*

186 O TASTE A CUP OF ENGLAND'S GENTLE TEA
England, September 1952.
1 handmade paper leaf, 17¾×12¼ inches; ink.
Anonymous poem written out for exhibition at the Tea Centre, London.
*Lent by P. W. Filby*

Mervyn Oliver was born in 1886 and died in 1958. He was a student of Edward Johnston (nos. 123–4) at the Royal College of Art and became one of the greatest British teachers of this century. He taught at the Central School of Arts and Crafts, London, Chelsea School of Art, St. Martin's School of Art and the Hampstead Garden Suburb Institute. Among his pupils in this exhibition are: Irene Base (147), Ann Camp (153), Heather Child (157–8), William Gardner (165), Freda Hands (167), Donald Jackson (171), Pat Russell (195), Lewis Trethewey (204), Mary White (211) and Pamela Wrightson (216–7). He was the author of the chapters on the design of manuscript books and inscriptions, and the development of illumination in *The Calligrapher's Handbook* (1956). His numerous commissions include war memorial and record books. He was awarded the M.B.E. (Member of the Order of the British Empire) in 1956. S.S.I.

His work and studio are continued by his daughter, Joyce R. Griffiths.

## *Wendy Parnell*

187 SINE SOLE SILEO: a decorative broadsheet on sundials
Bristol, England, 1961.
1 vellum leaf, 22×25½ inches; Chinese ink, watercolor, shell gold, raised burnished gold; title in pen-built capitals, text in a compressed foundational hand with some in a round foundational hand.
*Lent by the Artist*

V. Wendy Parnell was born in Bristol, England, in 1932. She attended the West of England College of Art, specializing in writing and illuminating under Irene Base (no. 147). She now teaches lettering at the West of England College of Art and executes private commissions. S.S.I.

## *Enid Eder Perkins*

188 POEM FROM "THE GARDENER" by Rabindranath Tagore
New York City, 1965.
1 vellum leaf, 11¾×8¾ inches; ink, tempera, gold leaf, shell gold.
*Lent by the Artist*

Enid Eder Perkins was born in New York City. She first studied at the Art Students League and later under Arnold Bank (no. 145) at the Brooklyn Museum Art School. For the past twenty years she has devoted herself to illuminating, and in 1960 she visited England for tuition in gilding with Irene Base (no. 147). The illuminated border of the poem shown is similar to that of an inscription she made for the Spanish Colonial Chapel of San Isidro in Palmira, Colombia. She is an associate member of the S.S.I.

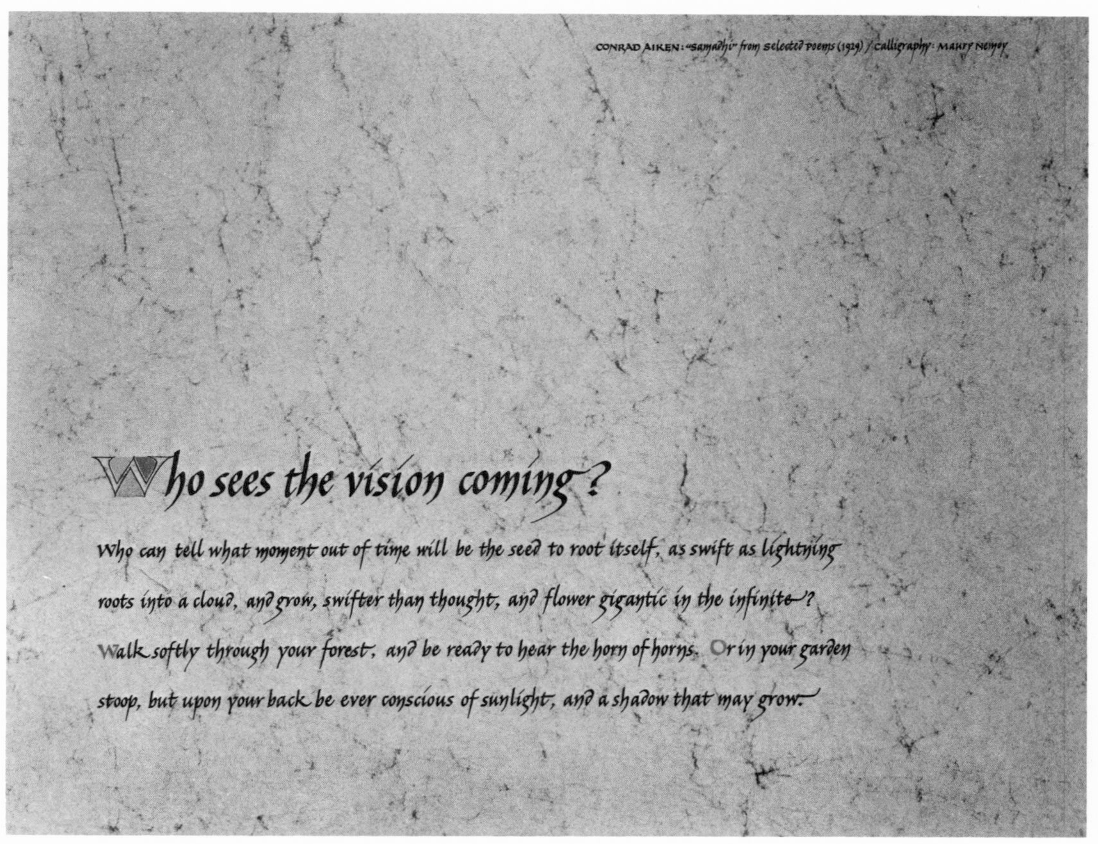


183. Conrad Aiken: Samadhi. Maury Nemoy. 1965

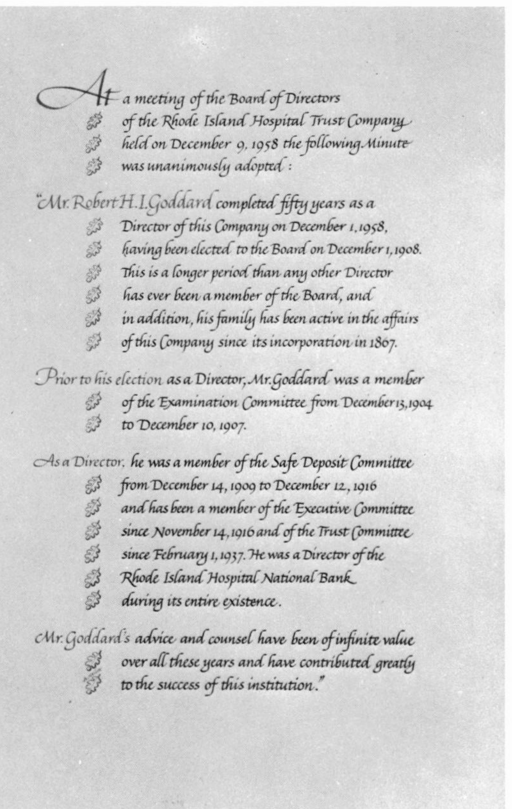

At a meeting of the Board of Directors
of the Rhode Island Hospital Trust Company
held on December 9, 1958 the following Minute
was unanimously adopted:

"Mr. Robert H. I. Goddard completed fifty years as a
Director of this Company on December 1, 1958,
having been elected to the Board on December 1, 1908.
This is a longer period than any other Director
has ever been a member of the Board, and
in addition, his family has been active in the affairs
of this Company since its incorporation in 1867.

Prior to his election as a Director, Mr. Goddard was a member
of the Examination Committee from December 13, 1904
to December 10, 1907.

As a Director, he was a member of the Safe Deposit Committee
from December 14, 1909 to December 12, 1916
and has been a member of the Executive Committee
since November 14, 1916 and of the Trust Committee
since February 1, 1937. He was a Director of the
Rhode Island Hospital National Bank
during its entire existence.

Mr. Goddard's advice and counsel have been of infinite value
over all these years and have contributed greatly
to the success of this institution."

184. Citation for Robert H. I. Goddard, Sr.
Alexander Nesbitt. 1958

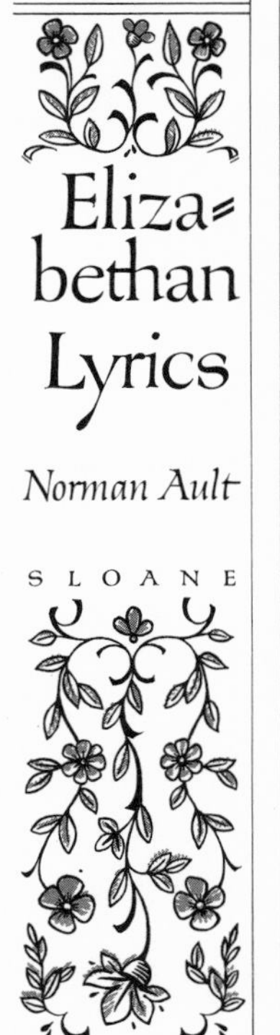


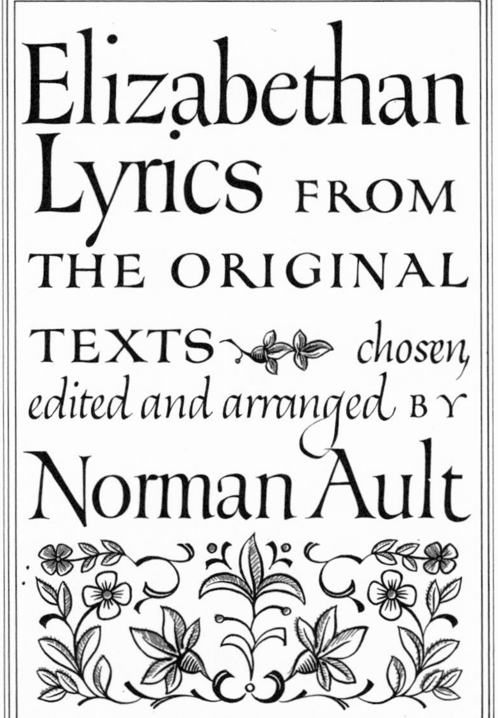


185. Book Jacket. Oscar Ogg. 1949

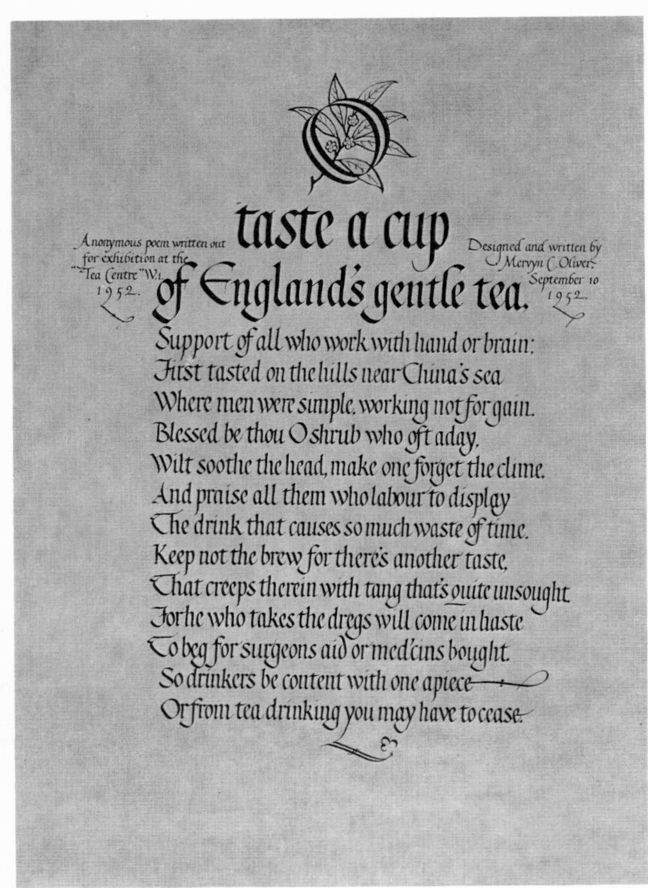


186. O Taste a Cup of England's Gentle Tea. Mervyn C. Oliver. 1952

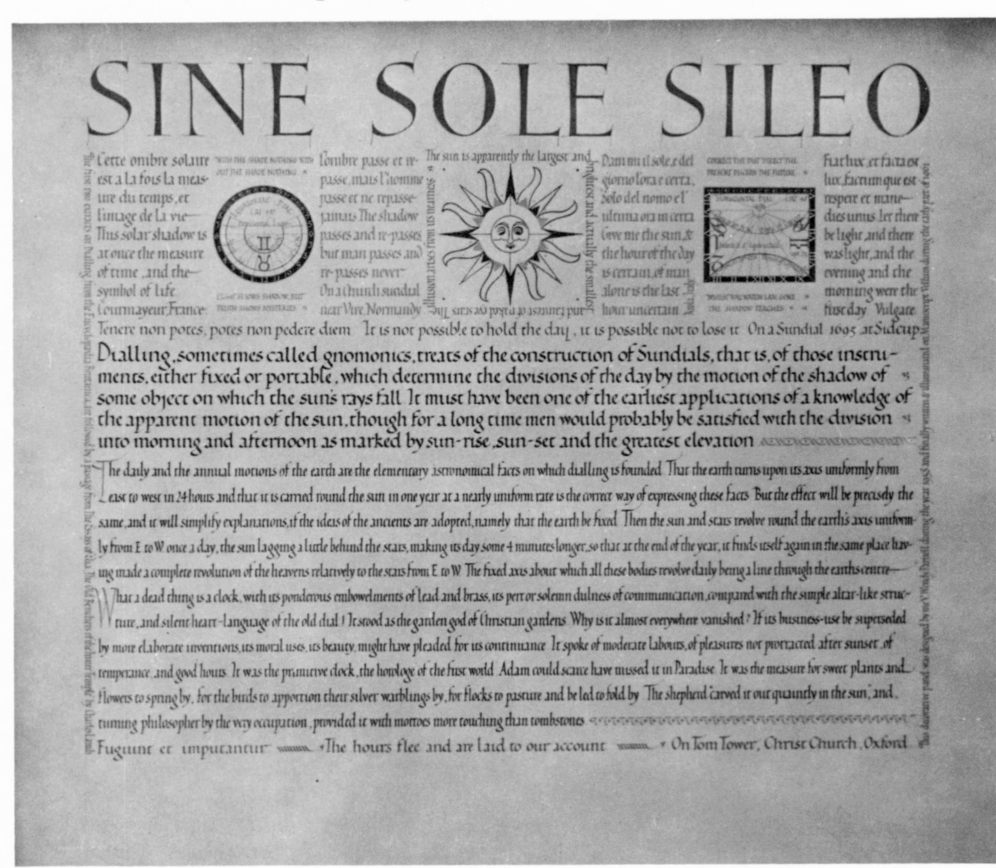


187. Sine Sole Sileo. Wendy Parnell. 1961

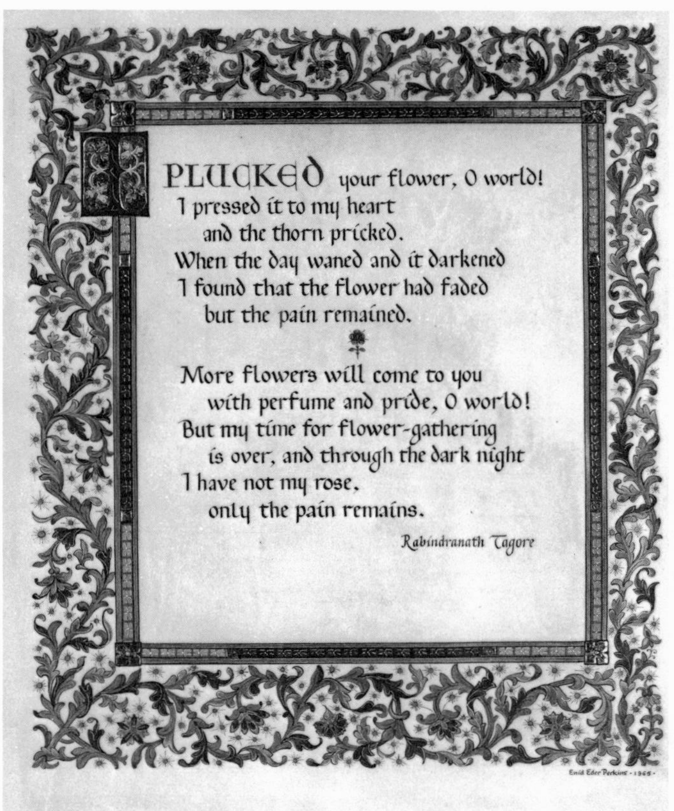


188. Tagore: Poem from "The Gardener." Enid Eder Perkins. 1965

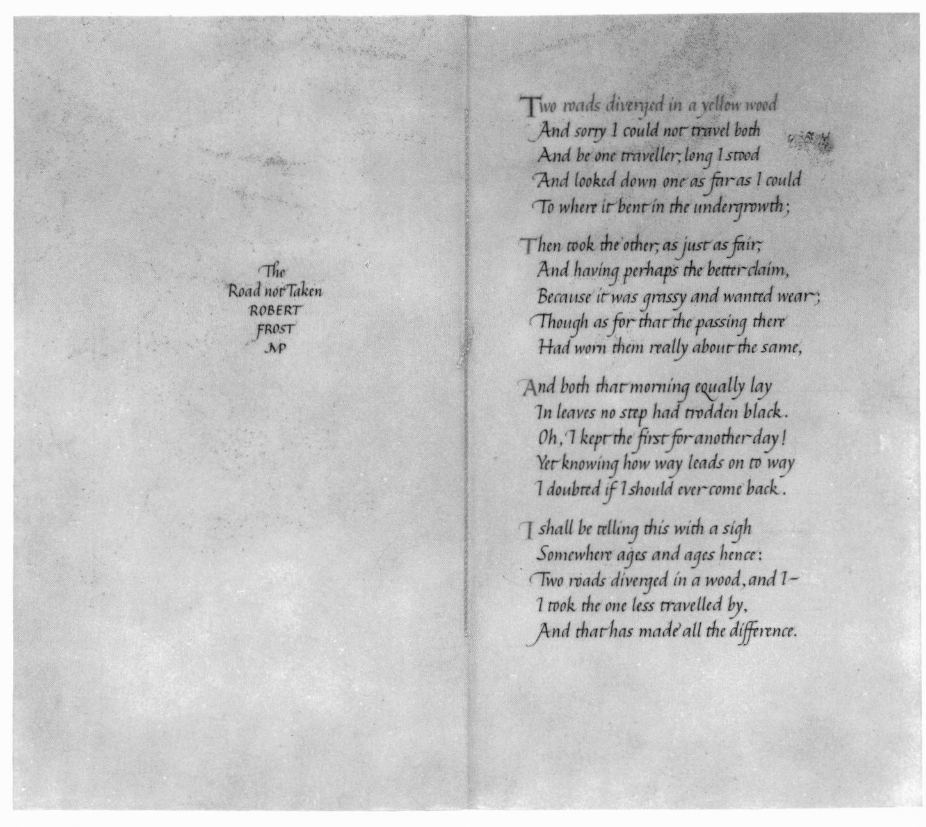


189. Robert Frost: The Road Not Taken. Joan Pilsbury. 1957

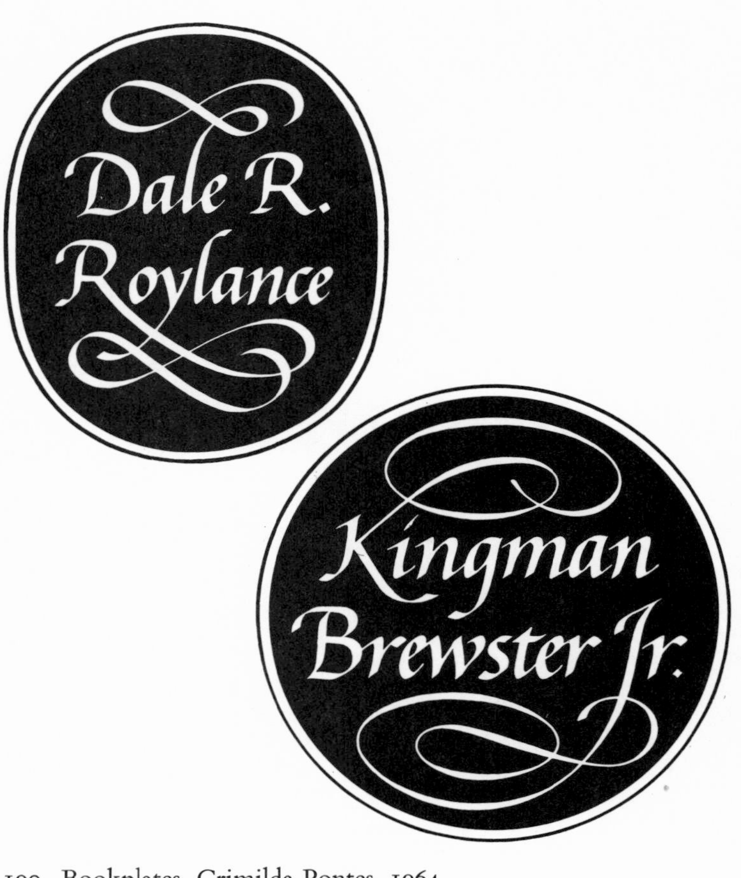


190. Bookplates. Crimilda Pontes. 1964

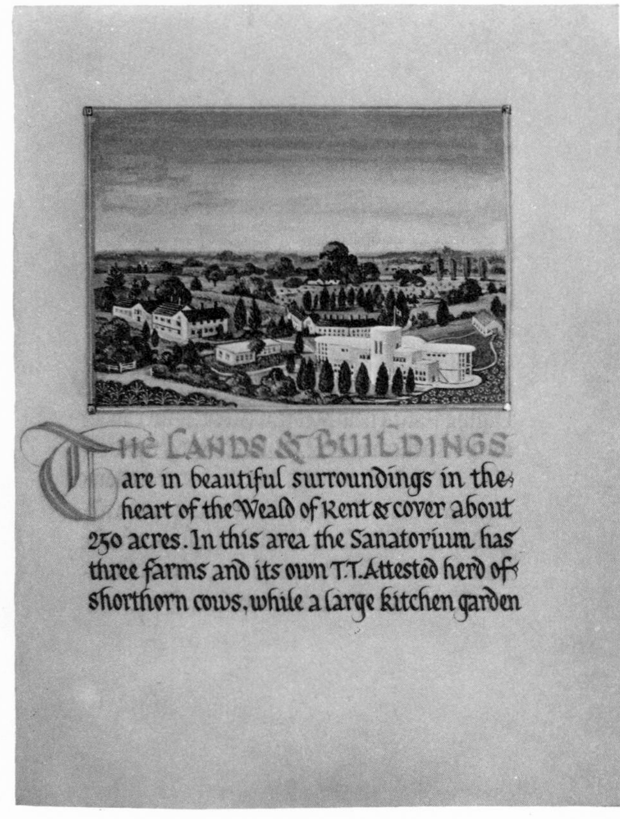


192. Benenden Book. Mildred M. Ratcliffe. 1950

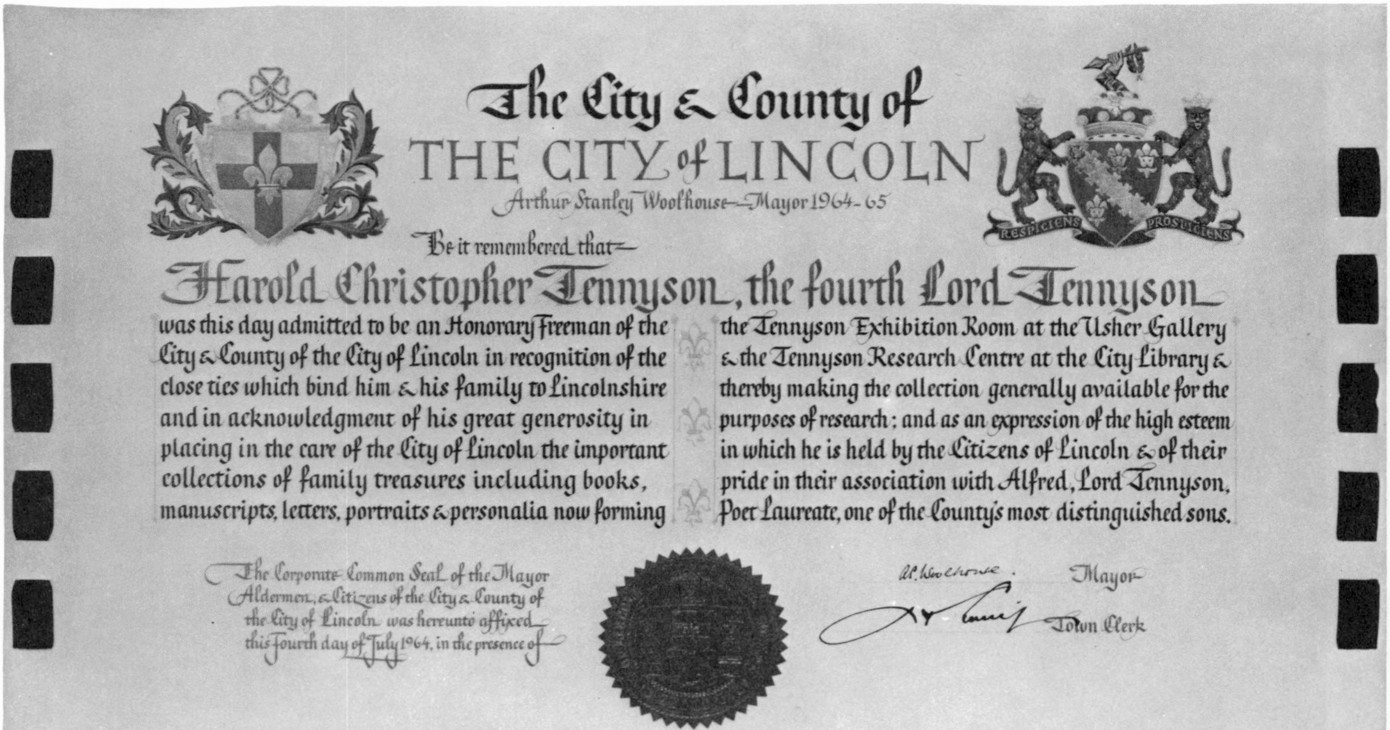

The City & County of
THE CITY of LINCOLN
Arthur Stanley Woolhouse—Mayor 1964–65

RESPICIENS PROSPICIENS

Be it remembered that—
Harold Christopher Tennyson, the fourth Lord Tennyson
was this day admitted to be an Honorary Freeman of the City & County of the City of Lincoln in recognition of the close ties which bind him & his family to Lincolnshire and in acknowledgment of his great generosity in placing in the care of the City of Lincoln the important collections of family treasures including books, manuscripts, letters, portraits & personalia now forming the Tennyson Exhibition Room at the Usher Gallery & the Tennyson Research Centre at the City Library & thereby making the collection generally available for the purposes of research; and as an expression of the high esteem in which he is held by the Citizens of Lincoln & of their pride in their association with Alfred, Lord Tennyson, Poet Laureate, one of the County's most distinguished sons.

The Corporate Common Seal of the Mayor Aldermen & Citizens of the City & County of the City of Lincoln was hereunto affixed this fourth day of July 1964, in the presence of

Mayor
Town Clerk

191. Freedom of the City of Lincoln Conferred on Lord Tennyson. Margery Raisbeck. 1964

## *Joan Pilsbury*

189 THE ROAD NOT TAKEN by Robert Frost
Twickenham, Middlesex, 1957.
2 vellum leaves, 9×5 inches; ink, color, burnished gold; italic hand. Binding: handmade paper board.
*Lent by Frederick B. Adams, Jr.*

Joan Pilsbury was born in 1925 at Amersham, Buckinghamshire. She studied at the Central School of Arts and Crafts, London, and later became part-time instructor there, assisting Irene Wellington (nos. 209–10), who considers her the best scribe of her generation. She is known for her decorative maps, and has collaborated on important commissions with Mrs. Wellington and with Wendy Westover (no. 152). Among her many outstanding works is the illuminated charter marking the 500th anniversary of the Drapers' Company, London. S.S.I.

## *Crimilda Pontes*

190 BOOKPLATES
New Haven, Connecticut, June 1964.
Paper, 1½×1½ inches; ink.
*Lent by the Artist*

Crimilda Pontes was born in 1926 at Somerset, Massachusetts. While at the Rhode Island School of Design she was in the workshop in calligraphy of John Howard Benson (no. 149). During her senior year she was apprenticed at Benson's studio, the John Stevens Shop, Newport, where she received her most valuable training, studying calligraphy, printing, wood engraving, layout for stone inscriptions and related arts. She designed, set and printed Palatino's *The Instruments of Writing*, Berryhill Press, 1948 (Chiswick Bookshop, 1953), and assisted in the revision of Benson and Carey's *The Elements of Lettering* (1950). She has been instructor of art at various institutions and was assistant typographer at Yale University Press from 1959 to 1964. She is now designer in the Editorial and Publications Division, Smithsonian Institution, Washington.

## *Margery Raisbeck*

191 FREEDOM OF THE CITY OF LINCOLN CONFERRED ON LORD TENNYSON
Harrogate, Yorkshire, 1964.
1 vellum sheet, 13×24 inches; ink, color, gold; Johnstonian hand.
*Lent by the Rt. Hon. The Lord Tennyson*

Margery Raisbeck was a pupil of Edward Johnston (nos. 123–4) at the Royal College of Art, London, and student assistant in his lettering class in 1934–1935. She uses a distinctive style—Johnstonian, or modern based on twelfth-century Winchester—and lavish illumination. Four examples of her work have been purchased by the Victoria and Albert Museum, and others are to be found in public and private collections all over the world.

Of the piece shown she writes: "The 'Freedom of the City' of Lincoln, England, was conferred on Lord Tennyson on the 4th July 1964, by means of this vellum scroll (recording the event), enclosed in a casket made from oak from Lincoln Cathedral. The Mayor, Alderman & Citizens wished to honour Lord Tennyson thus, since he had presented the City with a collection of books, Mss. etc, belonging to or concerning his great-grandfather, Alfred, Lord Tennyson, the poet (Laureate) who was a Lincolnshire man." S.S.I.

## *Mildred M. Ratcliffe*

192 BENENDEN BOOK
Maidstone, Kent, 1950.
1 vellum leaf, 8×6 inches; Chinese ink, watercolor; slightly compressed informal hand to suit the literary matter.
Part of a book of 8 pages given to Queen Elizabeth, the Queen Mother, in 1950. This page was done over because of a fault on the reverse side of the vellum.
*Lent by the Artist*

Mildred Ratcliffe was born in Rochester, Kent, in 1899. She left the Civil Service to study lettering at the Hammersmith School of Art under Madelyn Walker (no. 130) and later under Daisy Alcock, at the same time receiving instruction from Graily Hewitt (nos. 132–3) at the Central School of Arts and Crafts, London. In 1935 she studied gothic lettering in Munich under Anna Simons (no. 131). All four of her teachers had been pupils of Edward Johnston (nos. 123–4). She was one of the earliest craft members of the S.S.I.

## *Rosemary Ratcliffe*

193 PSALM XV
Buckinghamshire, 1953.
1 Japanese paper leaf, 15½×9½ inches; black ink, watercolor.
*Lent by the Victoria and Albert Museum, London*

Rosemary Ratcliffe was born in London and studied calligraphy there at the Central School of Arts and Crafts, London, where she succeeded Graily Hewitt (nos. 132–3) in 1930. She remained until 1940, also teaching at the Byam

Shaw School of Drawing and Painting, Kensington. Her ecclesiastical work is to be seen in many churches and cathedrals, and the recipients of her presentation addresses include General Smuts and Sir Robert Menzies. She aims "to get the true forms of the letters, yet with a dancing freedom—can only get the latter when confident enough to write freely and not trying *too* hard," and the example shown, written freely without preliminary draft, proves how well she achieves her aim. S.S.I.

## *Lloyd J. Reynolds*

194 THE ROUNDEL FROM "THE PARLEMENT OF FOULES" by Geoffrey Chaucer
Portland, Oregon, January 1965.
1 calfskin leaf, 14½×9 inches; Artone fountain pen india ink; based on twelfth-century script, refrain has cursive modifications.
*Lent by the Artist*

Lloyd Reynolds was born in 1902. He holds three degrees from Oregon State University and the University of Oregon. He left advertising lettering after one year because he "could find no adequate theoretical approach, no logic, that would apply to the letter arts." Some years after joining the Reed College faculty in 1929, he found the logical approach in Johnston's *Writing & Illuminating, & Lettering* and the study of historical alphabets with the edged pen in hand.

Lloyd Reynolds is self-taught (a method which he does not recommend), but acknowledges the help of Arnold Bank (no. 145) and Alfred Fairbank (no. 135). A long correspondence over the years and meetings with Fairbank in 1960 have greatly influenced his work. He is Professor of Fine Art, Reed College, Portland, where he has organized exhibitions and is the author of *Italic Lettering & Handwriting Exercise Book* (1957) and other manuals on calligraphy. His exhibition catalogue, *Calligraphy: The Golden Age and Its Modern Revival* (1958) undoubtedly inspired other exhibitions later held in America.

## *Pat Russell*

195 ST. FRANCIS OF ASSISI: paraphrase of the Lord's Prayer; translated by L. Sherley-Price
Abingdon, Berkshire, 1961.
12 paper leaves, 6¼×4 inches; shell gold, watercolor; formal italic hand. Binding: sheepskin vellum.
*Lent by the Artist*

Mrs. Russell was born in Wembley, Middlesex, in 1919. She studied under Mervyn C. Oliver (no. 186) at the Chelsea College of Art. Her work is to be seen in many institutions, and she was responsible for part of the American Air Force Remembrance Book in St. Clement Danes, London. S.S.I.

## *Hans Schmidt*

196 WO DER GEIST DES HERRN IST, DA IST FREIHEIT. A Biblical quotation
Mainz, Germany, 1958.
1 Japanese paper leaf, 20×26½ inches; woodcut; informal, roman capitals.
No. 8 of an edition of 10, signed. Purchased from the artist.
*Lent by the Library of Congress—Pennell Fund*

Hans Schmidt was born in Germany and is an instructor at the Werkkunstschule in Offenbach. His new forms, especially in woodcuts and linoleum cuts, are arousing great interest throughout the world. He is a painstaking and meticulous worker and a gifted writer and typographer.

## *Paul Standard*

197 RUBBING made from inscription in brass panel
New York City, 1963.
6×36 inches. The brass panel is affixed to the lectern containing Paul Standard's 100-foot scroll at the Federation Charities, New York City. Italic set hand based directly on Arrighi.
*Lent by the Artist*

Paul Standard was born in upstate New York and holds three degrees from Columbia University. He served for fifteen years as chief United States publicity officer for the Canadian Pacific Railway. Although he is widely known as a teacher, author, calligrapher and graphic arts consultant, his most remarkable achievement has been the pioneering introduction of Arrighi's chancery cursive to the American public. His article with instructional charts, *Our Handwriting*, published in 1947 in *Woman's Day* (circulation 4,000,000), was reprinted as a pamphlet and republished in five foreign countries. An extensive interview recorded in *The New Yorker* in January 1963, under the heading *Crusader* was another long step toward making the "outside" public aware of a movement already familiar to educational and technical circles. Recently he has converted more than a dozen private schools to the italic hand, including The Groton School, Massachusetts, The Chapin School in New York and The Potomac School in McLean, Virginia. For the last fifteen years he has been teaching at the Cooper Union Art School and the Parsons School of Design in New York.

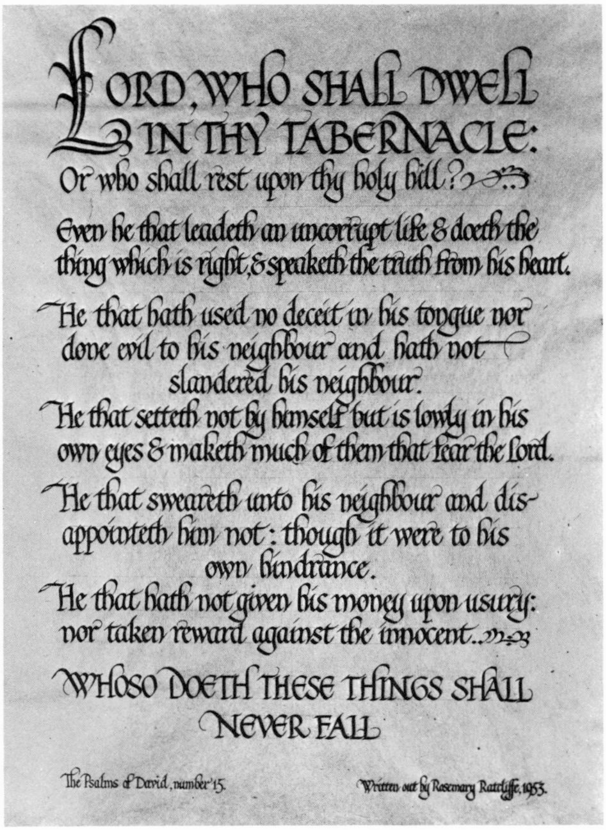

LORD, WHO SHALL DWELL
IN THY TABERNACLE:
Or who shall rest upon thy holy hill?
Even he that leadeth an uncorrupt life & doeth the
thing which is right, & speaketh the truth from his heart.
He that hath used no deceit in his tongue nor
done evil to his neighbour and hath not
slandered his neighbour.
He that setteth not by himself but is lowly in his
own eyes & maketh much of them that fear the Lord.
He that sweareth unto his neighbour and dis-
appointeth him not: though it were to his
own hindrance.
He that hath not given his money upon usury:
nor taken reward against the innocent.
WHOSO DOETH THESE THINGS SHALL
NEVER FALL

The Psalms of David, number 15. Written out by Rosemary Ratcliffe, 1953.

193. Psalm xv. Rosemary Ratcliffe. 1953

Qui bien aime a tard oublie

Now welcome somer with thy sonne softe
That hast this wintres weders over-shake
And driven awey the longe nightes blake!

Seynt Valentyn, that art ful hy onlofte—
Thus singen smale fowles for thy sake:

Now welcom somer, with thy sonne softe
That hast this wintres weders overshake.

Wel han they cause for to gladen ofte
Sith ech of hem recovered hath his make;
Ful blisful may they singen whan they wake;

Now welcom somer, with thy sonne softe
That hast this wintres weders overshake
And driven away the longe nightes blake

The roundel from Geoffrey Chaucer's The Parlement
of Foules. The Skeat edition.
Written out by Lloyd J. Reynolds on January 7, 1965

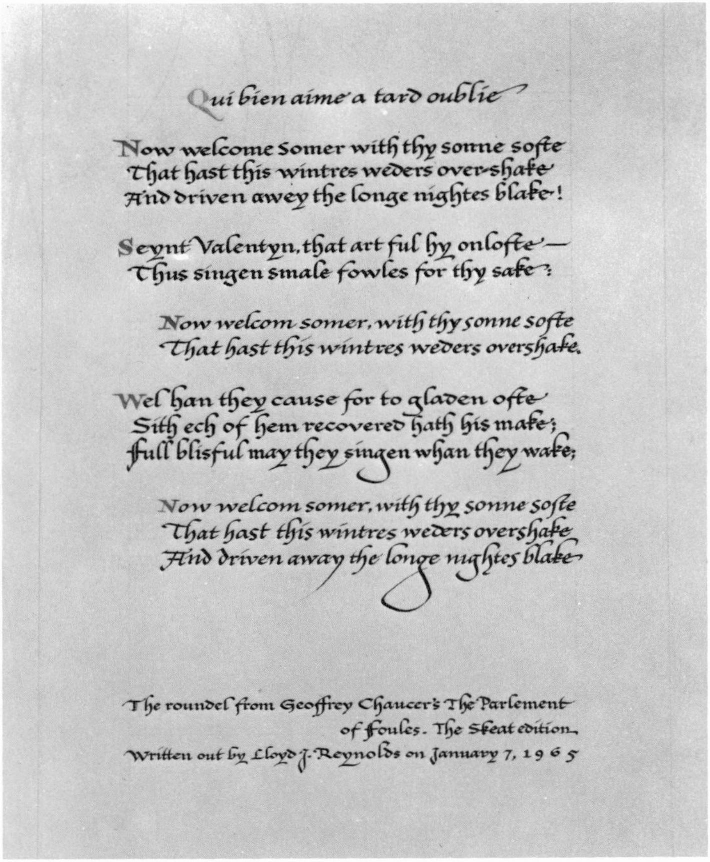

194. Chaucer: The Roundel from "The Parlement of Foules."
Lloyd J. Reynolds. 1965

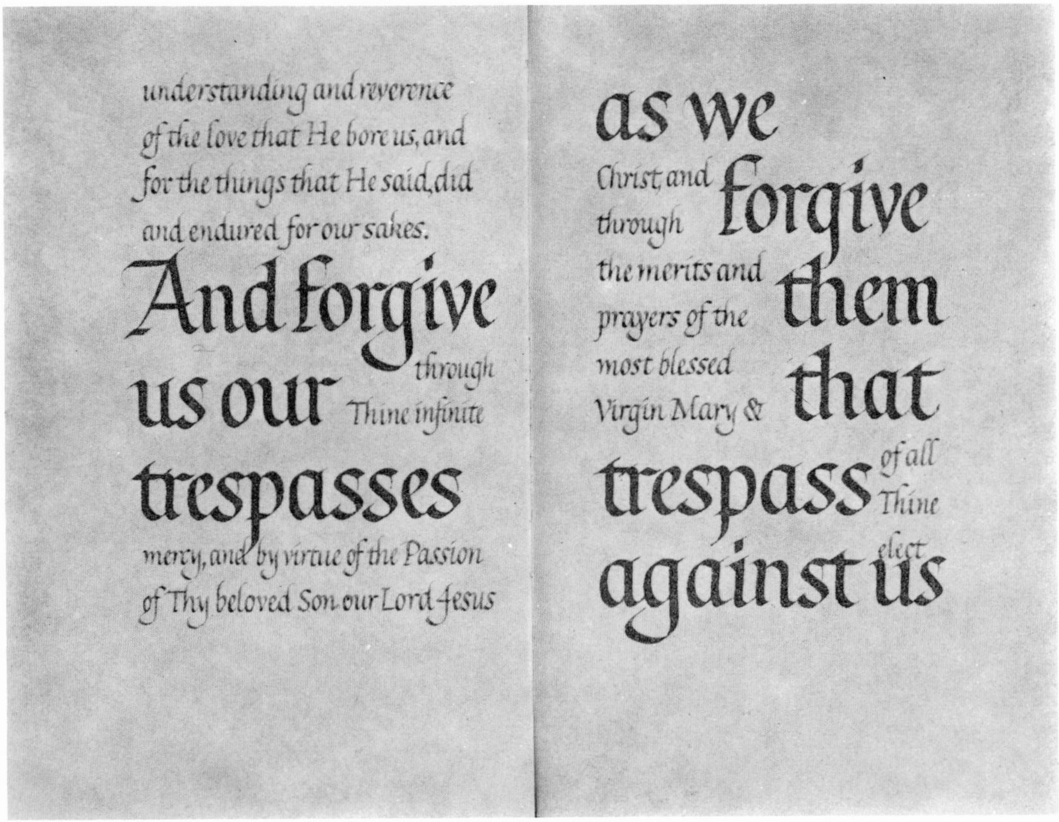

understanding and reverence
of the love that He bore us, and
for the things that He said, did
and endured for our sakes.
And forgive
us our through
Thine infinite
trespasses
mercy, and by virtue of the Passion
of Thy beloved Son our Lord Jesus

as we
Christ and
forgive
through
the merits and
them
prayers of the
most blessed
that
Virgin Mary &
trespass of all
Thine
elect
against us

195. St. Francis of Assisi. Pat Russell. 1961

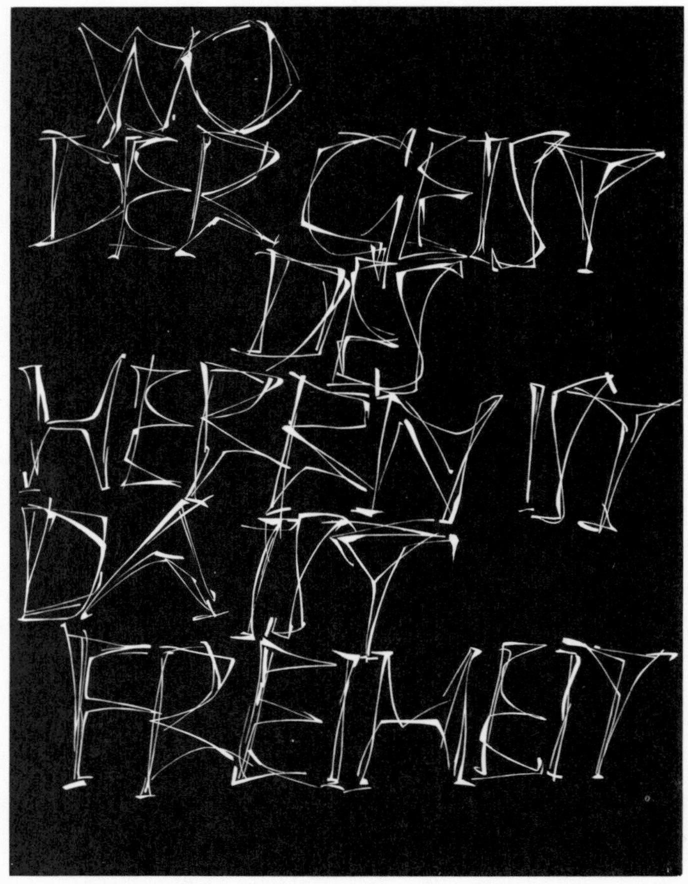


196. Wo der Geist des Herrn ist, da ist Freiheit. Hans Schmidt. 1958

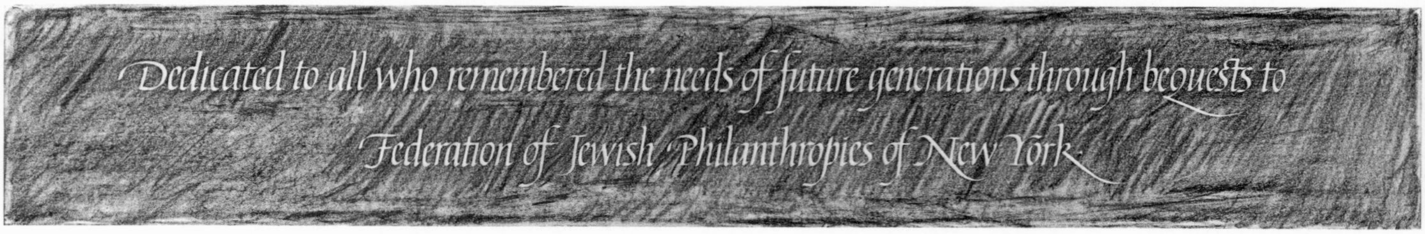

Dedicated to all who remembered the needs of future generations through bequests to
Federation of Jewish Philanthropies of New York

197. Rubbing made from Inscription in Brass Panel. Paul Standard. 1963

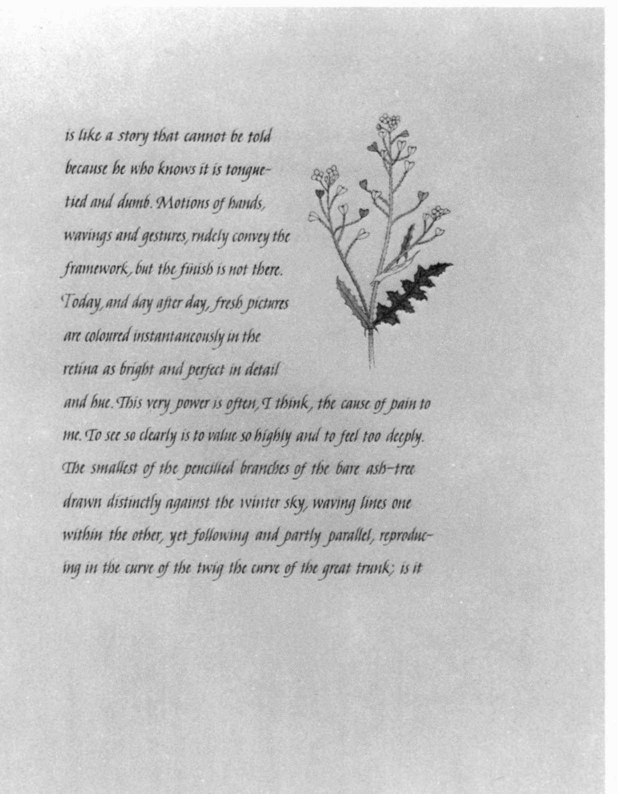

is like a story that cannot be told
because he who knows it is tongue-
tied and dumb. Motions of hands,
wavings and gestures, rudely convey the
framework, but the finish is not there.
Today, and day after day, fresh pictures
are coloured instantaneously in the
retina as bright and perfect in detail
and hue. This very power is often, I think, the cause of pain to
me. To see so clearly is to value so highly and to feel too deeply.
The smallest of the pencilled branches of the bare ash-tree
drawn distinctly against the winter sky, waving lines one
within the other, yet following and partly parallel, reproducing in the curve of the twig the curve of the great trunk; is it

200. Richard Jefferies: Open Air. Pamela Stokes. 1964–1965

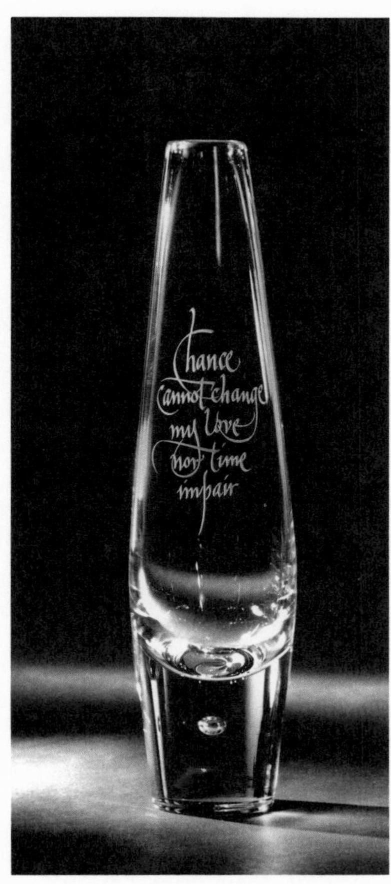


199. Steuben Glass. Robert Browning: Any Wife to Any Husband. Golda Goldblatt. 1958

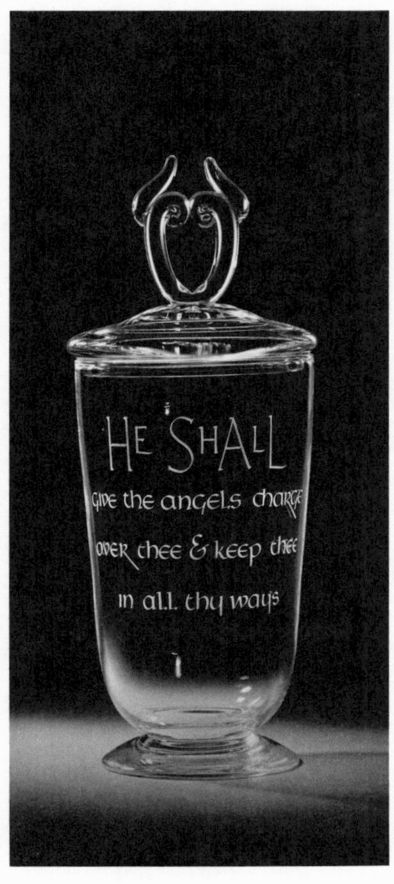


198. Steuben Glass. Psalm XCI. Elliot Offner. 1957

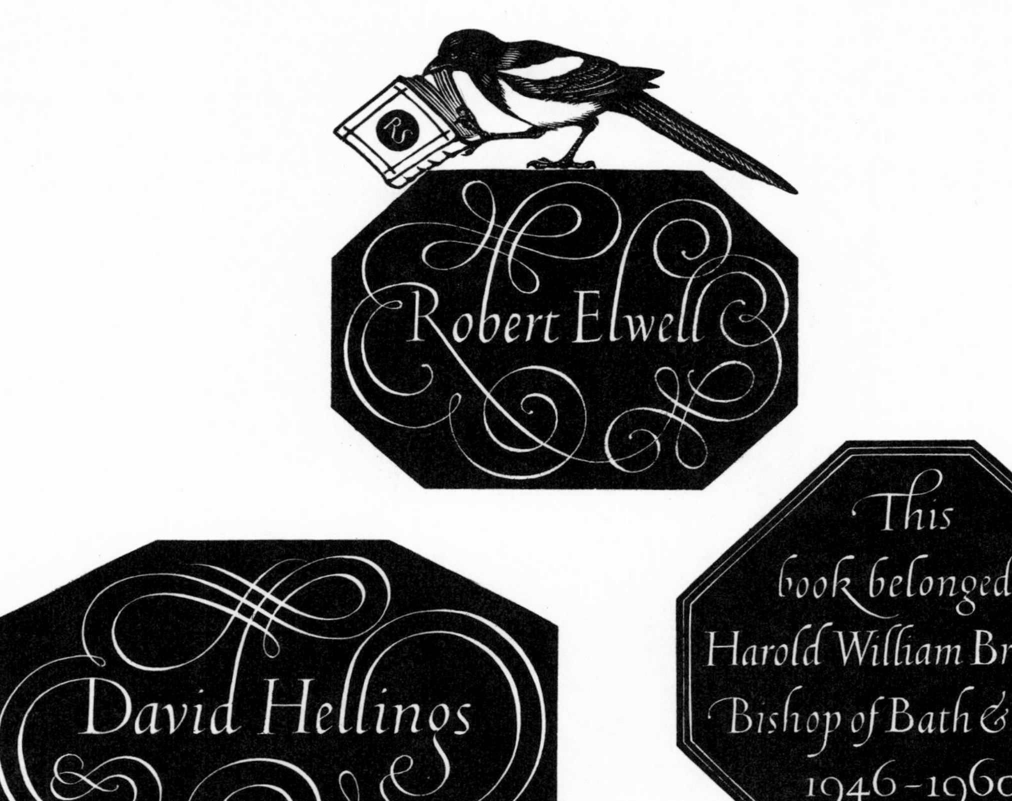


201. Book Labels. Reynolds Stone. 1960's

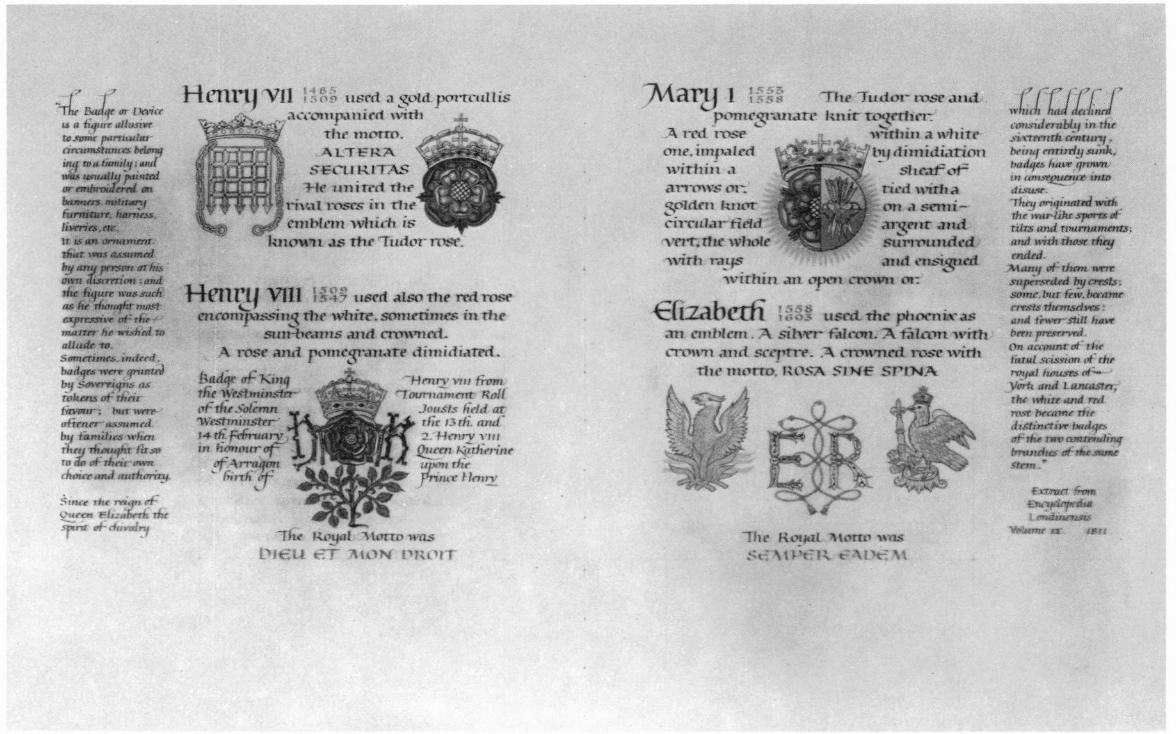


202. Heraldic Badges of English Tudor Sovereigns, 1485–1603. Thomas W. Swindlehurst. 1964

## *Steuben Glass*

198–199

Steuben Glass, founded in 1933, is the leading American maker of fine glass. Using crystal glass as its medium and hand craftsmanship as its method, it is dedicated to the advancement of glassmaking as an expression of the arts.

The administrative offices, design department and principal display rooms of Steuben Glass are located in New York City. The glass is made at Corning Glass Center, Corning, New York, where are located the glass blowers, cutters and engravers.

The design department of Steuben Glass is staffed with full-time artists, many with long experience in designing the form and decoration of glass. A considerable amount of their time is spent on experimental and advanced design.

In addition to the staff of its design department, Steuben retains a smaller group of "associate" designers—painters and sculptors—who submit original work and to whom special projects are assigned.

Steuben Glass has also from time to time commissioned original work from many independent artists throughout the world.

## *Elliot Offner*

198 INSCRIBED COVERED URN.
Verse from Psalm XCI
New York City, 1957.
Crystal glass, 8½×3½ inches; made and engraved by Steuben Glass.
(Steuben Glass, M-102.)
*Lent by Steuben Glass*

Elliot Offner was born in 1931 in Brooklyn, New York. He studied at Cooper Union Art School, where only a month with Paul Standard (no. 197) was sufficient to ignite the spark of interest in calligraphy. He obtained his M.F.A. from Yale in 1959. Serving as staff calligrapher for Steuben Glass from 1955 to 1957, he designed inscriptions for a number of unique pieces in private and museum collections. Others, such as the piece exhibited, are in general production.

Since 1959, with the exception of one year at the University of Massachusetts, he has taught sculpture and calligraphy at Smith College. His sculpture is exhibited at the Forum Gallery in New York.

## *Golda Goldblatt*

199 INSCRIBED BUD VASE. Line from Robert Browning's *Any Wife to Any Husband*
New York City, 1958.
Crystal glass, 8×2 inches; made and engraved by Steuben Glass.
(Steuben Glass, M-109.)
*Lent by Steuben Glass*

Golda Goldblatt (Fishbein) was born in New York City in 1934. She studied at the Cooper Union Art School under Paul Standard (no. 197) and George Salter. She worked for several years in the New York design department of Steuben Glass. For the last five years she has been a busy mother, but has found time to design book jackets for Random House and McGraw-Hill.

## *Pamela Stokes*

200 WILD FLOWERS. An Essay from *Open Air* by Richard Jefferies
Mainz, Germany, 1964–1965.
62 Dürer Bütten paper leaves, 11 4/5 × 9 3/5 inches; Chinese stick ink, watercolor, shell gold; italic hand. Binding: oasis morocco leather.
*Lent by Richard Harrison*

Pamela Stokes was born in Chesham Bois, England, in 1924. She started lettering and calligraphy "for the fun of it" while working for a press agency in Germany, and received private tuition in Hamburg from Frieda Wiegand, graphic artist, book designer and illustrator. Her works include manuscript books, diplomas, decorative maps, book jackets and television titles. She is a lay member of the S.S.I.

## *Reynolds Stone*

201 BOOK LABELS AND BLOCK
England, 1960's.
Paper; reproduced from wood engravings.
*Lent by the Artist and Robert Elwell*

Reynolds Stone was born in 1909 at Eton, where his father and grandfather were both masters at the College. After Eton and Cambridge, he joined the Cambridge University Press, and there learned typography from its great Overseer, F. G. Nobbs. After a short time spent with Eric Gill (137) he decided on engraving as a career, working on stone and slate as well as wood blocks for printing.

He showed his first bookplates in 1934, and these have been followed by a succession of letter headings, symbols and now famous trademarks, all unmistakably individual, much as they have been imitated. He designed the new British five-pound note, the royal arms of Her Majesty's Stationery Office and a number of Britain's commemorative stamps. One of his finest works is the double title page with engraved capitals and ornament for Stanley Morison's *The Typographic Book*, published by the Cambridge University Press (1963).

## *Thomas W. Swindlehurst*

202 HERALDIC BADGES OF ENGLISH TUDOR SOVEREIGNS, 1485–1603
Horsforth, Yorkshire, December 1964.
4 vellum leaves, 2 handmade endpapers, 12½×9½ inches; red and black ink, color and gold; based on Winchester tenth-century (foundational) hand, marginal writing laterally compressed and more freely written. Binding: cloth spine, paper-covered boards.
*Lent by Richard Harrison*

Thomas Swindlehurst was born in Yorkshire in 1900. He studied calligraphy and lettering under Edward Johnston (nos. 123–4) from 1924 to 1927. Until 1959 he taught at the College of Art, Leeds.

Although his work reflects the tradition and craftsmanship of his great teacher, he carries these into our own day by his individual verve. Some of his many commissions have been exhibited in Britain, Europe and America, and are to be seen in private and other collections, including the Victoria and Albert Museum. S.S.I.

## *Frank Taylor*

203 FOUR FREEDOMS. From the speeches of Franklin Delano Roosevelt
Leeds, Yorkshire, 1964.
Vellum broadside, 14×18 inches; ink, watercolor, raised and burnished gold; semiformal hand, modern versals.
*Lent by the Artist*

Frank Taylor was born in Bradford, Yorkshire, in 1911. He specialized in portrait painting and during World War II spent all his spare time working with war artists, both lecturing on art to Army personnel and painting for them. When a certain officer requested a portrait in the manner of Holbein, he discovered the fascination of the Roman Capital and his ignorance of it. His awakened interest led him to Alfred Fairbank's *Book of Scripts* and eventually to its author (no. 135), on whose advice he studied with Thomas Swindlehurst (no. 202) at the Leeds College of Art. Since 1957 he has taught calligraphy at the Swarthmore Centre for Adult Education and the Leeds College of Art, while holding a post as lettering-reproduction artist in a printing establishment. Many of his commissions are in American institutions.

## *Lewis Trethewey*

204 SONNET XXII by William Shakespeare
London, 1964.
1 vellum leaf, 12¾×9 inches; Chinese ink, color, gold; set cursive hand.
*Lent by the Artist*

Lewis Trethewey was born in 1925 at Newquay, Cornwall. He studied at the Central School of Arts and Crafts, London, and Hampstead Garden Suburb Institute where his teachers were Mervyn C. Oliver (no. 186), Irene Wellington (nos. 209–10) and Joan Pilsbury (no. 189).

Although a civil servant he has taught at the Central School of Arts and Crafts, City Literary Institute, Samuel Morley College and for eight years at the Mary Ward Centre, London. He has written articles for the *Journal of the Society for Italic Handwriting* under the pseudonym *Otis Tarda*, and under his own name. S.S.I.

## *Marjorie Tuson*

205 THE MAY MAGNIFICAT by Gerard Manley Hopkins
Compton Martin, Bristol, 1959.
4 vellum leaves, 9⅝×6¾ inches; Chinese stick ink, paint, raised gold; slightly compressed formal hand. Binding: by Sydney M. Cockerell.
*Lent by the Artist*

Marjorie Tuson was born in Woolton, near Liverpool. Her art education took place at Liverpool School of Art and later at the West of England College of Art, Bristol, where Irene Base (no. 147) was her teacher. She was a partner in the Sycamore Press, Leigh, designing and printing small commissions. She is now Head of the Art Department, Colston Girls' School, Bristol. She has been represented in a number of British exhibitions. S.S.I.

## *Jan van Krimpen*

206 THE RAVEN by Edgar Allan Poe
The Netherlands, c. 1950?.
6 paper leaves, 7¼×5⅛ inches; ink. Binding: paste paper wrappers.
Acquired from Menno Hertzberger, Amsterdam, 1964.
*Lent by the the Boston Public Library*

FREEDOM

Democracy alone of all forms of government, enlists the full force of mens enlightened will.... It is the most humane, the most advanced and the most unconquerable of all forms of human society. The democratic aspiration is no mere recent phase of human history. It is human history. ¶ In the future days, which we seek to make secure, we look forward to a world founded upon four essential human freedoms. The first is freedom of speech and expression everywhere in the world. The second is freedom of every person to worship God in his own way everywhere in the world. The third is freedom from want which translated into world terms, means economic understanding, which will secure to every nation a healthier peacetime life for its inhabitants everywhere in the world. The fourth is freedom from fear which translated into world terms, means a worldwide reduction of armaments to such a point and in such a thorough fashion that no nation will be in a position to commit an act of physical aggression against any neighbour anywhere in the world. The only thing we have to fear is fear itself: nameless, unreasoning terror which paralyzes efforts to convert retreat into advance.

From the speeches of Franklin Delano Roosevelt · President United States of America · on Freedom · scripsit Frank Taylor AD 1964

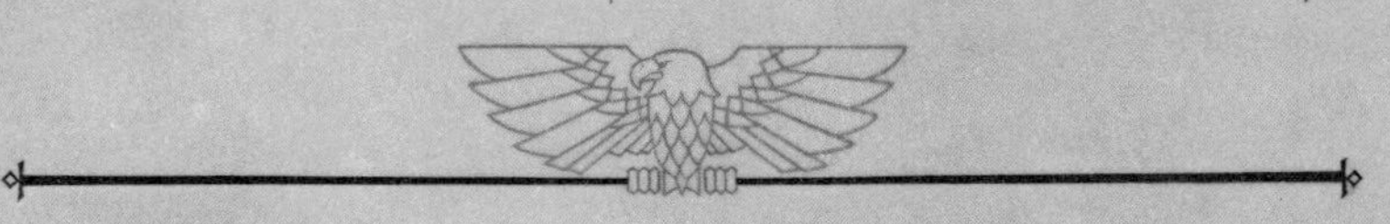

203. Franklin D. Roosevelt: Four Freedoms. Frank Taylor. 1964

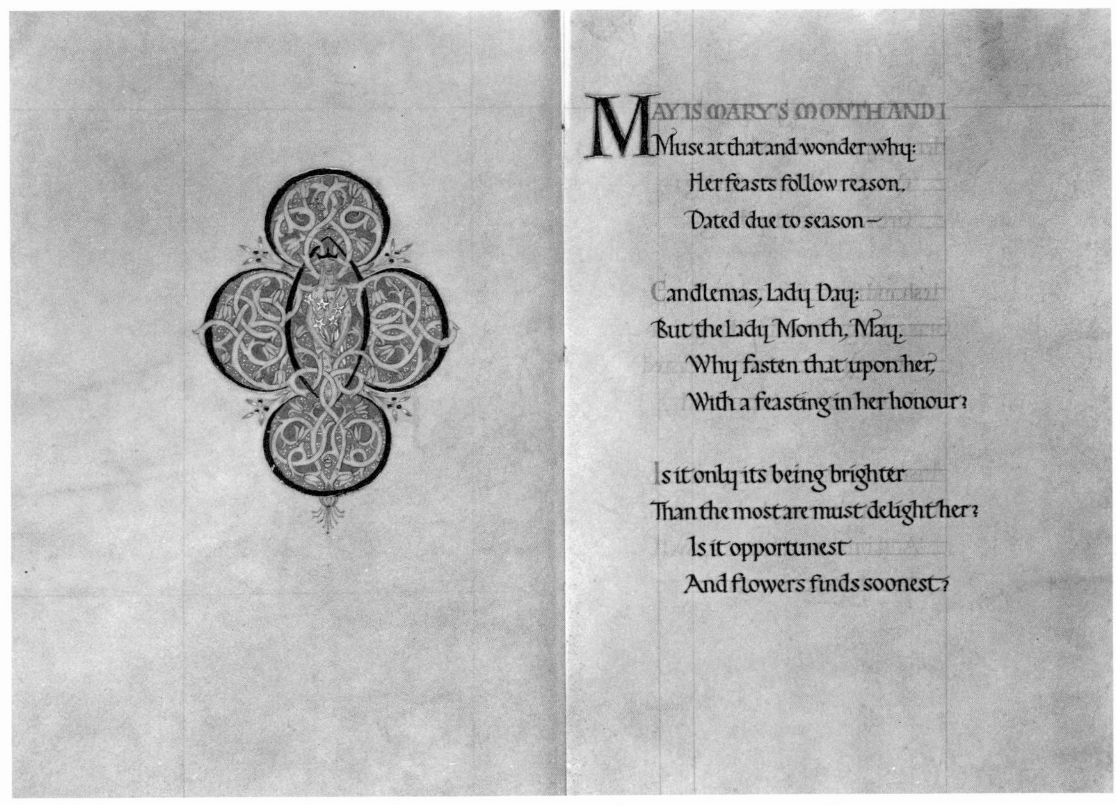


205. Gerard Manley Hopkins: The May Magnificat. Marjorie Tuson. 1959

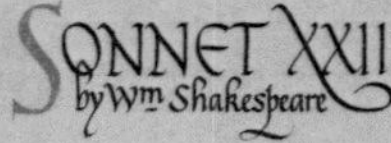
SONNET XXII
by Wm Shakespeare

My glass shall not persuade me I am old,
So long as youth and thou are of one date;
But when in thee time's furrows I behold,
Then look I death my days should expiate.
For all that beauty that doth cover thee
Is but the seemly raiment of my heart,
Which in my breast doth live, as thine in me:
How can I, then, be elder than thou art?
O, therefore, love, be of thyself so wary
As I, not for myself, but for thee will;
Bearing thy heart, which I will keep so chary
As tender nurse her babe from faring ill.
Presume not on thy heart when mine is slain;
Thou gav'st me thine, not to give back again.

204. Shakespeare: Sonnet XXII. Lewis Trethewey. 1964

ONCE upon a midnight dreary,
while I pondered, weak and weary,
Over many a quaint and curious
volume of forgotten lore,—
While I nodded, nearly napping,
suddenly there came a tapping,
As of some one gently rapping,
rapping at my chamber door.
''Tis some visitor,' I muttered,
'tapping at my chamber door:
Only this and nothing more.'

Ah, distinctly I remember
it was in the bleak December,
And each separate dying ember
wrought its ghost upon the floor.
Eagerly I wished the morrow;—
vainly I had sought to borrow
From my books surcease of sorrow—
sorrow for the lost Lenore,
For the rare and radiant maiden
whom the angels name Lenore:
Nameless here for evermore.

206. Poe: The Raven. Jan van Krimpen. c. 1950?

WE are the hollow men
We are the stuffed men
Leaning together
Headpiece filled with straw. Alas!
Our dried voices, when
We whisper together
Are quiet and meaningless
As wind in dry grass
Or rats' feet over broken glass

207. T. S. Eliot: The Hollow Men. Sheila Waters. 1965

loudlipped faces tocking the earth away:
slow clocks, quick clocks, pendulumed
heart-knocks, china, alarm, grandfather,
cuckoo; clocks shaped like Noah's whirr-
ing Ark, clocks that bicker in marble
ships, clocks in the wombs of glass wom-
en, hourglass chimers, tu-wit-tu-woo
clocks, clocks that pluck tunes, Vesuvius
clocks all black bells and lava, Niagara
clocks that cataract their ticks, old time-
weeping clocks with ebony beards, clocks
with no hands for ever drumming out time
without ever knowing what time it is.
His sixty-six singers are all set at different
hours. Lord Cut-Glass lives in a house and
a life at siege. Any minute or dark day now,

208. Dylan Thomas: Under Milkwood. Sheila Waters. 196

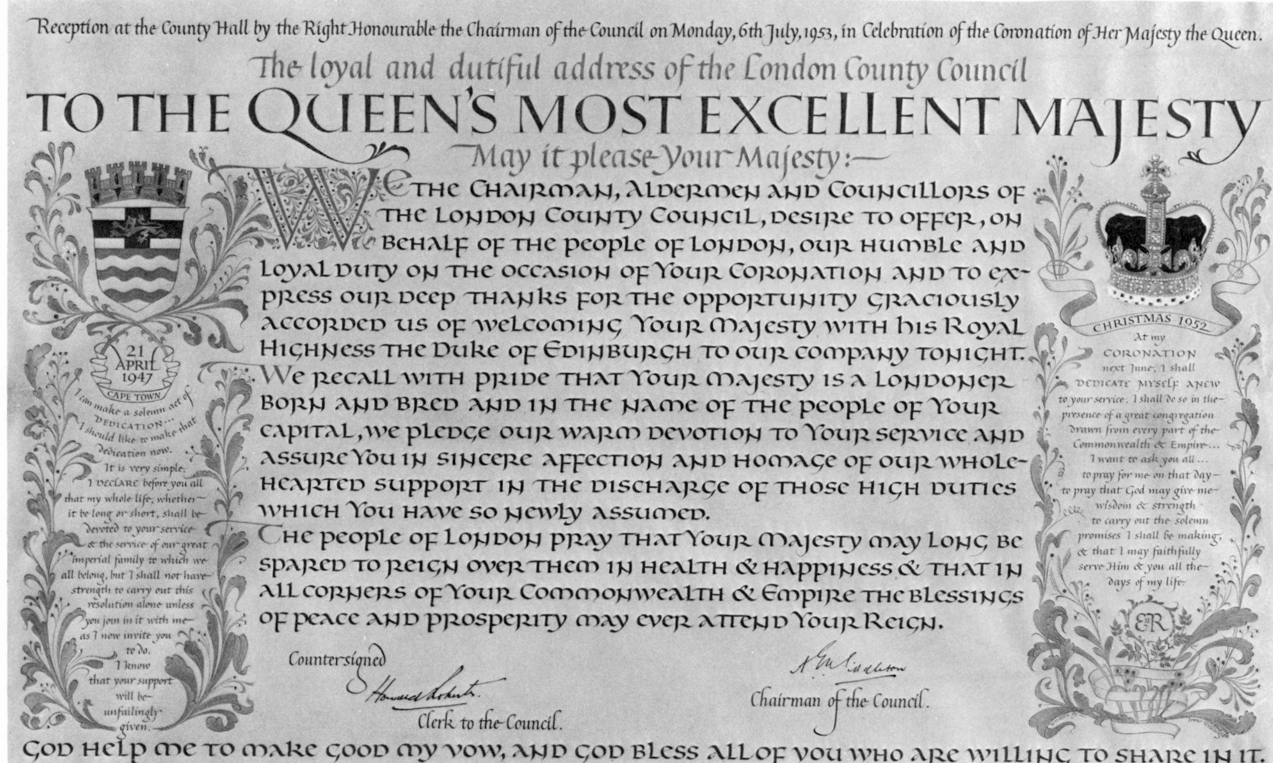

Reception at the County Hall by the Right Honourable the Chairman of the Council on Monday, 6th July, 1953, in Celebration of the Coronation of Her Majesty the Queen.

The loyal and dutiful address of the London County Council

TO THE QUEEN'S MOST EXCELLENT MAJESTY

May it please Your Majesty:—

We the Chairman, Aldermen and Councillors of the London County Council, desire to offer, on behalf of the people of London, our humble and loyal duty on the occasion of Your Coronation and to express our deep thanks for the opportunity graciously accorded us of welcoming Your Majesty with his Royal Highness the Duke of Edinburgh to our company tonight. We recall with pride that Your Majesty is a Londoner born and bred and in the name of the people of Your capital, we pledge our warm devotion to Your service and assure You in sincere affection and homage of our whole-hearted support in the discharge of those high duties which You have so newly assumed.

The people of London pray that Your Majesty may long be spared to reign over them in health & happiness & that in all corners of Your Commonwealth & Empire the blessings of peace and prosperity may ever attend Your Reign.

Countersigned

Clerk to the Council.

Chairman of the Council.

21 April 1947 Cape Town

I can make a solemn act of dedication... I should like to make that dedication now. It is very simple. I declare before you all that my whole life, whether it be long or short, shall be devoted to your service & the service of our great imperial family to which we all belong, but I shall not have strength to carry out this resolution alone unless you join in it with me—as I now invite you to do. I know that your support will be unfailingly given.

Christmas 1952

At my Coronation next June, I shall dedicate myself anew to your service. I shall do so in the presence of a great congregation drawn from every part of the Commonwealth & Empire... I want to ask you all... to pray for me on that day—to pray that God may give me wisdom & strength to carry out the solemn promises I shall be making, & that I may faithfully serve Him & you all the days of my life.

EIIR

God help me to make good my vow, and God bless all of you who are willing to share in it.

209. Coronation Address to Her Majesty Queen Elizabeth II from The London County Council. Irene Wellington. 1953

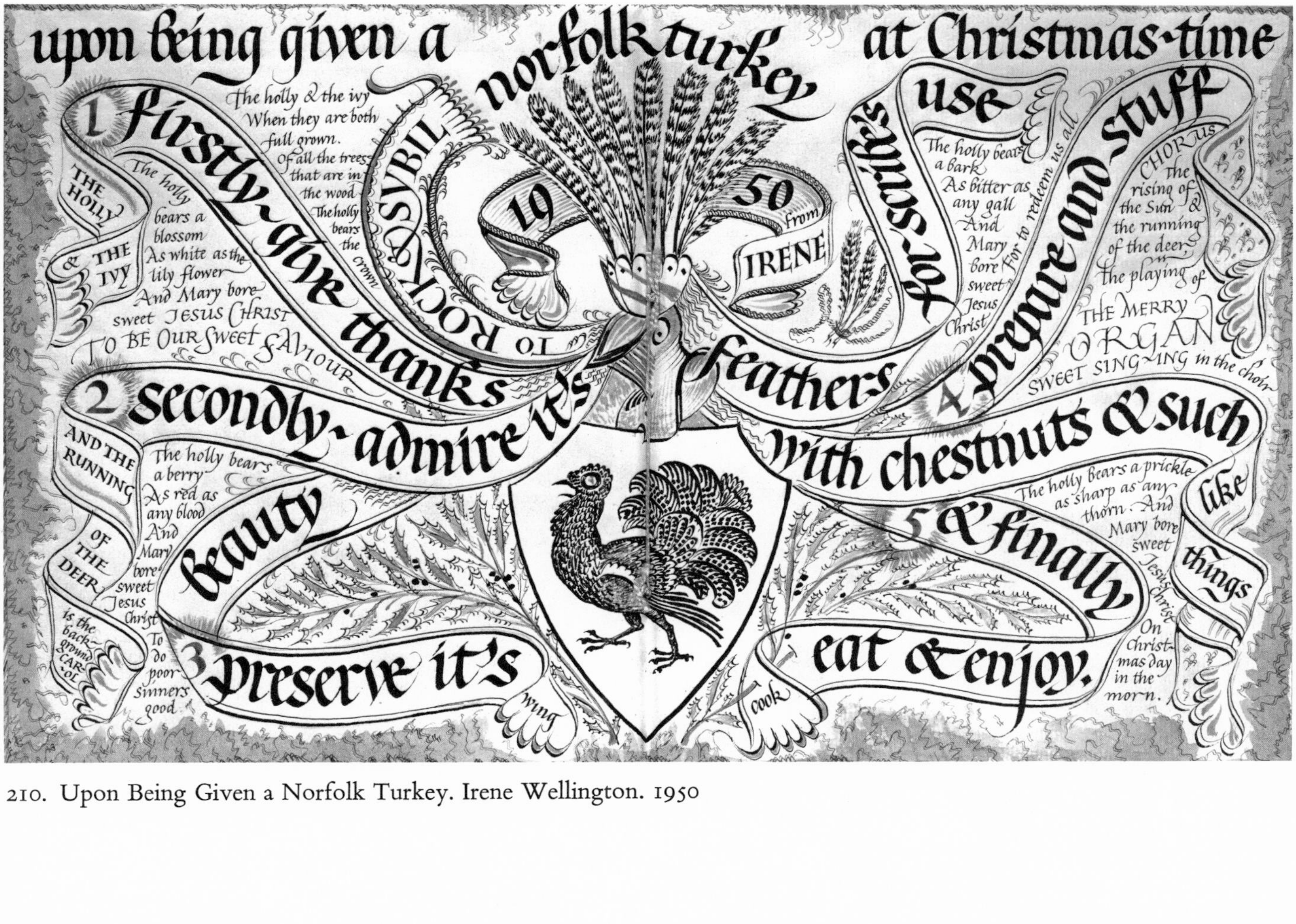

upon being given a norfolk turkey at Christmas-time

To Rockosybil 1950 from Irene

1 firstly give thanks 2 secondly admire it's beauty 3 preserve it's wing 4 prepare and stuff with chestnuts & such like things 5 & finally cook eat & enjoy. use for scribe's feathers

210. Upon Being Given a Norfolk Turkey. Irene Wellington. 1950

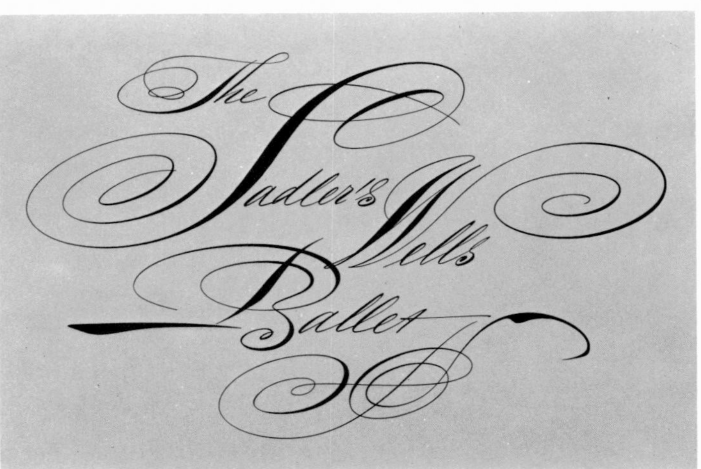


212. The Sadler's Wells Ballet. Martin Wilke. 1964

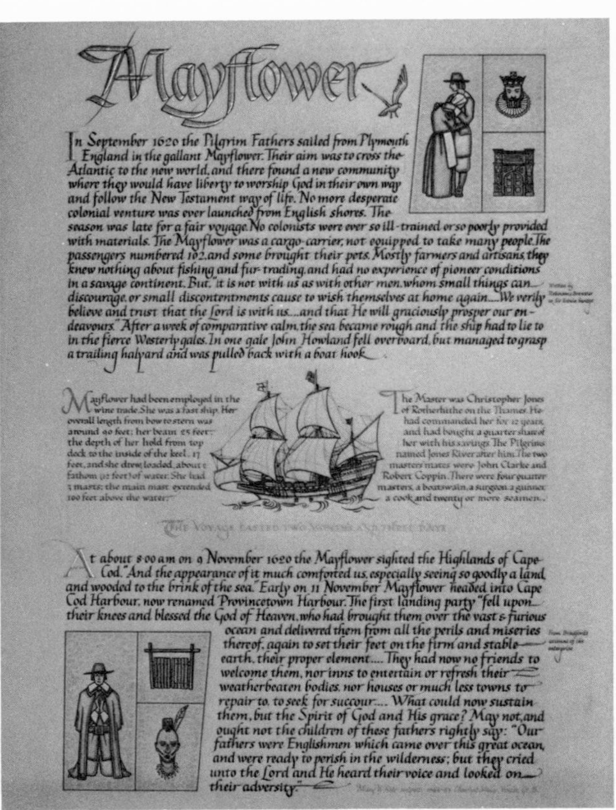


211. Mayflower. Mary White. 1964–1965

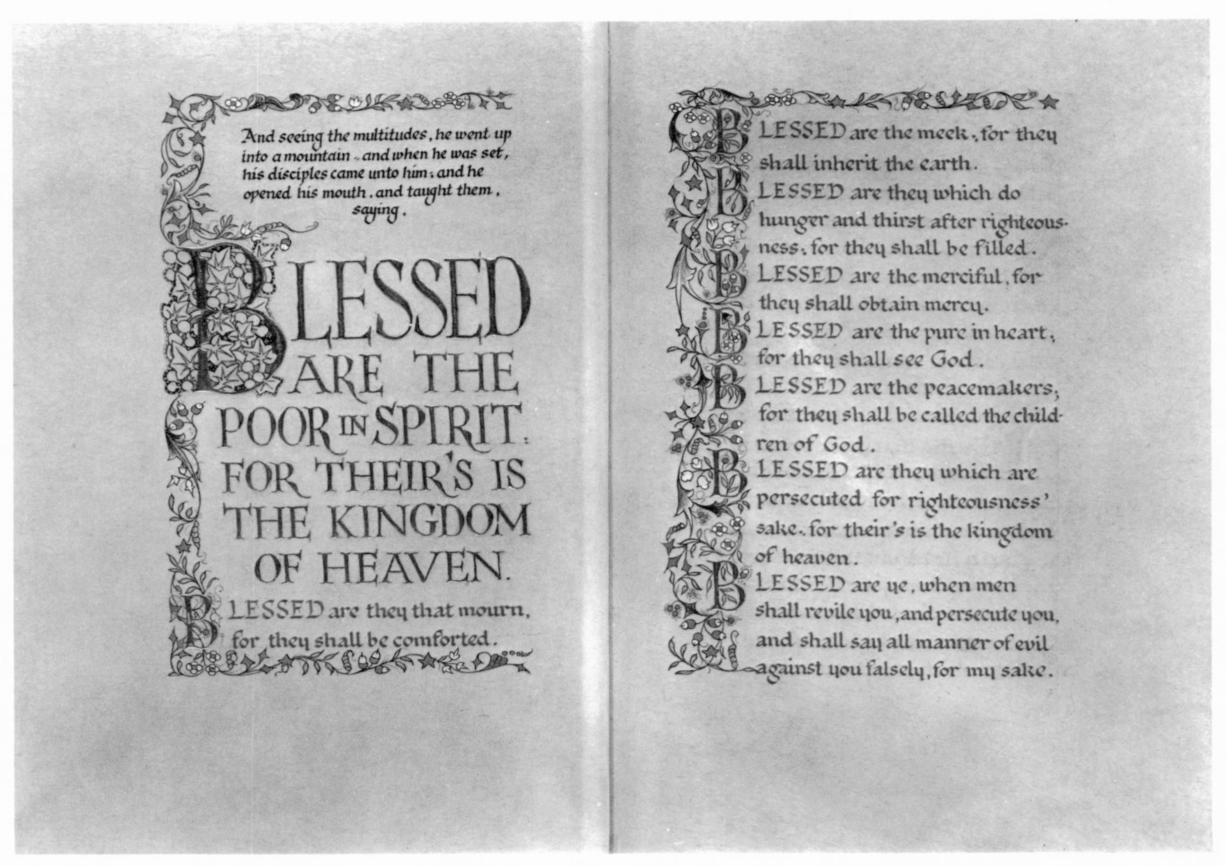


213. The Sermon on the Mount. Violet Wilson. 1957

Jan van Krimpen was born in Gouda, near Rotterdam, in 1892 and died in Haarlem in 1958. He attended the Academy of Art at The Hague and, like many others, was inspired by Johnston's remarkable handbook, *Writing & Illuminating, & Lettering*, in Anna Simons' translation. In 1912 he took up lettering and calligraphy professionally and adopted Palatino and other Italian writing masters as his models. In 1923 he first came into contact with Enschedé en Zonen, the Dutch printing firm, through his designs for postage stamps, and began an association which was to continue until his death. His *Lutetia* type was immediately successful, and was followed by *Romulus, Cancelleresca Bastarda, Spectrum* and others.

The beauty of his types brought him commissions in other fields, including the decoration of books, bindings, dust jackets and many items of formal calligraphy. The Stanbrook Abbey Press, Worcester, England, of today is in a sense his creation, for with the exception of one book set in Gill's *Perpetua*, this press is printed in his types and according to his principles of design and execution. Much of his accomplishment is recorded in *The Work of Jan van Krimpen* by John Dreyfus (1952).

## *Sheila Waters*

207 THE HOLLOW MEN by T. S. Eliot
Froxfield, Hampshire, 1965.
Paper, concertina opening out to show whole MS and both covers, 10×6 inches; ink, color, gold; based on ninth-century carolingian script. Binding: black oasis morocco with gold and blind tooling by Peter Waters.
*Lent by Richard Harrison*

208 UNDER MILKWOOD by Dylan Thomas
Froxfield, Hampshire, 1965.
1 vellum leaf, 8×5 inches; ink, color, gold; italic hand. Specimen pages with marginal illustrations from MS commissioned by Edward Hornby; in process of being written.
*Lent by the Artist*

Sheila Waters was born at Gravesend, Kent, in 1929. She studied at Medway College of Art and at the Royal College of Art, where she specialized in calligraphy under Dorothy Mahoney (no. 181). Among Miss Mahoney's other pupils was Peter Waters, who had already earned distinction as a bookbinder and was continuing his studies at the behest of Roger Powell, the eminent binder. Sheila and Peter Waters were married in 1953, and she continued to work and to teach at three art schools. A growing family has caused her to give up teaching; but, she writes, "I work at home free lance when three sons allow me to."

She was one of the group who executed the Royal Air Force Book of Remembrance under Alfred Fairbank's direction, and she has fulfilled a long list of important commissions of her own, demonstrating exceptional command of a variety of styles. She makes all drawings required by her husband and Roger Powell, who are now partners in bookbinding. She was responsible for the section on calligraphy in the recently published book *Lettering Today*. Members of the Society for Italic Handwriting will be familiar with her handsome design for the cover of its *Journal*. S.S.I.

## *Irene Wellington*

209 CORONATION ADDRESS TO HER MAJESTY QUEEN ELIZABETH II FROM THE LONDON COUNTY COUNCIL
Henley-on-Thames, Oxfordshire, 1953.
1 vellum leaf, 17×28 inches; ink, watercolor, matt and burnished gold; main text uncial hand, Queen's speeches semiformal hand. In cream pigskin tube, gold tooled.
*Lent by Her Majesty Queen Elizabeth II*

210 UPON BEING GIVEN A NORFOLK TURKEY (background carol, *The Holly and the Ivy*)
Henley-on-Thames, Oxfordshire, Christmas 1950.
1 paper leaf, 9⅜×15½ inches; ink and watercolor; cursive italic hand. Binding: boards, red leather spine by Sydney M. Cockerell.
*Lent by the Marquess and Marchioness of Cholmondeley*

Irene Wellington was born at Lydd, Kent, in 1904. From 1921 to 1924 she studied at Maidstone School (now College of Art), and from 1925 to 1930 at the Royal College of Art, where she was taught by Edward Johnston (nos. 123–4) and assisted him for her last two years there. From 1932 to 1943 she taught at Edinburgh College of Art, and then became instructor of calligraphy and illumination at the Central School of Arts and Crafts, London, from 1944 to 1959. Among her pupils were Marie Angel (nos. 141–3), Ann Camp (no. 153), Mary Duxbury, Tom Gourdie (no. 166), Joan Pilsbury (no. 189) and John Woodcock (no. 215).

In the *Creative Craftsman* John Farleigh lists her principal works, but it would be impossible to enumerate or describe them here. All are characterized by strength, freedom, grace and delicacy, from the most formal, like the coronation address shown, to the most spontaneous, like the Christmas card, which she describes as "sheer play, designed and executed within the spare time of three days."

Besides many rolls of honour and addresses to heads of state and other eminent persons, she executed the quotation from Shakespeare which Sir Winston Churchill sent to Harry Hopkins when the latter's son was killed in the war. The making of this inscription at Edward Johnston's behest is described in Priscilla Johnston's book about her father.

The first three of her *Irene Wellington Copy Books* have been published by Heinemann. S.S.I.

## *Mary White*

211 MAYFLOWER
Llantwit Major, Glamorgan, 1964–1965.
1 vellum leaf, 22×14 inches; Chinese ink, watercolor, gold, title in raised gold; simplified modern italic and conventional foundational round hand.
*Lent by the Artist*

Mary White was born in Croesyceliog, Monmouthshire, South Wales. She first studied at the Newport College of Art and Crafts, and then went to Hammersmith College of Art where she was taught calligraphy and illumination by Daisy Alcock and bookbinding by Vera Law (no. 178). While at the Goldsmiths' College of Art, London University, she studied calligraphy under Mervyn C. Oliver (no. 186) at Hampstead and architectural lettering under George Mansell at Hornsey. She has taught at grammar schools and the Swansea College of Art. She is now teaching in the Graphic Design Department of Atlantic College, St. Donat's Castle, Llantwit Major, where her husband is Head of the Art Department. Her broadcasts on calligraphy have been seen on the British television. S.S.I.

## *Martin Wilke*

212 THE SADLER'S WELLS BALLET
Berlin, 1964.
1 paper leaf, 7½×11¼ inches; ink.
*Lent by the Artist*

Martin Wilke was born in 1903 in Berlin, Germany, where he studied with O. H. W. Hadank and W. H. Deffler. His many lettering assignments have included the design of trademarks, and typefaces such as *Ariston*, *Caprice*, *Palette* and *Diskus*. For Photo-Lettering, Inc., in New York he designed *Wilke Halftone*. With the late Johannes Boehland he has long been responsible for much of the finest graphic design in the Berlin area.

## *Violet Wilson*

213 THE SERMON ON THE MOUNT.
*St. Matthew* V–VII
Wimbledon, 1957.
12 vellum leaves, 9¼×6¾ inches; ink, color, burnished gold; formal round hand. Binding: full crushed blue levant morocco by Sangorski & Sutcliffe.
*Lent by La Casa del Libro, San Juan, Puerto Rico*

Violet Wilson was born in 1902 in Wimbledon, Surrey. She studied calligraphy as a private pupil of Claire Evans. Books and decorative maps are now her favorite types of work. She has exhibited in many countries, and is one of the early craft members of the S.S.I.

## *Jeanyee Wong*

214 UNICEF CHRISTMAS CARD
New York City, 1962.
1 paper leaf, 4⅝×5¾ inches; ink, color; italic hand.
*Lent by the Artist*

Jeanyee Wong, calligrapher, designer and illustrator, was born in San Francisco, California. She has been interested in drawing and reading books since early childhood. She started to study Chinese at the age of three and has been influenced by the beauty of Chinese calligraphy. The love of this combination of drawing, reading and calligraphy is undoubtedly reflected in her work in the field of book-jacket design and illustration.

She studied sculpture and ceramics in high school, but her formal art education began at the Cooper Union Art School in New York. There, in addition to painting and sculpture, she studied design, lettering and advertising. Later she was associated with Fritz Kredel as an apprentice to learn illustration technique and woodcutting. At the same time she started free-lance art work which has continued to this day. In addition to book-jacket design and illustration, her work includes maps, Christmas cards, advertising lettering and testimonial award certificates. The greeting which she contributed to UNICEF for its Christmas cards has made its way into millions of homes throughout the world. She is now engaged in illustrating a book of Oriental fairy tales compiled by Pearl Buck.

Jeanyee Wong has illustrated or decorated more than thirty books, some of them completely hand written. Quite a number of the books contain Oriental or medieval themes which are especially suitable to the decorative style of the artist who likes pen or brush line work and flat colors.

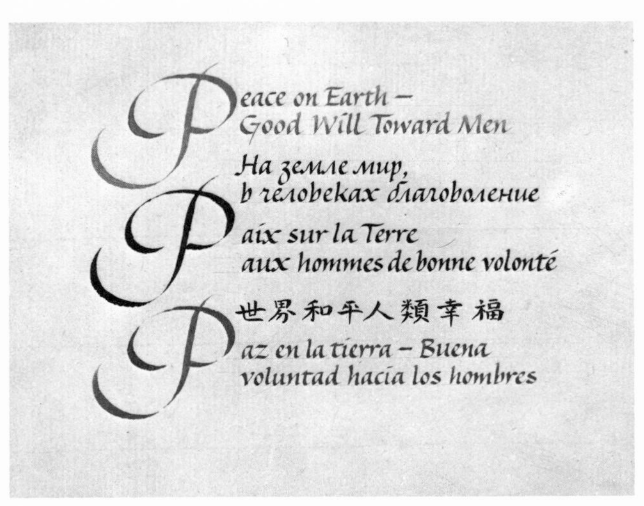


214. UNICEF Christmas Card. Jeanyee Wong. 1962

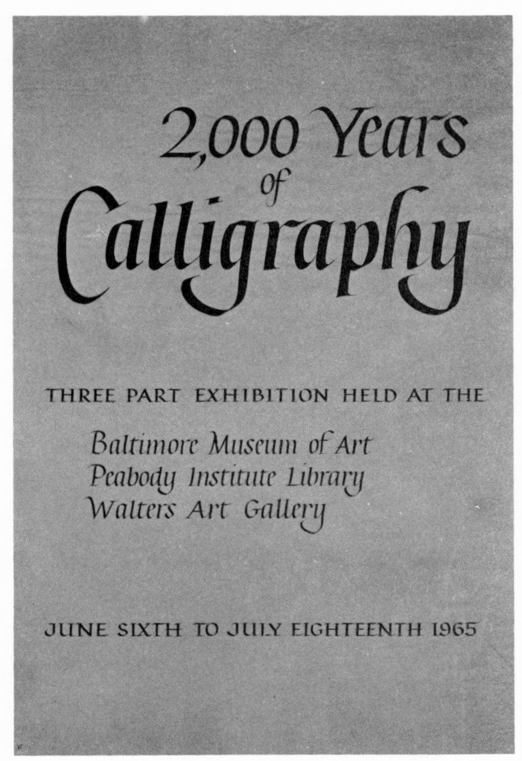


217. Poster announcing Baltimore Calligraphy Exhibition. Pamela Wrightson. 1965

POSTREMO PENSANDUM
*Finally, we must consider*
QUANTA DOCTRINAE COMMODITAS SIT
*what pleasantness of teaching there is*
RICHARD DE BURY IN LIBRIS, PHILOBIBLON 1:9
*in books,*
QUAM FACILIS, QUAM ARCANA·
*how easy, how secret!*
QUAM TUTO LIBRIS HUMANAE IGNORANTIAE
*How safely we lay bare the poverty of human ignorance to books*
PAUPERTATEM SINE VERECUNDIA DENUDAMUS!
*without feeling any shame!*
HI SUNT MAGISTRI QUI NOS INSTRUUNT
*They are masters who instruct us*
SINE VIRGIS ET FERULA, SINE VERBIS ET CHOLERA,
*without rod or ferrule, without angry words,*
SINE PANNIS ET PECUNIA· SI ACCEDIS, NON DORMIUNT;
*without clothes or money· If you come to them they are not asleep;*
SI INQUIRENS INTERROGAS, NON ABSCONDUNT;
*if you ask and enquire of them, they do not withdraw;*
NON REMURMURANT SI OBERRES;
*they do not chide if you make mistakes;*
CACHINNOS NESCIUNT, SI IGNORES·
*they do not laugh at you if you are ignorant·*

215. Richard de Bury: Philobiblon: John Woodcock. 1964

# PREAMBLE OF THE CHARTER OF THE UNITED NATIONS

NOUS, PEUPLES DES NATIONS UNIES RESOLUS

*à préserver les générations futures du fléau de la guerre qui deux fois en l'espace d'une vie humaine a infligé à l'humanité d'indicibles souffrances,*

*à proclamer à nouveau notre foi dans les droits fondamentaux de l'homme, dans la dignité et la valeur de la personne humaine, dans l'égalité de droits des hommes et des femmes, ainsi que des nations, grandes et petites,*

*à créer les conditions nécessaires au maintien de la justice et du respect des obligations nées des traités et autres sources du droit international,*

*à favoriser le progrès social et instaurer de meilleures conditions de vie dans une liberté plus grande,*

ET A CES FINS

*à pratiquer la tolérance, à vivre en paix l'un avec l'autre dans un esprit de bon voisinage,*

*à unir nos forces pour maintenir la paix et la sécurité internationales,*

*à accepter des principes et instituer des méthodes garantissant qu'il ne sera pas fait usage de la force des armes, sauf dans l'intérêt commun,*

*à recourir aux institutions internationales pour favoriser le progrès économique et social de tous les peuples,*

AVONS DECIDE D'ASSOCIER NOS EFFORTS POUR REALISER CES DESSEINS·

WE THE PEOPLES OF THE UNITED NATIONS DETERMINED

to save succeeding generations from the scourge of war, which twice in our lifetime has brought untold sorrow to mankind, and

to reaffirm faith in fundamental human rights, in the dignity and worth of the human person, in the equal rights of men and women and of nations large and small, and

to establish conditions under which justice and respect for the obligations arising from treaties and other sources of international law can be maintained, and

to promote social progress and better standards of life in larger freedom,

AND FOR THESE ENDS

to practice tolerance and live together in peace with one another as good neighbors, and

to unite our strength to maintain international peace and security, and

to ensure, by the acceptance of principles and the institution of methods, that armed force shall not be used, save in the common interest, and

to employ international machinery for the promotion of the economic and social advancement of all peoples,

HAVE RESOLVED TO COMBINE OUR EFFORTS TO ACCOMPLISH THESE AIMS·

NOSOTROS LOS PUEBLOS DE LAS NACIONES UNIDAS RESUELTOS

*a preservar a las generaciones venideras del flagelo de la guerra, que dos veces durante nuestra vida ha infligido a la humanidad sufrimientos indecibles,*

*a reafirmar la fe en los derechos fundamentales del hombre, en la dignidad y el valor de la persona humana, en la igualdad de derechos de hombres y mujeres y de las naciones grandes y pequeñas,*

*a crear condiciones bajo las cuales puedan mantenerse la justicia y el respeto a las obligaciones emanadas de los tratados y de otras fuentes del derecho internacional,*

*a promover el progreso social y a elevar el nivel de vida dentro de un concepto más amplio de la libertad,*

Y CON TALES FINALIDADES

*a practicar la tolerancia y a convivir en paz como buenos vecinos,*

*a unir nuestras fuerzas para el mantenimiento de la paz y la seguridad internacionales,*

*a asegurar, mediante la aceptación de principios y la adopción de métodos, que no se usará la fuerza armada sino en servicio del interés común, y*

*a emplear un mecanismo internacional para promover el progreso económico y social de todos los pueblos,*

HEMOS DECIDIDO AUNAR NUESTROS ESFUERZOS PARA REALIZAR ESTOS DESIGNIOS·

МЫ, НАРОДЫ ОБЪЕДИНЕННЫХ НАЦИЙ ПРЕИСПОЛНЕННЫЕ РЕШИМОСТИ,

*избавить грядущие поколения от бедствий войны, дважды в нашей жизни принесшей человечеству невыразимое горе, и*

*вновь утвердить веру в основные права человека, в достоинство и ценность человеческой личности, в равноправие мужчин и женщин и в равенство прав больших и малых наций, и*

*создать условия, при которых могут соблюдаться справедливость и уважение к обязательствам, вытекающим из договоров и других источников международного права, и*

*содействовать социальному прогрессу и улучшению условий жизни при большей свободе,*

И В ЭТИХ ЦЕЛЯХ

*проявлять терпимость и жить вместе, в мире друг с другом, как добрые соседи, и*

*объединить наши силы для поддержания международного мира и безопасности, и*

*обеспечить принятием принципов и установлением методов, чтобы вооруженные силы применялись не иначе, как в общих интересах, и*

*использовать международный аппарат для содействия экономическому и социальному прогрессу всех народов,*

РЕШИЛИ ОБЪЕДИНИТЬ НАШИ УСИЛИЯ ДЛЯ ДОСТИЖЕНИЯ ЭТИХ ЦЕЛЕЙ·

*Done at the city of San Francisco the twenty-sixth day of June, one thousand nine hundred and forty-five·*

*Transcribed by Hermann Zapf Frankfurt am Main 1960*

218. Preamble of the Charter of the United Nations. Hermann Zapf. 1960

## *John Woodcock*

215 EXTRACT FROM "PHILOBIBLON" by Richard de Bury
Kingswood, Surrey, 1964.
1 paper leaf, 13¾×20¾ inches; ink, color; free roman capitals, italic gloss.
Acquired at the Crafts Centre of Great Britain, 1964.
*Lent by the Boston Public Library*

John Woodcock was born in 1924 at Cudworth, Yorkshire. He was trained at Barnsley School of Art and the Royal College of Art, where his teachers were Dorothy Mahoney (no. 181) and Irene Wellington (nos. 209–10). He wrote the chapter on the design of formal scripts in *The Calligrapher's Handbook* (1956). The admiration that his work has aroused in many exhibitions has earned him innumerable commissions. S.S.I.

## *Pamela Wrightson*

216 PATER NOSTER [*Not illustrated.*]
London, 1961.
1 blue Ingres paper leaf, 18½×12 inches; white designer color; foundational and semiformal italic hand.
*Lent by the Artist*

217 POSTER announcing Baltimore Calligraphy Exhibition, 1965
London, 1965.
1 yellow Japanese paper leaf, 37×25 inches; black ink, dark brown designer color; foundational and italic capitals.
*Given by the Artist*

Pamela Wrightson (Barnett) was born in London in 1928. She studied at Henrietta Barnett School, and later under Mervyn C. Oliver (no. 186). As permanent scribe for Heal & Son, Ltd., a large London store, she has achieved fame for her posters, which have been acclaimed at many exhibitions. The outstanding poster shown was made for this exhibition. S.S.I.

## *Hermann Zapf*

218 PREAMBLE OF THE CHARTER OF THE UNITED NATIONS
Frankfurt am Main, 1960.
Mould-made paper broadside, 18¾×25 inches (in gilded frame, 24½×34⅞ inches); Chinese ink, black, red, blue; roman and italic together with Cyrillic italic hands.
Polyglot in French, English, Spanish and Russian.
Commissioned by the Pierpont Morgan Library.
*Lent by the Pierpont Morgan Library*

Hermann Zapf was born in 1918 in Nuremberg, Germany, and taught himself lettering from the manuals of Rudolf Koch (no. 125) and Edward Johnston (123–4). He was first exposed to typography in the studio of Paul Koch in Frankfurt am Main in 1938, and later in the same year was engaged by Stempel Foundry, where he became art director from 1947 to 1957. During World War II, while an officer in a German mapping unit, he started to write out small manuscript books in his spare time, and had completed over fifty of them by 1948. He taught lettering at the Werkkunstschule in Offenbach from 1948 to 1950, and has made several lecture tours in the United States.

His thirty-odd type designs include *Palatino*; *Michelangelo* and *Sistina Titling*; *Optima*; several Greek, Arabic and Cyrillic faces; *Melior*, a newspaper type; and a dozen poster and display types plus ornaments. Among the examples of his book design are his own works, originally published in Frankfurt. They include *About Alphabets, Some Marginal Notes on Type Design* (Typophile Chap Book 37, 1960) translated, with a preface by Paul Standard. Of special interest to calligraphers is his *Pen and Graver. Alphabets and Pages of Calligraphy* (1952), published in this country by Museum Books, as are his superb *Manuale Typographicum* with one hundred typographic arrangements in sixteen languages (1954) and his latest book, *Typographic Variations* (1964).

# *Index*

*Numbers refer to catalogue entries, those in italic being main examples or descriptions. Since the index, like the catalogue, was prepared by the three compilers independently, some variations in emphasis will be apparent.*